299.5

— Daoist Modern —

Innovation, Lay Practice, and the

Community of Inner Alchemy

in Republican Shanghai

Harvard East Asian Monographs 313

Daoist Modern

Innovation, Lay Practice, and the Community of Inner Alchemy in Republican Shanghai

Xun Liu

Published by the Harvard University Asia Center
Distributed by Harvard University Press
Cambridge (Massachusetts) and London 2009

© 2009 by the President and Fellows of Harvard College

Printed in the United States of America

The Harvard University Asia Center publishes a monograph series and, in coordination with the Fairbank Center for Chinese Studies, the Korea Institute, the Reischauer Institute of Japanese Studies, and other faculties and institutes, administers research projects designed to further scholarly understanding of China, Japan, Vietnam, Korea, and other Asian countries. The Center also sponsors projects addressing multidisciplinary and regional issues in Asia.

Library of Congress Cataloging-in-Publication Data

Liu, Xun, 1959–

Daoist modern : innovation, lay practice, and the community of inner alchemy in Republican Shanghai / Xun Liu.

    p. cm. -- (Harvard East Asian monographs ; 313)

    Includes bibliographical references and index.

    ISBN 978-0-674-03309-2 (cloth : alk. paper)

    1. Taoism--China--Shanghai--History--20th century. 2. Chen, Yingning, 1880–1969--Influence. 3. Shanghai (China)--Religious life and customs. 4. Social change--China--Shanghai--History--20th century. 5. Laity--China--Shanghai--History--20th century. 6. Mind and body--Social aspects--China--Shanghai--History--20th century. 7. Community life--China--Shanghai--History--20th century. 8. Shanghai (China)--Social conditions--20th century. 9. Shanghai (China)--Politics and government--20th century. 10. China--History--Republic, 1912–1949. I. Title.

    BL1910.L565 2009

    299.5'1409510904--dc22

                                                                                               2009002498

Index by the author

∞ Printed on acid-free paper

Last figure below indicates year of this printing

18 17 16 15 14 13 12 11 10 09

Dedicated to

My teacher and friend Charlotte,

My parents Xiang Shugui and Liu Dengqi

And my family Sherry, Rujun, and Mengdan

Whose enduring love and support

made the book possible

Acknowledgments

From its first stirrings on a hot summer day in the reading room of the Stanford University Library in 1994 to its final completion in the basement office of my home in East Brunswick, New Jersey, on a cool spring evening in 2008, this book has taken more than thirteen years to complete. Like a Daoist inner alchemist in pursuit of his or her goal, I have also entered a network of personal friendships and professional ties that includes my teachers, friends, colleagues, relatives, and strangers. Without their understanding and support, their insightful comments and constructive criticisms, this book would not have been possible. So even though I have by no means accomplished the legendary Daoist feat of immortality, it is nonetheless timely and appropriate that I give my heartfelt thanks to those who have sustained me throughout the journey.

To my mentor and friend Charlotte Furth, I am forever indebted. It was she who brought me into the field of history at USC in 1990 when I was still searching for a direction in my professional career. In the years that followed, I have had the good fortune of studying with her and learning from her exemplary scholarship about how to be a historian. My discipleship with her has since grown into a friendship that has continued to inspire and sustain my professional and personal growth beyond the graduate school. Her careful readings of and critical comments on the manuscript over the years from its early dissertation drafts to its present finished book chapters have significantly improved the book. To Charlotte, I dedicate this book.

My book journey first started at USC, where I benefited from the advice and fellowship from my other teachers and fellow graduate students as I was preparing my dissertation. To John E. Wills, Gary Seaman, Gordon Berger, Michael Robinson, Connie Orliskie, and Pedro Loureiro, I give my thanks.

My post-graduate sojourns took me to the Fairbank Center at Harvard University, the Institute of Society, Religion, and Laity (G.S.R.L.) at CNRS in Paris, and the Center for Chinese Studies at UC Berkeley. I am most appreciative of the fellowships and grants from these institutions, which supported the revisions and rewritings of the various versions of the book manuscript. At Harvard's Fairbank Center, Wilt Idema, Paul Cohen, Michael Puett, Merle Goldman, Ellen Widmer, Xiao Yang, Steven Miles, and Zhang Hong provided both time and support to the book project. Their comments given both formally at the Center's seminars and informally over lunch and in the aisles of research cubicles helped greatly during the early stages of manuscript revision. I am particularly indebted to Professor Idema, the director of the Center, whose unfailing support of my manuscript project led to the symposium entitled "Between Eternity and Modernity: Daoist Tradition and Transformation in Twentieth Century China" at Harvard in the summer of 2006. The comments and suggestions I received from the participants in the symposium helped improve the manuscript. To my co-organizer of the symposium, David Palmer, and fellow presenters and discussants Vincent Goossaert, Paul Katz, Everett Zhang, Kristoffer Schipper, Ken Dean, Franciscus Verellen, Prasenjit Duara, Livia Kohn, Elena Valussi, Lee Fongmao, Lai Chi-tim, Robert Weller, Mayfair Yang, Alain Arrault, Li Dahua, Fan Guangchun, Lü Xichen, Gai Jianmin, Yang Der-ruey, Adeline Herrou, Wang Ka, and Liu Zhongyu, I express my deep sense of gratitude. At Berkeley, where I completed and presented much of the revised manuscript, I benefited from informal conversations and formal suggestions given at seminars and presentations from Wen-hsin Yeh, the late Frederic Wakeman, Robert Sharf, Jr., Bao Weihong, Linghon Lam, David Johnson, Christian Henriot, Kevin O'Brien, and Feng Yi.

Acknowledgments

Several versions of the book manuscript were presented at CNRS in Paris and Augsburg University in Germany in the fall of 2004. I thank the audience there for their useful comments, which contributed to the improvement of the manuscript. At the Academia Sinica symposium "The City and Chinese Modernity" in Taipei in the summer of 2007, the comments and suggestions I received from Professors Dorothy Ko, Paul Katz, Huang Kewu, and Fan Chunwu were particularly useful for rethinking the issues of religious modernity among the urban elite in Republican Shanghai.

In Beijing, Shanghai, and Sichuan, where much of the early archival research and fieldwork was done, I received help from Professors Chen Yaoting, Qing Xitai, Li Yangzhen, Li Gang, and Lu Guolong, the late Ms. Yu Zhongjue, Dr. Wu Yakui, Dr. Yan Zhonghu, Dr. Yin Zhihua, the late abbot Lü Zong'an of the White Cloud Monastery in Shanghai, and several other Daoist clerics in Beijing.

This book would not have been possible without the active support provided by some of the survivors of the Republican Shanghai community of the lay Daoist practitioners, especially the late Dr. Zhang Zhuming, and his son, Dr. Wei Zhongyao. For a decade, from 1995 to 2005, Dr. Zhang and Dr. Wei graciously granted me several long interviews from which I learned a great deal about the personal, social, and institutional dimensions of the Shanghai inner alchemic practice and community. Their contribution to whatever merits this book may have is beyond description. I have also benefited from the comments of the two anonymous reviewers for the Harvard University Asia Center's Publications Program and from the editorial assistance of the program's staff.

At my current institutional home, Rutgers University, my colleagues Don Roden, Indrani Chatterjee, Jackson Lears, Paul Clemens, Jennifer Jones, Julie Livingston, and Ziva Galili have supported this project. To them, I also give my thanks. I alone am responsible for all the faults and mistakes of the book.

My mother, Xiang Shugui, and my father, Liu Dengqi, and my sister, Rose E. Liu, have been my steadfast supporters over the years. Their unconditional love and unswerving support have sustained me through the critical moments of my life and career. To them I owe my life, and, of course, this book.

Last but not least, to my wife, Sherry Yin, and our children, Christine and Milton, I dedicate this book. They deserve most of the credit this book may possess, since they have made the greatest sacrifice by enduring my long absences and unintentional parental and spousal neglect. To them, I am eternally indebted. I can only hope that this book will start to repay what I owe them as a husband and a father.

X.L.

Contents

	Figures	xii
	Abbreviations	xiii
	Introduction	1
1	Late Qing and Early Republican Daoism	21
2	A Journey from Anqing to Shanghai	40
3	Innovating Immortals' Body: Nationalism, Antiquity, and Science	77
4	Practice Makes Perfect: Inner Alchemic Techniques and Regimens	122
5	The Inner Alchemic Community	173
6	The Print Culture and Revival of Inner Alchemy	231
	Conclusion	273
	Epilogue	277

Reference Matter

Notes	285
Selected Bibliography	339
Index	369

Figures

1	Chen Yingning in Shanghai, ca. 1933	42
2	The White Cloud Monastery in Shanghai	50
3	Portrait of Lü Bicheng	60
4	South Market district, Shanghai	69
5	An immortal's ascent by flight (*Feisheng tu*)	78
6	Universal vista (*Puzhao tu*)	97
7	Inner illumination (*Neizhao tu*)	99
8	The Heart and the Kidneys (*Xinshen tu*)	105
9	The Heavenly Orbit (*Zhoutian tu*)	107
10	Chen Yingning's diagram of the Way	108
11	Triple Rings, late Ming	139
12	Selecting sites for practice: a view of Mount Huang	141
13	Dr. Zhang Zhuming, ca. 1933	181
14	Mr. Chang Zunxian, ca. 1933	183
15	Mr. Hong Tai'an at practice	213
16	Women's beginning practice	222
17	Female inner alchemy	223
18	Mr. Zhang Xuetang, founder of Yihuatang	235

Abbreviations

For bibliographic information on the items cited here, see the Selected Bibliography, pp. 339–68.

DXHK	*Daoxie huikan* 道協會刊
DZ	*Daozang* 道藏
DZJY	*Daozang jiyao* 道藏輯要
DZJH	Xiao Tianshi, *Daozang jinghua* 道藏精華
DZJHL	Ding Fubao, *Daozang jinghua lu* 道藏精華錄
ESWS	Shanghai guji chubanshe, *Ershiwu shi* 二十五史
XD	*Xiandao yuebao* 仙道月報
YS	*Yangshan banyue kan* 揚善半月刊
ZWDS	Hu Daojing et al., eds., *Zangwai daoshu* 藏外道書

— Daoist Modern —

Innovation, Lay Practice, and the

Community of Inner Alchemy

in Republican Shanghai

Introduction

This book tells a story about Daoism's encounter with modernity and its modern transformation by tracing the life and career of Chen Yingning 陳攖寧 (1880–1969) in early twentieth-century Shanghai. In his day, Chen was arguably the most influential theoretician and practitioner of the Daoist self-cultivation practice known as "inner alchemy" (*neidan* 內丹). He led a group of fellow lay practitioners in promoting Daoist practices as techniques for ensuring personal health and healing, as venues for pursuing individual spirituality, and as ways of forging cultural self-identity, building community, and even strengthening the nation. Amid the social and political crises of the first three decades of the Republican era, the pursuit of Daoist inner alchemy by urban lay practitioners became intricately linked with the rise of nationalist and scientific discourse, the revolution in social and gender relations, the increase in state control and reform of religions, and the proliferation of mass media in the modernizing urban metropolis of Shanghai and beyond. This encounter with the ideologies and processes of modernity helped transform, reshape, and continue the Daoist tradition of self-cultivation in the early twentieth century.

My interest in telling this story was inspired by my reading of two very different texts dealing with the state of China's indigenous religion in modern times. A few years ago, I happened on a vignette of a street scene in Shanghai during the Japanese occupation in the early 1940s, as depicted by the incomparable Eileen Chang:

> A Daoist priest is begging for alms along the street. Dressed in a black Daoist robe that has faded to a yellowish hue, the Daoist wears his hair in a dusty topknot on his head, not unlike the upswept coiffure worn by a modern lady. His narrow slit eyes, like his hairdo, slant up and backward. He wears the expression of a wretched woman. It's hard to tell his age. Because of malnutrition, his lanky gaunt frame makes him look like a seventeen- or eighteen-year-old lad who has outgrown himself.
> "Tuh, tuh." He beats a piece of hollow bamboo resting along the length of his forearm. The sound is like a pendulum that marks a different kind of time, like the inching motion of the setting sunray on an ancient monastery located deep in the mountains. Like space, time also has some expensive segments, as well as large patches of barrenness. There are segments of time, of which you cannot buy even an inch with ten thousand pieces of gold. As for those who would sell their whole life spans just to earn a bite, their time is worthless (even if they were willing to sell their next life, the future of their posterity!).
> Now the Daoist, carrying with him all that surplus yet worthless time comes to this high-speed metropolis with its shiny billboards, shops, and stores, with its cars blowing their horns. He is a man from some ancient romance in which he dreams the Yellow Millet dream. Yet he has merely slumbered without ever dreaming that dream and awakens only to feel ever more at a loss.

Eileen Chang then describes the profound indifference of urban shoppers to the Daoist beggar, as he perfunctorily kowtows to the shops in equally profound indifference to others and his surroundings.[1]

Chang's depiction of the Daoist beggar has since been read by many of her fans and scholars of modern China alike as a common street scene in modernizing Shanghai, as well as of all other modernizing Chinese cities. Yet it is precisely the seeming ordinariness of this scene and the serendipity of her use of the Daoist beggar as an icon that intrigue me. For into this simple street encounter, Chang embedded complex layers of emotions. On one level, the image of the uncouth Daoist beggar, like the other mundane things Chang observed on her shopping trip to her neighborhood market, evokes the quotidian rhythm of everyday life in the city, which quietly but stubbornly continued despite the Japanese occupation and other tribulations history had hurtled at it. There is something persistent and unchanging about the scene. It was her sense of being connected to the daily pace of this tenacious reality that inspired Eileen Chang's depiction and instilled in her a quiet sense of confidence about the future of her city and her nation.[2]

Yet on another level, Chang's sympathy for the plight of the Daoist beggar is imbued with a subtle nostalgia for a timeless and transcendent past, encapsulated in the remote Daoist mountain temple fading in the setting sun, of which the Daoist cleric was a metonymic reminder. Buried in the nostalgia is an unmistakable feeling of both temporal and spatial dislocation and incoherence. The Daoist past set in the rustic and dreamlike mountain and embodied in the unkempt and undernourished Daoist beggar appears jarringly at odds with modern Shanghai's glitzy neon lights, department stores, automobiles, and other trappings of modernity. The dramatic juxtaposition serves only to highlight the apparent incongruities between Daoism and modernity. Chang's Daoist beggar—disheveled, malnourished, frail, and, most of all, indifferent to himself and everything around him—appears to symbolize the general decline of Daoism in modern China.

More important, the literary imaginary Chang created resonates with established conventional wisdom about the decay of Daoism, which has been shaped by a combination of influences, from Song neo-Confucian historiography to the sixteenth-century Jesuit missionaries' views of Chinese religions to the modern Chinese states' religious policies. Chang's seemingly serendipitous use of the Daoist beggar as an icon of an irretrievable past reflects this persistent vision of Daoist decay in late imperial China. Although recent scholarship has begun to dispel this view by revealing a more complex picture of Daoism in the late imperium, the Daoist decline thesis, first perpetuated by the Song neo-Confucians, still lingers among many scholars of Daoism and modern China. This thesis perceives Daoism as a grand philosophical system developed by sages and philosophers during the pre-Qin golden age. Daoism steadily declined in both influence and power beginning with the Song dynasty, and the deterioration accelerated after the seventeenth century.[3] Typical of this Confucian critique are the comments of the Southern Song scholar Ma Duanlin 馬端臨 (1254–1323). In his widely read and influential *Wenxian tongkao* 文獻通考, a bibliographic review of pre-Yuan literary and philosophical writings and compilations, Ma characterized Daoism and its practices as being "a promiscuous hodgepodge" (*za'er duoduan* 雜而多端). Following earlier Song literati critics of Daoism such as Ouyang Xiu 歐陽修 (1007–72) and Zhu Xi 朱熹 (1130–1200), Ma defined Daoism narrowly as a system of moral and philosophical teachings about the attainment of spiritual purity, tranquility, and non-action (*qingjing wuwei* 清靜無為). He dismissed the cult of divine immortals (*shenxian* 神仙) and rejected other practices often associated with Daoism, such as refining cultivation (*lianyang* 煉養), drug ingestion (*fushi* 服食), gymnastics (*daoyin* 導引), and talismans (*fulu* 符籙), as being "vulgar and shallow" (*biqian* 鄙淺) and "deviating far and wide from the true teachings of Laozi."[4]

Ma's elitist view of Daoism as primarily a moral philosophy influenced many later generations of scholars. Privileging the early classics by Laozi and Zhuangzi, Ma's interpretation saw the history of Daoism from the medieval era on as a process of decline and decay, a liturgical corruption of the classicism of the pre-Qin era. Widely cited by many post-Song scholars in their discussions of Daoism, his remarks have become a standard critique of Daoism. In this critique, post-Song Daoist institutions and practices, which flourished by incorporating Confucian and Buddhist teachings, were naturally seen as derivative, and not important or worthwhile. This elitist focus on the early philosophical writings as the core of Daoism has directed much scholarly attention to the classical period at the expense of the late imperial and modern periods of Daoist history.

In the early sixteenth century, the neo-Confucian critics of Daoism found an unlikely ally in the Jesuit missionaries in China. In their efforts to define themselves vis-à-vis the Confucian orthodoxy and other indigenous cults and practices, Matteo Ricci and others extolled the official state ideology of Confucianism, characterizing it as a system of moral wisdom, while describing Daoism and other popular indigenous rituals and practices as "deluded beliefs" (*mixin* 迷信), a term they introduced to the Chinese. As their perception of

Daoism gradually gained acceptance among the Europeans of the Age of Enlightenment and then through them among the modern Chinese intellectuals of the late nineteenth and early twentieth centuries, Daoism came to be seen as a backward and unenlightened mishmash of irrational beliefs and practices.[5]

For many Chinese scholars of Daoism, the decline of Daoism was hastened in the late nineteenth and early twentieth centuries by the forces of modernity. In a recent major survey of Daoist history, Ren Jiyu and several other leading Chinese scholars write of the Daoist decline in the late Qing period as part of the general and pervasive decay of the Qing empire. They attribute the decline to such factors as the state-led antisuperstition campaigns and other secularizing projects. This view is shared by the authors of another recent multivolume history of Daoism.[6]

The Daoist decline thesis may be more muted in the West, but it persists in western writings on Daoist history, where it is often couched in more nuanced arguments centering on state persecution and sectarianism, such as those advanced by early sinologists like J. J. M. de Groot. Writing at a time of intense and often violent cultural clashes between China and the West, de Groot held that many of his European compatriots entertained a romantic notion about Chinese religious tolerance, first popularized by Enlightenment thinkers such as Voltaire whose knowledge of China, ironically, came from the writings of Jesuit missionaries like Matteo Ricci. In light of popular antimissionary sentiments, which erupted as the Boxer uprising throughout north China in 1900, de Groot vowed to "endeavour to show that the favorable opinion entertained by the world at large about the tolerance and liberality of China on religion is purely chimerical." Having culled the Chinese classics, penal codes, court decrees, and recorded customs, de Groot concluded that state persecution of and ideological hostility toward non-Confucian religions and cults had been extensive and rampant throughout Chinese history. Implicit in de Groot's study is the thesis of Chinese religious decline and destruction by imperial state persecution and sectarianism.[7]

Although few scholars now share de Groot's view of societal and state attitudes toward religion in China, subtler and more nuanced variations of the decline thesis still persist. In a popular primer on Daoism, Kristofer Schipper, the esteemed scholar of Daoism and an ordained Daoist cleric, rectifies de Groot's self-serving argument by stressing the role of western influence in the "progressive decline of Daoism over the last centuries." For Schipper, the destruction of Daoism, which began in the sixteenth century, must also be understood as the result of a series of collusions, first between the proselytizing Jesuits and the Ming Confucian officials, then among European-influenced Chinese intellectuals and the modern state, and finally with Marxist-inspired socialist state policies and the mass movement of the Great Proletarian Cultural Revolution. Yet even his admirable rectification of the historical record accepts the thesis of Daoist decline in the face of advancing modernity in China.[8]

But was Daoism really in decline in modern China, as embodied by the sickly Daoist beggar? Had Daoist monasteries, lineages, ideas, techniques, and practices become as irrelevant to the modern world as the Daoist beggar appeared to be in the modern metropolis of Shanghai? How did contemporary Daoist practitioners experience the modern world as symbolized by Shanghai, with all its new physical, social, and cultural trappings? How did they envision and explain their encounter with modernity in their own daily life?

Very different responses to these questions emerged in the books, articles, and poems by Chen Yingning and his fellow practitioners of Daoist inner alchemy that appeared in the journals they published in Shanghai from the 1920s to the 1940s. In their writings, I encounter a different picture of what modern Daoism meant and how it fared during the same decades when Eileen Chang was growing up and writing her classic sketches of modern Shanghai. I can still recall my own sense of wonder and excitement more than a decade ago when I first read a poem composed by one of Chen Yingning's fellow practitioners of inner alchemy:

> One
> Marry the Bridegroom Golden Lad in a timely way;
> Betroth the Beautiful Maid at the age of sixteen.
> Quietly wait to sequester the Sweetheart in the
>   Golden Chamber,

And in ten moons the Pearly Fetus matures into a
   Fragrant Infant.
                     Two
Nourish the Fetus of Peace and Beauty to come out
   of the Dark Pass.
Fear not the nine years of toil and hardship.
Ply to and fro to bathe in Lake Kunming,
Await quietly the Scarlet Summons to depart
   the Mud Ball.

The poet was Chang Zunxian 常遵先 (1873–?), a devoted practitioner of the ancient Daoist meditative technique of inner alchemy. In this verse, inspired by a Ming adept's poem on the practice, Chang displayed his classical learning and his erudition in inner alchemy. Drawing on a rich repertoire of inner alchemic metaphors for the vital energies (the Beautiful Maid and the Golden Lad), Chang discussed his own sense of the delicate timing needed for uniting, refining, and perfecting these vitalities within the location in the lower abdomen known as the Golden Chamber for the goal of gestating and engendering a new self. He further affirmed that through persistent meditative care and nurture, figuratively described as "bathing," the newborn "Fetus of Beauty and Peace" would answer the "Scarlet Summons" of the celestial realm and ascend from the "Pass of Darkness" in the lower abdomen through the Mud Ball within the head to achieve the ultimate freedom of an immortal.[9]

When he was not writing about his inner alchemic practice or doing editorial work for *The Biweekly to Promote the Good* (*Yangshan banyue kan* 揚善半月刊), which was published every two weeks in the city, Chang ran a small private clinic and practiced Chinese medicine for a living in the bustling South Market, right off the Bund. Originally from Xiangtan in Hunan province, Chang came from a literati family steeped in Confucian learning. Well versed in the Classics and widely traveled, he joined the anti-Qing revolutionary movement in the early 1900s and served as a ranking official in the first Republican regime in Guangdong after 1911. But when the northern warlords seized the reins of power in the new Republican government, Chang left his post and retired to his home in Xiangtan. While observing the mourning rites for his father in the late 1920s, Chang found himself the target of the communist-led local peasant movement in Hunan. Like many other Hunanese literati, Chang had to flee for his life. He finally settled in the booming city of Shanghai, where he turned to practicing Chinese medicine for a living. In his spare time, Chang engaged in Daoist inner alchemic meditation, wrote and published poems and articles on the practice, and served as one of the contributing editors for the biweekly.

And Chang was not alone. Among the tens of thousands who came to seek shelter and food, fame and fortune, in the expanding treaty port city of Shanghai, many followed a life centered on the Daoist inner alchemic meditation and other ascetic practices, even though most of them were not ordained or consecrated Daoist clerics (*daoshi* 道士). For almost a decade, from 1933 to the early 1940s, many of these lay practitioners were the readers, writers, contributors, and editors of the *Yangshan* biweekly and its successor, *The Immortals' Way Monthly* (*Xiandao yuebao* 仙道月報). Using these journals as their forum, they wrote articles and poems, exchanged correspondence, and offered testimonials on the subject of Daoism and inner alchemy. Many of their fellow readers and practitioners enthusiastically read and responded to their publications.

Under the leadership of Chen Yingning, Chang and this group of Shanghai practitioners actively promoted traditional Daoist teachings and inner alchemy as "Immortals' Learning" (*xianxue* 仙學). In the eight years from 1933 to the Japanese takeover of the foreign concessions in Shanghai in December 1941, Chen and his fellow advocates published these two journals, which became public forums where they and likeminded practitioners of Daoist inner alchemy pushed for a wider and more public understanding of Daoist history and geography and Daoism's contribution to Chinese civilization. They vigorously promoted a national organization to link the various Daoist sects and lineages, as well as ordained clergy and lay practitioners. They established and operated a small but popular seminary in the French Concession to teach and disseminate the Daoist classics and inner alchemic meditation practice. As they sought to make the Daoist self-cultivation tradition more appealing and accessible to their readers and followers in and beyond Shanghai, Chen and his colleagues reformulated traditional teachings and practices of Daoist inner alchemy by adopting and appropriating ideas from the modern discourses of nationalism and science then spreading in China. Over the eight-year period, they actively promoted this reinvented Daoist inner alchemy through the publication and distribution of these journals, personal communication and travels, and meetings of the journal editors, their readers, followers, and practitioners. Out of these connections and activities, a sense of community was engendered and strengthened. A network of inner alchemic practitioners connected through their common interest and ties to the journals gradually emerged, with a membership that extended from Shanghai to Chongqing, from Luoyang to Luzon in the Philippines.

After the greater Shanghai area fell to the Japanese in the autumn of 1937, Chen and other members of the lay-centered inner alchemic network withdrew to the International Settlement and the French Concession. From inside these zones in the city, which were known as the Solitary Isle (*gudao* 孤島), they endured, continuing their publication of the monthly and their operation of the journal-supported network of Daoist inner alchemy practice for another two and a half years. It was only in the winter of 1941 when Japanese forces attacked Pearl Harbor and took over the Solitary Isle in the heart of Shanghai that the lively *Xiandao* monthly ceased publication, and its network of practitioners disbanded.

But the legacy of the Shanghai Daoist group has continued to assert itself well into the post-1949 era in both mainland China and Taiwan. In the 1950s, Chen Yingning played a significant role in the emerging self-cultivation and healing movement known as *qigong* 氣功, a practice that stresses healing and health through a range of Daoist- and Buddhist-inspired breath regulation, meditation, and trance techniques. He was active in state-approved Daoist organizations in the PRC and led a host of Daoist reform projects until his death in 1969. In Taiwan, a journal run by a group of his disciples and devoted to the dissemination of Daoist inner alchemy and self-cultivation practice was published from the early 1950s into the 1990s. Since the 1980s, his writings have been reprinted and circulated widely. His teachings have continued to inspire and influence communities of contemporary *qigong* practitioners and Daoists in China and beyond.[10]

Chen Yingning, Chang Zunxian, and many of their colleagues and followers embodied a Daoist tradition and their experience manifested a history of Daoism different from the one centered on monastic decline or clerical corruption. Their lives and careers represented a vastly different encounter with the forces of modernity in early twentieth-century China. Yet their story has so far remained largely unknown.

This book seeks to tell their story. It is a story about how modern lay Daoist practitioners such as Chen Yingning sought to renew the Daoist tradition by incorporating the new into the old and by reinventing the ancient Daoist practice of inner alchemy through a close engagement with nationalism, science, the religious reform movement, new urban print culture, and other forces of modernity. It is a story about the Daoist encounter with modernity, a story about resilience, reinvigoration, and revival through innovation of a Daoist tradition known as "literati Daoism" (*wenren Daojiao* 文人道教) in early twentieth-century China.

Defining "Literati Daoism" and Inner Alchemy

If Eileen Chang's vignette of the Daoist beggar was meant to evoke a familiar picture of the clerical and monastic Daoism of the late imperial and early Republican eras, the life and careers of urban educated lay practitioners such as Chang Zunxian and Chen Yingning constitute a less familiar dimension of Daoism. Their obscurity stems in part from the fact that they do not fit our conventional categories of what or who constituted Daoism and Daoist identity. Neither ordained nor affiliated with any specific Daoist monasteries or sects, Chen and Chang were lay Daoists by devotion and practice. They were part of the lay Daoist tradition that Timothy Barrett and Russell Kirkland have recently termed "literati or gentry Daoists," the members of the educated, often salaried or landed elite in traditional China who embraced the Daoist ethos, shared a Daoist outlook on life, and most of all pursued various Daoist techniques of self-cultivation in search of spirituality and self-identity. Although their devotion to Daoist pursuits defined their religious identity, their social and cultural status as part of the elite often defied conventional definitions.

Indeed, as noted above, Daoism has long been defined by three mutually related sets of influences: the Song neo-Confucian interpretation, the early missionary definition, and the modern state's regulatory efforts in China. Both the early neo-Confucian vision of Daoism as a moral and philosophical tradition centered on sages such as Laozi and Zhuangzi and the later Jesuit dismissal of it as a collection of primitive rituals and superstitious beliefs rooted among rural peasants have had lasting impacts on Daoist historiography. In the late nineteenth and early twentieth centuries, as the Qing and the Republican states sought to modernize themselves in the image of the western powers, they redrew the boundaries between the public and the private, the secular and the sacred, by granting legal protections only to those well-organized religious institutions and sects that could be integrated as organized "religions," and by outlawing the more diffused community-based rituals and practices as "superstitions." As a result, only two well-organized Daoist groups, the liturgical Orthodox One (Zhengyi 正一) sects and the monastic Complete Perfection (Quanzhen 全眞) lineages, managed to have gained legal status through formation of a national organization and local registration in the early twentieth century.[11]

The effects of Confucian historiography and modern state policies toward religion can still be felt in debates about what constitutes Daoism, or who is a Daoist, albeit in subtler and more implicit terms of subject matter or subjects treated as "Daoist." Although we have clearly moved away from the early sinologists' almost exclusive focus on philosophical Daoism, most scholars today still concentrate on two main groups of people and institutions: the Zhengyi liturgical specialists, who trace their origins to the earlier Celestial Masters (Tianshi 天師) sects, and their ritual-centered practices based in rural communities; and the organized Daoist clergies such as the Quanzhen sects and their monastically based practices, communities, and lineages.[12] Reflecting the sociological and historical turn in the field of Chinese religious studies, the shift in attention to rural ritual specialists and monastic practitioners seeks to situate and understand

Daoism in the historical and social contexts of "popular religion." But, since few of these recent studies examine the Daoist experience outside these two settings, they may have inadvertently reinforced the old boundaries for defining Daoism as being composed of organized lineages and monastic orders on one hand and the "diffused" rural ritual specialists and their communities on the other.

As such, they still do not adequately encompass and explain the richness and complexity of the Daoist experience in Chinese history and society. For example, they cannot account for the role and contributions of "gentry Taoism" during the Tang period, a time when many of the educated and bureaucratic elite, such as Sima Chengzhen 司馬承禎 (647–735), Wu Yun 吳筠 (?–778), Cheng Xuanying 成玄英 (fl. 630s–650s), and Li Bai 李白 (701–62) were actively engaged in promoting and disseminating Daoist ideas and techniques of self-cultivation through their writings.[13]

The analytical limits of the earlier paradigms have prompted scholars of Daoism such as Timothy Barrett and Russell Kirkland to stress the importance of paying attention to the "diverse social backgrounds of the various historical leaders and shapers of the various streams that formed the tradition." To Kirkland, the involvement in Daoism of the educated elite, or what he terms "literati Taoists," can be traced to the early Louguan Daoists, who through their representative work, "Scripture of Western Ascension," advocated a model of self-cultivation that would appeal to literati of all ages. He points out that literati Daoists such as Ge Hong 葛洪 (283–343) played a pivotal role in both refining and promulgating many characteristically Daoist ideas and techniques, including alchemical practices as a means of self-transformation in the early medieval period. In the twelfth and thirteenth centuries, literati Daoists such Wang Zhe 王嚞 (1113–70) and his followers were instrumental in developing the early eremitical and individually based practices of inner alchemy into the monastically centered regimens and lineage orders that still endure today.[14]

Implicit in this and other studies is the view that literati Daoism, which stressed personal engagement with a variety of self-cultivation techniques, has been a continuous tradition from the medieval period to the late imperium. The tradition was embodied and carried on through and by socially affiliated groups whose membership changed over time, from the aristocrats of the Eastern Jin dynasty in southeast China through the elite members of the Tang court based in Xi'an down to assorted civil service examination aspirants, landowners, merchants, and diviners of the early thirteenth-century Jurchen empire in north China. As the studies by Barrett and Kirkland show, these educated elite practitioners were neither ordained Daoist clerics nor temple managers nor villager ritual specialists. Indeed, the literati or gentry Daoists became so by virtue of a variety of factors or reasons, ranging from their faith in Daoist beliefs to intellectual and personal ties with Daoist institutions and clergy to, more fundamentally, their embrace of the Daoist vision and ideas, their observance of Daoist precepts, and their pursuit of Daoist longevity and self-cultivation techniques.

Daoist inner alchemy formed the core of traditional literati Daoist endeavors. As a self-cultivation meditative technique, inner alchemy is generally considered to have matured around the late Tang and early Song periods. It combines earlier speculative cosmologies derived from the *Book of Changes* (*Zhouyi* 周易), yin-yang (陰陽) and Five Phases (*wuxing* 五行) theories; nourishing life (*yangsheng* 養生) techniques and regimens such as regulated breathing (*huxi* 呼吸); gymnastics; and bedchamber arts (*fangzhong shu* 房中術). It used the symbolic terminology inherited from the early "outer" or "laboratory alchemy" (*waidan* 外丹). Ideologically, inner alchemy has since its inception been characterized by its capacity to incorporate Confucianist teachings and Buddhist elements, a syncretic disposition that became even more pronounced during Ming and Qing times.[15]

The ultimate goal of inner alchemy has remained the attainment of immortality, a goal that for some meant unification with Nature and for others eternal life. Since at least the twelfth century, inner alchemy has been a definitive and integral part of monastic life among the major Daoist lineages and schools, and its meditative techniques and cosmology have inextricably been associated with the literati pursuits of health, longevity, wisdom, and transcendence.[16]

But literati Daoism as an analytical category is not without its critics and limits. One objection has to do with the analytical usefulness of the category. If the term "literati Daoist" refers simply to the personal spiritual self-cultivation beliefs and practices of individual members of the educated elite, then the "literati Daoist" is easily submerged in the larger social group we call scholar-officials or the gentry. But, even though the Daoist ordination rites are sometimes compared to the rigorous Confucian civil service examination system, they could never compete with the latter in granting both prestige and status to the successful candidates. Although ordained Daoist clerics gained a special status and authority as ritual specialists or monastic practitioners with privileged access to the spiritual world, their vocational skills and social status often excluded them from membership in the scholar elite as defined by orthodox Confucians, who tended to treat them with scorn and disdain. For that reason, the term "literati Daoist" does have the advantage of highlighting the learned culture of the Daoists as a social group distinct and separate from the gentry.

But what is more important and relevant, "literati Daoism" fittingly describes the unique contributions that many lay literati individuals and groups outside Daoist monastic or liturgical sects made to Daoist institutional, praxical, and intellectual traditions in Chinese history. As an analytical concept, it takes more seriously the personal and private beliefs and practices of lay Daoist practitioners and seeks to understand them in their own historical and social contexts, rather than explaining away their lives as the products of general cultural trends or idiosyncratic habits.

Literati Daoism and Its Modern Fate

For that reason and many others, the story of urban lay Daoist practitioners like Chang Zunxian, Chen Yingning, and their colleagues in 1930s Shanghai is significant. First, the story offers a rare opportunity to examine the history and transformation of the literati Daoist tradition in early twentieth-century China, a topic still largely unexplored in Daoist studies. Since Liu Ts'un-yan's pioneering studies of the Ming literati's intellectual debt to and involvement in Daoism more than three decades ago,[17] historians and scholars have paid closer attention to both the roles of literati Daoists in Chinese society and politics and the social, political, and cultural interaction between the literati elite and Daoist institutions, ideas, and individuals during the late imperial period. Huang Zhaohan's studies on the emergence of the Western Lineage in Daoist inner alchemy explores the active participation of the local literati elite in the creation and dissemination of Daoist inner alchemic writings and practice in late eighteenth- and early nineteenth-century Sichuan. Zeng Shaonan, Farzeen Baldrian-Hussein, Yang Ming, and others have examined the writings and practice of several influential literati Daoists from the Song to the late Qing period.[18] Yet, few of these studies have dealt with the literati Daoists' modern transformation in early twentieth-century China. The prominent exception is Vincent Goossaert. Although his recent pathbreaking study focuses on the social and institutional changes affecting Daoist clerics and their temples, Goossaert has also carefully traced the transformation of some urban-based Daoist lay practitioner groups in the context of the emerging self-cultivation market both in and around Beijing in the late nineteenth and early twentieth century.[19] My own study seeks to further expand the investigation of the subject by tracing historical changes and continuities within the literati Daoist tradition in the first few decades of twentieth-century Shanghai.

Second, the focus on the early Republican era offers a unique opportunity to study and examine the nature and process of the Daoist encounter with modernity. As a major treaty port opened to foreign settlement, trade, and missionary activity in the 1860s, Shanghai experienced the rapid spread of western cultural and material influences in terms of industrial expansion, demographic growth, urban culture, and civic self-governance during the late nineteenth and early twentieth centuries. While living and practicing in this fast-changing and modernizing city, Chen and his associates engaged with many of the modern intellectual and cultural currents and movements that shaped modern China. Their nativistic advocacy of the Daoist inner alchemic meditation as the genuine "national learning," their polemics against the Japanese-influenced Pure Land Buddhist sects in Shanghai, their incorporation of western scientific ideas and values into the traditional Daoist cosmology and inner alchemy, their use of modern mass media and seminars as means of teaching and disseminating Daoist learning and practice, and their efforts at national organization of both lay and clerical practitioners combined to shape the trajectories of the Daoist engagement with modernity in early Republican China.

Third, the story of Chen Yingning and the Shanghai "Immortals' Learning" group does not end with the 1941 Japanese takeover of the foreign concessions in Shanghai. Their legacy continued to unfold and helped shape developments in Daoism after 1949 through Chen's continuing personal involvement in the emergence of *qigong* movements in the early 1950s and later through the publication of his writings in the contemporary, post-Mao era. The story of the Shanghai network of urban lay Daoist inner alchemy practitioners is crucially relevant to our understanding of Daoism and its practice as a living tradition in modern China today.

Sources and Outline of the Narrative

The primary source materials for this book are the *Yangshan* biweekly and the *Xiandao* monthly. These journals published essays, correspondence, commentaries, serialized books, poems, and testimonials written by Chen Yingning and fellow practitioners of inner alchemy in Shanghai and other parts of China. Supplementing these journals are several published monographs by Chen and members of the Shanghai group, as well as an unpublished manuscript composed by Chen and circulated among his associates and followers. In these writings, Chen and his fellow practitioners not only expounded their view of Daoist cosmology and inner alchemic theories of the body but also outlined how the practice of inner alchemy might lead to the transformation of the self and even the salvation of the nation. Lastly, I have also relied on notes taken during my initial field research in China in the fall of 1994 and on my interviews of and private correspondence with surviving members of the Shanghai group between 1995 and 2004.

The book consists of six chapters and an epilogue. Chapter 1 outlines several major historical developments and cultural currents during the late nineteenth and early twentieth centuries as background for understanding both the innovative reformulation and reinvigoration of the Daoist tradition of inner alchemy and the emergence of a flourishing Daoist inner alchemy community between the 1920s and the 1940s.

Chapter 2 traces the life and career of Chen Yingning from 1880 to the 1940s as a key leader of the urban lay-centered Daoist revival in inner alchemy in Republican Shanghai. Chen's lifelong pursuit of inner alchemy grew out of an early childhood experience of a nearly fatal illness. But in the late Qing cultural, political, and intellectual contexts, the culmination of Chen's search for a cure of his illness in his pursuit of Daoist inner alchemy intersected with China's national search for power and wealth and for modernity. As such, it took on much larger public and cultural meanings. I show how this intersection of a personal search and the national quest helped forge Chen's vision of the Daoist tradition and foster a remarkable albeit brief revival of Daoism and inner alchemic self-cultivation practice during the 1930s and 1940s.

Chapter 3 examines how Chen and his associates constructed modern Daoist inner alchemic theories of cosmology and the body by selectively integrating traditional inner alchemy with scientific and nationalistic discourses. These reformulations of Daoist inner alchemy and cosmology were meant not only to inform the individual pursuit of spirituality and transcendence but also to define and shape the "authentic" Chinese body and character for the nation. Rejecting as foreign and culturally inferior both the Buddhist mind-centered body and the western biologically driven body, Chen and his fellow practitioners argued for an "authentic" Chinese body as the only way to achieve the national and moral liberation of China. In favor of what they called "vitalism" (weisheng zhuyi 唯生主義), Chen and his colleagues located this "authentic Chinese" body in the Daoist inner alchemic tradition, which sought to transcend the divide between the mind and the body by uniting the mental and psychological energies of the Spirit (shen 神) and the physical vital forces of qi 氣 through persistent meditative practice. In this way, the Daoist inner alchemic body became the site and conduit for the production of cultural nationalism, and the personal pursuit of self-transformation came to be linked with the Republican state's quest for a new citizenship and cultural norms in the 1930s and 1940s.

Chapter 4 investigates both the normative discourse and the practice of modern Daoist inner alchemy by Chen Yingning and his Shanghai group of practitioners during the 1930s and 1940s. By closely analyzing the practice manuals, poems, testimonials, and letters of members of the Shanghai group, I reconstruct the normative and experiential dimensions of the modern inner alchemic practice as imagined and carried out by Chen and many of his fellow practitioners. I show that although modern inner alchemic practice continued to be influenced by tradition in its assumptions, regimen, and techniques, it also employed and appropriated concepts and practices of modern science and medicine in its reinvention and in its adaptation to the changed political, social, cultural, and material conditions of modern China.

Chapter 5 examines the social and cultural milieus of modern Daoist inner alchemy practice. By following the stories of how individual practitioners and small groups came to be involved in Chen Yingning's advocacy and pursuit of the Immortals' Learning, I show that the modern practitioners of Daoist inner alchemy came from a variety of personal, social, and professional backgrounds. They embraced the practice for a range of reasons, such as concern for physical health and well-being, spirituality, and cultural or national identity. During the early decades of the twentieth century, they faced a host of daunting national crises, political and economic difficulties, and numerous personal obstacles as they took up the practice. In overcoming traditional difficulties and new challenges, these practitioners demonstrated remarkable resilience, courage, persistence, and ingenuity.

In telling the stories about individual practitioners and self-cultivation groups in Shanghai and beyond, I also trace their origins and the evolution of urban-based and lay-centered Daoist inner alchemic practice from small and private circles of friends and enthusiasts to the geographically far-flung network of a self-conscious public community, which extended beyond the city from the 1920s to the early 1940s. I argue that this transformation took place because

Chen and his follow practitioners conceived of the Daoist tradition as a resource and spiritual space to be shared by the public. Through their journals and published writings, they created an open forum and public space for Daoist inner alchemic practice throughout the 1930s. As it changed from an "esoteric" pursuit of the few into a public practice by many, Daoist inner alchemy offered its modern practitioners both practical means of caring for the body and the mind and a new venue to forge and maintain a new cultural or religious identity in the modernizing society of early Republican China.

Chapter 6 delineates the main institutional developments and innovations of the Daoist revival during the 1930s and early 1940s. By focusing on the role of journal publication and circulation by the Yihuatang 翼化堂 publishing house, I show how Chen Yingning and his associates used the emerging mass print culture to create a vibrant and thriving public sphere of Daoist practice. Through their active promotion of the Immortals' Learning, Chen and his colleagues redefined modern Daoism by appropriating sacred symbols from the early sage lore of China and by incorporating concepts of modern science to purge traditional Daoist inner alchemy of elements that could be identified with Buddhist idealism. Chen and his associates helped forge a sense of identity and fellowship among their followers through the nexus of writing, communicating, and publishing centered around the journals. Emerging from these writings and correspondence and the circulation of the journals was a vibrant community and fellowship of modern inner alchemy practitioners. This thriving Daoist revival was aborted only by the Japanese occupation of all of Shanghai in December 1941.

The Epilogue traces Chen Yingning's career in the 1940s and early 1950s, especially his transformation from a Daoist scholar and practitioner to a leading Daoist reformer under the changed political and cultural circumstances of the PRC. I argue that despite the new restrictions on the practice of inner alchemy, Chen sought to preserve and continue the Daoist tradition of inner alchemic practice by reformulating it as part of "Daoist learning" (*daojiao zhi xueshu* 道教之學術) closely associated with the now-sanctioned discourse of science, and by promoting it as the new *qigong* practice and an efficacious self-healing and public health alternative to the limited resources of western medicine at the time. I conclude with some reflections on the significance of the achievements of the Daoist reforms throughout the 1930s and early 1940s and their ramifications for understanding the dynamics between Daoism and modernity and the process of religious secularization in modern China.

1

Late Qing and Early Republican Daoism

The modern transformation of the literati Daoist tradition and inner alchemy has to be understood in the context of several major social and cultural developments at the turn of the twentieth century: the growth of nationalism, the spread of science, the increasing attention to personal health and well-being among the urban population, the emergence of the gender revolution, and the state-sponsored and intellectual-driven reform of religion. All these encouraged both intellectuals and ordinary people to search for new forms of spirituality and religion in the face of advancing modernity. Chen Yingning and the Shanghai Daoist inner alchemy community were integral parts of that search in the early twentieth century.

For the Chinese, the nineteenth century was catastrophic and traumatic. Violent uprisings, destructive rebellions, and humiliating defeats at the hands of foreign powers alternated to form the main historical rhythm of the late nineteenth and the early twentieth centuries. The Opium War in 1840, the mid-nineteenth-century Taiping Uprising, the defeat by Japan in 1895, the abortive 1898 Reforms, the Boxer Rebellion in 1901, and the collapse of the Manchu dynasty in 1911 not only highlighted China's obvious weakness but, in the eyes of many intellectuals, revealed a deep systemic national and cultural crisis.

To understand the causes of China's weakness and the secrets of Western power, China's cultural elite turned to a comparative examination of Chinese and Western cultures for answers and solutions. Their collective soul-searching began in the aftermath of the Taiping Uprising and accelerated after the humiliating defeat by Japan in 1895. Although the cultural elite clung to the sinocentric vision of Chinese moral superiority in the post-Taiping "self-strengthening" reforms, many grudgingly began to acknowledge the material or technical superiority of the West. For them, the cure for China's weakness was to import and graft western technologies onto the Chinese moral and cultural core. For many, the obvious manifestations of western strength were the physical health and vigor of foreigners. Indeed, around the turn of the century, physical health and vigor became inextricably intertwined with a rising nationalist discourse informed by social Darwinist theories about racial survival and advancement.[1]

Reflective of this emerging concern for the health and physical vigor of the nation was the renewed interest in the traditional discourse of "nourishing life" (yangsheng 養生). Some saw the traditional regimen of physical self-cultivation as relevant to the task of developing a healthy and robust nation. Among the host of traditional nourishing-life texts published during the latter half of the nineteenth century were some that incorporated the western hygiene and health techniques. As early as 1858, Pan Wei 潘蔚, a ranking Qing official and reform advocate, published a reprint of an early Qing classic on traditional self-cultivation under the new title *Essential Techniques for Guarding Life* (*Weisheng yaoshu* 衛生要術). In 1881, the work was again reprinted under a different title: *An Illustrated Treatise on Inner Practice* (*Neigong tushuo* 內功圖說).[2] In 1935, another reprint appeared under a much more modernized title, *The Path to Health* (*Jiankang zhi lu* 健康之路),[3] as the notion of health (*jiankang* 健康) and hygiene became increasingly popularized.

The most representative late Qing intellectual to advocate the pursuit of health through self-cultivation practice was the well-known reform advocate, thinker, and entrepreneur Zheng Guanying

鄭觀應 (1842–1921). Zheng wrote the influential *Alarming Words for Prosperous Times* (*Shengshi weiyan* 盛世危言) and was keenly aware of the value and relevance of physical health and vigor to the survival of the nation. An avid practitioner of Daoist self-cultivation, Zheng befriended many Daoist adepts, including Fangnei sanren 方內散人 (AKA Wan Ligeng 萬立賡, z. Ganchen 干臣, h. Qiyingzi 啓英子,1848–?) and Huang Suizhi 黃邃之 (?–1937), who later became an associate and friend of Chen Yingning. From these adepts, Zheng learned various Daoist meditation techniques and practiced them all his life in search of health and spiritual well-being. He used his personal wealth unsparingly to preserve and distribute Daoist classics and scriptures. Zheng's Daoist self-cultivation pursuits and his patronage of efforts to collect and distribute Daoist scriptures remain largely overlooked and unknown. His interest in Daoism went far beyond a personal hobby. It stemmed partly from his personal quest for health and partly from his vision of Daoism as a repository of China's cultural essence. In 1909, Zheng published a supplement to his early famous reform tract. The entire opening volume is devoted to his essays and correspondence on the importance of Daoist technologies (*dao shu* 道術) to the task of strengthening the nation and the pursuit of self-cultivation. He also sought to synthesize Chinese health regimens with Western hygiene practices in his 1890 compendium *Essentials for Protecting Life from China and Abroad* (*Zhongwai weisheng yaozhi* 中外衛生要旨).[4]

No one did more to shape late Qing intellectual discourse on the vital connection of personal physical health to national power than Yan Fu 嚴復 (1854–1921) with his influential 1895 essay "On Power" ("Yuanqiang" 原強). Writing in the immediate aftermath of China's humiliating defeat at the hands of Meiji Japan, Yan commented that one source of the national strength of European powers was their attention to cultivating robust physiques (*tipo qiangjian* 體魄強健) among their citizens, especially women. By contrast, Chinese men who smoked opium and women who bound their feet and breasts enervated the vitality and fertility of the nation. Yan argued that in the West, men and especially women were unfettered by these physically restricting and debilitating practices. Physically vibrant and robust, they bore healthy and strong offspring. Zheng argued, "Since the mother is healthy, her son will be stout. By cultivating its earlier generation, the race advances forward" (gai mujian er hou erfei, pei qi xiantian er zhong nai jin 蓋母健而後兒肥, 培其先天而種乃進). Reflecting the influence of social Darwinism, Yan Fu and many of his generation perceived human history as a process of competition among the nations of the world. Physical health, sexual prowess, fertility, and bodily strength thus became the direct expressions of national strength. As such, the body was envisioned as the repository of potential national power. The proper care and continued rejuvenation of the body held the key to the survival and prosperity of a race (ren zhong 人種).[5]

Yan's argument on physical strengthening as a way to national power in turn influenced his generation and led many to view and stress physical education and health as the key to nation-building and racial viability.[6] A healthy and robust physique meant not just bodily well-being and vitality but also national power and wealth. It even justified the very existence of a nation. In the words of one late Qing, early Republican medical reformer, the secret of national power lay in the health of the individual:

A person's spirit (jingshen 精神) lives in the body. The Original Qi (元氣) of a nation lies in the bodies of its people. There is a saying by a western sage: "A healthy mind lives in a healthy body." If we extrapolate from this, then "a healthy nation resides in a healthy population." The protection of health is the role of hygiene (weisheng 衛生). In the world of living things, the Way of survival and competition does not abate for even one instant.[7]

Even outside the emerging state medical establishment, the youth and intellectuals of the May Fourth era were convinced of the vital importance of individual health and physical vigor to national survival. Writing in the popular journal *New Youth* (Xin qingnian 新青年), an impassioned Mao Zedong 毛澤東 (1893–1976) warned readers of the national crisis that arose from China's collective weakness:

Our nation is wanting in strength. The martial spirit has not been encouraged. The physical condition of the population deteriorates daily. If this state of affairs continues, it will become an extremely disturbing phenomenon. Our weakness will increase further if our bodies are not strong. We will cower at the sight of enemy soldiers. Then how can we attain our goals and make ourselves respected?[8]

For Mao and many of his generation, the pursuit of health and physical cultivation became an integral part of national salvation. Such thinking gave rise to a series of state-sponsored medical reforms undertaken by the late Qing court and then the expanding Republican state to modernize public health and medical care by establishing western-style medical schools, hospitals, and standards of medical practice, primarily in urban areas and for the urban elite. With the establishment of a modern medical profession and public health institutions, procedures, and standards, both the state and urban media actively promoted concepts of public health, sanitation, and personal and domestic hygiene for the purpose of improving the quality and strength of the nation.[9]

In this way, the care and discipline of the body became an intense focus of Chinese state-building. Foot binding, opium smoking, and other "unhealthy" bodily practices became the target of public censure and prohibition after the Republican revolution. Public health, domestic and personal hygiene, healthcare for women and children, and the martial arts were actively promoted in the emerging urban media in cities across China. With their feet unbound, women also increasingly turned to activities and practices aimed at the better care and health of their bodies. As the concepts and practices of personal hygiene and physical health came to be promoted and linked with the goals of strengthening the nation and the race (*qiangguo qiangzhong* 強國強種), women, especially urban and educated women, like their male counterparts, also participated increasingly in a host of bodily practices ranging from personal and household hygiene to dietary regimens to physical exercise to the spiritually oriented pursuit of self-cultivation.

Cultivation for the Nation: Late Qing and Early Republican Self-Cultivation

Indeed, aside from the state-centered initiatives and propaganda for physical health and prowess, the popular pursuit of self-cultivation practices (*xiulian* 修煉) for health and physical vigor also spread across China in the first two decades of the twentieth century. For many proponents of self-cultivation, the practice became more than just a simple pursuit of physical health and prowess. Self-cultivation in the form of various physio-spiritual regimens became the venue for re-experiencing and reinventing the cultural and spiritual traditions of China's past and for constructing a new cultural and religious identity in a time of great change.

The widespread interest in self-cultivation was in part engendered and sustained by the well-established religious traditions of Buddhism, Daoism, and especially by the various resurgent popular Buddho-Daoist-inspired millenarian devotional groups that Prasenjit Duara and others have termed "redemptive societies." Two of the most active redemptive societies were the Common Benevolence Society (Tongshan she 同善社) and the Society of the Way and Its Virtues (Daoyuan 道院; also known as the Morality Learning Institute, or Daode xueshe 道德學社), which spread throughout China during the late Qing and especially the early Republican periods. Most of these redemptive societies prescribed a variety of self-cultivation techniques, such as quiet-sitting meditation, scriptural recitation, and breathing exercises, as part of a strict daily regimen for their followers.[10]

In what Vincent Goossaert has called the "self-cultivation market,"[11] one of the most popular and widespread forms of meditative sitting was developed and promoted by the famous philosopher and public intellectual Jiang Weiqiao 蔣維喬 (1873–1958). Named after its author's sobriquet, *Master Yinshizi's Method for Quiet Sitting* (*Yinshizi jingzuo fa* 因是子靜坐法) became an instant best-seller when it was first published in 1914. People from all walks of life, especially college and high school students suffering from chronic illnesses and physical frailty, responded enthusiastically to the book. Many quiet-sitting practice groups and societies sprang up in schools and other institutions across the country. Practitioners and enthusiasts wrote to Jiang with inquiries and comments. The first edition of more than several tens of thousands of copies quickly sold out. Demand for the book remained high. Barely three years after its initial publication, a second, revised edition of the best-seller had to be printed. This was followed by a separate volume on quiet sitting specifically devised for Buddhist practitioners in 1922.[12]

Jiang's book on self-cultivation resonated with the cultural currents of his times on several levels. The book offered readers informative and helpful instructions for meditation, but it was more than just a practice manual. It was also a powerful testament to the resilience and survival of the cultural body of a nation. In the book, Jiang revealed intimate details about his history of suffering since childhood from an extremely frail constitution, a condition further aggravated by his habitual masturbation and his consumptive disorders during adolescence. Enumerating an array of symptoms that included night sweats, nocturnal emissions, dizziness, tinnitus, a sore back, palpations, recurrent fevers, and bloody coughs, Jiang's narrative about his mental anguish, physical afflictions, and final triumph over his illness-ravaged body struck a deep chord with his audience, especially students and youth. Like Jiang, many saw their own infirmities and poor health not only as personal afflictions and bad luck but also as emotional symbols of cultural enervation and national failure.

The occasion that prompted Jiang to write and publish his tract was also significant. In the preface to the 1917 edition, Jiang recalled the sharp twinge of embarrassment he felt when he first read two popular translations of books on quiet sitting by Japanese self-cultivation experts. For him, the popularity of these two books in China testified to the superior national character of the Japanese people and, by contrast, the shortcomings in the Chinese "national character" (*guomin genxing* 國民根性).

I have quietly observed the fundamental character of my own nation. Be it scholastic excellence or technical expertise or productive acumen, we Chinese tend to regard [such things] as private secrets to be concealed for one's own use, but never to be shown to others or shared with the public for study or exploration. From time immemorial to the present, those who mastered all the consummate arts and techniques but chose never to transmit them were truly many in number. The people of our eastern neighbor are, however, different in this respect. Whenever they obtained a technique from us, they presented it for public study and investigation. The results are far superior to ours, and we have to learn and obtain the techniques back from them.[13]

For Jiang, the decisive factor in modern Japan's success in gaining power and wealth was none other than the spirit of thorough study and investigation of things, which they acquired from and then applied to their pursuits of Chinese quiet-sitting techniques. In fact, the Japanese interest in China's ancient self-cultivation practice only served to affirm the power and efficacy of the tradition. Jiang hoped that his countrymen could cultivate the same kind of inquisitive and studious spirit in their pursuit of the indigenous tradition, since the practice of quiet sitting would foster perseverance and perceptiveness in its practitioners. He wrote in the preface to his book:

> Nowadays, our "national character" is still too frivolous and wavering. When faced with an event, many of us cannot fully comprehend its cause or reason, but simply follow it blindly and passively, much like a mob. We begin, but seldom finish. If our national character is such, aren't our country's days numbered! I want to save it through the quiet-sitting technique. Isn't it the perfect medicine prescribed by Bian Que of Lu? I shall pray for that result with this book.[14]

As implied by this allusion to the legendary physician Bian Que 扁鵲 of the Warring States period (475–221 BC), Jiang looked to China's antiquity as the ultimate and pristine source of inspiration for national reconstruction and cultural rejuvenation. Elsewhere he identified the inner practice (neigong 內功) that had evolved from China's ancient times as the origin of his own popular method. For Jiang, this ancient tradition of inner cultivation originated with the early Daoists and embodied the true spiritual and moral essence of the Chinese national character, which had since become corrupted and lost.[15] Through quiet-sitting practice, Jiang urged his audience to recover and re-experience the lost tradition both physically and spiritually. As they rejuvenated their physique, they also recovered their common tradition and culture.

Daoism as the Source and Essence of the Chinese Nation

Indeed, China's antiquity, especially its Daoist tradition, would for many Chinese play a great part in the nation's urgent search for a new identity in an age of change and turmoil. Like Jiang, many intellectuals around the turn of the century looked to China's ancient past and identified Daoism as a repository of the Chinese cultural essence and a promising resource for national renewal and salvation. The newfound interest in Daoism was in part driven by the reform thinkers' perception and embrace of an evolutionary cosmology that affirmed and reified such Darwinian values as change, adaptation, and progress. For some, Daoist philosophy offered parallels to and support for western notions of history and change. Daoist-informed concepts such as constant change (yi 易) or transformation (bian 變) as the fundamental principle of the natural, social, and moral orders reverberated with the newly introduced western theory of biological evolution and social progress. For late Qing reformers and intellectuals like Kang Youwei 康有爲 (1858–1927) and Tan Sitong 譚嗣同 (1865–98), such indigenous ideas not only inspired them intellectually but also validated their political reform programs by giving them a strong sense of cultural authenticity and historical inevitability. For Kang and Tan, the egalitarian social and political ideals espoused by ancient sages and attempted by early religious Daoists also provided intellectual and ideological inspiration for reform and action.[16]

The late Qing reformers' interest in Daoism can be traced to the evidentiary learning (kaozheng 考證) school of the eighteenth and early nineteenth centuries. Departing from the Confucian elite's prejudice toward Daoism, some evidentiary learning scholars began to explore the Daoist Canon (Daozang 道藏), the enormous encyclopedic corpus of Daoist writings, as a repository of knowledge in all branches of learning from China's past. For these scholars, questions of dating, authorship, and provenance of the texts in the Canon were more than just the objects of scholarly exegesis. Rather, the evidentiary learning scholars treated these questions as part of their collective search for the Way and truth. Because of their researches, the Daoist Canon as an object of scholarly study entered into the consciousness of many late Qing scholars and intellectuals.

One intellectual who pioneered the study of Daoism was the renowned evidentiary Confucian scholar and court official Yu Yue 俞樾 (1821–1907). Despite his jinshi degree and service as a Qing official, Yu exhibited little of the traditional Confucian scholarly disdain toward Daoist scriptures. Following the example of the great early Qing scholar Hui Dong 惠棟 (1697–1758), Yu Yue regarded Daoist writings as sharing the same cultural and intellectual origins as classical Confucianism. As such, Daoist works revealed the same principles or truth (*li* 理) manifested in Confucian classics. In annotating the Daoist popular scripture *Tract of Taishang on Action and Response* (*Taishang ganying pian* 太上感應篇) and in investigating Daoist hagiographies and magic, Yu brought the same high level of scholarly rigor and thoroughness to bear as he would have applied to any Confucian classic.[17]

The late Qing scholar and renowned Buddhist practitioner and lay activist Yang Wenhui 楊文會 (z. Renshan 仁山, 1837–1911) approached Daoist scriptures from a Buddhist perspective. Yang had converted to Buddhism early in his life. Through the Jinling Scripture Carving Bureau 金陵刻經處, which he established in Nanjing, Yang issued the first edition of the Buddhist Canon (Da zangjing 大藏經) published since 1738. Through his friendship with Japanese monks, Yang retrieved many Buddhist scriptures considered long lost in China. By the early twentieth century, under his leadership, centers devoted to circulating Buddhist scriptures were set up in Beijing, Shanghai, Tianjin, and other cities in China. He was also responsible for establishing the Buddhist Study Society (Foxue yanjiuhui 佛學研究會), the first such group in China, which led to the creation of the well-known Institute of Buddhist Learning (Neixue yuan 內學院).[18]

In his youth, Yang had also been attracted to Daoist learning and had been extremely fond of reading and collecting Daoist texts and books. A syncretist at heart, Yang saw Daoist scriptures as renditions from a different culture of the same truth manifested in Buddhist texts. Between 1896 and 1904, Yang returned to his earlier interests and edited and published at least four books of annotations on Daoist scriptures.[19] In a preface to one of these works, Yang wrote of his rediscovery of Daoism:

When I was young, I relished reading esoteric books (*qishu* 奇書). Whenever [I ran across] Daoist books, books of military strategy, or books by the early non-Confucian masters, I would buy them without fail. I acquired four annotated editions of *Yinfu jing* and I also handcopied the original (*zhengwen* 正文) as my own reading text. But I could not ascertain its subtle meaning yet. Later as I devoted myself to learning Buddhism, I put away all the texts of "miscellaneous learning" (*zaxue* 雜學) in the attic for over twenty years.

I happened on the handcopied version of the *Yinfu jing* scripture while sorting through my bookcases. After glancing through it, I found its arguments particularly extraordinary. So much so that it could only have been written by someone who had transcended the mundane and entered sagehood (*chaofan rusheng* 超凡入聖). So I cogitated and mulled it over in my heart. It then dawned on me that the profound meaning of the teaching transmitted by the ancient sages correlates with the Buddhist scriptures. Complying with their local speech (*fangyu* 方語), their respective languages appear distinctly different, but their meanings interpenetrate (*yishi xiang guan* 義實相貫).[20]

Both Yu Yue's and Yang's interest in Daoism reflected the pervasive influence of traditional syncretism, which had remained strong since the Song era. Yet behind their syncretist motives also lay their shared perception of Daoism as a legitimate body of knowledge worthy of scholarly investigation and intellectual reflection.

Indeed, by the early twentieth century, Daoism began to be increasingly viewed as an untapped legacy of Chinese culture. Its vast literature was seen as the records of historical change in religious, social, political, and cultural life in China. In the first few decades of the twentieth century, a new generation of scholars and western-trained historians turned their attention to Daoism. In 1910, Liu Shipei 劉師培 (1884–1920), a highly respected scholar and staunch anti-Manchu intellectual at Peking University, become one of the first modern scholars to peruse the entire Daoist Canon. In the detailed and useful notes he prepared on a large body of scriptures from the Daoist Canon, Liu brought his formidable erudition on philology and the Classics to bear. Through careful comparison and cross-examination with sources both in and outside the canon, he was able to provide accurate historical dates and trace the textual evolution of many of the scriptures.[21] Concurrent to Liu, other leading intellectuals such as Hu Shi 胡適 (1891–1962), Xu Dishan 許地山 (1892–1941), Chen Yinke 陳寅恪 (1890–1969), Chen Yuan 陳垣 (1880–1971), and Fu Qinjia 傅勤家 (fl. 1934) published historical studies of Daoism during the first three decades of the twentieth century.[22]

Changing Perceptions of the West

Even as Chinese intellectuals' attitude toward Daoism and Daoist knowledge was undergoing fundamental changes, their perception of the West and western learning was being transformed by events at home and abroad. By the early twentieth century, after several decades of learning and adopting from the West, the results were at best mixed. The Republican revolution appeared to have deteriorated into constant strife among western-backed warlords scrambling for power and spheres of influence. While the few treaty ports saw growth and expansion, the vast rural hinterlands remained in deepening poverty and bankruptcy. The educational reforms of the late Qing exposed China's youth to new areas of knowledge, but they had also induced in many of them a new discontent with the social and political realities surrounding them. The shortcomings of the West as a model were exposed at the 1919 Versailles Peace Conference, when the Allied powers snubbed China by transferring Germany's colonial privileges in China to Japan, even though China had fought on the side of the Allies.

In Europe, the devastation wrought by the Great War led intellectuals to ponder and rethink the spiritual and moral ramifications of technology and materialism. In the aftermath of the May Fourth movement, European antirationalism, skepticism, anarchism, and the criticism of materialism and technology filtered through to China, providing Chinese intellectuals with new perspectives and points of departure in their ongoing search for cultural identity and their efforts at redefining the sino-western encounter.

The most vivid and influential expression of this process of Chinese cultural reflection came in the form of a series of impassioned articles published by several leading intellectuals during the 1920s and 1930s. Appropriately named the debate between "science and the outlook on life" (*kexue yu rensheng guan* 科學與人生觀) or "science and metaphysics" (*kexue yu xuanxue* 科學與玄學), the ongoing intellectual dispute became the forum where divergent intellectual responses to the sino-western encounter were voiced. Sparked by a lecture that preached spiritual autonomy from science in early 1923, the debate involved leading Chinese intellectuals and scholars whose different perspectives on the relationship between science and life divided them into two camps. For the science camp, represented by the British-trained geologist Ding Wenjiang 丁文江 (1887–1936), science as a positivist methodology alone could confirm the natural world as the ultimate reality for humans. They thus affirmed the primacy of scientific knowledge derived from the natural world. Zhang Junmai 張君勱 (z. Jiasen 嘉森; also known as Carsun Zhang in the West, 1887–1968), whose initial lecture at Qinghua University in Beijing set off the debate, was the main spokesman for the camp of metaphysics or life outlook.

Moving away from the earlier sinocentric vision that focused on the Chinese moral core and western applications (ti yong 體用), the "science and outlook on life" debate of the 1920s initially centered on the cultural dichotomy between East and West, typically characterizing Asia as spiritual, quietistic, backward, pacific, and traditional and defining the West as scientific, dynamic, advanced, aggressive, and modern. Convinced of the innate relevance and viability of Chinese tradition to the modern world, disenchanted with the devastation of the Great War, and gravely concerned over the prospect of western cultural domination of China, many Chinese intellectuals involved in the debate sought to conceptually redefine the sino-western encounter. They stridently affirmed the autonomy of Chinese culture and rejected the claim to universality of western civilization by characterizing Chinese culture as historically unique. In the 1923 debate, intellectuals like Zhang Junmai went even further and viewed western science as a culturally specific product, even though scientific knowledge claimed to be universal. Reflective of their profound belief in free will and human autonomy in relation to science, Zhang and others also stressed the differentiation of various forms or branches of human knowledge. They argued for the distinction and separation of science, which was knowledge about nature, from what they called the "life outlook," which was about ethics, spirituality, philosophy, and psychology. They insisted that the latter existed outside the realm of objective material nature and addressed issues of human existence; they were, therefore, not subject to the same laws as science.[23]

The critique by Zhang and his colleagues in the metaphysics camp sprang from their profound skepticism about the function, nature, and limits of scientific knowledge. They were critical of science's exclusive focus on the material and natural world. They argued that the great discoveries of modern scientists had only contributed toward a sort of mechanical determinism, resulting in a modernity wherein the human soul and spirit were increasingly alienated by machines and technologies. Yet for them, the human soul remained the last territory beyond the reach of science. For that and other reasons, Zhang and his colleagues held that scientific knowledge gained through the study of the natural world had its limits. They argued that moral and religious insight and wisdom and other forms of what they called "metaphysics" or "life outlook" were an entirely autonomous system of knowledge independent of science, because they were acquired through intuition and other nonscientific means.[24]

The debates about eastern and western cultures and about "science and metaphysics" had profound intellectual significance for a generation of Chinese intellectuals beset with spiritual and cultural anguish over the conflicts between western modernity and Chinese tradition. For many Chinese, these debates demonstrated the limitations of western civilization, epitomized by the scientific and technological achievements, as revealed by the tragic events of the Great War. Science, and by extension western civilization, were viewed as being too materialistic (*weiwu* 唯物) and lacking in spirituality and morality. Further, many felt that science did not enjoy a monopoly over human knowledge. As part of a knowledge system, science was just one of many disciplines, and its sphere of knowledge applied only to the material world. Since human action and free will constituted a distinct realm of knowledge, one not susceptible to the laws of science, science could not and must not serve as the basis for moral or spiritual knowledge.

Many Chinese intellectuals held that since western culture arose from specific historical conditions and held no claim to universality, China could not and must not rely on the West as the model for its cultural evolution. The cultural relevance of China's own history was thus affirmed. For many, the debates not only revealed the "cultural deficiency" of science-centered western civilization but also valorized the autonomy of Chinese tradition and justified the search for solutions within China's past to compensate for the perceived shortcomings of science and western culture. The cultural and intellectual ramifications of these debates could hardly be overestimated.

Daoism in the Late Qing and Early Republican Period

Alongside these changing cultural and intellectual crosscurrents ran another, even deeper series of developments in Daoism that began in the Ming and Qing periods. In contrast to the widely held perception of a general decline in cloistered and liturgical Daoism since the Song dynasty, recent studies have shown that Daoism during the late imperial period was characterized by robust institutional renewal, innovative writings, and the extensive circulation in Chinese culture and society of Daoist concepts, techniques, and influences through the proliferation of Daoist scriptures and books. These developments, which have yet to be studied in full, formed the historical background to the renewed interest in Daoism around the turn of the twentieth century.

During the mid-seventeenth century, under charismatic leader Wang Changyue 王常月 (?–1680), the Longmen sect of the monastic Quanzhen sect at the White Cloud Monastery in Beijing witnessed a remarkable moral and institutional renewal. For the next century, this sect thrived. Its influence spread throughout the Jiangnan region, and it became one of the main formal religious organizations of the Qing dynasty.[25] Recent studies have also shown that up until the end of the imperial era in 1911 Daoism continued to be a vital political, cultural, and religious force in local communities in the frontier provinces of Gansu and Yunnan under the Ming, in the Qing capital of Beijing, and in the Henan, Jiangnan, and Guandong regions. By working with local officials, literati elites, and rural communities, Daoist monasteries and clerics of both the Quanzhen and the Zhengyi sect continued to maintain and expand their influence in local culture, politics, and society.[26]

Alongside monastic and liturgical Daoism during the Ming and Qing periods, Daoist inner alchemy practice also thrived and spread.

Over several centuries, many adepts of inner alchemy within the Quanzhen sects, such as Wu Shouyang 伍守陽 (1552–1640), Liu Huayang 柳華陽 (1736–?), Liu Yiming 劉一明 (1734–1821), and Min Yide 閔一得 (1758–1837), produced a remarkable and influential body of writings on the practice of inner alchemy.[27] Meanwhile, outside the cloisters of Quanzhen Daoism, Daoist knowledge, especially of inner alchemy, became integrated into popular beliefs and literature through the numerous inner alchemy writings produced and circulated from the late Ming through the Qing periods. The proliferation of Daoist concepts and practices in both the popular and the literati imagination was evidenced in the widespread presence of themes and characters informed by Daoism in popular novels, plays, and literary sketches.[28]

But parallel to its dissemination among monastic Daoists and in popular writings, the practice of inner alchemy also gained popularity among literati scholars and lay practitioners outside the Daoist monastic orders. Through their writings, many literati and other lay practitioners—notably Lu Xixing 陸西星 (1520–1606), Cao Heng 曹珩 (fl. 1630s), Qiu Zhao'ao 仇兆鰲 (1638–1713), Tao Susi 陶素耜 (fl. mid-1600s), Fu Jinquan 傅金銓 (1796–1850), Li Xiyue 李西月 (1796–1861), and Wang Qihuo 汪啓濩 (1838–1917)—emerged as leading proponents of Daoist inner alchemy during the late imperial period. Writings by these adepts and others added greatly to the corpus of Daoist alchemic scriptures. In addition, many of these inner alchemists were actively involved in collecting, editing, printing, and circulating scriptures and inner alchemy texts that had not been included in the 1444 and 1607 editions of the Daoist Canon. Their collective efforts played a vital role in propagating inner alchemic practice in the late imperial period.[29]

The enthusiasm for Daoist knowledge was evident in the continuous efforts undertaken at various times throughout the Qing dynasty at supplementing and compiling new Daoist canonical compendia.[30] Fueled in part by the renewed interest in Daoism among late Qing intellectuals and lay practitioners, efforts to preserve, reprint, and expand the Daoist Canon continued well into the early twentieth century, culminating in the 1926 reprinting of the full version of the canon sponsored by Xu Shichang 徐世昌 (1855–

1939), the onetime president of the Beijing government under the Beiyang clique. Meanwhile, other private individuals, such as Ding Fubao 丁福寶 (h. Shouyi zi 守一子), also worked to preserve and reprint essential texts found both inside and outside the Ming Daoist Canon.[31]

The cumulative effect of these developments was a continuous tradition of Daoist learning and practices, much of which centered on inner alchemic self-cultivation. As China's imperial order crumbled, Daoist activists and intellectuals could build on these traditions as they sought to reclaim and revive the heritage of Daoism in modern times.

The Buddhist Revival

The late nineteenth- and the early twentieth-century efforts at preserving and propagating Daoist knowledge and practice were stimulated by several external factors. The widespread Buddhist revival, which began in the mid-nineteenth century and burgeoned in the first few decades of the twentieth century, reinvigorated Buddhist practice by incorporating many innovative ideas and institutions. Under the leadership of charismatic clerical and lay Buddhists, a host of new forms of Buddhist education were introduced to train and educate Buddhist clergy and lay practitioners after Buddhism lost imperial protection and patronage in 1900. To promulgate Buddhist teachings in an increasingly secular and modernizing world, and to resist state confiscation of temple properties to serve as schools, many modern Buddhist educational institutions, from advanced seminaries (*Foxue yuan* 佛學院) to elementary schools, were established from the 1910s to the 1940s. During the same period, national and cross-regional Buddhist associations were formed to integrate and protect the interests of local Buddhist monasteries and practitioners. Buddhist publications and printing flourished in many urban centers across the country. Buddhist lay activism and social philanthropy also expanded greatly.

As part of the effort to make Buddhism a truly world religion, Chinese Buddhist laity and monks also became actively engaged in international exchanges and communications. Contacts with Buddhist organizations and individuals in Japan, India, Tibet, Southeast

Asia, and Europe during the early decades of the twentieth century greatly advanced the prestige and status of Buddhism as a world religion and promoted the international flow of ideas and institutional exchanges. The interactions with the Japanese Buddhist community proved to be the most complicated and even controversial. From the Tang to the Ming dynasties, China had exported Buddhism to Japan, but that process was reversed during the late nineteenth century. The effort was spearheaded by the Higashi Honganji sect of Japanese Pure Land Buddhism. Despite its announced goal of purifying Chinese Buddhism for the sake of strengthening China, the Japanese Buddhist mission was inextricably entangled in Japan's political, military, and cultural designs on China. As early as 1871, Etō Shinpei, one of the Meiji reform leaders, had proposed using Buddhist missions as part of Japan's overall strategy of conquering China. It is not clear if Etō's proposal played any role in initiating Japan's Buddhist mission to China, but later events would reveal the close cooperation between Japan's Buddhist missions and Japanese military and political expansion in China.

Following Japan's defeat of the Qing in 1895, Japanese Buddhists in China put themselves in a politically and morally ambivalent position by becoming involved in local Buddhist efforts to resist the Qing state's confiscation of temple land and properties to set up new schools. From the 1895 Sino-Japanese war to the 1900 publication of Etō's notorious proposal to the infamous Twenty-one Demands in 1915 to the full-scale invasion of China in 1937, Japanese Buddhist missionary activities could never escape the stigma of aiding and abetting Japan's political and military ambitions in China. Aside from its perceived collaboration with the expansionist state, Japanese Buddhism was also viewed by many in China as tainted by secularism and modernism. Japanese monks, who married and ate meat, appeared to most Chinese clergy and laity to lack the spiritual piety and ascetic rigor crucial to the Buddhist faith. As a result, Japanese Buddhist missions headed by Pure Land and other Buddhist sects became objects of intense scrutiny and interfaith polemic in a time of rising nationalism among Chinese religious communities and beyond.[32]

But Chinese Buddhist successes in educational, intellectual, and monastic reform, scriptural publications, lay expansion and social activism, and international contacts during this period proved to be a source of both inspiration and inter-religious rivalry for the Daoist inner alchemy community in Shanghai and elsewhere.

It was against this larger historical background that the Shanghai Daoist renewal and reformulation of traditional inner alchemy began. The political, intellectual, and cultural currents of the time helped stimulate and shape the reforms and reformulations of the values, ideas, institutions, and techniques of modern inner alchemy. The major catalyst and leader of these reforms was Chen Yingning, to whose life we now turn.

— 2 —

A Journey from Anqing to Shanghai

> Having heard our parting words, the wind and rain wail.
> My eyes, teary, follow you to the earth's ends.
> Our decade of gathering the elixir seems but a dream
>   in the mountain;
> Now in the fifth moon you sail afloat the raft laden
>   with our friendship.
> It takes you to observe the metamorphosis of the Fish
>   and Dragon;[1]
> But soon, like a simian and a crane, you will laugh at
>   fleeting fame.[2]
> I yearn to join you in cultivating perfection on Mount Lu,[3]
> Till we carve out an empyrean to affirm our old covenant.[4]

With these lines, Chen Yingning bid farewell to Hu Yunchang 胡允昌, his friend and fellow practitioner of inner alchemy, on a windy and drizzly May day in Shanghai in the early 1920s. Hu was leaving on a voyage to north China, where he would engage in the self-transforming practice of Daoist inner alchemy, here alluded to as the "metamorphosis of the Fish and Dragon." Such retreats were common among devotees of the practice.[5] The close mutual bonds, the years of shared travels and arduous ascetics, the rejection of "fleeting fame" in favor of self-cultivation, and the resolve to transcend this world by "carv[ing] out an empyrean," so movingly captured in the poem, reflect the life and career of Chen Yingning himself, arguably the most influential practitioner, thinker, and reformer of modern Daoism and inner alchemy in twentieth-century China.

Early Life and Education of Chen Yingning

Born in the twelfth month of 1880, Chen Yingning (original name Zhixiang 志祥; z. Yuanshan 元善 and Zixiu 子修) came from a scholarly family of landlords in Huaining 懷寧, in western Anhui in central China (Fig. 1). His ancestors had long resided in a village called Xinchen geng 新陳埂, located in Hongzhen township 洪鎮鄉, an area dotted with lakes, canals, and rice paddies west of the Huaining county seat.[6] In 1260, the town of Huaining merged with the adjacent river port of Anqing 安慶 to serve as the joint seats for both Huaining county and Anqing prefecture. Since the Ming, the region had been known for its rich traditions of Confucian learning and merchant culture. It was also home to many famous doctors and healers. In the nineteenth century, Anqing became the provincial capital of Anhui. The Chens, like many gentry families, left their native village to settle in the nearest market town as absentee landlords. In Anqing, they pursued Confucian learning in hope of gaining office under the Qing.

Situated at the confluence of the Wan 皖水 and the Yangtze rivers, Anqing is a major port of call and a center of trade and commerce in the middle stretch of the Yangtze River valley. As a strategically vital link on all the main water and land routes in central China, Anqing has frequently been a major battleground for dynastic contenders and foreign invaders. During the Taiping rebellion, control of the provincial capital and port city was hotly contested between Qing forces and the Taiping rebels, and Anqing changed hands several times.[7]

As a major hub on the Yangtze River, Anqing received and distributed material goods and human traffic by boat from and to outlying regions throughout southern Anhui, northern Jiangxi, and eastern Hubei as well as downstream to the vast lower Yangtze delta

Fig. 1   Chen Yingning in Shanghai, ca. 1933
(YS, no. 13 [Jan. 1, 1934]: 208).

region. Like the rice, fish, cotton, silk, and other famous local goods that crowded Anqing's markets, the region's other renowned "products"—doctors, healers, and magicians—also converged on the port city to serve the needs of sojourning merchants, absentee landowners, shop owners, craftsmen, and other residents. From Anqing, they also journeyed to other major cities and markets up and down the Yangtze to ply their trade and sell their skills.

Anqing was also the center of ritual and religious life for the region and home to many Buddhist and Daoist temples. The roots of Daoist monasticism there can be traced to the early Ming period. Daoist influence peaked toward the end of the nineteenth century, when at least thirty-two Daoist temples and abbeys dotted the landscape of the Anqing region.[8] In addition to temples and monasteries, Anqing had an extensive network of Zhengyi at-home or hearth Daoist ritual specialists (huoju daoshi 火居道士). Almost every neighborhood in the city had its own ritual center, known locally as the "altar" (tan 壇) and maintained by the hereditary Daoist ritual specialist known as the "altar master" (*tan zhu* 壇主). The neighborhood altar was operated by the altar master and his assistants, who were either his sons in apprentice or hired ritual assistants known as "guest adepts" (*ke shi* 客師). They provided funerary services, led communal sacrifices, and conducted seasonal festivals for the residents of their neighborhood. Each altar strictly observed the territorial boundaries of its own neighborhood that had evolved over the years. Between 1928 and 1943, a total of 1,198 Zhengyi ritual specialists operated the neighborhood altars in Anqing and its surrounding market towns and villages.[9]

The most powerful and largest Daoist monastic institution in Anqing during the Qing period was the Quanzhen Daoist Monastery of the Sage Guardian (Yousheng guan 祐聖觀). The monastery was built on the site of an early Ming Daoist temple and was renovated and expanded several times with official funds during the Kangxi reign. Unlike the Zhengyi hearth ritual masters, who could marry and reside with their families, the Quanzhen Daoist clerics at the Yousheng monastery were celibate. Compared with the Zhengyi hearth specialists, the Quanzhen clerics enjoyed much greater power and influence. They were not restricted by the boundary lines that constrained the Zhengyi practitioners and could undertake ritual services for clients throughout the Anqing region. Anqing's other Quanzhen monastery was the Chunyang daoyuan 純陽道院, which was founded in the center of the city in 1719. Like its bigger counterpart, the Yousheng monastery, the Quanzhen abbey honored the memory of the late Tang Daoist immortal Lü Dongbin 呂洞賓.[10] Patriarch Lü was one of the most popular Daoist deities in Anqing area and was considered particularly powerful. Local legends celebrated the divine efficacy of Immortal Lü's cure-all elixir, as well as his exorcist prowess and swordsmanship, both of which were purportedly achieved through years of inner alchemic self-cultivation practice. Throughout Anqing, an area prone to both flood and drought, Lü was particularly revered as a skillful slayer of evil dragons and a successful diviner of wells. These local memories of Lü's exploits as a consummate alchemist, an immortal, and a great healer were perpetuated through the annual temple festivities held on Lü's birthday in the fourth month at the Quanzhen monasteries in Anqing.[11]

Growing up in such diverse social and ritual milieus in Anqing, Chen was early exposed to an array of cultural and intellectual influences—Confucian orthodoxy, Daoist ritual techniques and beliefs, and various local cults. His father, Chen Jingbo 陳鏡波, was a scholar of repute in Anqing. Having gained a *juren* degree in the provincial civil service examinations, the elder Chen, like many of his contemporaries, found it difficult to secure an official post. He had to earn a living by teaching the Classics at his own private school, which he ran from his home. Like many adherents of the Confucian evidentiary learning school from the region during the Qing period, the elder Chen had a fondness for the Daoist learning of the Yellow Emperor and Laozi (*Huang Lao zhi xue* 黃老之學).[12]

Despite his own lack of success in officialdom, the elder Chen was determined to see his son succeed on the civil service exams. From early childhood, Chen Yingning followed a strict and rigorous Confucian curriculum to prepare for the examinations. Reflecting on this experience later, Chen claimed that he started to learn to read while sitting on his father's lap. From childhood to early adolescence, Chen attended his father's school and took formal lessons from his father. By six, Chen had read the Four Books (*Sishu* 四書). By eleven, Chen had not only finished studying the Five Classics (*Wujing* 五經) but had also begun to compose poems in various classical styles and to write essays in the format required for the examinations.[13]

Yet in spite of his progress, Chen became bored with the long hours of reading and memorizing the Confucian classics and began exploring other topics. Much to his father's dismay, Chen developed an intense interest in Daoism, an interest that ironically may have derived from the elder Chen himself and the scholarly company he kept. One of the elder Chen's close friends was Hu Yuanjun 胡遠浚 (z. Yuanru 淵如, h. Tianfang sanren 天放散人; 1869–1933), a prominent scholar of Daoist philosophy. Hu came from a merchant family with a long tradition of learning. His father, Hu Chun 胡椿, founded and operated a well-known and successful local food-processing business.[14] Hu himself studied the Confucian classics with an uncle who was a renowned poet and calligrapher in Anqing. Like the elder Chen, Hu also held a *juren* degree, which he obtained in

1891. Later, in 1906, Hu was retained by Yan Fu, one of the most seminal minds and reform advocates in late Qing China, to teach the Classics at the newly established Anhui Advanced College (Anhui gaodeng xuetang 安徽高等學堂) in Anqing. An accomplished calligrapher and poet, Hu was also a well-known scholar of Daoist classics and wrote two influential exegeses on the *Laozi* and *Zhuangzi*.[15] Living and working in the same town, Hu and the elder Chen were social and intellectual friends who shared an interest in the Daoist classics. Hu took a special interest in his friend's precocious son by occasionally quizzing the youngster on passages from *Zhuangzi* and other classics.

Exposed to older scholars like Hu Yuanjun, Chen Yingning developed a taste for Daoism. His readings quickly expanded from the Daoist classics to hagiographies of immortals and deities. At the age of ten, Chen read *Biographies of the Divine Transcendents* (*Shenxian zhuan* 神仙傳), which was attributed to Ge Hong, and aspired to become an immortal. Years later Chen recalled with evident relish how he had read Ge Hong's hagiography by placing it in his lap while pretending to be reading Confucius' *Analects* spread out on the desk. When he was thirteen, Chen avidly read two hand-copied classics of Daoist alchemy he found in his father's treasured collection: *A Treatise on the Mysterious Essentials* (*Xuanyao pian* 玄要篇), attributed to the early Ming Daoist Zhang Sanfeng 張三丰, and *The True Oral Secrets on the Earthly Origin* (*Di yuan zhenjue* 地元眞訣) by the Song Daoist Bai Yuchan 白玉蟾 (1194–1229). But reading Daoist books alone could not satisfy Chen's curiosity. He became equally intrigued by the ritual services and magic performed by the local Zhengyi liturgical masters and Quanzhen clerics. Before long, Chen began to sneak out of the classroom and wander the streets of Anqing, where he spent time with the Daoist practitioners, buying scriptures and learning talisman writing (*hua fu* 畫符) and other ritual skills from them.

Chen's father soon found out. The elder Chen took a dim view of his son's excursions in Daoist learning. As Chen reported decades later, his father immediately sought to rectify his waywardness by burning the Daoist books he had purchased and gave him a severe scolding. When that failed, a sound whipping followed.[16]

But even physical punishment proved insufficient. Along with Daoism, Chen became exposed to late Qing reformist ideas by reading the new journals published in Shanghai. According to his biographers, when Chen first sat for the *xiucai* degree examination in Anqing, he turned in an essay in which he criticized Qing policies on the grounds that they impoverished the people and weakened the country. Fortunately, the chief proctor, a close friend of the elder Chen, spotted the offensive essay. Shocked, he discreetly removed it and informed his friend of the younger Chen's folly and recommended stricter supervision.[17]

After failing the exam, Chen heeded his father's reproaches and his mother's pleas to mend his ways. The following year, he retook the exam and attained the *xiucai* degree at the youthful age of fifteen. His prospect for a career in learning and officialdom seemed bright. But around this time, just as the already weakened Qing empire suffered yet another blow in its humiliating defeat by Japan, Chen confronted a life-threatening illness.

Chen had been coughing badly and was diagnosed with "pupils' consumption" (*tongzi lao* 童子癆), a pulmonary wasting disorder common among overstressed and malnourished youth. His doctors declared his condition beyond help. Decades later, Chen would attribute the illness to years of stress and mental overexertion, lack of exercise, and poor diet often associated with the rigorous preparations for the civil service examinations. With his son's life hanging in the balance, the elder Chen no longer had the heart to push him to spend long hours poring over books. Chen himself was devastated by the diagnosis and grew more despondent by the day.[18]

Help came from a granduncle who was a doctor of Chinese medicine and known for his learning and virtue throughout the Anqing region. From 1896 to 1900, Chen studied Chinese medicine under his granduncle's tutelage in an effort to find ways to cope with his condition. During this period, Chen read major medical classics such as *The Inner Canon of the Yellow Emperor* (*Huangdi neijing* 黃帝內經), *Canon on Problematic Cases* (*Nanjing* 難經), and *The Treatise on Cold Damage Disorders* (*Shanghan lun* 傷寒論). Chen later recalled that although he had gained theoretical knowledge through the systematic study of these medical classics, he failed to find in them any practical therapeutic solutions to his condition. But in the course of his medical studies, Chen came across a discussion about the self-cultivation methods attributed to Daoist transcendents and immortals. Intrigued, Chen tried the practice. Despite an initial lack of success, he persisted, and gradually his condition improved.[19] It was around this time that Chen adopted the personal name Yingning 攖寧. The phrase comes from Zhuangzi and means "tranquility after overcoming disturbance, or a profound inner peace or perfection achieved by quelling the disturbance."[20] The adopted name not only reflected Chen's fascination with Zhuangzi but also vividly captured his desire and determination to gain control over his debilitating condition.

While Chen was engaged with his self-healing practice, he did not lose sight of the national crisis emerging in the wake of the first Sino-Japanese war. He closely followed the reformist writings appearing in journals published and distributed from Shanghai and was particularly impressed with the influential treatise *Alarming Words for Prosperous Times* written by Zheng Guanying, the well-known entrepreneur, reform advocate, and a patron and proponent of Daoist self-cultivation practice.

In the aftermath of the Sino-Japanese war, the Qing court came under great pressure at home and abroad to reform. Gradually, the Qing court implemented a series of reform initiatives and programs that began with the abortive Hundred Days' Reforms in 1898 and culminated in the court-sanctioned New Policies (*xin zheng* 新政) of 1901. These reforms focused on improving central and local administration, defense, foreign relations, and education. As part of this state-building project, the Qing court and local administrators established new schools as additional or alternative ways of training a much-needed official and technical elite. In 1905 when the Qing court abolished the traditional civil service examination system, the new schools and colleges, whose curricula stressed western science and technology, became the main means of training and selecting the governing elite.

Like many of his generation, Chen was exposed to western learning through the new education system. By 1900 his health had improved, and Chen branched out from his studies of medicine and

Daoist self-cultivation practice into the natural sciences. This shift was in part inspired by his elder brother, an accomplished scholar said to be well-versed in the new learning (xin xue 新學). Under his tutelage, Chen read widely in science between 1900 and 1905. Decades later, Chen would recall with fondness the days and nights he spent reading books on various subjects in the natural sciences. With his brother as his mentor, Chen studied the translations of texts on physics, chemistry, biology, and other natural sciences published by the Jiangnan Arsenal (Jiangnan zhizao ju 江南制造局), the leading contemporary institution of western learning and industrialization.[21]

But Chen's new pursuits came to a halt with his brother's death from a pulmonary hemorrhage (tuxue zheng 吐血症). In 1905, Chen switched to the study of law. That year, after passing an entrance examination, he enrolled at the new Anhui Provincial Advanced College of Law and Politics (Anhui gaodeng fazheng xuetang 安徽高等法政學堂) in his hometown of Anqing. The college was part of the Qing government's efforts to modernize the training of administrative and judicial officials. Chen spent nearly two years studying legal, social, and scientific theories with Yan Fu and perhaps Hu Yuanru and other teachers at the college.[22] But in 1907, Chen had to suspend his studies and return home when his pulmonary wasting disorder flared up again. Decades later, Chen recalled that this relapse and his brother's death two years earlier so shocked him that he nearly despaired. It dawned on him that the Daoist healing regime he had been practicing was not sufficient to stem this illness. With no help from medicine, Chen felt his only hope lay in learning more advanced Daoist self-cultivation practices.[23]

Early Travels and Encounters with Buddhism and Daoism

To pursue his goal, Chen decided to leave Anqing and travel to Buddhist and Daoist centers located in mountains in other parts of the country. There he hoped to study with Buddhist and Daoist adepts who could transmit to him the secrets of a healing practice. Known as "travels of search and inquiry" (xun fang 尋訪), such journeys were common among seekers of alchemic, medical, or religious truths. They often took years and were costly, with little assurance of success. Chen's brother-in-law, Dr. Qiao Zhongshan 喬仲珊, a doctor trained in western medicine, came to the rescue. Like Chen, Dr. Qiao suffered from a frail constitution and shared Chen's interest in traditional meditation as a way of self-healing and health. Hoping that Chen's travels would lead to discovery of a cure, Dr. Qiao offered to subsidize Chen's travels.

When his condition stabilized the following year, Chen set out on a journey that first led him to visit several renowned Buddhist masters throughout the lower Yangtze River valley and the Jiangnan region. He met and befriended the eminent Master Yuexia 月霞法師 (1857–1917) on Jiuhua Mountain 九華山 in Anhui, Master Dixian 諦閒法師 (1858–1932) in Ningbo, the Eight-Fingered monk (Bazhi heshang 八指和尚, Jing'an 敬安,1851–1912) on Tiantong Mountain 天童山 near Ningbo,[24] and Monk Yekai 冶開和尚 (1853–1922) in Changzhou in Jiangsu. None, however, proved helpful to Chen. He later commented that the self-cultivation methods taught by these Buddhist masters emphasized refining the mind-nature (*pian zhong xin xing* 偏重心性) but were of little use in the care of the flesh body (*rou shen* 肉身). They could neither cure physical illness nor lengthen life. Disappointed but undeterred, Chen extended his travels to famous Daoist sacred mountains, such as Mount Wudang 武當山 in northwestern Hubei, Mount Lao 嶗山 in Shandong, Mount Mao 茅山 in Jiangsu, and Mount Qiongbei 邛北山 and Mount Jin'gai 金蓋山 in Zhejiang. At these places, Chen met many ordained Daoist clerics, but few impressed him. He reported that many of the Daoist priests knew less than he did about Daoist self-cultivation practices. Some could not even understand his questions.[25] After spending several years in a vain search for a knowledgeable master, Chen decided that he would be better off studying the subject of self-cultivation by reading the Daoist Canon on his own. Shortly before Chen reached this conclusion, Qiao had moved to Shanghai to practice medicine there, and he invited Chen to join him and his family in Shanghai in 1912.

Around the turn of the century, the White Cloud Monastery (Baiyun guan 白雲觀) in Shanghai was among the handful of Daoist

Fig. 2   The White Cloud Monastery (Baiyun guan) in Shanghai.
(*Upper*) entrance alley to the monastery; (*lower*) the scriptorium
(photographs by the author, November 1994).

universal monasteries (*conglin* 叢林) that still possessed a copy of the prized Daoist Canon first printed during the Zhengtong reign (1436–49) of the Ming dynasty (Fig. 2). Located in the bustling South Market District (Nanshi 南市) just off the famous Bund, the monastery was established as a small cloister in 1874 by Wang Mingzhen 王明眞 (?–1880?), a Quanzhen Daoist cleric from the Longmen Daoist Monastery of Manifest Perfection (Xianzhen guan 顯眞觀) in Hangzhou. After several major expansions in the 1880s, presiding abbot Xu

Zhicheng 徐至成 (1835–90), who succeeded Wang, cultivated close ties with the White Cloud Monastery in Beijing. In 1887, Abbot Xu converted the expanding private cloister into a Quanzhen universal monastery. A year later, through his ties with the prestigious White Cloud Monastery in the capital, Xu acquired from the Qing court a copy of the prized Daoist Canon, which he housed in a specially constructed two-storied scriptorium at the center of the monastery compound.[26] Viewed as the repository of the secrets of Daoist magic and power over the universe, the canon was treasured by the Daoist clergy. Access was restricted and rarely granted to the public.[27] But through Qiao's local connections, Chen gained special permission from the abbot to read the monastery's prized collection. Between 1912 and 1915, Chen was a regular visitor. On the first and fifteenth of each month, Chen submitted a list of the titles to the cleric in charge of the scriptorium. After burning incense and paying homage to the deities, the cleric would then remove the books from their shelves and bring them to Chen to read at a desk inside the scriptorium. By the end of 1914, Chen had read the entire canon.[28]

The New Republican State and Its Religious Reforms

Chen's arrival in Shanghai and his studies there between 1912 and 1915 coincided with a sea change in the Chinese religious world. The religious views of the new political and intellectual elites who rose to dominate the state and the public sphere in the late Qing and early Republican era differed from those of their predecessors. Trained in the West or influenced by western science and Enlightenment beliefs in the separation of church and state, many of these new intellectuals and politicians either helped devise or supported the late Qing court's and the Republican state's push for reforms aimed at modernizing and maximizing the modern state by reducing the influence of Buddhist, Daoist, and folk religions and by expropriating their resources. During the abortive Hundred Days' Reforms in the summer of 1898, the Guangxu emperor, at the instigation of Kang Youwei and other reformers, had decreed the confiscation and conversion of temple properties into new-style schools as a means of modernizing and expanding popular education in the empire. In 1912, the new Republican state, equally bent on modernizing and expanding its power, continued the expropriation of temple properties for the new education system. But the new Republican state differed from its imperial predecessors in one important way. The imperial governments had sought to control religions by distinguishing the "orthodox" (zheng 正) from the "heterodox" (xie 邪). Only those religious cults and beliefs radically opposed to Confucian ideology were suppressed as heterodoxies. The vast array of rural cults and practices, few of which met the test of orthodoxy, were by and large left alone because they did not openly challenge the imperial state's ideology. But the new Republican state, under the influence of science and western Protestantism, sought to reduce the number of cults and regulate religions by introducing a new set of definitions and by marking and policing the boundaries between the secular and the sacred. Continuing a trend of emulating the West to modernize and strengthen the nation, many early Republican reformers saw Christianity as a model for creating and reforming institutional and hierarchical religions in China, and they sought to remold traditional Chinese religions by emulating the Roman Catholic hierarchy and the organizational structure of Protestant churches, with their doctrinal emphasis on the laity. The Enlightenment model of secularization by restricting churches' access to the public sphere came to inform the Republican government's religious policies and was embodied in a set of far-reaching proposals for managing and regulating religions. First published in Shenbao 申報 in the summer of 1912 by the Ministry of Education, the "Proposals on Managing Religions" ("Guanli zongjiao yijian shu" 管理宗教意見書) promulgated a set of criteria for distinguishing religions (zongjiao 宗教) from superstitions or deluded beliefs. Religions were defined as "social organizations" with "pure" and socially beneficial doctrinal, spiritual, and ethical systems, and devoid of any superstitious elements such as liturgies and rituals.[29]

Implicit in the 1912 proposals was the new Republican state's vision of religion. This vision proclaimed a hierarchical church-like structure and social and utilitarian missions as the new norms for state-sanctioned religion, but it rejected the cellular and egalitarian nature of Chinese religious traditions, their locally based organization, and their individualistic pattern of monastic life and lay worship.[30] The 1912 proposals made unequivocally clear what reforms the new Republican state expected of traditional religions in China.

Having weathered the initial 1898 Qing policy of temple expropriation and subsequent state and local official encroachments and seizures of temples, Chinese monastic leaders and lay activists, especially among Buddhist circles, were quick to sense the approaching crisis. Long before the issuance of the 1912 proposals, many Buddhist lay activists and monastic leaders had begun to reform monastic education, promote lay social activism, establish regional organizations among monasteries, clerics, and lay devotees, engage in international collaborations and exchanges, and actively publish and disseminate Buddhist scriptures.

Much of the Buddhist reform effort in the early 1900s was centered in Shanghai and the greater Jiangnan region, where Buddhism had traditionally been strong. While Chen Yingning was engaged in Daoist studies in Shanghai between 1912 and 1915, he became directly involved in the Buddhist reforms and befriended many of the major reform leaders and activists, such as the influential and industrious lay activist and thinker Yang Wenhui and the charismatic and innovative monastic leaders Yuexia, Taixu 太虛 (1890–1947), and Yinguang 印光 (1861–1940). From the late 1890s to the early 1910s, Buddhists from around the country joined in efforts to establish a national Buddhist organization with a headquarters, provincial chapters, and regional branches at major Buddhist monasteries throughout the country. They established Buddhist seminaries and hermitages, recarved and distributed Buddhist scriptures, and promoted both intersectarian and international exchanges among various Buddhist sects. The inauguration of many Buddhist journals and newspapers resulted in the formation of nationwide Buddhist media. Numerous lay societies (*jushi lin* 居士林) flourished in different parts of the country, creating a national network of lively and vigorous lay Buddhist practice. These experiments and reforms revitalized Buddhism both institutionally and doctrinally and generated much energy and excitement in- and outside Buddhist circles in China.[31]

While in Shanghai, Chen actively participated in these Buddhist reforms. He registered for scriptural studies at the prestigious

Buddhist Pinjia Hermitage (Pinjia jingshe 頻迦精舍) at the Hardoon Gardens in the fall of 1913. The seminary was founded by the renowned Huayan lineage master Yuexia. It was funded by the wealthy Mrs. Hardoon and backed by Shanghai's Buddhist lay elite activists including Kang Youwei and Wang Zhen 王震 (z. Yiting 一亭; 1867–1938).[32] While attending the seminary at the Pinjia Hermitage, Chen befriended the famous lay Buddhist activist and practitioner Gao Henian 高鶴年 (z. Yeren 野人, h. Yinshi 隱士; 1872–1962). Gao was a compatriot from Guichi 貴池 in Anhui. Although Gao later became known for his Pure Land Buddhist faith and ascetic practice, he had spent his youth as an acolyte at the famous Daoist monastery on Mount Qionglong (Qionglongshan daoyuan 穹窿山道院) near Suzhou. His literary sobriquets, which he adopted in adulthood, reflected his continuing interest in Daoism, even well after his conversion to Buddhism at the age of eighteen.[33]

At the time, both Chen and Gao had just completed years of travels to Buddhist and Daoist sacred mountains in search of teachers. They now settled down in Shanghai to pursue scriptural studies. Even as Chen explored Buddhism, he remained committed to the Daoist vision that the human flesh body may be perfected and made immortal through ascetic techniques and proper practice. A devotee of Pure Land doctrine, Gao stressed the importance of ascetic practice for self-transformation of the mind; the goal of this asceticism was to deliver the soul from the flesh body to the Buddhist paradise. At the Pinjia Hermitage in Shanghai, Chen often engaged Gao in long hours of discussing and debating the Buddhist scriptures. Yet despite their differences, the two became fast friends, each appreciative of the other for his commitment to ascetic practice. In the summer of 1913, when Gao decided to undertake a pilgrimage to the sacred Buddhist site of Mount Wutai 五臺山 in Shanxi, Chen inscribed Gao's travel cap to show support. In three poems he composed for the occasion, Chen praised Gao for his undaunted spirit in pursuing Buddhist ascetics through the pilgrimage, but gently reminded his friend that the Buddhist paradise of the Pure Land could and must be achieved in the present, not the next, world. While wishing Gao well on his journey, Chen exhibited his competitive side by telling Gao that he was a kindred spirit poised to take his own "immortal's raft" (xian cha 仙槎) for a voyage to Qingdao, the gateway to the Quanzhen Daoist Mount Lao, in June of that year.[34]

Together with Gao, Chen was at the center of the exciting Buddhist revival in education, doctrine, and lay activism. While attending the seminary, Chen also served as the assistant to the monk Yuexia, who founded the Huayan Seminary (Huayan daxue 華嚴大學) at the Hardoon Gardens. Chen proofread and hand-copied Yuexia's famous lectures on the Vimalakītri Sūtra (Ch. *Weimo jing* 維摩經) delivered at the institute. Even though he knew Chen to be a dedicated Daoist practitioner, Yuexia treated him with respect and courtesy and spent time with Chen discussing many issues related to Buddhist scriptures and history. At the seminary, Chen perused the popular and influential portable edition of the Buddhist canon, which had been printed with support from Mrs. Hardoon.[35] But three months after its founding in 1914, the Buddhist seminary had to move to Hangzhou, because of a tiff with Mrs. Hardoon.[36]

In spring 1915, Chen followed the seminary to its new home in the famous Buddhist Haiyan Temple (Haiyan si 海嚴寺) in Hangzhou, where it became one of the most exciting centers of Buddhist learning. It continued to offer stimulating seminars on Buddhist scriptures and practice. The institute was open to both Buddhist clerics and lay practitioners. Although it invited famous monastic masters such as Yuexia to give lectures, lay activists and supporters played a vital role in its daily management. Impressed with its lay-centered and stimulating intellectual environment, Chen spent nearly two years at the institute.[37]

Years later Chen recalled that having just completed his studies of the Daoist canon in Shanghai, he felt a need to study Buddhism and participate in the ongoing reforms. Before the late 1930s, when his position toward Pure Land Buddhism hardened, Chen was receptive to Buddhist teachings and open to syncretism. He argued that the three teachings of Confucianism, Buddhism, and Daoism must not be perceived as mutually exclusive. From his own experience of having studied all three, he did not see any barriers among them.[38]

What also excited Chen about the Buddhist reform movement in Shanghai and Hangzhou was its daring engagement with the new and modern. Early Republican reformers assiduously portrayed

Buddhism as a "study" or "learning" (*xue* 學) and downplayed the religious or sectarian aspects (*jiao* 教) of its teachings and practice. Monk Yuexia and his Huayan Seminary were among the first to adopt the modern educational terminology of "institute" (*daxue* 大學) as the venue for teaching and transmitting Buddhism in modern China.

Yet despite his admiration for the early Buddhist reformers, Chen remained unconvinced by the Buddhist vision of the body, which at its extreme regards physical illness, and even the body itself, as nothing more than delusions of the mind. But Chen's illness and his recovery through Daoist meditation practices convinced him that the body was the center and the site of human reality.

Shortly after his return from Hangzhou to Shanghai in 1915, Chen journeyed north to Beijing. His purpose, according to his recollections decades later, was to visit Daoist specialists in self-cultivation practice in the capital. There Chen studied meditative self-cultivation techniques at the White Cloud Monastery and at a small temple dedicated to Patriarch Lü (Lüzu ge 呂祖閣) in western Beijing.[39]

Chen's sojourn at the capital in 1915 came as Daoism was attempting to deal with the changing social and political conditions of the Republican era. His visits to the major Daoist temples in the capital followed a spurt of Daoist attempts at reforms just a few years earlier. Like their Buddhist counterparts, a group of Quanzhen Daoist clerical leaders and lay activists from several major Daoist monasteries in Beijing, Manchuria, Henan, Shanghai, and Xi'an had gathered at the White Cloud Monastery and established the national Central Daoist Association (Zhongyang Daojiao hui 中央道教會) in July 1912. Provincial chapters and regional branches were envisioned.

Under the leadership of Chen Mingbin 陳明霦 (1854–1936), the abbot of the White Cloud Monastery, Daoist leaders from the provinces drafted a public declaration and planned associations aimed at meeting the challenges and demands of the 1912 proposals. In countering the 1912 proposals' outright dismissal of Daoism as an illegitimate religion, these leaders characterized Daoism as the "national religion" (*guojiao* 國教) and highlighted the indigenous origins of Daoism and its historical roles as the promoter and disseminator of transcendent Chinese moral values and spirituality. They also emphasized Daoists' traditional functions as advocates and providers of social welfare and public services, and downplayed "superstitious" practices such as talismans, rituals, divinations, and other magical techniques.[40] Further, in their efforts to "modernize" Daoism and make it look more like the Protestant church model embraced by the Republican state, Abbot Chen and his fellow Daoist leaders proposed Sunday services at the national headquarters and provincial and county chapters of the new Daoist association. These five-hour-long services would begin at eight in the morning and end at one in the afternoon, with one hour devoted to ritual and confessional services (*li chan* 禮懺) and the remaining four hours spent on sermons and lectures (*jiang shuo* 講說).[41]

The deliberate elision of Daoist rituals and liturgy from the founding declaration of the first modern national Daoist organization reflected Daoist leaders' efforts to accommodate the Republican state's criteria for distinguishing "legitimate religion" from "superstitious beliefs and practices." It also reveals the early struggles of Daoist monastic leaders to redefine what constituted Daoism and to decide what parts of the Daoist tradition could be accommodated within the fast-changing political, social, and cultural boundaries of religion in the new Republican era. It is striking yet not surprising to see that these early Daoist reformers chose to stress Daoist self-cultivation practices such as inner alchemy and other meditative techniques as one of the defining features of Daoism.[42]

When Chen Yingning arrived in Beijing in late 1915, the capital's "self-cultivation market" was abuzz with popular and elite interest in Buddhist and Daoist self-cultivation practices. Some of this interest was linked with the Quanzhen White Cloud Monastery, which was located just outside the southwestern gate of the capital. Since the 1220s, the monastery had been one of the major centers of Quanzhen Daoism and its inner alchemic meditation practice and teaching. During the late nineteenth and early twentieth centuries, several Daoist clerical and lay adepts with ties to the Quanzhen monastery had become known to the public as advocates and teachers of self-cultivation practices through their writings and teaching in and around the capital. Abbot Gao Rentong 高仁峒 (1841–1908) cultivated a wide following among Qing court elites and taught Daoist self-meditation techniques to elite women during his tenure between 1881 and 1908. Almost concurrently, Master Liu Mingrui 劉名瑞 (1839–1932), a Quanzhen adept with lineage ties to the famed Longmen sect at the monastery, actively practiced Daoist ascetics and transmitted Quanzhen teachings and meditation techniques among his disciples in the suburbs of the capital. According to Vincent Goossaert, Liu's renown as an adept of Daoist self-cultivation practice was greatly enhanced by one of his disciples, the great lay Daoist proselytizer Zhao Bichen 趙避塵 (1860–1942). A native of the Changping 昌平 district of Beijing, Zhao learned self-cultivation techniques from a variety of masters and actively promoted self-cultivation practices incorporating elements of western science in and around the capital. His teaching found a wide following among the new urban middle class of merchants, Nationalist party officials, and government clerks, as well as prominent opera singers and militarists in the capital.[43]

Another driving force behind the popularity of self-cultivation practice came from new sectarian groups such as the Common Benevolence Society and the Morality Learning Institute. Indeed, many of Zhao Bicheng's disciples were involved in these sectarian organizations, which had mushroomed in the capital and beyond. Growing out of the traditional Buddho-Daoist millenarian sects and popular cults of the Ming-Qing era in Sichuan and other regions, these new redemptive cults soon spread to the capital and proved attractive to businessmen, government clerks, and military and professional elites in the early Republican years. Like their Ming and Qing predecessors, these redemptive groups featured various forms or techniques of self-cultivation practice as the core components of their daily regimens.[44]

Beyond these monastic and redemptive society circles, popular self-cultivation practice was also connected to public campaigns by the modernizing Qing and Republican states and some leading public intellectuals for personal hygiene, public health, and a new citizenry. Although self-cultivation practice had long been part of traditional literati life, modern public intellectuals like Jiang Weiqiao now promoted it as a means to both personal health and national strength. With the publication of Jiang's *Master Yingshizi's Method for Quiet Sitting* in 1914, quiet sitting became the rage among young students, clerks, and professionals in cities like Beijing and Shanghai.

At the core of these varied strands of self-cultivation practice was the body. For the sectarian practitioners and the followers of the Daoist monastic adepts, the body was the site where they created a spiritual or religious identity. For those like Jiang more concerned with strengthening the nation, the individual pursuit of health and vigor was a prerequisite of national reinvigoration and modernization.

An Encounter with the Modern Practitioner: Lü Bicheng

While sojourning in Beijing between 1915 and 1916, Chen began to teach Daoist techniques of self-cultivation to students selected from among his intellectual and social peers. One of his first disciples at the capital was the famous poet and women's rights advocate Lü Bicheng 呂碧城 (z. Shengyin 聖因 and Lanqing 蘭清; 1883–1943) (Fig. 3). A prodigy and compatriot from Jingde 旌德 in Anhui, Lü came from a family with a long tradition of classical learning. Her father, Lü Fengqi 呂鳳岐 (?–1895), served as educational commissioner in Shanxi between 1882 and 1885. Her mother, Yan Shiyu 顏士瑜, was an accomplished poet and taught Lü and her sisters the Classics and poetry. After her father died, Lü's family fell on hard times. An intralineage inheritance dispute deprived her widowed mother of her share of the income from her husband's estates and left her and her family in dire poverty. To survive, Lü's mother sent her to live with her maternal relatives. Growing up in such adverse family circumstances, Lü became independent and strong-willed. At twenty-two, she left her abusive uncle in the port of Tanggu and made her way to the thriving modern city of Tianjin. There she impressed the editor of *Dagong bao* 大公報, a popular modern newspaper, with her poetic talents and writing skills, and made a living as an editorial assistant at the newspaper.[45] Soon her poems, which appeared in the journal, caught the eyes of the public. Attracted by her

Fig. 3   Portrait of Lü Bicheng, dates unknown
(Li Baomin, *Lü Bicheng ci jian zhu*, illus. 1).

beauty and talent, literary and political elites from Tianjin and the capital, such as Yuan Shikai 袁世凱 (z. Weiting 慰亭, h. Rongan 容庵; 1859–1916) and Fan Zengxiang 樊增祥 (z. Fanshan 樊山; 1846–1931), sought her friendship by exchanging poems and letters with her. Because of her personal experiences with poverty and adversity, Lü became interested in promoting women's education and welfare. She learned to parley her literary renown and her political ties into support for women's rights and education. In 1904, she published a host of articles in *Dagong bao* 大公報 and other journals to push for women's educational rights. Her appeal found support from the reform-minded Yuan Shikai, then the governor-general of Zhili. In November 1904, with funding support from the Maritime Customs at the Tianjin-Tanggu ports, the North China Women's College (Beiyang nüzi gongxue 北洋女子公學) opened for admission with Lü as its provost.

By virtue of her literary renown and her commitment to women's education and rights, Lü became a vocal spokeswoman for the emerging women's rights movement around the turn of the century. Although Lü remained politically conservative throughout her public career, she was sympathetic to the anti-Qing revolutionary cause and befriended such radical revolutionaries as Qiu Jin 秋瑾 (1875–1907). In July 1907, when Qiu Jin was executed for her attempted assassination of a Manchu official, Lü's open sympathy and personal connections with the anti-Manchu revolutionaries nearly cost her own life. Yet in spite of the threat to her life, Lü later assisted in building tombs for Qiu and several other martyred Republican revolutionaries in Hangzhou.[46]

Yet Lü's sympathy for the revolutionaries never led her to endorse the kind of political radicalism exemplified in Qiu Jin's assassination attempt. Her traditional upbringing, her belief in education as the means of national salvation and social change, and her conviction that literary enlightenment was the way of individual liberation inevitably put her at odds with the political and cultural radicalism of her late Qing contemporaries. What suited her intellectually and politically was a moderate approach that sought gradual social and cultural change through spiritual cultivation and moral transformation on an individual level.

Outside her career as a poet, educator, and women's rights advocate, Lü grew interested in traditional techniques of self-cultivation and healing. Frail and suffering from chronic illnesses, Lü was attracted to self-cultivation practice early in her life. Dedicated to poetry and public work, she had sworn off marriage while in her twenties, a decision that caused much concern among her senior male mentors and friends such as Yan Fu. Lü's interest in Daoism was signaled by her initial correspondence about Daoist philosophy with Jiang Weiqiao, the advocate and practitioner of the Daoist quiet-sitting practice in Beijing, as early as 1911.

While Chen Yingning sojourned in the capital in 1916, Lü sought him out as a teacher in Daoist self-cultivation practice. In her first encounter with Chen Yingning, she raised critical questions and argued tirelessly with him about the practice of female inner alchemy (*nüdan* 女丹). In a poem composed after their contentious meeting, she reflected on the occasion:

> I lament not having fully known your wondrous teachings
>   at first.
> In vain I have made all the evaluations and judgments.
> Regretful, my sophistication and intellect are my own ruin,
> I beseech you to forgive my maidenly conceit.
> Having taken root in the Dust, a hundred affairs sadden me;
> Yet one is free to travel between the Void and the
>   Bright Realms.[47]
> A myriad of red petals, the spring is like a sea,
> But having renounced the gossamer skirt, I shall never
>   turn back.[48]

Deeply reflective, the poem subtly reveals the inner struggle Lü was undergoing. Along with her fame as an accomplished poet and her achievements as an ardent social activist for women, she also cherished an intense yearning for spiritual transcendence. Earlier in her life, the death of her father and the ensuing squabble over the division of the family property left her widowed mother penniless. This poverty caused the family of Lü's betrothed to break the engagement. The social stigma of being spurned left a deep scar on the teenager. Later, after she had become famous, Lü rejected overtures from many qualified suitors. Her unconventional decision to remain single and her association with many famous literary and political men led to much gossip and insinuations in the media, causing much chagrin and grief among relatives and friends. The pressures of her personal life aside, in the years leading up to 1916 when Lü began her study of Daoist self-cultivation with Chen Yingning, Beijing witnessed constitutional crises, political chaos, and social tumult, culminating in the death of Yuan Shikai, her old patron, in 1916. In the late summer of 1915, when Yuan and his supporters were clamoring for the restoration of the monarchy, Lü resigned her post as secretary to then-President Yuan.[49] Deeply disappointed and saddened by what she alluded to as the "hundred affairs of the Dust," Lü sought refuge in Daoist meditative practice and aspired to an immortal's freedom to move at will between the mortal and the divine realms. But although treasuring this opportunity to query an adept on the practice of achieving the dream of return, she could not help showing the independent streak and analytical intellect of a poet in her first exchange with Chen Yingning, as she critically "evaluated and judged" (*ping liang* 評量) his teaching. She struggled with her strong will and intellect, which she deemed impediments to her newfound practice. But even her self-doubts failed to deter her resolve, as Lü vowed to renounce her attachment to the secular world symbolized by the images of "a myriad of red petals" and "the gossamer skirt" (*qing ju* 輕裾).

Perceiving in her a genuine spirituality, Chen Yingning consoled her self-conscious anguish by pointing out that a true immortal was a radical critic at heart, transcending social conventions in both spirit and conduct. In a poem rhymed after her original, Chen heartily encouraged her to carry on her pursuit of Daoist learning:[50]

> Well versed in both Zhuangzi and the Mysterious Learning,[51]
> Your talent matches the erudite Ban Chao.[52]
> No need to blame your sharp arguments,
> An immortal is by nature proud and unflinching.
> Sad and past were the Emerald Feathers and Bright Pearls,[53]
> But your transfigured body comes from the Petal Palace.[54]
> The Celestial Flowers scattered, the Void becomes the Phenomenon;[55]
> In the Azure Heaven clouds above, the Crane is yet to return.[56]

Appreciative of Lü's career as a social reformer and women's rights advocate, Chen sought to affirm the uncompromising and critical spirit in Lü by implicitly comparing her social activism to the pursuit of immortality. Like her social activism, which aimed at reforming present conditions, Chen assured her that the Daoist pursuit of immortality rested on the assumption of the imperfection of the present life and the need for improvement. Indeed, it conceived one's present existence as a "transfigured body" from a pristine past or the "Petal Palace" inhabited by immortals dressed in "Emerald Feathers and Bright Pearls." For both Chen and Lü, this imagined pristine past provided the ideal and the goal for the present existence. Through a proper regimen of meditative cultivation, Chen advised, one could succeed in repairing imperfections by replenishing the atemporal *qi* in the body, until the perfected body became alchemically ripened or matured in the form of the "Celestial Flowers." Then, the pristine realm of the immortals, here alluded to as the Void, would become one with the phenomenal world of the Dust. Yet to realize this dream, one must begin with the cultivation practice of "returning," or replenishing, the body's vitalizing energy, or *qi*, much like the soaring Crane that has yet to return to its empyrean nest in the poem.

Under Chen's encouragement and guidance, Lü pursued the study and practice of female alchemy in earnest. One of the main texts Chen chose for her was *A Poem on Female Alchemy by Sun Bu'er* (*Sun Bu'er nüdan shi* 孫不二女丹詩), a practice poem attributed to the Jin female Daoist Sun Bu'er (1119–82). Chen prepared an annotated version of the poem as the instructional manual for Lü's practice. Lü also read *Ten Rules on Female Alchemy* (*Nüdan shize* 女丹十則), a late Qing text on female meditative practice, which Chen later edited and annotated. Based on her reading of these texts, Lü produced a list of thirty-six questions for Chen on issues such as the basic concepts of inner alchemy, techniques and procedures of the practice, and key loci in the female body and their relevance to the practice. In his written response, Chen engaged Lü in an equally open and detailed discussion of the technique of breast massage for the circulation of *qi* in the female body and the various stages of menstrual flow as relevant to the practice. The written format of the exchange, which centered on scriptural texts, allowed both Lü and Chen extraordinary freedom to explore these rather personal and sensitive issues related to the female body, sexuality, and sexual feelings in the context of women's inner alchemic practice.

The plain and direct style of the written exchange reveals Chen Yingning to be a learned, patient, and charismatic teacher, and Lü an inquisitive, intelligent, and eager disciple. The queries and answers are also revealing of the private and personal context of the teaching and transmission of Daoist inner alchemy at this early stage of Chen's career and of the larger problems traditional Daoist inner alchemy faced in the changing social and cultural conditions of early Republican China. As evidenced in Chen's encounter with Lü Bicheng in 1916, his early teaching career still followed the traditional pattern of transmission. Instruction still remained a private and personal undertaking between the master and the chosen disciple away from the public eye. As practice guides, Chen prepared for his disciples individually tailored textual commentaries and dialogues on the relevant scriptures. The choice of textual commentary and written dialogue as means of teaching was not accidental. It reflected Chen's and his disciples' shared elite social, cultural, and intellectual background and upbringing. The learned format of textual commentary and written dialogue provided both distance from and connection with the original text, allowing the master and the disciple to criticize its content, extrapolate its untapped meanings, and even postulate their own views. As such, they created a private sanctuary, with remarkable freedom to discuss otherwise sensitive and even controversial subjects, and this resulted in a formalized intimacy between the master and the disciple, as evidenced in the 1916 poems and written exchanges between Chen and Lü.[57]

Yet the 1916 exchanges also revealed certain limits on the traditional way of teaching and transmitting Daoist knowledge and the new challenges to traditional Daoist inner alchemy. The old one-on-one teaching methods could reach only a small audience. Further, the arcane terminology and obscure language of the Daoist inner alchemy scriptures made them difficult for even educated intellectuals like Lü Bicheng to understand and further impeded the spread of Daoist knowledge and practice among the public, which was becoming increasingly used to the vernacular language in both public and private communications.

The language problem was further complicated by the fact that Daoist inner alchemy now faced increasing competition from monastic Daoists and Buddhists, as well as many other traditional and new sectarian and scientific visions of the body and self-cultivation practice. Traditional elite men and women had always been interested in self-cultivation, but Lü's interest in Daoism was more than just an iconoclastic whim or fad.[58] Hundreds of thousands of students, government clerks, and intellectuals were trying the quiet-sitting practice advocated by Jiang Weiqiao or joining Common Benevolence Society chapters in Beijing or attending lectures at the Buddhist Huayan Seminary in Hangzhou, and Lü's interest in female inner alchemy was part of this widening quest among the emerging urban professional elite for a cultural identity, spirituality, or other forms of meaning in the early Republican era. Accommodating the yearnings of people like Lü presented a great challenge to the traditional Daoist inner alchemic vision of the body and its self-cultivation practices.

For that reason, Lü's initial contentious meeting with Chen, her subsequent pointed and skeptical queries about inner alchemy, and, above all, her brief discipleship to Chen Yingning served only to highlight the new challenges to inner alchemy. The late Qing scripture Chen assigned Lü to read mirrored the existing social and gender hierarchies of late imperial China in its admonitions to women practitioners to await their deliverance (dai du 待度) by celestial deities, instead of attaining transcendence on their own as did their male counterparts. What was even more troubling was that such gender-biased precepts were rooted in a prevalent cosmology of the body in the Daoist inner alchemic discourse of late imperial China. In advising women beginners in the practice of inner alchemy, *Ten Rules on Women's Alchemy* stipulates: "Generally speaking, a woman is weak in nature and prone to distraction in intention. Her sentiments are shallow, and her *qi* susceptible to agitation. Since her heart of varied impure thoughts is hard to subjugate, how could her body be conserved for eternity, and how could any practice be of help to her!"

Even after a woman has succeeded in transforming her body, she must be vigilant against the residual yin elements in her nature (*yinning zhi xing* 陰凝之性), which purportedly prevent a woman from ascending to the immortals' paradise on her own. Instead, she must wait patiently to be liberated by other divine transcendents. The *Ten Rules* advises the woman practitioner about the intricacy of the final stage before her ascension:

Why must a woman await her deliverance? Because even though she has, by way of the inner practice, purified her body of depletion and blood into the body of *yang qi* energies, her new *yang* body has not yet been completely refined of its proclivity toward *yin* condensation. She still lacks the practice of returning to the Void and has not fully achieved the wondrous transformation of heaven and earth. So the reason why she cannot yet soar above and transcend the world is due to her infirm physical constitution. Hers is not like the male body, which will have been refined into the diamond body beyond corruption. With the practice of returning to the Void, the male body can nurture its divine brilliance to fill up between heaven and earth. So it does not need to wait for deliverance. It can complete the Way and achieve perfection on its own.

The scripture goes on to admonish women to engage in socially worthy deeds after they accomplish their alchemic perfection so that they could accumulate sufficient merits (gongde 功德). Then they will be summoned to advance into the Daoist pantheon of immortals.[59]

Chen was keenly aware of these incongruities with the changing social and cultural conditions of the early Republican period. Yet, Daoist practice had proved for Chen an efficacious way of managing his health problems. His two decades of travels and scriptural studies had also convinced him of its cultural worth and spiritual viability. Making this tradition both meaningful and appealing to his social and intellectual peers like Lü Bicheng became a pressing challenge for him.

Marriage and the Early Circles of Inner Alchemic Practice

This sense of urgency was further hastened by Chen's widening circles of social and intellectual friends and especially his marriage to Dr. Wu Yizhu 吳彝珠 (1882–1945), his longtime friend and a fellow practitioner. In the fall of 1916, Chen ended his sojourn in Beijing and returned to Shanghai, where he married Dr. Wu, whom he had befriended on his earlier sojourn in Shanghai around 1908. At the time, Dr. Wu was attending medical school, but she shared Chen's passionate interest in Daoist learning.[60]

Born in 1882, Wu was originally from Wuxing 吳興 county in Zhejiang. After her parents passed away when she was still young, she followed her paternal uncle to Wuhu 蕪湖, a busy commercial port on the Yangtze River known for its rice markets and located downstream from Anqing. Wu attended school in Wuhu and later completed a course of medical studies in gynecology and obstetrics at the Sino-Occidental Medical College (Zhongxi yixue yuan 中西醫學院), a school of western medicine in Shanghai. After graduating in 1911, Wu first served as the director of medicine at the Red Cross Hospital in Wuchang 武昌. She then moved to Shanghai and practiced obstetrics at the Second Hospital there before joining the medical staff at Shangxian Hospital 尚賢醫院 in the city. Outside her practice at the hospital, she also taught courses in gynecology and obstetrics at the Renhe Advanced School of Obstetrics (Renhe fuchan gaoji xuexiao 仁和婦產高級學校) in Shanghai.[61]

Wu had apparently developed a keen interest in Daoism and self-cultivation practice early in her childhood. Like Chen, she longed for the "way of the immortals" in her teenage years. Although trained in western medicine and practicing modern obstetrics, Wu remained passionate about the Daoist pursuit of the elixir. She and Chen first met as fellow cultivators of the Way (daolü 道侶). The two had intended to maintain that relationship, but concerned over public misperceptions of their relationship, they decided to marry and continue their shared pursuit of the elixir as husband and wife. For that purpose, they decided against having children.[62]

By the time she and Chen married in 1916, Wu had quit her job at the hospital and set up a private clinic on Minguo Road 民國路 near the busy Yu Garden 豫園 in the South Market District of Shanghai (Fig. 4). Chen worked at the clinic, helping his wife by managing the daily administrative chores. By all standards, their union was unconventional. Both Chen and Wu were in their thirties when they married. With her medical practice, Wu was the main breadwinner in the family. Chen contributed by earning small stipends as a private tutor in the Classics. The unconventional partnership brought both emotional and economic stability. Living and working so closely with a specialist in gynecology and obstetrics helped Chen acquire an intimate and up-to-date knowledge of Western medicine, especially biology and physiology. The daily routine at the clinic also allowed Chen the leisure to continue his studies of both traditional and new subjects. He would later recall that during the 1920s he had had time to read two or three books a day after completing his work at the clinic. His readings covered a range of topics from the practices of self-cultivation techniques to history, literature, philosophy, science, and medicine.[63]

A Journey from Anqing to Shanghai

Fig. 4 Two scenes of the South Market district, Shanghai. (*Upper*) Minguo Road (now People's Road); (*lower*) Yihuatang Bookstore on Yuyuan Road (now Lishui Road) (photographs by the author, November 1994).

Outside their work at the clinic, the couple cultivated a circle of close friends and associates among their social and intellectual peers who shared their passion for Daoism, especially Daoist techniques of self-cultivation. This small circle included members of Shanghai's business, political, professional, and religious elites. Huang Chanhua 黃懺華 (z. Canhua 燦華, h. Fengxi 風兮; 1885–1972), for example, came from Shunde 順德 in Guangdong province. He had graduated from Imperial Tokyo University, where he studied philosophy and literature. Upon his return from Japan, Huang and his wife first settled in Shanghai. There Huang became involved with the Southern Society (Nanshe 南社), the conservative literary society of prominent poets and writers, such as Lü Bicheng, Chen Qubing 陳去病 (1874–1933), Liu Yazi 柳亞子 (1887–1958), Su Manshu 蘇曼珠 (?–1918), and Ma Junwu 馬君武 (1881–1940). While living in Shanghai in the 1910s, Huang and his wife were neighbors of the Chens at their residence on Minguo Road. Other members of their close circle included Huang Suizhi of Nanchang, Zheng Dingchen 鄭鼎臣 of Beijing, Xie Jiyun 謝季雲, and Gao Yaofu 高堯夫. Both Huang and Zheng were veteran adepts of Daoist inner alchemy. Zheng was an erudite master of inner alchemy admired by both Chen and Huang.[64] Chen had befriended Huang during his early years of travels. Huang was also a close associate of Fangnei Sanren, another influential inner alchemist of the late Qing and the early Republican eras. Both Huang and Fangnei made a living by teaching Daoist inner alchemy practice to patrons in Shanghai such as Zheng Guanying, the late Qing reformer, entrepreneur, and advocate of self-cultivation. When Chen was editing the manuscript on Sun Bu'er, which he had prepared for Lü Bicheng, for publication, Huang endorsed the book by composing a preface for it.[65]

Experimenting with the Way: Early Outer Alchemy and Spirit Writing

On weekends at their residence near the City God Temple (Yimiao 邑廟) in Shanghai, the Chens hosted informal gatherings of their friends. Over tea or wine, they engaged in hours of discussion about Daoism and techniques of self-cultivation. Between 1916 and 1928, one of the recurring subjects at their weekly gatherings was outer alchemy (*waidan* 外丹). Huang Suizhi participated in many of the alchemical experiments at the Chens' residence in Shanghai in the early 1920s. He vividly recalled how Chen Yingning and his colleague Zheng Dingchen carried out regimens of alchemical experiments whatever the weather:

Both of them are most diligent and fearless of the toils involved in the experiments on the origin of the Earth (*di yuan* 地元). Over the years, they both pored over the furnaces and attended to the cauldrons despite the heat of the summer or the chill of the winter. Even repeated fiendish obstacles and setbacks could not daunt their resolve.[66]

Their collective interest in outer alchemy was driven by several factors. One likely motive was the age-old yearning for longevity among practitioners of Daoism who had historically pursued the practice as a means of producing the coveted elixir of immortality. Commenting on the use of outer alchemic terminology in *Ten Rules*, Chen wrote:

The Scarlet Flora, the Purple Meridian, the Yellow Shoots, the White Snow, the Ruby Powder, and Purple Sand, these terms refer to real substances refined over the furnaces of outer alchemy. They really possess their respective forms. You can see them with your eyes, and hold them in your hand. You can also swallow them into your stomach. So they are called Golden Elixir (*jindan* 金丹). . . . Since we Chinese were not willing to divulge the technique of transforming mercury into gold, we have lost its transmission and let the foreigners claim its invention in the end. As for the elixir of long life and no aging, we Chinese dared not to acknowledge to have first developed it, so as to let the foreigners take the credit. A country with five thousand years of civilization and a nation of four hundred million civilized people have completely forgotten their ancestral tradition. We have lost our Way and have to beg for it from foreign nations. How deplorable![67]

But what Chen deplored may well have been what motivated him and his friends to pursue outer alchemy throughout the 1920s. At the time, Daoist alchemy was being linked to the origins and history of modern chemistry by sinologists, chemists, and historians of science in the West and Japan. In these writings, Chinese alchemy and Daoist alchemic experiments, which arose as part of the search for wealth and immortality, were viewed as iatrochemistry, or the forerunner of modern chemistry.[68]

Published in easily accessible popular science journals and books in English and circulated widely in the United States and Japan, the western discourse about the possible connections between ancient Chinese Daoist alchemy and modern chemistry could conceivably have become known among Chen's friends and colleagues, many of whom were doctors, scientists, and scholars educated either abroad or at the new universities in China. It may thus be more than a coincidence that Chen and his circle of close friends and associates were pursuing Daoist outer alchemic experiments around this time in Shanghai. In a letter to Huang Chanhua in 1935, Chen reminisced about these experiments. He recalled that he and Wu had set aside two rooms at their Minguo Road residence for the experiments. The front courtyard of their house was always filled with supplies of cinnabar, mercury, and lead, and stacked with heaps of charcoal, as well as furnaces, alembics, and crucibles. On weekends, amid the hustle and bustle of the South Market District, Chen and his friends would be poised over stoves and furnaces, smelting down chemical ingredients to ascertain their alchemic qualities or the processes of a compound. These activities and discussion centered on the outer alchemy would carry on well into the nights, with Chen and his friends debating and arguing about the various alchemic formulas and self-cultivation methods. According to his own estimates, Chen and his associates carried out over a hundred such experiments in the makeshift lab at his home in Shanghai, in order to test the many secret instructions and formulas he had found in the Daoist Canon.[69]

Like his early pursuits in self-healing, Chen's outer alchemic experiments had a lasting influence on him and his approach to Daoism. Experimenting with various chemical compounds and observing their reactions reinforced in Chen a strong aversion to empty talk and speculative abstraction in self-cultivation practice. It helped shape in him an equally strong inclination toward the primacy of the physical, the material, and the living, toward a more concrete approach to exploring the ultimate. These two orientations were to surface as the dominant features of his approach to Daoist inner alchemy, or what he called "Immortals' Learning," later in his career.

But if modern science in part framed Chen and his colleagues' probes into Daoist outer alchemy, its perceived limits may also have inspired their less "scientific" explorations in Daoist learning. In the aftermath of the Great War, as self-doubt and criticism of the promise and prowess of science and technology emerged in Europe, Chinese intellectuals also began to question the cultural worth and epistemological limits of western science. The famous debates between the opposing camps of Science and Life Philosophy in the 1920s best exemplify contemporary cultural skepticism and doubts about the universal claims of science. Indeed, the cultural critique of science and its limitations by Zhang Junmai and others resonated tangibly with Chen Yingning's own thinking about the relevance of nonscientific and intuitive forms of human knowledge. Chen conceived of spirit-writing as a means of looking into unsolved mysteries and uncovering esoteric truths (xuan li 玄理) unknown to modern science. He argued that as long as we lack full knowledge about the composition of the universe and about the genesis of all species, religion cannot be dismissed. It would continue to be indispensable to us as mode of knowledge. Any attempt to destroy religion would result only in great social turmoil.[70] It was against this immediate cultural background that Chen and his associates explored the practice of spirit-writing in Shanghai during the 1920s.

The appeal of spirit-writing (jixian 乩仙, fuji 扶乩, or fuluan 扶鸞) or séances to Chen and his friends also derived from its long history in China. It continued to be popular among both elites and commoners during the late Qing and early Republican periods.[71] The popularity of the practice during the 1920s may also have reflected the worldwide interest in paranormal psychology in Europe, Japan, and the United States, where many Chinese students and intellectuals had been exposed to scientific studies in mesmerism, hypnotism, and other paranormal psychological phenomena while studying abroad. In the fall of 1917, with the endorsement of Yan Fu, several intellectuals and practitioners established the first scholarly organization dedicated to "the pursuit of psychical research and the exploration of the mystery of spirits and ghosts of the yonder world." With the establishment of the Shanghai Psychical Research Society (Shanghai Lingxue hui 上海靈學會) in 1917, the divinatory practice of spirit-writing became part of the global popular interest in parapsychology in the early twentieth century.[72]

The practice of spirit-writing Chen and his friends carried out in Shanghai typically involved a chief inquirer and several assistants. The chief inquirer would present questions to the descending deity or immortal on issues of interest to the participants. The deities' responses were channeled through a T-shaped stick suspended over a sandbox and manipulated by the chief inquirer. The scribbled messages in the sandbox were then read aloud and interpreted by the chief inquirer and recorded by his assistant.

For lay practitioners such as Chen and his associates, the practice of spirit-writing promised direct and unmediated access to the divine pantheon, access that was once the purview of specially ordained Daoist clergy. Since a séance involves direct interaction with the perceived presence of a descending deity, the experience is thus evocative of the Daoist encounter with immortals.[73]

Throughout the 1920s, Chen and his wife and their colleagues pursued the practice with great interest. Chen recalled that he began his studies of spirit-writing with a Daoist priest at the White Cloud Monastery in Shanghai by writing talismans as a means of invoking deities. But his lack of success with talismanic writing led Chen to believe that the key to summoning deities lay in the inner perfection of the heart rather than the skillful writing of talismans. So Chen gave up talismanic writing, which he had learned in his youth with Daoists in the streets of Anqing, and focused on meditation practice as a way of inducing the gods during the séance. About two months into the practice, Chen reported that the gods descended and wielded the pen to write in the sandbox. The initial writings were hardly legible. But Chen persisted, and about half a year later, with help from his wife and his niece, he felt he was able to channel the gods at will to conduct the spirit-writing sessions. Before long, the Chens were holding regular séances with their friends and colleagues on all seasonal holidays, and sometimes even at locations away from their home.[74]

Several poems composed by the descending deities at the time addressed the issues of self-cultivation practice for healing and longevity. In one poem evocative of the trope of the divine encounter, the descending immortal, the Scribe of the Jade Flower Palace (Yuhua gong shishu xianzi 玉華宮侍書仙子), preached on the importance of inner alchemic practice, exhorting the séance attendees to refrain from the bountiful immoral excesses to be found in the city and to conserve their *qi*, the True Fluid (*zhen ye* 眞液), in the body for further cultivation toward immortality:

I have just accompanied the Queen Mother's chiming chariot.
Playful, I descend through the bright effulgence onto the
    colorful plume.[75]
The settled dust of the mundane seems but a dream in the
    cloud and rain;
For long I have not seen the chill of the snowy frost on the
    Jade Rostrum.[76]
Fall or soar, all hangs on the weight of one's passions
    and thought.
Suffering or bliss, heavenly and human realms are worlds apart.
Treasuring my predestined bond, I enlighten those late
    in awakening:
Conserve your True Fluid to tide over the aging decay.[77]

On another level, the pursuit of spirit-writing by Chen and his associates also reflected a common practice among the growing lay-centered self-cultivation and spirituality movements during the early Republican period. The practice of spirit-writing was central to the operation, organizational integrity, and identity of popular redemptive organizations like the Common Benevolence Society in Beijing and Tianjin, because it also offered lay cult leaders and members unmediated, authenticating access to the divine.[78] In the case of Chen Yingning and his associates, spirit-writing expressed the urban-based Shanghai lay practitioners' quest for spiritual autonomy and self-reliance. It was also consistent with Chen's early dissatisfaction with the monastic and liturgical Daoist specialists who claimed special access to the divine realm. In that context, Chen's emphasis on the individual's inner sincerity through meditation, rather than the Daoist cleric's technical proficiency in talismanic writing, as a means of inducing deities to descend during a séance is indicative of the lay practitioners' ambivalence toward and distrust of liturgical clerics and their craft. Further, as in the redemptive cults, spirit-writing provided Chen and his lay colleagues an extraordinary means of accessing and producing Daoist esoteric knowledge, thus legitimizing and authenticating their own vision and experience of Daoism.

Even more important, Chen's pursuits in outer alchemy and spirit-writing can best be understood in the larger context of the ongoing efforts of Daoist intellectuals to reform Daoism since the early 1910s. By trying out and sorting through various components of Daoism, Chen and his fellow lay practitioners were also making conscious selections from the Daoist tradition to deal with the changing social and cultural conditions of early Republican society. In that sense, it was by no means accidental that the issue of Daoist self-cultivation and the body frequently appeared in their séances during the 1920s.

— 3 —

Innovating the Immortals' Body

Nationalism, Antiquity, and Science

> Over the Realms with three thousands merits attained;
> I soar, delighted and free of this yin-yang sack.
> Roaming unfettered far and wide, in and out of sight,
> My Spirit, intoxicated, will never return to Ninghai.[1]

Reciting these words, the Jin Daoist nun Sun Bu'er was said to have ascended to Heaven in broad daylight on the nineteenth day of the twelfth month of 1182. The poem is remarkable because it speaks of the mysterious experience of "flying to Heaven in broad daylight" (*bairi feisheng* 白日飛升), the ultimate expression of the Daoist pursuit of self-transformation and transcendence.[2] After a long and arduous practice of inner alchemic cultivation, alluded to here as the "three thousand merits attained" (*sanqian gong man* 三千功滿),[3] the perfected being known as the Yang Psyche (*yang shen* 陽神) in Sun Bu'er soared above the present world, here referred to as the Realms, that is, the three Buddhist realms of Desire (*yu jie* 欲界), the Phenomenal (*se jie* 色界), and the Nonphenomenal (*wu se jie* 無色界). As she ascends to the empyrean, Sun sheds her mortal body of the "yin-yang sack" (*yinyang bao* 陰陽包) and acquires the ultimate freedom of transcendence through her new alchemically perfected

78 Innovating the Immortals' Body

Fig. 5   An immortal's ascent by flight (*Feisheng tu*, 1615) (*Xingming shuangxiu wanshen guizhi*, juan ji, 45a).

immortal's body, a body that allows her to appear and disappear at will. To enthusiasts of Daoist inner alchemy since her times, the appeal of Sun's poem lies in its jubilant celebration of the ecstasy, joy, and freedom experienced through the alchemic body, a body that transcends the limits of time and space and defeats the karma of life and death (see Fig. 5).

Body Cultures: Competing Visions in Early Twentieth-Century China

The subject of the body and Daoist self-cultivation (*xiulian*) was very much on the mind of Chen Yingning and his associates after Chen's return from Beijing in 1916. Their interest in exploring self-cultivation techniques is apparent in the queries they raised during the weekend séances at the Chens' residence in Shanghai throughout the 1920s. Chen Yingning's 1926 study on women's inner alchemic practice is devoted to a discussion of Sun Bu'er's celebratory poem. Based on the practice manual Chen had prepared for Lü Bicheng a decade earlier, the 1926 annotations of Sun's poem also reflected efforts among intellectual and religious elites to explore traditional Daoist self-cultivation techniques as a means of creating both personal meaning and cultural identity in the changing social and cultural landscapes of early Republican China.[4]

Indeed, in the larger contexts of late Qing and early Republican culture and politics, an interest in Daoist self-cultivation practices was also directly connected with the new intellectual and political agendas behind the religious reforms. These reforms sought to transform Chinese religious traditions both by recasting their relationship with the emerging modern state and by reconstituting and reformulating their contents. In this elitist and reformist vision of what constituted a modern religion, traditional Daoist self-cultivation techniques were perceived not only as means for attaining personal goals of health, longevity, and transcendence but also as vital instruments for preserving national culture and identity, and even strengthening the nation by perfecting the bodies and spirits of individual citizens. Additionally, in the context of the reformist goal of exorcising Daoism and other religions of their "superstitious" elements, leading Daoist lay and clerical reformers had come to favor individual and body-centered self-cultivation techniques over local and communal deity cults, rituals, and liturgical techniques as the proper constituents of religious practice in modern China. It was no accident that the program of the 1912 Central Daoist Association specifically cited the traditional self-cultivation techniques of "withholding the consciousness" (she nian 攝念), "ceasing the gaze" (zhiguan 止觀), and inner alchemy over the liturgical and ritual techniques as constituting the true meaning (zhendi 眞諦) of Daoism, the meaning that was to be disseminated by the newly established national Daoist organization.[5]

At the core of self-cultivation practice is a vision of the body. Various religious and spiritual traditions and schools in China had historically offered different and sometimes competing visions of and approaches to the body in their respective efforts to shape individual selfhood, community, and the culture at large. During the late Qing and early Republican eras, these competing visions were influenced by larger social, political, and cultural events, forces, and processes:

the late Qing self-strengthening movement, the Hundred Days' Reforms, the founding of the Republic, the introduction and spread of science, the New Culture and May Fourth movements, religious reforms, the emergence and proliferation of modern mass media, and Japan's militaristic expansion in China. In the first few decades of the twentieth century, partly in response to the expanding Qing and Republican states' demand for change and reform and partly driven by the internal need to renew themselves, Confucianism, Buddhism, and Daoism vied with newcomers such as the Common Benevolence Society and other redemptive societies and with modern science to redefine and assert their respective visions of the body and its cultivation. For many, the body was more than just a physical space. It was also a cultural arena where the renewed and divergent constructions of the body and bodily practices not only aimed to shape individual selfhood and spirituality but also consciously strove to reform the culture and the nation.

Much of the rivalry in envisioning the authentic body of self-cultivation and of the new national religion played out in the new popular media of newspapers and magazines in major urban centers across the country in the early twentieth century. As the old Buddhist and Daoist monasteries and new redemptive societies such as the Common Benevolence Society began to organize themselves in response to state initiatives for religious reform and control, they employed the popular media as means to communicate and disseminate among themselves and to the public their own religious visions and views. When Quanzhen clerics and lay activists first attempted to promote a national organization in the summer of 1912, they chose the widely circulated *Shenbao* as a venue for announcing to the public and their fellow Daoists the bylaws, program, and mission of the national Central Daoist Association. During this period, Buddhist clerical and lay reformers and their organizations led the way in establishing the new religious print culture, publishing more than four hundred journals devoted to the discussion and dissemination of Buddhist teachings. The charismatic monk and reformer Taixu alone was responsible for publishing some of the most influential Buddhist journals during the Republican period, such as *The Buddhist Monthly* (*Foxue yuebao* 佛學月報; 1913–18?), *The Journal of the*

Enlightenment Society (Jueshe congkan 覺社叢刊; 1918–20), and The Tidal Roar (Haichao yin 海潮音; 1920–49).[6]

As Chen Yingning traveled and sojourned in Beijing, Shanghai, and other places between the 1890s and the 1940s, he and many of his colleagues became both witnesses to and participants in the renewed sectarian competition to shape the vision of the body and reformulate self-cultivation practice for the modern public. In 1933, when Chen was invited to serve as a special contributor to and editor at large of the newly established *Yangshan Biweekly* in Shanghai, he found a forum in this competitive market for expounding and promoting his vision of the body.

Chen's vision derived initially from his pursuit of Daoist self-cultivation practice for health and spirituality in the 1890s and evolved and took shape gradually in close dialogue with the intellectual, cultural, and religious crosscurrents of his times in the first half of the twentieth century. His search for a new vision of the body began with a critique of Confucian learning. Having been schooled in both Confucian and modern western learning, Chen, like many of his contemporaries, developed a complicated relationship with the Confucian tradition. On one hand, Chen came from a family of Confucian scholars and owed much of his formidable knowledge of the Classics to that education. On the other, he was witness to many unsavory and unjust social and physical practices, which had by his times come to be associated with Confucian culture. As he was exposed to other traditions of learning—Buddhism, Daoism, and western science—Chen became ambivalent about and even critical of what he saw as the Confucian tolerance of concubinage, foot binding, and opium smoking and other social and bodily practices deemed enervating and deleterious to the emerging new nation and culture. He argued that Confucianism was concerned primarily with how to be human in secular society but offered no real solutions to the fundamental problems confronted by every person: illness, aging, and death. For Chen, Confucian culture used the body primarily for procreation and the continuation of the family and society; it allowed little opportunity for individual liberation and transcendence. Driven by the desire to succeed socially, the Confucian body and its vital energies were expended in trying to pass the civil service examinations, which had become irrelevant in the changed social and political realities of modern times. Having developed a wasting disorder in his youth in pursuit of such goals, Chen, like many of his contemporaries, viewed his own childhood illness and his chronically weak constitution as both direct consequences and manifestations of the limits of Confucian culture. Chen's critique of the Confucian body culture was evidenced in his rejection of paternity, the most important of all Confucian responsibilities. In his eyes, Confucianism represented a failed cultural and political legacy and had little to offer in terms either of the care and strengthening of the individual body or of the rejuvenation of the national body politic.[7]

In early 1920s, Chen was equally critical of Buddhism. His critical stance on Buddhism was shaped by his fruitless inquiries of eminent Buddhist monks for a cure for his wasting disorder between the 1890s and 1912. His subsequent systemic study of Buddhism and personal involvement in Buddhist reforms in Shanghai and Hangzhou between 1912 and 1915 did not fundamentally change his critical views of Buddhism. Although he was clearly impressed with the rigor and magnitude of the Buddhist revival in the 1910s and 1920s, Chen remained critical of Buddhist ambivalence toward the flesh body and related self-cultivation practices.

He was particularly critical of some contemporary Buddhists for what he perceived to be their neglect of the body and body-centered techniques of self-cultivation. Reviewing the religious landscape in China in the 1920s, Chen wrote that although Buddhism alone had succeeded in establishing itself as a religion in modern China, four of its major sects—the Contemplative (Chan 禪) school, the Tiantai 天台 school, the Pure Land (Jingtu 淨土) school, and the increasingly popular transplant, the Japanese Shingon (眞言; Ch. Zhenyan) school—had long abandoned the emphasis in the authentic Buddhist tradition on the importance of the body and body-centered self-cultivation pursuits. Chen deplored the focus among all four dominant sects on the perfection of the mind (weixin 唯心) of the practitioner and their failure to provide practical solutions to the real threats to the body every practitioner faced: birth, aging, illness, and death (sheng lao bing si 生老病死). Chen assailed the growing trend among the four major Buddhist schools of favoring the Pure

Land sect's practice of reciting sutras or chanting the Buddha's name as the principal means of self-transformation.[8]

For Chen, the modern Buddhist shift away from more body-based, rigorous practices not only betrayed what he saw as the authentic traditions of self-cultivation within Buddhism but also, and more important, relocated the center of self-cultivation and transformation from within the practitioner's body to deities outside the body. This resulted in spiritual and religious dependency on the Buddha for individual liberation, a dependency that was growing because of the popularity of the Pure Land sect. For Chen, the Pure Land stress on reciting scriptures and chanting the Buddha's name as the means of salvation amounted to spiritual lethargy and religious defeatism.

In the context of Japan's defeat of China in 1895 and its infamous Twenty-One demands in 1915, Chen's sharp attacks on the Pure Land sect and the increasingly popular Japanese esoteric Shingon sect demonstrate his strong sense of cultural and religious nationalism. After initial difficulties in their missionary activities, major Japanese Buddhist monasteries managed to expand and build branch temples in major treaty ports in China, especially in southeastern Chinese cities like Shanghai, Hangzhou, and Xiamen, after 1896. The most dominant and aggressive of these Japanese missions were those led by famous Pure Land monasteries such as the Higashi-Hongan ji 東本願寺, based in Kyoto. Although the announced goal of these missions was to support the Chinese sangha, the general public and even Chinese Buddhists suspected they had another agenda. In 1895, many Japanese Buddhist Pure Land missions encouraged their Chinese counterparts to declare their temples branches of Japanese Pure Land home temples to gain extraterritoriality and thus be able to fend off the threats of expropriation by the local governments. This tactic proved so successful that in the early 1900s the Qing court felt compelled to relax its policy of confiscating local temples to establish new schools. Once the court dropped its policy of temple seizures, the rush to affiliate with Japanese temples fizzled out.[9] But the open interventions by the Japanese Pure Land missions in China's domestic religious disputes fostered suspicion among both the Chinese public and Buddhist clerics, who grew wary of Japanese intentions after 1915.[10]

These nationalistic sentiments further complicated Chen's personal attitude toward Buddhism, especially the Pure Land sect, during the 1920s and 1930s. Indeed, Chen's pursuit of Buddhist scriptural studies and meditation techniques did not change his earlier assessment of Mahayana Buddhism (Dasheng Fojiao 大乘佛教).[11] On the contrary, his erudition in Buddhist learning only served to solidify his rejection of the Buddhist view of the body. It was no accident that this fundamental criticism and rejection of Buddhism paralleled the Japanese expansion in China throughout the 1930s and early 1940s.

Chen's rejection was based on philosophical as well as nationalistic grounds. To Chen, Buddhism, especially Mahayana Buddhism, failed to comprehend and confront the reality of life. In an article published in the *Yangshan Biweekly* in 1937, Chen reflected on the life story of Sakyamuni:

When Sakyamuni left home for self-cultivation, wasn't he also motivated by the same dreariness and fear of the impermanence of life (*wu chang* 無常)? He encountered a dotard at the eastern gate, a sick man at the western gate, and a dead corpse at the southern gate of his princely city. Only then did he resolve to go into the mountains to practice ascetics. It is a pity that he should have the misfortune to have been born in India instead of China. The two teachers he encountered were not very wise and sagacious in learning. As a result, he never developed a thorough approach to the solid and veritable practice that would prevent and allow him to rid himself of the three sufferings of aging, illness, and death. The repertoire of self-cultivation he evolved, which he put on show for a full forty-nine years of his life with gusto and aplomb, can be summed up in a single word: "enlightenment" (*jue* 覺). I am not saying that there should not be any enlightenment in life. The only pity is that there is not the slightest shred of a method for preventing and repelling aging, illness, and death, except for that single word. But neither sitting in contemplation (*canchan* 參禪) nor refining the gaze (*xiuguan* 修觀) nor reciting scriptures (*songjing* 誦經) nor intoning mantras (*chi zhou* 持咒) can attain the goal. Even if a sudden enlightenment does come, of what use is it?[12]

For Chen, the futility of this method arises from the Buddhist view of the world and the body as nothing more than figments or appearances of the Mind. He argued that the Buddhist rejection of the physical world and bodily experience as illusory and unreal (*fei zhenshi* 非真實) was ontologically unsound and profoundly at odds with observed facts. Furthermore, Chen held that because of its denial of materiality, Buddhism imposed an artificial distinction between the Realm of the Dharma (*fajie* 法界) and the Body of Phenomena (*seshen* 色身). He argued that this distinction destroyed the unity between the spiritual and the physical dimensions of the body. Consequently, any enlightenment achieved through mind-centered self-cultivation remained but an illusion of the mind itself and had no effect on the material world. As Chen reasoned:

> People who seek immortality stress only practice, but not enlightenment. They certainly cannot attain any transformative powers of divinity and efficacy through enlightenment. This is because any transformative powers of efficacy and divinity are intimately connected with the Material. But the Buddhist enlightenment is too detached from the realm of the Material (*wuzhi zhi jingjie* 物質之境界). Even if you reach a consummate enlightenment, the Material outside the Mind is not changed, not by a shred or an iota.[13]

Chen further argued that the Buddhist view of reality and the body had since ancient times produced devastating results in China. Again, writing in the summer of 1937, a time when Japanese military and cultural expansion in China reached new heights, Chen reasserted his sense of religious nationalism by impugning the Buddhist epistemology of the body as a totally alien and culturally bankrupt vision. Chen even claimed that the adoption of Buddhism in the second century CE had brought cultural disaster to the Chinese nation:

> Ever since coming to the East, Buddhism has inculcated in the minds of millions of Chinese its abstruse and sophisticated Mahayana philosophy, which should have [made China] far exceed the three dynasties of the Sages in both achievements and virtue. But why does our country still languish in so much difficulty? Why are popular mores so diluted daily, livelihood so impoverished, and the vitality of the nation so enervated? How is it that we have suffered from the upheavals of the Five Barbarians' dynasties and Sixteen States, the division between the Southern and the Northern Kingdoms, the succession of the Five Dynasties, and the shame of subjugation by the Liao and Jin, the agony of conquest by the Yuan and Qing dynasties, and the current anxiety of aggression by foreign powers? Aren't these all that Mahayana acumen and perfection have amounted to?[14]

Thus, as Japanese expansion unfolded from the early 1930s through the 1940s, cultural nationalism fueled Chen's scathing criticism of the Buddhist visions of the body and the world. But more important, they also inspired him to seek an alternative vision of the body and the world distinctly different from Buddhism.

To Chen, the Buddhist fallacy about the body was embedded in its excessive idealism, which valued the mental and the psychological over the physical and the bodily. This fallacy was best exemplified in the worship of relic bones (*sheli* 舍利). In their single-minded focus on perfecting the Mind-Nature, the Buddhists missed the true transformative potentials of the somatic and physical energies of the body. Instead, they came to worship relic bones, which, Chen argued, were only the decayed remnants of the vitalizing energies of Essence (*jing* 精) and *qi* 氣 in the body. Chen argued that the Nature of the Heart (*xin xing* 心性) was nothing but the Psyche (*shen* 神) of the body, whereas relic bones were the Essence and *qi*, which represented the Life Force of the body (*ming* 命). But to the Buddhist, only the Psyche was imperishable and beyond the cycle of life and death. So when a Buddhist died, only his or her Psyche would be able to transcend the phenomenal realm, and his or her Essence and *qi* were left to linger in the form of relic bones in the world. By contrast, Chen argued that a perfected Daoist would be able to integrate both the spiritual Psyche and the physical Essence and *qi* in the body through inner alchemic practice and thus achieve a superior transcendence wherein both the *shen* and *qi*, the Mind-Nature and the Life Force would be united:

The Daoist, on the other hand, cultivates both the Mind-Nature and the Life Force in the body. The Essence, *qi*, and *shen* are mingled into a union. Through the practice of firing along the Orbit of the Heaven, the Daoist refines and cultivates another body out of the present body. In the new body, Psyche, Essence, and *qi* coexist without distinction or division. So when the Daoist transforms by disintegration, regardless whether he or she does so by transforming the flesh body into *qi*, or by levitating the Yang Psyche out and dissolving the corpse, there is nothing left behind such as relic bones. Occasionally when some Daoists do leave behind relic bones in sitting disintegration (*zuo hua* 坐化), their previous daily practice must have leaned more toward the Buddhist way: too mindful of the Mind-Nature while remiss of the Life of their body. Dual cultivators of both the

Nature and the Life (*xingming shuangxiu zhi shi* 性命雙修之士) solidify the Essence, *qi*, and the Psyche of their bodies into a union of effulgence and vitality. All their bones and flesh are transformed at the same time; all the pores and cavities of their bodies are harmonized; their blood is like the silvery cream; their body is like a flowing fire,[15] spreading free and unobstructed to the four limbs and in between the Hundred Joints. It shines and glows in the Void Realm of purity and tranquility. That is why their bodies can ascend and descend beyond any predication, appear and disappear at will. This is the difference between Buddhism and Daoism.[16]

In Search of an Immortal's Body

Chen's critique of the Buddhist vision of the body reflected his ongoing efforts in searching for and defining what he perceived to be the authentic body for modern self-cultivation practice, which could be clearly demarcated from the body as defined by other religious and cultural traditions. From the 1910s to the 1940s, Chen wrote and edited a score or so monographs on the subject of Daoist self-cultivation techniques, which he termed the "Immortals' (or Transcendents') Learning" (*xianxue* 仙學), a name that reflected the contemporary attempt of religious reformers to present Daoism more as a tradition of scholarly learning (*xue* 學) than as a religion or faith (*zongjiao* 宗教). From 1933 to 1941, in his capacity as editor at large for *Yangshan Biweekly* and its successor journal, the *Immortals' Way Monthly*, Chen wrote and published books, essays, poems, and letters on the subject of Daoist inner alchemic cultivation. Together, these writings form a corpus of his thinking on the new body of Daoist inner alchemy. Of these, the best-known and most widely circulated are *Lectures on the Yellow Courtyard Scriptures* (*Huangting jing jiangyi* 黃庭經講義), *Annotations to Sun Bu'er's Poem on Female Alchemy* (*Sun Bu'er nüdan shizhu* 孫不二女丹詩注), *Explorations in Oral Secrets* (*Koujue gouxuan lu* 口訣鉤玄錄), *Vernacular Annotations on the Ode to the Great Way of the Numinous Origin* (*Lingyuan dadao ge baihua zhujie* 靈源大道歌白話注解), and an unpublished manuscript entitled "Learning Immortals Will Surely Succeed" ("Xuexian bicheng" 學仙必成).

Personal interest in the subject aside, Chen's motives in writing and producing these texts have to be understood in the context of the widening public interest and participation in various self-cultivation techniques as advocated by Daoist and Buddhist clerics, the redemptive societies, and elite lay practitioners such as Jiang Weiqiao. The growing public interest, especially among women, also presented inner alchemists like Chen Yingning with both theoretical and practical challenges. First, the obscure terminology and difficult language of traditional inner alchemic scriptures made them unfathomable even to the learned, let alone the general public. For women, the problem was compounded by their lack of access to the few scarce texts on women's inner alchemic practice. Second, traditional inner alchemic theories centered on the male body and rarely discussed the female body and its related practice. Partly out of the need to address the public demand for accessible texts and partly in response to internal issues within the traditional inner alchemic theories and practice, Chen began to use simple, vernacular language to edit and compose commentaries and annotations on early Daoist inner alchemic scriptures.

Although written and published at various times, these writings have much in common. One important feature of all of Chen's writings is that they were composed with actual practice in mind. *Annotations* began as a manual to instruct Lü Bicheng in women's inner alchemic meditation in Beijing in 1916. *Lectures* was a practice manual for his friend Wang Pinsan 王聘三 in Shanghai in the early 1920s. His *Vernacular Elucidations* was prepared and delivered as a series of lectures over the summer of 1938 to a small group of practitioners who gathered every weekend to practice quiet sitting in the unoccupied French concession in western Shanghai.[17]

Another important shared feature is the format of Chen's commentaries. Chen's adoption of the established practices of textual commentary was driven by several practical factors. On one hand, his preference for this format reflected his own literati roots and suited his scholarly disposition. On the other, the format cast him in the role of an elucidator of the early masters, a persona that would have appealed to the taste and predilections of his educated audience. The format also fulfilled the practical need for question-and-answer dialogues that mimicked the adept-acolyte relationship. It authenticated Chen's personal authority through his erudition while reinforcing the disciple's own sense of being an informed and confirmed practitioner. Additionally, Chen's commentaries allowed both affiliation with and distance from the canonical text. As such, it best fitted Chen's need for innovative interpretations and adaptations in the context of practice. Furthermore, Chen's preference for the textual commentary may have reflected the modern inner alchemist's concern to avoid being associated with the now much maligned "superstitious and quack" practices often transmitted through secret oral teachings among less literate practitioners.

But Chen's use of early Daoist inner alchemy classics as the basis for his commentaries also revealed his cultural-nationalist desire to trace and locate the authentic modern alchemic body within the indigenous Chinese tradition. In this earlier and more pristine Daoist tradition, Chen found both the "historical" origins and the cosmological foundations of the modern alchemic body, a body whose antiquity and history differentiated it from the non-Chinese Buddhist tradition and whose materiality connected it to the teachings of modern science.

The History of the Body: The Yellow Emperor and the Divine Transcendents

Chen first traced the origins of his "Immortals' Learning" and the authentic alchemic body to the legendary Yellow Emperor (Huangdi 黄帝). In his study of a late Qing inner alchemic text, Chen identified the ancient tradition of the Divine Transcendents (shenxian jia 神仙家) as the origin of the modern "Immortals' Learning" and defined the theories and techniques of the early tradition as "the transcendents' or supermen's philosophy" (chaoren zhexue 超人哲學). He located the earliest written record of the Divine Immortals tradition in the purported instructions by the legendary transcendent Guangcheng zi 廣成子 to Xuanyuan 軒轅, the Yellow Emperor, on the art of governance and the techniques of longevity and immortality.[18]

Chen's claim of filiation to the Yellow Emperor was aimed at establishing the school of the Divine Immortals as the origin of all intellectual, cultural, and religious traditions in China. Encompassing the art of governing the world on one hand and techniques for transforming the body on the other, the Divine Immortals tradition thus originated over 4,600 years ago in China's antiquity and continued through the early Xia and Shang dynasties through the Daoist philosophers of the Zhou era such as Laozi all the way down to the modern period. It gave rise to the late Zhou schools of the Daoist philosophers (daojia 道家) and the Confucians (rujia 儒家). Although it differed from Daoism, the Divine Immortals' Learning formed the core and essence of Daoism. For Chen, much of the Divine Immortals' teachings on the arts of refining the body were handed down and preserved in the oral secrets of Daoist inner alchemy. In a small tract composed in the early 1930s and serialized in the *Yangshan Biweekly* between the summer of 1934 and early 1937, Chen shared with his audience his reflections on the origin of the ancient tradition and its relationship with Daoism and Confucianism:

After the Yellow Emperor's times, China underwent many more dynasties and was until the time of Laozi of the Zhou dynasty dominated by Daoists whose teachings were consummate and systemic. When applied externally, its teachings can govern the state and harmonize the family (*zhiguo qijia* 治國齊家). When used internally, they can refine the body and nurture the mind (*xiushen yangxing* 修身養性). . . . The Confucian teachings began with Confucius. But before Confucius, there existed only the Daoists, but not the Confucians. At the time, Confucius himself had received teachings from Laozi. He admitted that he only transmitted but did not create his teachings, and that he believed in and was fond of the ancients. So we know that Confucianism had come from Daoism.

Reflecting on his own training in the Confucian historiographical tradition, Chen portrayed what he termed "religious Daoism" (*daojiao* 道教) as a distinct and derivative tradition characterized by its ritual and liturgical techniques.[19]

Chen's attempts to differentiate and distance the Immortals' Learning from the Daoist liturgical and other magic-based techniques mirrored his elitist and reformist agenda. He wanted to cleanse Daoism of its "superstitious" and magical elements and present what he saw as the quintessence of the early Daoist Immortals' Learning tradition as foundational to the culture and history of the Chinese nation. The centrality of the Yellow Emperor in Chen's reconstruction of the Daoist tradition also reflected the common intellectual roots that modern Daoist reformers like Chen shared with the rising Han-centric cultural-nationalist discourse about the origin and ethnicity of the Chinese peoples (*Zhonghua minzu* 中華民族) in the early twentieth century. At the core of this ideology was the veneration of the Yellow Emperor as the founder and creator of Chinese culture and the Chinese nation.[20]

The Cosmology of the Body

The body of the Divine Transcendents that emerged in the writings of Chen Yingning from the 1920s to the 1940s was a body perfected through the optimal integration of the physical and the spiritual—the bodily contours and constituents of the flesh and the intelligent powers of the mind-heart. It was a body composed of the two most primary and fundamental cosmic energies: the generative and substantive power known as *qi* and its closely related counterpart, the Psyche or psychic energies called *shen*. The genesis and perfection of the alchemic body lie in the union of these two basic energies within the practitioner's body.

The Body of Energies and Temporalities. In Chen's vision of the alchemic body, both the *qi* and the *shen* energies were divided into a pair of interrelated modes of temporality: atemporal (*xiantian* 先天) and temporal (*houtian* 後天). In his *Annotations*, Chen used the opening couplet of Sun Bu'er's poem to capture the quintessence of that vision:

> Before my body comes into being,
> The Unitary Qi has long been in existence.

For Chen, the atemporal *qi*, here alluded to as the "Unitary Qi" (*yi qi* 一氣), was the most fundamental generative energy of the universe. It existed outside the confines of time and prior to the moment when material, human, and conscious genesis began, and distinction and multiplication subsequently emerged. It was the potent creative force that engendered the initial division of the undifferentiated realm into the dynamic duo of yin and yang and sustained their subsequent ceaseless rounds of transformation into a myriad of beings and things.[21]

In the Five Dynasties classic *The Book of Metamorphosis* (*Huashu* 化書) by Tan Qiao 譚峭 (z. Jingsheng 景昇; fl. 907–60), Chen found the most lucid illustration of atemporal *qi*'s creative process in which the *qi* of the substantive Void (*xu* 虛), the original undifferentiated state of the cosmos, transformed from its atemporal ethereal *qi* into the temporal forms of human life:

> The Void transmutes into the Psyche; the Psyche transfigures into *qi*; *qi* is transformed into Blood; the Blood into the Embryonic Form; the Embryo gestates into the Fetus; the Fetus matures to an Infant; the Infant grows into a Youth; then the Youth matures into Adult; and then through Adulthood to Dotage, and finally returns to Death.[22]

For Chen Yingning, Tan Qiao's eloquent description illustrated the progressive interaction of *shen* and *qi*, as they transform from the atemporal realm into the temporal realm in the creation and growth of human life. In their respective atemporal modes, *shen* was known as the Original or True Psyche (*yuan shen* 元神, *zhen shen* 眞神), and *qi* as the Original or True Vitality (*yuan qi* 元氣, *zhen qi* 眞氣). As they interacted and crossed the threshold into the temporal realm, these two most basic generative energies of the atemporal began to assume different functions and forms in the human body. There they constituted the very substance and function of human life: from its bodily fluids to its bone and flesh to its sensory and intelligent powers and mental faculties. Chen provided further details of this vision of the body formed through the constant interaction between *shen* and *qi* by citing these lines of the Song female immortal Cao Wenyi 曹文逸 (ca. 1101–25):

> No need to distinguish the mucus, saliva, semen, or blood,
> All are but of the one and same Origin.
> It never has a fixed location,
> And mutates instantly at the Heart's whim.
> When feeling hot in the body, it changes into sweat;
> At a melancholy sight, it turns to tears.
> It flows as Essence, as desires rise in the Kidneys;
> It discharges as mucus when wind blows into the nose.
> Far and wide it circulates and moistens the whole body;
> In origin it stems from the Divine Fluid,

A Fluid that is hard to describe and known to but
a few.
It grows out of the True Vitality.[23]

For Chen, Cao's verse reveals the subtlety of the transformative journey of the atemporal *qi* in the genesis and growth of the body. In *Vernacular Annotations*, Chen identified the Divine Fluid (*shen shui* 神水) as the intermediate generative energy produced at the transformative fulcrum between the atemporal and the temporal body. As the True Vitality mutates into the fluid, it crosses the threshold that separates the atemporal and the temporal realms. Circulating in the body, the Divine Fluid, still a formless energy, responds in perfect synergy with the Psyche, which is temporally embodied as the conscious mental and psychic powers of the body. As the Heart's Intentions (*xinyi* 心意), which are the functions of the Psyche, react to the varied stimuli of the surroundings, the Divine Fluid hastens to respond to the "whims of the Heart" by transforming itself into sweat, tears, mucus, blood, semen, and various bodily fluids. In this way, the atemporal *qi* changes from the formless ethereal energy, through the intermediate phase of the Divine Fluid, to take its final form of the vital constitutive fluids of the temporal body.[24]

It is precisely this continuous process of interactive transformation between the Psyche and *qi* that first creates and then sustains human life. Like earlier alchemists such as Tan Qiao, Cao Wenyi, and Sun Bu'er, Chen viewed the symbiotic affinity between *qi* and *shen* as the foundation of life itself and their integration within the body as the only path to transcendence and perfection:

> *Shen* is the Function of the Heart, and *qi* is the Stuff of Life;
> When *shen* does not wander, *qi* settles within firm and secure.
> Who can be more intimate: the two are of one origin;
> Losing both, how can your life hold on?
> Blend them into a unity without ever remembering it;
> You can then be coeval with the Origin of Creation.[25]

"Going Along with It": Restoring the Atemporal Body. The transformative journey from life to death so eloquently described by Tan Qiao conveys a sense of the innate proclivity of the atemporal

energies of *shen* and *qi* toward this end. In the traditional discourse of Daoist inner alchemy, the natural proclivity of the atemporal energies to transmute into the temporal forms of life was known as "conforming" or "going along with it" (*shun* 順). This tendency was most prominently manifested in the realm of human procreation. But inner alchemists viewed the body born of this natural process of conformity as impermanent and prone to the ravages of time, illness, and death. They argued that going along with the natural predisposition toward transmutation led only to becoming a mortal (*shun ze chengren* 順則成人).[26]

For both early inner alchemists and modern practitioners such as Chen Yingning, to be human was to err and to deviate from the Way of the Divine Transcendents. For them, human imperfection began at the very instant the atemporal energies of *qi* and *shen* first evolved to assume the heavier and more turbid forms of semen, blood, breathed air, saliva, sweat, and other bodily secretions and fluids.[27] Thus the natural transmutative journey of both *shen* and *qi* from their atemporal state to the temporal realm was often viewed as a degradation, a fall from the pristine original perfection. The natural body was thus vulnerable to physical toil, mental anguish, illness, aging, and ultimately death. Chen Yingning dwelled on Sun Bu'er's contemplation on the fragility of the natural body:

> It begins originally within Nothingness;
> Who expects it to fall into the temporal realm!
> Barely has the first cry left the mouth,
> The three-inch tongue thereafter holds sway over the body.
> Worn and dreary, how can it withstand the ravages of illness?

For Chen and his followers, the body born through the process of "going along" with *qi*'s natural transmutation led a precarious existence. As the infant leaves the womb, it falls immediately under the control of its postnatal breathing, figuratively referred to here as the "three-inched tongue" (*san cun* 三寸). Further, the infant's newfound and growing sensory and cognitive powers can hasten the natural decay of the body. Using the familiar Buddhist term "the Six Dusts" (*liu chen* 六塵), Chen described how the infant's increasing abilities to see, hear, smell, taste, touch, and discern exhaust the powers of its heart and the vitality of its body (*laoxin laoli* 勞心勞力). As the infant grows, its sensory and intellectual powers render the body susceptible to various harmful stimulations and temptations, enervating and threatening it with exhaustion, anguish, illness, and even premature death, and deprive it of any chance of longevity and transcendence.[28]

For Chen and his fellow practitioners of inner alchemy, both the ultimate source of human vulnerability and the beginning of liberation lie in the "natural" process of human procreation. If the original alienation of *shen* from *qi* and their continued separation are the root causes of the body's congenital frailty and impermanence, they are also the starting point for the body's rejuvenation and perfection. Chen again found an affirmation of his vision in Sun Bu'er's verse:

> But just as a robust Son benefits the Mother,
> Never say that it will not come back around.
> Withhold your breath to focus on *shen*,
> And *qi* will arise from the East.[29]

In the same way that a healthy robust newborn could add to his mother's health, Chen explained that postnatal breathing (*houtian qi* 後天氣) could fortify the atemporal *qi* (*xiantian qi* 先天氣) within the body so that the body could reverse *qi*'s natural transmutation, and restore and return it to its original atemporal realm. The key to reversing the transformative mechanism (*nizhuan zaohua* 逆轉造化) was to regulate one's breathing (*qi*) while focusing the mental energies (*shen*) in the body so that the two blended into one. He urged fellow practitioners to persist in this practice at propitious hours while facing east and to cultivate and gather the Unitary Qi from within the atemporal Aperture of Original Creation (*you zaohua ku zhong qu xiantian yiqi* 由造化窟取先天一氣).[30]

It is clear that *shen*, even in its postnatal temporal forms of the sensory and intellectual powers and functions of the body, plays a particularly vital role in both the destruction and the revitalization of the body. The practitioner's ability to focus and integrate *shen* with *qi* remains the key to the rejuvenation of the body. Chen identified the *shen* and its powers as the most mysterious thing, which defied reason and held the key to achieving transcendence.[31]

The Bodyscape: Apertures, Nexuses, and Channels. The body Chen Yingning envisioned for modern practitioners was also a landscape in which the interactions of the atemporal energies shaped the destiny of the body. Drawing on the Shangqing classic *Yellow Courtyard Scriptures* and other medieval Daoist inner alchemic writings, Chen delineated the body of modern inner alchemy as a sacred landscape made up of strategically situated "imperial palaces, mansions, passes, and channels." This complex network of nodes, loci, and central points in the body form an intricate web of circulatory pathways and resting places, on and through which the *shen* and *qi* energies are cycled and refined so that the process of "bucking," or reversing, their natural journey can commence. Chen argued that as one focused one's psychic energies of *shen* and directed the flow of the *qi* through the body's key loci and channels, the two merged and reunited to recover their original unity in the atemporal realm.

For Chen, the central locus of the body is the Yellow Courtyard (*huangting* 黃庭). In his *Lectures*, Chen explained that both the color and the centrality of this locus are meant to evoke the image of an imperial palace. To Chen, the Shangqing Daoist scripture's roundabout way of describing the locus serves only to enhance its physical and functional centrality in the body:

> The Numinous Soul above and the Original Pass below;
> Young Yin is to the left, and to the right, Grand Yang.
> The Secret Door is in the back, and the Gate of Nativity to
>   the front;
> Out breathe the Sun; in breathe the Moon.
> Robed in scarlet is the Perfected One of the Yellow Court;
> Joined in coitus are the Yin and Yang sides of the Original Pass.
> Solemn and noble, it is hemmed in by the Gate of Nativity;
> Delicate and subtle is the Qi of Essence in the Cinnabar Field.

In *Lectures*, Chen explained to his modern audience how the Yellow Courtyard locus was defined in relation to an array of surrounding loci within the abdomen. Above the Yellow Courtyard is the Numinous Mansion (*lingfu* 靈府), where the Heart Deity (*xinshen* 心神), also known as the Numinous Soul (*hunling* 魂靈), resides. Below is the Pass of Origin (*guanyuan* 關元). To the front of the Yellow

Innovating the Immortals' Body 97

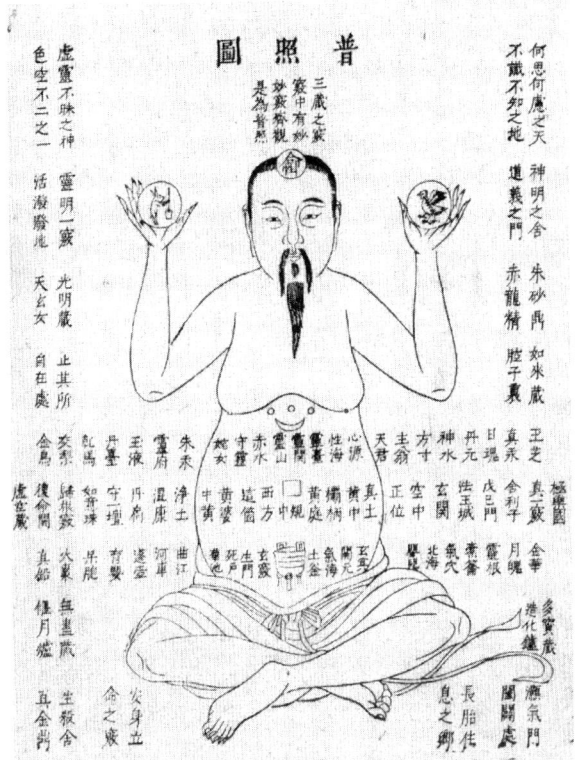

Fig. 6 A universal vista (*Puzhao tu*, 1615). Note the locus of the Yellow Courtyard near the navel on the body (*Xingming shuangxiu wanshen guizhi*, yuan ji, 20b).

Courtyard is the Gate of Nativity (*shenmen* 神門). Opposite the Gate of Nativity at the back of the body is a locus called the Secret Door (*mihu* 密戶), also known as the Gate of Life (*mingmen* 命門). Smack at the intersection of the Numinous Soul–Pass of Origin axis and the Gate of Nativity, the Secret Door axis is the Yellow Courtyard,[32] just above the navel of the body (see Fig. 6).

Chen further explained that "yellow" alludes to the physical and functional centrality of the vital locus. "Yellow" is the symbolic color for Earth (*tu* 土). In the theory of the Five Phases, an important component of inner alchemy, the Earth occupies the center of the alignment of the Five Phases and symbolizes the center of the universe. The word "courtyard" signifies an empty space or void at the center of the body. To Chen, this vacant center plays a pivotal role in the balance of the body:

> Of our body, the part above the navel is the upper half. It is much like the trunk of a plant with its vitality growing upward. Below the navel is the lower half. It is like the root of the plant with its vitality growing down. In a plant, the pivot of life and the source of primal energy of both the upper and the lower halves is at the divide between the trunk and the root. But in the human body, it is at the navel.
>
> When the fetus is still in the womb, its nose does not breathe. The umbilical cord functions as its breathing. At the moment when the infant is born, its umbilical cord ceases to function, and its nostrils open up for breathing. But the oral secrets of the divine immortals value fetal breathing (*taixi* 胎息). What is fetal breathing? It is just a name for returning each breath to the Root (*xixi guigen* 息息歸根). What is the Root? It's simply the Void within the thorax. This Void within the thorax is the Yellow Courtyard.[33]

The Yellow Courtyard locus is thus the center and the pivot that simultaneously separates and connects the upper and lower halves of the body. It is also the threshold between the atemporal and the temporal realms within the body. As the last vestige from the undifferentiated past, the Yellow Courtyard locus can also serve as the fulcrum that enables the practitioners to restore and return their temporal body to its atemporal perfection.[34]

The Body of Viscera, Orbs, and Coituses. Following early Daoist and medical notions of the body, Chen Yingning also envisioned the inner alchemic body to be composed of the Five Viscera and Six Orbs (*wuzang liufu* 五臟六腑), as well as the meridians (*mai* 脈), sinews (*jin* 筋), flesh (*rou* 肉), bones (*gu* 骨), skin (*pi* 皮), and fluids (*ye* 液). Drawing on the medical classic *The Inner Canon of the Yellow Emperor*, Chen, like his predecessors, saw the proper management of the equilibrium among the five viscera—the Heart (*xin zang* 心臟), the Lungs (*fei zang* 肺臟), the Liver (*gan zang* 肝臟), the Kidneys (*shen zang* 腎藏), and the Spleen (*pi zang* 脾臟)—as the key to the body's health, longevity, and ultimately its immortality, because each of these viscera functioned as the repository and host for its correlated forms of *shen* and *qi* within the body[35] (see Fig. 7).

Innovating the Immortals' Body 99

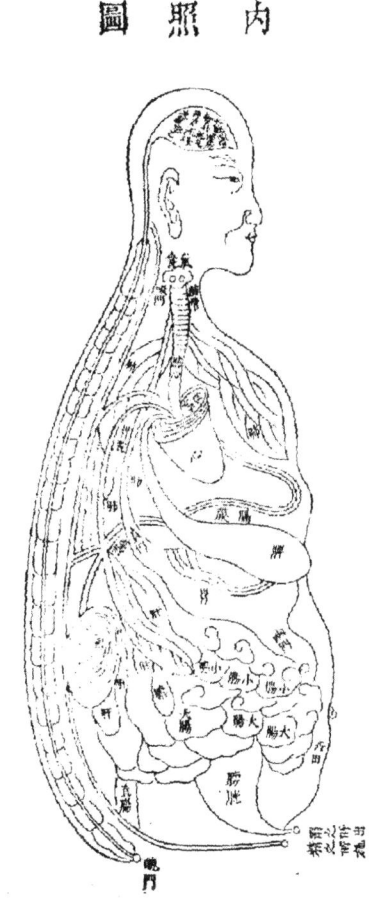

Fig. 7 Inner illumination (*Neizhao tu*, 1615).
Note the Five Viscera in the body. (*Xingming
shuangxiu wanshen guizhi, yuan ji*, 22b).

In Chen's construct of the modern alchemic body, the Heart was still the primary organ among the five viscera. Perched over the Yellow Courtyard, the Heart is the locale where the Heart Deity, also known as the Numinous Soul, resides. It is where the psychic and conscious *shen* of the body converge and concentrate. It is therefore the central nexus that encompasses and controls all bodily functions. Elaborating on a passage in the *Yellow Courtyard Scriptures*, Chen wrote:

The reason the human body and its viscera can function is entirely because *shen* holds sway over them (*shen wei zhuzai* 神爲主宰). The Heart and *shen* are one and the same thing. When it is tranquil, it is known as the Heart. When it moves, it is called *shen*. All the Five Viscera and Six Orbs possess the capacity of natural movement and operation without the slightest error or lapse. Hence it is said that they cycle around the heavenly orbit within the Heart. But the viscera and orbs of an ordinary person move day and night without rest. Sooner or later come the day of fatigue and weariness and the time of depletion and impairment. So the cultivators of the Way must first hold to the tranquil in order to regulate the moving. Then conserve *shen* so as to pacify the Heart. Next, empty the Heart to refine *shen* so that they mutually benefit. So the circulation of *qi* and the Blood within the viscera and orbs may be slowed and calmed and in turn rested and cultivated so as not to cause such ills as being stout outside yet withered inside in the body, being hastily imperious and out of regulation, restlessly unsettled and without peace in the Heart. Then one can enjoy prolonged life.

Under the viscera of the Lung in our thorax is the Heart. Its shape is like a lotus flower about to bloom. Its function is to regulate the Blood. As the Blood is regulated, life is then put in order, and the body is fully freshened and glistening with moisture.

Chen thus imagined the Heart and the Psyche (*shen*) as two sides of the same coin. The Heart is defined by its alternating states of action (*dong* 動) and quietude (*jing* 靜). *Shen* is manifested in the *qi*'s activation of the faculties and functions of the body (*qidong wei zhi shen* 氣動謂之神), whereas the Heart is seen as the alternative state of *shen* in which the natural faculties and functions of *qi* are calmed (*qijing wei zhi xin* 氣靜謂之心). It is this state of tranquil and calmed *shen* toward which an inner alchemic practitioner must strive.[36]

Underlying the stress on tranquility is the inner alchemist's fundamental understanding of the Heart's function and its relationship with several other key viscera and loci of the body. This understanding draws heavily on traditional Chinese theories of the Five Phases, yin-yang, and the intervisceral symbiosis of traditional medical discourse. For Chen Yingning, the chief function of the Heart is to keep the focal gaze of *shen* on the Yellow Courtyard locus, the center of the body and the gateway to immortality. As the practitioner keeps the Heart Deity focused on the Yellow Courtyard, the psychic and conscious energies of *shen* are infused into the *qi* of breathing, and the *qi* in turn enwraps *shen* to form the phenomenon of yin-yang coitus (*mu pin zhi xiang* 牡牝之相). Quoting the alchemic classic *Cantongqi* 參同契, often ascribed to Wei Boyang 魏伯陽 of the Eastern Han period, Chen argued that this majestic union in the recesses of the Yellow Courtyard behind the Pass of Darkness (*xuanguan* 玄關) facilitates the rise and flow of the vital *qi* from the Lower Cinnabar Field (*xia dantian* 下丹田) just below the Yellow Courtyard, and so it is coeval with Heaven and Earth.[37]

The centrality of the Heart among the five viscera is also highlighted through its vital relationships with two other important visceral epicenters of the *qi* energies: the Lungs, which control the life-sustaining breathing in the upper part of the body, and the Kidneys, which preside over the generative fluids in the lower part of the body. The Heart-Lung nexus is manifested in the *shen-qi* relationship, underscoring the vital importance of the Lungs. The Pulmonary Palace (*feibu zhi gong* 肺部之宮) is seen as the key locus of *qi* in the form of breath, just as the Heart is seen as the seat of *shen* in the form of psychic and intelligent faculties. The coitus between the Heart and the Lungs forms a special nexus vividly captured in these lines from the *Yellow Courtyard Scriptures*:

> The Pulmonary Palace resembles a canopy,
> Below it sits an Infant Boy inside the Jade Manor.

Like the canopy above an emperor's carriage (*hua gai* 華蓋), the Pulmonary Palace hovers over and nurtures the Heart below it. This symbiosis is further underscored by the reciprocally beneficial properties ascribed to the Heart and the Lungs based on Five Phases theory. Chen argued that the Lungs are aligned with the Phase of Metal and associated with the color white. Hence, the Lungs are also known figuratively as the Jade Manor (*yu que* 玉闕), home of the pulmonary deity known as the White Origin (*bai yuan* 白元). In contrast, the Heart is aligned with the Fire Phase and associated with the color red. So the Heart is known as the Purple Palace (*jiang gong* 絳宮), which is where the Heart Deity dwells. Chen Yingning went on to describe the Heart as the Son of the Seven Origins (*Qi-yuan zhi zi* 七元之子). He invoked the mutually beneficial numbers to underscore the reciprocating nexus of *shen* and *qi*: the number seven represents the Fire in the Heart, and the number nine stands for the Metal in the Lungs. The joining of the two propitious numbers signifies the transformative union of *shen* and *qi*, of the Fire and the Metal.[38] Since the Lungs control the vital function of breathing, Chen described the replenishing function of proper breathing:

> If one can apply the practice of regulating breathing so as to preserve the Essence and Psyche within the body [and prevent them] from leaking, his body will be a good cause for celebration. If he accumulates by the day and by the month and circulates his breathing within the Square Inch (*fang cun* 方寸), he will not only have established the Root of Life (*ming gen* 命根),[39] but can also use the Original Qi within his own body to attract and collect the Essence and Psyche from the Void, so that all their depletion since birth may be replenished and returned to his body. He shall have no worry about ever growing old.[40]

The technique of embryonic breathing was seen as the key to the reintegration of *shen* and *qi* within the body. In *Lectures*, Chen further elaborated on the technique for his audience:

> The most treasured secret of the Immortals' Way is to obtain *qi* with *shen*. Cause *shen* to enter within *qi* and *qi* to envelop *shen* from the outside. Hammer to bind the two into a single blade. Solidify it into a ball. Twist it into a thread so that the integrated *qi* is condensed into a point. In this way, the breathing returns to the Root and will not scatter to roam and disperse at random. It will gradually develop into a path that can be followed. Persist in this practice, and you can achieve embryonic breathing.
>
> What is embryonic breathing? In embryonic breathing, the breathed *qi* circulates and permeates the whole body. As the inner breathing opens and closes, all the pores on the body correspond with it. In contrast, the nose no longer feels any air flowing in and out, until even the inner breathing stops completely, and its opening and closing ceases. By then one is not far from the time when one arrives at Stillness so that pure Yang *shen* may finally appear.[41]

Chen's metallurgical imagery underscores the meditative breathing techniques of reuniting *shen* and *qi*. In this symbiotic dynamic, the coitus of the Heart with the Lungs further manifests the mutual dependence and indispensability of *shen* and *qi* in the body. Natural aging and bodily decay are understood as consequences of failure to reunite the two through breathing.

In contrast to the Lungs, which play a key role in regulating breathing in the upper body, the Kidneys control the operation of the generative fluids in the lower body. Whereas the Lungs are envisioned as perched above the Heart, the Kidneys, also known in Shangqing texts as the "Dual Lords of Water" (*liangbu shuizhu* 兩部水主), are pictured as an orb situated below the Heart and the central locus of the Yellow Courtyard. In Chen's construct, the Kidneys are closely associated with the Lower Cinnabar Field recessed somewhere behind the navel in the lower abdomen. In male and female bodies, the Kidneys have also been identified by various names evocative of their generative powers.[42] Citing a Shangqing scripture, Chen discussed the location of the Kidneys in the body:

> The Renal Palace is the rotund Alcazar of Darkness;
> It takes charge of the Fluids of the Six Mansions and
>   Nine Apertures.
> Hasten to focus on it when stricken by hundreds of ills
>   and plagues
> The Dual Lords of Water are opposite from the Gate
>   of Nativity
> They can lengthen one's life and make one ascend to
>   the Ninth Heaven.[43]

As with the Lungs, Chen consecrated the body by envisioning the Kidneys as the Renal Palace (*shenbu zhi gong* 腎部之宮) and by invoking their old Shangqing name: the Alcazar of Darkness (*xuan que* 玄闕). They are described as the potent source of all the generative fluids that nourish the internal organs and orifices of the body, here alluded to as the Six Mansions and Nine Apertures (*liufu jiuqiao* 六府九竅). In the Five Phases and medical theories, the Kidneys are aligned with water and regarded as the storehouses of vital fluids (*jin ye* 津液). Chen advised his audience that bodily ailments were directly attributed to the depletion of vital fluids in the Kidneys and could be prevented by conserving *shen* inside the Kidney:

The Kidneys are of the Water; so they are the source of the vital fluids for the Six Orbs and the Nine Apertures. As the renal *qi* is depleted, a hundred illnesses will rise. The cultivator often causes the Fire of the Heart to copulate downward with the Water of the Kidneys so that the Fire will not flare upward to scorch, and the Water will not leak out downward. As the Water of the Kidneys and the Fire of the Heart are harmonized, the elixir will gestate. . . .

If a man can always conserve his *shen* immovable between the Kidneys and the Navel so as to establish the foundation of his allotted life, he then shall not find it difficult at all to achieve eternal life.

Chen's elaboration emphasizes the potentially fatal instability of both the Heart and the Kidneys when each functions alone and unsupported by the other. By nature, the Kidney Water (*shenshui* 腎水) tends to flow downward and leak out (*xialou* 下漏) in the form of semen and menses, gradually depleting the reservoir of generative *qi* in the Kidneys and triggering illness in the body. Similarly, the Fire in the Heart (*xinhuo* 心火) tends to blaze upward (*shangyan* 上炎), resulting in a constantly restless and excited state. In turn, the restless and agitated Heart threatens to set the Lungs, the storehouse and the organ of *qi* as breath, on fire. For once the Heart becomes restless, *qi* is consumed and gradually leaks out by way of the tongue. Thus, when the Heart and the Kidneys become estranged, their respective innate tendencies will lead to diminution and depletion of the vital fluids and energies of the body[44] (see Fig. 8).

To prevent this fatal alienation of the Heart from the Kidneys, Chen cautioned readers that *shen* in the Heart must be brought to focus on the Kidneys and bring its flame down to heat the Water of the Kidneys into a union, thus reversing the latter's tendency to leak and dissipate. To achieve this, Chen again cited the *Yellow Courtyard Scriptures* and advised the practitioner to close all exterior conduits to the Heart, such as the eyes, ears, and mouth—the Triple Lights (*san guang* 三光) and the Five Orifices (*wu qiao* 五竅)—and redirect their conscious gaze (the Divine Effulgence, *shen guang* 神光), to focus inward on the Kidneys (the Dark Nether, *xuan ming* 玄冥).[45] Citing a couplet from the *Cantongqi*, Chen elaborated on the technique of shutting and redirecting the Triple Lights:

> Let the Three Lights sink and dwell in the deep,
> To incubate the Pearl of Son in warmth.[46]

Again following traditional medical and early Daoist concepts of the body, Chen viewed the external orifices of the body as direct

Innovating the Immortals' Body 105

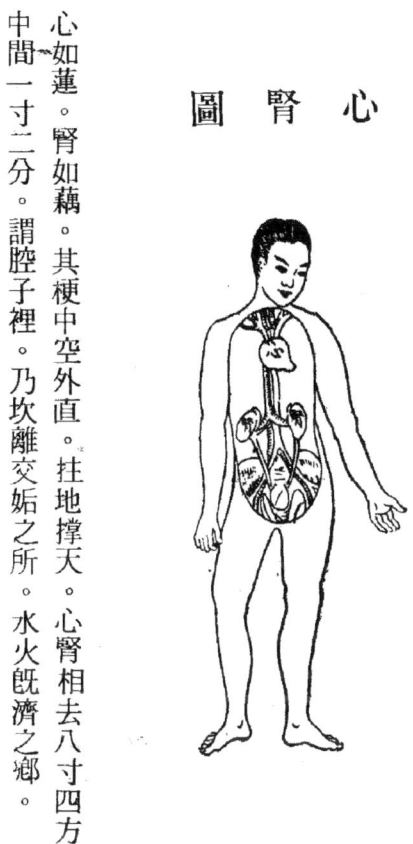

心如蓮。腎如藕。其梗中空外直。拄地撐天。心腎相去八寸四方中間一寸二分。謂腔子裡。乃坎離交姤之所。水火既濟之鄉。

Fig. 8 The Heart and the Kidneys (*Xinshen tu*, ca. 1933) (Hong Wanxin, *Wuda jiankang xiulian fa*, p. 70).

conduits to and extensions of the internal orbs and loci. Since they controlled the flow of the *shen* and *qi* energies of the body, their proper management would lead to health, balance, and possible transformation of the body.

So the nexuses of the Heart with the Lungs and the Kidneys form the two most important connections within the body. The body's health, balance, and ultimately its transformation depend on the intricate dynamics among the three organ systems. Chen advised his readers of the wondrous effect of regulated breathing in which the Psyche of the Heart becomes bound with *qi*:

At the moment when the cultivator's breathing is regulated and harmonized, his mouth will have engendered the Sweet Cool Saliva (*ganliang zhi jinye* 甘涼之津液). Swallow it up and guide it straight down. Then apply the Divine Fire to refine it, transforming the Saliva into *qi*. Saturate and permeate the body throughout with the *qi*. Return and hold it in the Lower Cinnabar Field so as to foster and cultivate the Stalk of Life.

The union of the Heart and the Lungs triggers a chain of reactions. First, the nourishing Saliva is produced and transformed by the Divine Fire of the Heart into the generative and nourishing *qi*, which permeates and circulates throughout the body. Then the *qi* is brought into the renal domain of the Lower Cinnabar Field for gestation into the seed or stalk of eternal life. The Heart-Lung nexus manifested in the union of *shen* and *qi* is thus intricately and inseparably linked with the Heart-Kidney nexus embodied in the coitus of the Fire and Water in the body's transformative process.[47]

The Body in Motion: The Orbits of Heaven and the Circulation of Qi. Chen also envisioned the modern alchemic body as one in constant motion. This motion was embodied in the intricate web of channels and pathways known as the "Orbits of Heaven" (*zhoutian* 周天), along which the commingled *shen* and *qi* travel and are refined (see Fig. 9). Drawing on early medical and inner alchemic traditions, Chen described the orbits as composed of two interconnected circulation pathways located, respectively, along the front and the back of the body and corresponding roughly with the Conception Channel (*renmai* 任脈) and the Superintendent Channel (*dumai* 督脈) as defined in traditional medical models of the body. The upward flow of the commingled *qi* along the dorsal Superintendent Channel is known as the "advance of the Yang Fire" (*jin yanghuo* 進陽火), and its downward descent along the ventral Conception Channel is called "withdrawal of the Yin Talisman" (*tui yinfu* 退陰符). The full cycle of the *qi* flow through the Orbit of Heaven is known as the mechanism of the "frontal descent and back ascent" (*qianjiang housheng* 前降後升) in Daoist inner alchemy. The advance of the Yang Fire follows the dorsal Superintendent Channel along the spinal cord. It extends from the Tailgate locus (*wei lü* 尾閭) at the base of

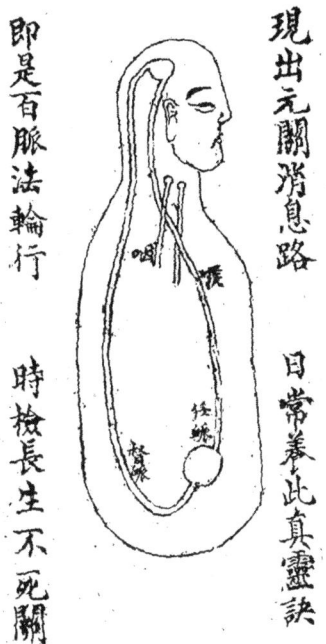

Fig. 9 The Heavenly Orbit (*Zhoutian tu*, 1919). Note the conjoined Ren and Du channels (Xi Yukang, *Neiwai gong tushuo jiyao*, p. 411).

the spine, rising to the Mud Ball (*ni wan* 泥丸) in the head. The withdrawal of the Yin Talisman follows the ventral Conception Channel, descending from the Mud Ball to end in the Sea of Qi (*qi hai* 氣海) in the renal domain of the lower abdomen,[48] as shown in a late Qing inner alchemy text (see Figs. 9 and 10.)

The dorsal ascent path is straddled by a series of vital loci. The starting point of the *qi*'s ascent, however, is located at the Sea of Qi, an inner locus approximately three inches below the navel in the lower abdomen. The nascent *qi* is then directed to move downward along the imagined pathway until it reaches the pivotal connection point of the Lower Magpie Bridge (*xia queqiao* 下鵲橋), slightly above the perineum of the Converging Yin (*huiyin* 會陰), and then crosses over the anus to link with the Tailgate locus, situated behind the coccyx, to begin its ascent journey to the Mud Ball.

The Tailgate is the first of the three major passes (*guan* 關) along the *qi*'s dorsal ascent path. From there *qi* moves upward to reach the

108 *Innovating the Immortals' Body*

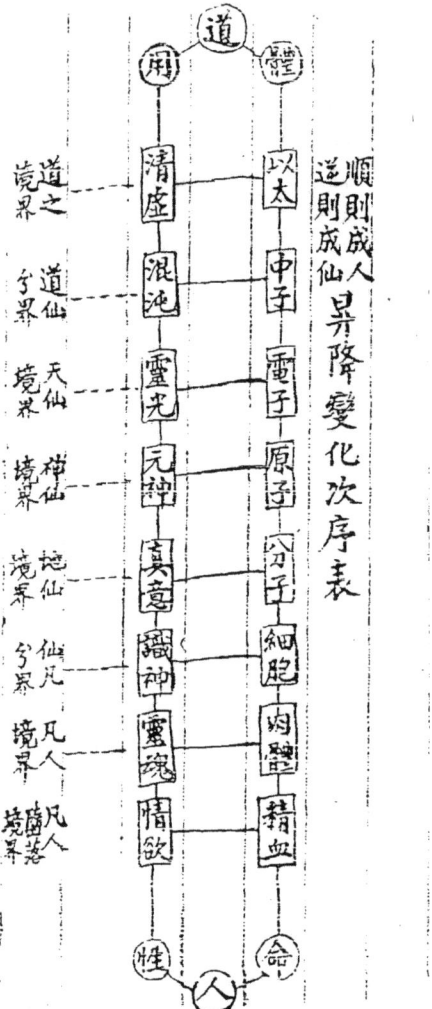

Fig. 10 Chen Yingning's diagram of the Way (ca. 1945) (Chen, "Xuexian bicheng," 35a).

second pass, the Narrow Bluff (*jia ji* 夾脊). Also known as the Double Pass (*shuang guan* 雙關), the locus is located at the midpoint of the spinal column, corresponding to the Gate of Life behind the Yellow Courtyard of the body, and roughly level with the elbow joints. As the *qi* flows higher up the ascent path, it encounters the third major pass, the Jade Pillow (*yu zhen* 玉枕). Located above the nape, roughly behind the occipital bone at back of the head, the Jade Pillow locus is considered the smallest pass on the ascent path and therefore the most difficult one for the ascending *qi* to cross. For that reason, the locus has since the Ming been known as the Iron Wall (*tie bi* 鐵壁).[49] As the *qi* reaches the Mud Ball, it completes the dorsal ascent.

From the Mud Ball in the top of the head, the *qi* then begins the ventral descent of "withdrawing the Yin Talisman" along the Conception Channel. Like the dorsal ascent, the ventral descent of *qi* flow also traverses several major loci situated along the descent path before reaching its final destination in the Lower Cinnabar Field in the abdomen. These key loci perform the vital function of refining and sublimating the commingled *qi* energies. But unlike the dorsal ascent, which is experienced as the flaring Yang Fire of the *qi* rising up the back, the ventral descent of *qi* down from the Mud Ball is envisioned as a process of cooling and refining the commingled *qi* flow.

As the ascending flow of *qi* departs the Mud Ball, it first crosses a vital link nestled deep in the recess behind the Mountain Root (*shan gen* 山根) locus between the eyebrows. Known as the Upper Magpie Bridge (*shang queqiao* 上鵲橋), it is one of the first vital links that connects the *qi*'s ventral descent from the Mud Ball to its destination in the Lower Cinnabar Field.

As the flow of *qi* enters the mouth, known as the Jade Pond (*yuchi* 玉池), by way of the Upper Magpie Bridge, it cascades downward as the Sweet Saliva to descend into another key locus of the Dark Bosom (*xuanying* 玄膺), hidden away below the tongue. The Dark Bosom is viewed as the aperture that generates the nourishing Sweet Saliva fluid (*shengjin zhi qiao* 生津之竅), moisturizing and nurturing the body.[50]

From the mouth, the Sweet Saliva cascades downward into another major vital locus on the ventral descent known as the Crimson Palace (*jiang gong* 絳宮). Also known as the Twelve Stacked Pavilions (*shi'er chonglou* 十二重樓), the Crimson Palace is located in the front of the chest along the bronchial trachea. It stems from the Bright Hall (*ming tang* 明堂) in the upper chest and reaches up into the lower jaw to connect with the Upper Magpie Bridge. As the cascading Sweet Saliva travels down through the Twelve Stacked Pavilions and enters the Bright Hall, it is transformed into the refined *qi* ready to be returned to the Lower Cinnabar Field in the lower abdomen, completing the full cycle of the Orbits of Heaven in the body.

In his writings, Chen Yingning encouraged the practitioner to repeat this transformative cycle as often as possible. The efficacious powers of the repeatedly cycled flow of *qi* in the form of the Sweet Saliva would double and triple. Chen claimed that when perfected, this process produces communion with the divine and numinous:

> Get the Saliva from the Dark Bosom to enter the Bright Hall
> Irrigate down the Throat to coalesce with the Divine
>   and Effulgent.[51]

Indeed, the repeatedly cycling flow of *qi* would ultimately yield an elixir so refined that it is believed to have acquired the psychic and intelligent properties and powers of a deity or the Psyche, becoming divine and numinous. The refined and numinous *qi* accumulated in the Lower Cinnabar Field is to be further recirculated upward and deposited ultimately into the locus of the Mud Ball.

Next to the starting point of the Sea of Qi in the abdomen, the Mud Ball in the head is the most vital locus on the transformative Orbits of Heaven. It is envisioned as the highest point of the embodied landscape, and the dwelling place for the nascent transcendents, who are born of the refined numinous energies in the body (*zhenren zhi suozai* 眞人之所在):

> Ever present,
> The Psyche exists in the Mud Ball and the Hundred Joints.
> Supreme is the Mud Ball, the deity of deities.
> Within, the Nine Perfected Transcendents reside in
>   their chambers.
> At the center like a circle in a square is the one-inch Vertex.

Inspired by the Shangqing vision of the Mud Ball as the sacred abode of the divinities in the body, Chen portrayed the locus as the residence for the Perfected Transcendents made of the refined and sublimated atemporal energies of the Original Trio (*san yuan* 三元): the Original Essence (*yuan jing* 元精), the Original Qi (*yuan qi* 元氣), and the Original Psyche (*yuan shen* 元神). Divided into nine chambers, the Mud Ball is inhabited by the central transcendent Lady Mud Ball (*niwan furen* 泥丸夫人) and her eight sub-divinities known as the Eight Pure Ones (*ba su* 八素). Together, they are the supreme chief and lords of the human body (*wei renshen zhuzai* 爲人身主宰), presiding over all its vital functions.⁵²

But where the *Yellow Courtyard Scriptures* conceived of the locus as the sacred abode of the bodily divinities and transcendents, Chen chose to stress the locus as the repository of the refined and sublimated numinous material or energies that he called the Brain Marrow (*naosui* 腦髓). He described the Brain Marrow as a special "numinous material" (*lingzhi* 靈質), which was "transformed from the Original Qi" (*yuan qi huasheng* 元氣化生) generated and refined through the *qi* circulation of the dorsal ascent and ventral descent.⁵³ Chen's description of the Brain Marrow reflected the influence of Chinese medical and late imperial inner alchemic classics, which had distanced themselves from the early Shangqing vision of the body as the abode of divinities. Instead, they perceived the alchemic body as consisting of sublimated energies of *qi* and *shen*.

Although both of these visions of the body were present in the early Shangqing classics such as the *Yellow Courtyard Scriptures*, Chen's choice of the body of refined energies over the body of divinities in his reinterpretation reflected both a subtle cosmological shift in the modern conception of the alchemic body and a conscious response to the cultural and religious contexts of the early Republican era. In contrast to the classical Shangqing vision of the body ("the Mud Ball, and each and every one of the hundred joints of the body, contains its own divinity"; *niwan baijie jie you shen* 泥丸百節皆有神), Chen Yingning had come to visualize the ontological foundations of the modern inner alchemic body primarily in terms of its energies and substance. In this modern vision of the body, although *shen* and *qi* energies still possess numinous powers, they are no longer envisioned as deities residing in the body. Instead of relying on the early Shangqing techniques of focusing on and visualizing (*cun xiang* 存想) these deities to achieve personal salvation and transcendence, the modern practitioner was urged to rely on bodily and meditative techniques of regulating breathing and other ascetics to attain immortality.

Behind this subtle disenchantment, or "de-divinization," of the body were the larger historical context of the state-sponsored antisuperstition campaigns and the modern religious reforms led by intellectuals like Chen Yingning himself in the first few decades of the twentieth century. Modern professional and urban-based elite practitioners would find a body formed of sublimated *qi* and *shen* energies more appealing than a body composed of deities.

Chen's elevation of the Mud Ball locus as the site of the atemporal *shen* energies further reveals his reformist response to the modern biological model of the body. In his construction of the modern alchemic body, Chen conceived of two modes of the *shen* and *qi* energies: the atemporal and the temporal. In *Annotations*, Chen distinguished the atemporal Original Psyche from the temporal Intelligent Psyche (*shishen* 識神). He argued that the Original Psyche was atemporal in origin and therefore indestructible, whereas the Intelligent Psyche comes from the postnatal realm and can be refined and restored to its origins.[54] Their differences in temporality aside, the Original Psyche and the Intelligent Psyche are also distinguished by their different locales within the body. Chen envisioned the head and the brain as the places where the refined and numinous psychic powers of the atemporal Original Psyche gather and dwell, whereas the Heart was the primary locale on which the energies of the temporal Intelligent Psyche converged. For him, as the repository of the refined Numinous Marrow, the Mud Ball locus housed a much higher form of intelligence and wisdom than the Heart's conventional forms of mental and intelligent faculties. As such, Chen argued that the Mud Ball constituted the most vital element in the transformation of the self into an immortal:

The Mud Ball is the Upper Cinnabar Field (*shang dantian* 上丹田). It is located in the center of the top of the head. Acupuncturists call it the locus of Hundred Convergences (*baihui* 百會). It is the brains, the most important key for the inner alchemic cultivator. When conducting the practice of cycling the Heavenly Orbits and Firing, the flow of *qi* must be lifted along the back and lowered along the front of the body. The ascending *qi* flow terminates in the Mud Ball, and the descent begins from it. This is what is called "returning the Essence to replenish the Brain" (*huanjing bunao* 還精補腦). The substance of the Brain Marrow is most refined. The powers of the Brain Marrow are the most efficacious. It is engendered indirectly through the transformation of the Original Qi. When depleted, it cannot be directly replenished from any kinds of materials. . . .

By the mechanism of the ascending *qi* in the back and its descent in the front, the Numinous Matter is engendered through transformation. By daily and monthly accumulation, the practice can gradually expand and replenish the Brain Marrow, restoring it to its original state, and even to a higher level than before. . . . Although this is not immortality yet, it is not far from it.[55]

The cosmological primacy Chen attached to the Brain and the Mud Ball locus reflected a Daoist reformer's desire to bring the traditional Daoist vision of the body more in line with the biomedical model of the body of the early twentieth century, wherein the head with its brain figured exclusively as the site of human intelligence and knowledge. Thus Chen's construct of the modern alchemic body represented a departure from the traditional Shangqing body model in which the psychic and intelligent powers of the deities were present throughout the body and converged in the Heart. By elevating the Mud Ball locus in the head as the site of the convergence of the material but numinous marrow, Chen wittingly or unwittingly made the Daoist alchemic body cohere with the modern biological body.

Between Cosmology and Science: Toward a Vitalistic Body

Indeed, science figured prominently in Chen Yingning's and his associates' rethinking and reformulation of Daoist inner alchemy. Chen's education and extensive readings in science from the late 1890s to the early 1910s and his extensive contacts with the western-educated social and professional elite had from early on given him an appreciation of the importance of science in the modern world and, especially, its cultural implications for Daoism. During the 1930s and 1940s, as Chen began to promote the Immortals' Learning among the public, he and his associates made a serious effort to incorporate new scientific principles and concepts in their reinterpretation of Daoist cosmology and inner alchemy.

Some of Chen's thinking on science was first made widely public in a series of published correspondence with a Buddhist friend in the fall of 1934. There Chen categorized world civilizations into three major schools: Materialism (*wuben zhuyi* 物本主義), represented by European civilization (*Ouhua* 歐化); Mind-Centered Idealism (*xinben zhuyi* 心本主義), represented by the Buddhist culture of India (*Tianzhu fohua* 天竺佛化); and Life-Centered Vitalism (*shengben zhuyi* 生本主義), represented by the Daoist culture of China (*Daojia wenhua* 道家文化).[56] For Chen, both Western materialism and Buddhist idealism were either deficient or excessive in their perspectives. He argued that neither grasped the subtle reality of the world around us, since each focused on only one aspect of it:

Idealist philosophers of ancient and modern times have held that the material realm of the universe is only an illusion (*huan wang* 幻妄). Everything is nothing more than a manifestation of the mind. As ideas arise in the mind, the external world is engendered. As the mind is extinguished, so is the phenomenal world. But this kind of theory knows only the function (*yong* 用) without understanding its substance (*ti* 體). On the other hand, experimental scientists know man only as an aggregate of various materials, but they cannot explain human will, thought, feelings, and desire. This is knowledge of only the substance without understanding its function.[57]

For Chen Yingning, the unity of the substance and the function was the key to understanding reality. Knowing just one aspect of reality failed to capture its totality. For that reason, Chen argued that only Daoist Vitalism truly intuited and reconciled both aspects of reality, since it sought to bridge the chasm between materialism and idealism. For that purpose, Chen found science, the quintessence of western materialism, the most effective remedy for rectifying the excesses of the Buddhist mind-centered model of the body.

For Chen, the Buddhist idealist cosmology and vision of the body had also found its way into the Daoist discourse of inner alchemy during the late imperial era. For Chen, the most telling evidence of Buddhist influence was the Daoist acceptance of the Buddhist insubstantiation of the body since the late Tang era. Chen argued that as the early Daoist outer alchemy began to be replaced by the emerging inner alchemy, Daoist self-cultivation practitioners turned away from the physical and material dimensions of the Daoist self-transformation tradition and increasingly focused inward on refining the elusive mind as a means of achieving transformation. For Chen, the most vivid example of this Daoist turn toward the Buddhist insubstantiation of the body was the adulation of the Void (*xu* 虛) in Daoist inner alchemic writings of the late imperial period:

"Smashing the empty Void or pulverizing the vacuous Emptiness" has been the catchphrase in Daoist books of later periods. No such phrases are found in the classics of the ancient immortals. This is because most of the ancient immortals began cultivation in the outer alchemy. Their practice was closely engaged with the material and the substantive (*wuzhi de* 物質的). It did not concern the empty Void at all. Nor did it work on the flesh body yet. But fearful of the complexities and hardships of outer alchemy, self-cultivators of later times preferred the simplicity and ease of inner practice. They switched to cultivating the Essence, *qi*, and the Psyche (*jing qi shen* 精氣神) of the body. They subsequently evolved the theory of refining the Essence into *qi* (*lianjing huaqi* 煉精化氣), refining *qi* into the Psyche (*lianqi huashen* 煉氣化神), and refining the Psyche to return to the Void (*lianshen huanxu* 煉神還虛). Since they later felt the theory to be insufficient, they put in an additional level of refining the Void to unite with the Way (*lianxu he Dao* 煉虛合道). As a result, the Way of Alchemy had since then become linked with the empty Void.[58]

For Chen, the most catastrophic consequence of this Buddhist turn was the valorization of the mind over the body, to such a degree that the materiality of the body was suppressed and even rejected. Symbolic of this rejection was the modern practitioners' contentment with the mere deliverance of the Yang Psyche from the body and their all-too-ready dismissal of "ascent by flight in broad daylight." For inner alchemists, this feat should epitomize the true union of the spiritual and the physical realms, in which the ancient immortals purportedly soared up into the empyrean with not only their perfected Yang Psyche but also their perfected flesh body (*routi* 肉體), achieving the rare wonder of the perfection of both the body and the spirit (*xingshen jumiao* 形神俱妙).[59]

To achieve this wondrous union, the body with all its physical and material resources and powers must be reclaimed as the foundation for true transcendence. It was for that task that Chen turned to science. Chen saw a strong affinity between science and the teachings of the ancient immortals on the cosmology of the body. Rejecting an article arguing for syncretism between science and Buddhism in 1935, Chen pointed to what he perceived to be practical and positivist tendencies within the Divine Immortals' tradition as the points of convergence with science. He argued that because of its emphasis on practice and veritable results, the Divine Immortals' learning was similar to science, and those who possessed scientific thought and knowledge would also find in the Immortals' Learning a kindred spirit, most accessible and easiest to understand.[60]

The fully evolved expression of Chen Yingning's thinking on the fundamental correlation between science and inner alchemy appears in Chen's unpublished manuscript entitled "Learning Immortals Will Surely Succeed," which he first drafted in early 1945 and revised later in 1947. Intended as a primer for people interested in the practice of the Immortals' Learning and Daoist inner alchemy, the manuscript is written in a simple and plain vernacular, and the discussion is presented in the dialogue format. Although never published in Chen's lifetime, it was eagerly hand-copied and circulated among Chen's associates, disciples, and the circles of Daoist inner alchemic practitioners in and beyond Shanghai in the 1940s and later in post-1949 China.

In this manuscript, Chen incorporated concepts from physics and biology in explaining the fundamental ideas, procedures, and methods of Daoist cosmology and inner alchemy. The most intriguing aspect of Chen's reformulation of the traditional discourse of inner alchemy is seen in its ontology, as demonstrated in a chart drawn by Chen (Fig. 10).

In the chart, Chen attempted to incorporate elements of atomic and organism theories in formulating a new and materialistic interpretation of Daoist cosmology and inner alchemy. The Way (Dao 道), the ultimate reality of the universe, manifests itself as the unity of two embodied and dialectically interrelated aspects: substance and function. These are two sides of the same coin: substance is the material base of function, and function is the formal application or power of substance. For Chen, the relationship between the two is not a metaphysical abstraction. The substance of the Way is not void or empty but concrete, physical, and unmistakably material in nature.

By incorporating scientific concepts of the physical structure of matter and animal life, Chen redefined the otherwise ephemeral and inscrutable *qi* as a physical continuum of energy and matter—the ether (*yitai* 以太), neutrons (*zhongzi* 中子), electrons (*dianzi* 電子), atoms (*yuanzi* 原子), molecules (*fenzi* 分子), cells (*xibao* 細胞), flesh bodies, and semen and blood. The various ephemeral categories of traditional Daoist cosmology, such as the Pure Void (*qingxu* 清虛) and the Passions and Lust (*qingyu* 情欲), were ontologically grounded in their material and physical counterparts. As Chen incorporated concepts of modern physics and biology in defining *qi*, the most basic constitutive element of the cosmos and body, he also reconceptualized and reformulated Daoist cosmology and the body in a new epistemic framework, imparting an unequivocal materiality to the substance of the Way.

Implicit in the physical continuum as the substance of the Way was also the concept of evolutionary change. In Chen's chart, from the level of ether down to the level of generative substance of the paternal semen and maternal blood, each of the physical and biological categories represents an interconnected stage in the continuous transformation of *qi*. Chen further developed the implied principle of evolutionary transformation by reformulating the cosmogony described in *Laozi*:

The phrase "The Way begets the One" means that "ether" congeals into the Neutron, also known as the Nucleus. The expression "One begets the Duo" means that the Neutron splits into the Yin Electron (Negatron) and the Yang Electron (Positron). As for the sentence "The Duo begets the Trio," it means that the Yin and Yang electrons form all kinds of atoms through different combinations. The sentence "The Trio begets a Myriad Beings" means that atoms of one, two, or three kinds combine to form numerous and most minuscule units of any matter, which are known as molecules. The sentence "A Myriad Beings yoke the yin and embraces the yang" means that regardless of what kind of matter, and despite the differences in form, all are based on atoms. Each atom contains a nucleus. The nucleus is a neutral particle. It is combined together with the Yin and Yang electrons. But it inclines more toward the Yang. Further, there are more or fewer additional Yin Electrons revolving around the nuclei. Hence the saying "Yoking the Yin and embracing the Yang." In their normal state, all atoms are neutral and harmonized in nature. In other words, no matter how numerous the Yin Electrons, their total negative electrical charge is always equal to the total positive charge of the electrical nuclei. So it does not show any electric discharge from the outside. This is what the book of *Daodejing* refers to as "intermeshing into harmony."[61]

Here Chen reinterpreted classical Chinese cosmogony using the terms and principles of subatomic structure and change and rendered the abstruse speculations of Daoist metaphysics as observable and verifiable facts of modern physics.

In a similar fashion, Chen also employed the principle of evolution and the biology of organisms to reinterpret the processes of human procreation and growth. The traditional Daoist notion of the atemporal *qi*'s transformation as the underlying principle of human procreation was now reconceptualized in concrete terms as the union of the paternal semen and the maternal egg (*fu jing mu luan* 父精母卵). Chen argued that underlying the biological continuum from the most primitive cell to the most complex and fully evolved organism was the same principle of evolution underlying all forms of life in the world:

Our parents are preceded by their parents. If we ask, "Where did our first parents come from?" They did not fall from the sky, nor did they burrow out of the earth. They are naturally evolved from an advanced species of animals (*gaodeng dongwu* 高等動物) that was similar to but not quite yet human. The advanced species in turn evolved from a lower species (*dideng dongwu* 低等動物), which came from a species even further down. One level after another, it evolved ultimately upward from the lowest level of the primitive cell.[62]

Beyond the level of the cell, Chen linked the biological organism of life to the process of cosmogony through the deeper structure of molecule, atom, electron, neutron, and ultimately the ether. So matter as a continuum of the Way was not only imperishable but also continuously evolving and transforming from one state or level to the next without end. Chen concluded, "Matter can neither be created nor extinguished, but it can undergo tens of thousands of transformations."[63]

Chen's use of science in stressing the material nature of the cosmos and the body did not, however, lead to his acceptance of a dichotomy between spirit and matter, mind and body. For Chen and his fellow practitioners, the spiritual and the physical realms remained an intricately and inseparably connected unity. One could not exist without the other. For Chen, all material things and beings existed as powers or functions of their substance:

All matter in the universe possesses appropriate energy or power (*nengli* 能力). The energy must stem from a kind of matter. Energy cannot be created just from sheer emptiness (*ping kong* 憑空). Matter is the substance, whereas power is its application. Both substance and application are the two aspects of one thing (*yiwu ermian* 一物二面).

So for Chen, each and every stage of the material substance existed as a specific function or application on the continuum of the Way. He deemed this function or application to be inherent to the substance of the Way. Ether, for example, manifested its supreme efficacy in the form of the Pure Void state, whereas the generative forces of the paternal semen and the maternal egg expressed themselves as the Lustful Passions (*qing yu* 情欲). In the inherent tendency of the Way to manifest its power also lay the so-called natural mechanism of transformation, which constantly propelled the continuum of change to evolve from the higher atemporal state of the Way (*dao zhi jingjie* 道之境界) to the lower temporal state of Degeneracy (*duoluo jingjie* 墮落境界). Hence the saying, "To go along with the natural mechanism of change is to become a mortal."[64]

But that is only half the story. Chen's emphasis on the materiality of the cosmos and the body never led to a materialist determinism in his reformulation of Daoist inner alchemy. Rather, Chen continued to impute a dynamically transformative power to the spiritual manifestations of the Way. Indeed, Chen maintained that through careful and intentional manipulation of the differentials between the various levels of the manifested powers on the continuum and in the body, a practitioner could stem the tide of bodily aging and decay. He argued that the Intelligent Psyche, which manifests itself at the level of the cell, could be properly employed through meditative cultivation to assist the transformation of the flesh body into the higher level and beyond. As the practitioner gradually transforms the lower-level substances of semen and blood into the higher-level substance of *qi* by focusing the Intelligent Psyche on breathing, he or she could ultimately transform the body to reach perfection.

For Chen, it was also here that science and the Immortals' Learning parted ways. Both science and the immortals accept the physicality or materiality of the cosmos and the body, but the scientist deals exclusively with the substance or materiality of the Way (*dao zhi ti* 道之體), resulting ultimately in a materialist determinism that ignores the spiritual potentials of man. In contrast, Chen argued that the Immortals' Learning focuses on the manifested powers or spiritual applications of the Way (*dao zhi yong* 道之用), leading to Vitalism (*weisheng zhuyi* 唯生主義), which seeks to unite the substance and the application of the Way. He advised his readers that through the persistent practice of focusing on the conscious and spiritual aspects of the body, they could reverse the natural mechanism of transformation and attain immortality (*ni ze chengxian* 逆則成仙):

> The extreme materialist scientists recognize only the flesh body. As for the function of human consciousness, they see it as no more than just the impulse of part of the flesh body. There is no so-called soul (*ling hun* 靈魂). When the flesh body is destroyed and its substance disintegrates beyond any means of organization, human consciousness perishes. If you insist on discussing any life beyond the flesh body, they will laugh at you, regarding it merely a dream. We followers of the Immortals' Learning must strive for a great accomplishment. We must practice hard and solidly attain the feat of "perfection of both the form and the spirit." Only then we can command respect and admiration from these scientists.[65]

For Chen and his fellow practitioners, the materiality of the body was not a barrier to achieving the perfection of the body and the spirit. It was the very foundation and venue for this transformation. They perceived their own body as the microcosm of the Way, and as such, it contained the seeds for effecting a reversal of the natural transformation of the body. For them, this wondrous reversal could be achieved only through practice within the body by uniting both the functional and the substantive dimensions of the Way.

In affirming the transformative and transcendent spiritual powers of the substance, Chen's reformulated Immortals' Learning and his vision of the alchemic body also show fascinating parallels to the Vitalist philosophy of Henri Bergson (1859–1941), first introduced to China by intellectuals like Zhang Junmai in the 1920s. Although both Chen and Bergson sought a transcendent explanation of the physical world, they came to their respective vitalistic visions of the body differently. Bergsonian vitalism arose from a discontent with mechanistic and biological interpretations of the physical world around the turn of the twentieth century. Chen arrived at his vitalistic body because of his profound disillusionment with the Buddhist idealist view of the physical world. Whereas Bergson rejected the notion that living processes may be explained in terms of the material composition and physio-chemical properties of the body, Chen came close to embracing such a view. Chen's profound aversion to Buddhist idealism propelled him to affirm the vitalistic powers of the material and physical, whereas Bergson's distrust of the material world led him to seek a transcending principle of the *élan vital* outside the confines of the physical world.

But Chen never succumbed to the deterministic tendencies of scientific materialism, even as he made an all-out effort to integrate scientific concepts and the principles of science into his reinterpretation of Daoist cosmology and inner alchemy during the 1930s and 1940s. Indeed, he remained true to his earlier Daoist vision of human subjectivity and the human capacity to ultimately transcend and harmonize the schism between the material and the spiritual realms. Reflecting in March 1935 on the divide between matter (*wuzhi* 物質) and spirit (*jingshen* 精神), Chen opined:

> In my opinion, human thought must not be constrained by science. If thinking cannot escape the sphere of science's influence, it should not be called "thinking." Thinking belongs to the spiritual realm, whereas science is part of the material realm. Modern human beings cannot yet break down the divide between the spirit and matter. Therefore, their consciousness and reality are often at war with each other. So in order for humans to be the subject, we must be able to control matter with our spirit, and not let matter conquer our spirit. Only then we can speak of happiness in life. Otherwise, all will be in great chaos.[66]

For Chen Yingning and his associates, it was the vitalistic powers of the material that could bridge what they perceived as lacking in both western materialism and Buddhist mind-centered idealism. For them, only the Daoist alchemic body could realize the fullest potential of human life. For them, it was thus the quintessential Chinese body, the body that every practitioner of inner alchemy must strive for.

— 4 —

Practice Makes Perfect

Inner Alchemic Techniques and Regimens

Having long heard of the nobility of the Immortals' Way,
I have vowed to learn the art of long life.
But I had no one to discuss alchemic secrets with;
And the mountains hem me in, further impeding my travels.
Having slain the dragon,
I find it hard to realize the dream of riding the crane.
On this night of bitter rain and weeping wind,
My heart aches with sorrow in the ancient city of Ye.[1]

In this early 1937 poem, entitled "My Aspirations While Living in Solitude," a Miss Dong of Anyang in northern Henan shared her anxieties over the difficulties she was encountering in practicing inner alchemy with the readers of the *Yangshan Biweekly*. Many of her fellow practitioners of Daoist inner alchemy faced similar problems in the Republican era. Worsening social and political conditions aside, the most daunting challenge to many urban practitioners was securing the prerequisites of the practice: the Method, Funds, Fellowship, and Locale (*fa cai lü di* 法財侶地). Access to these elements determined the outcome of one's practice.

In the early decades of the twentieth century, Daoist inner alchemic practice was complicated by a host of factors. The social order, political stability, and personal wealth presumed by traditional

Daoist inner alchemic discourse hardly existed for many modern practitioners. Further, Daoist monastic institutions and clerics, who had traditionally provided the institutional setting for both preserving and transmitting Daoist inner alchemic practice, had been under attack since the turn of the twentieth century. State ideological campaigns against "superstitions and excessive cults" and increasing encroachments on temples since the late nineteenth century had largely discredited Daoist monasteries and their clerics. They had come to be seen as bastions of backward and irrational beliefs and practices, even though these institutions were historically a major source of Daoist knowledge on inner alchemic self-cultivation techniques for lay practitioners. Miss Dong's home province of Henan was among the hardest hit in this regard. Beginning in 1927, under the military governorship of the iconoclastic warlord general Feng Yuxiang 馮玉祥 (1882–1948), a province-wide campaign was launched to promote popular education by expropriating temple lands and properties. The campaign to "smash temples" (*da miao* 打廟) led to the disbandment of Daoist and Buddhist monastic institutions throughout the province. In addition, the incessant wars among warlords for dominance in north China created extensive social chaos and political instability in both rural and urban China throughout the 1920s and 1930s.[2] These hard times were the background to Miss Dong's lament. General social, political, and economic conditions were inimical to inner alchemic practice in much of China.

Yet the acquisition of the four prerequisites continued to be considered key to successful practice. In traditional Daoist inner alchemy, the Method refers to the principles, procedures, and techniques of the practice. Often encrypted in the format of oral secrets (*kou jue* 口訣) or alchemic instructions (*dan jue* 丹訣), the Method could be acquired only from a willing teacher whose experience and knowledge would ensure the proper decryption and interpretation of the oral secrets. Chen illustrated the relevance of practice experience to understanding the oral secrets:

Without acquiring the oral secrets, one does not know where to begin practice. But if one has only the oral secrets, one will find it difficult to succeed without the benefit of experience. The oral instruction can be said in a few words, but it must constantly be illuminated by experience so that the "medicine may be applied to the proper symptoms." The oral secrets are rigid and inflexible, but the experience is lively. If one's experience is not rich, one is not qualified to teach others.³

But acquiring the Method was only the beginning. The success of the practice also hinged on securing sufficient funds, reliable fellow practitioners and assistants, and the proper locale. Meeting these needs was a concern of every practitioner from Miss Dong to Chen Yingning himself. In a host of writings published from the 1920s to the 1940s, Chen Yingning and many fellow practitioners confronted these problems and addressed issues of how to secure the four prerequisites and how to conduct inner alchemic practice. In these writings, Chen Yingning sought to define for his audience what constituted inner alchemic practice, and how, where, and with whom such practice must be pursued. His instructions show that despite the stories in the traditional hagiographies of successful practitioners soaring to the empyrean, the practice of inner alchemy began with a range of mundane activities—travel, meditative and dietary regimens, and the planning and management of work and family life. All these activities were seen as serving specific purposes conducive to the ultimate goal of attaining perfection and were to be pursued with zeal and diligence.

Securing the Prerequisites of the Practice

Quest for Oral Secrets (xun jue 尋訣)

Like their predecessors, inner alchemists in early twentieth-century Shanghai continued to regard the transmission and reception of oral secrets as the key to successful practice. Their awareness of the primacy of oral secrets is vividly illustrated in a work Chen published in serialized format in the *Yangshan Biweekly* from autumn 1934 to autumn 1935. Entitled *Explorations in Oral Secrets* (*Koujue gouxuan lu* 口訣鉤玄錄), Chen's writing was based on two books by the influential late Qing inner alchemist Huang Shang 黃裳 (fl. 1840s): *Lectures on Daodejing* (*Daodejing jiangyi* 道德經講義) and *Quotations from the Hall of Joyful Cultivation* (*Leyutang yulu* 樂育堂語錄). In his work, Chen explained why oral secrets (*jue* 訣) took precedence over principles or theories (*li* 理) in the practice:

> Although Daoist books circulating in the market are numerous in titles and categories, those that discuss the theoretical principles of the practice do not address issues of the oral secrets, whereas those that discuss the oral secrets of the practice do not discuss its principles. Hence, when learners read them, either they will find them too empty and general for actually engaging in practice, or they will hold stubbornly to one particular method while remaining ignorant of [the need for] flexible adaptation. In the end, their hair turns white without their achieving anything at all. This is why Master Huang stressed both principles and secrets when he was teaching the practice to people. The learner must first understand the principle clearly and then come to know the oral secrets. For the supreme wondrous secrets (*wushang mijue* 無上秘訣) of the practice are quite different from those "side doors and petty techniques" (*pang men xiao shu* 旁門小術). Once you know the secrets, you will be able to deepen your understanding of the principle. This is the truth that unites all and differs from empty talk and general discourse (*kongtan fanlun* 空談泛論). This is why I introduce his learning to those who are fond of the Way today.[4]

Like their predecessors, modern practitioners like Chen were keenly aware of the tension between the oral secrets and the textual traditions in Daoist inner alchemy. Yet unlike earlier participants in the controversy, Chen did not see the two as mutually exclusive and contradictory. Following Huang Shang, Chen warned his readers of the pitfalls of following one or the other tradition. He chose to see both traditions as complementary. But Chen's eclectic approach was not merely a philosophical choice. It stemmed from his personal experience of the practice. He had gained his own understanding and expertise through both a rigorous perusal of the Daoist Canon and years of persistent acquisition of oral secrets from a score of adepts he had befriended between 1895 and 1916. His insistence on the relevance of Daoist inner alchemic scriptural knowledge reflected his own literary background in classical and textual learning, and his valuation of oral secrets mirrored his years of experience as a practitioner who truly appreciated how the secrets derived from and were applicable to practice. It also reflected modern lay practitioners' relative lack of access to oral secrets. Chen was one of their few sources for such knowledge.

In "Learning Immortals Will Surely Succeed," Chen discussed issues surrounding the origin, transmission, and reception of oral secrets. For Chen and his fellow cultivators, the principles and the oral secrets together constituted the Method. But even though some oral secrets may have been written down and transmitted through the traditional texts of inner alchemy, "knowing" what these oral secrets meant for each individual's practice required much more than just the printed words. According to Chen, the oral secrets did not simply evolve out of sheer necessity in ancient times when writing instruments and written records were scarce. The oral secrets came into existence because they encapsulated the most essential and salient elements of practice experience in the memorable format of rhymed verse.[5]

Since oral secrets captured and preserved the most essential elements of alchemic truth, their transmission and reception were traditionally guarded with the utmost care and secrecy. For Chen Yingning, the tradition of oral secrets dated to "primordial times" and survived into the era of written and printed transmissions, as attested by this passage Chen quoted from Wei Boyang's *Cantongqi*:

> I divulge it only to the worthy in secret.
> How dare I lightly put it down in writing?
> But if I commit myself to silence,
> I may incur the crime of extinguishing the Way.
> Writing my feelings down on bamboo and silk,
> Terrified I am to have divulged the Heavenly talisman.
> Sigh after sigh, how hesitant I am;
> Casting my head up and down, how could I end this insanity!
> There are methods and rules for refining and firing the elixir,
> But to divulge them, I am not at such liberty.[6]

To Chen Yingning and his fellow practitioners, Wei Boyang's hesitation reflected the painful dilemma of a transmitting adept. If fully written down, the oral secrets might fall into the wrong hands. But an adept who kept silent ran the risk of "extinguishing the Way" by breaking its transmission (*jue daomai* 絕道脈). Underlying Wei's uncertainty is another fundamental concern: the moral and spiritual fitness of the potential recipient of the oral secrets. This worry highlights the adept's overriding need to find a suitable vehicle for carrying the Way (zai Dao zhi qi 載道之器). Chen addressed another concern among transmitting adepts that their oral secrets, if easily obtained, might be treated casually or even slighted. He cautioned his audience that possible ramifications of a casual transmission of the secrets might deter adepts.[7]

Another issue for the transmitting adept was to match the potential recipient with instructions suited to that individual. Since the oral secrets had evolved from the experiences of different masters under different practice conditions and for different purposes, they were necessarily divided into different categories and ranks. Matching the method and techniques to the novice under proper physical, spiritual, and financial conditions had a direct bearing on the success or failure of the practice. For Chen, these considerations were causes for hesitation and unwillingness on the part of the teacher.[8]

The issue of reciprocity constituted another concern for the transmitting adepts, who possessed varying levels of perfection and entertained different expectations of their disciples. These differences were thought to have a direct bearing on the adept's willingness to transmit his secrets. Chen pointed out in his analysis of the oral secrets tradition that their transmission was a joint moral and spiritual enterprise between the adept and the disciple, involving a delicate reciprocal process in which the interests and needs of both the adept and the disciple had to be served. The recipient of the oral secrets was expected to offer financial and other forms of support to assist the master in his pursuit of perfection. For the master and the disciple, this process meant a profound spiritual, moral, and financial commitment. In sum, the transmission of oral secrets was meant to forge a lasting covenant and a master-disciple hierarchy among inner alchemic practitioners.[9]

Finally, as evidenced in Wei Boyang's words, the oral transmission of alchemic knowledge was protected by rituals. A master might risk punishment for breaching his own oath of secrecy and proper transmission. The grave potential consequences of improper transmission were reflected in secret rituals involving oath taking and sacrifice that preceded the transmission. Citing a verse from the *Yellow Courtyard Scriptures*, Chen reminded his audience of the solemnity of transmission rituals:

> Addressing the transmitting master, the recipient takes an oath to heaven.
> Silk of clouds and chiffon of phoenix are offered entwined with gold bands,
> Hair is cut so that the sinews and skin are preserved whole and sound,
> Hand in hand, ascend the mount to smear the cinnabar fluid on the mouth,
> Only then can the Gold Scriptures and Jade Effulgence be revealed.[10]

If the consequences of breaching the oath made on such a solemn occasion were only implied in this passage from the ancient Shangqing scriptures, the threat of violence became much more explicit in the oath sworn by a modern practitioner of inner alchemy. In Chen's views, these oaths bound the transmitting adept to extreme caution in divulging oral secrets:

> As a master, he must have sworn an oath at the time when he was taught his own oral secrets, such as "I must not casually pass it on to an inappropriate person. If I do, I will bring calamity on myself" (bi zao zaihuo 必遭災禍). This is just a very ordinary oath. There are more severe ones such as "If alive, condemned to die by man and Heaven; and when deceased, subject to the sufferings of the Earth's hell." Having taken all these vows, a master cannot but feel anxious at heart, apprehensive lest he breach his own vow by his lapse of caution. So he will not easily part with his secrets.[11]

Chen himself lived up to what he preached, adhering strictly to the ancient rituals of transmission. In 1936 when his wife, Dr. Wu Yizhu, decided to learn female inner alchemy as a means of recuperating from a breast cancer operation, both Chen and Wu took the extraordinary precaution of observing every one of the rituals of initiation and transmission. Only after Dr. Wu had been properly initiated as his disciple did Chen transmit to her the secrets of the female practice designed to aid her recovery.[12]

In the early twentieth century, transmission of inner alchemic secrets was further complicated by the rise in nationalist sentiments. For Chen and many of his followers, inner alchemy was seen as an ethnically bound practice. Transmission to non-Chinese became problematic and potentially disastrous for the Chinese as a nation. Chen Yingning elaborated on how the issue of nation affected revelation of the oral secrets:

> Buddhism and Christianity are world-bound religions by nature. Daoist learning and the techniques of the Immortals (*daoxue xianshu* 道學仙術) are ethnically bound. Universal religions always welcome you to join their church organizations regardless of your ethnicity (*zhongzu* 種族). If you don't believe, they try to persuade you to believe. Once you believe, they talk you into joining them.
>
> As for Daoist learning and the Immortals' techniques, just the opposite position is true. If you are not a descendent of the Chinese nation and a son and grandson of the Yan and Huang emperors (*Yan Huang zisun* 炎黃子孫), don't even dream of acquiring a shred of true secrets from a master.
>
> When I was learning the Way, I also took the routine vow never to reveal the secrets for fear that foreigners may obtain them and spare nothing in putting them to practice. If they succeeded in achieving perfection, that would be just like adding wings to a tiger (*ru hu tian yi* 如虎添翼). We Chinese would be left further behind, only to sigh over the dust left in their trail (*wangchen xingtan* 望塵興嘆). We would be better off preserving the little heritage bequeathed to us by our ancestors. That would still leave us with a few hopes. Perhaps, in the future, we may be able to utilize the efficacious power refined through our flesh body to overpower the deadly war machines of science and suppress into submission all the murderous fiends. Hence the unwillingness to pass on the secrets.[13]

Consistent with Chen's conception of the alchemic body, Daoist inner alchemy was also imagined as a nationally bound practice and quintessentially Chinese. Since the practice refined the body, divulging its secrets to non-Chinese amounted to both physical and spiritual depletion of the nation. For Chen and his followers, oral secrets were still perceived not only as the essence of the practice but also as an epistemological crystal through which one gained truthful insight into the reality of the world and achieved immortality. In the social, political, and economic contexts of the 1930s, this belief led Chen and his followers to perceive the oral secrets as embodying the cultural and national essence of China. As such, they held the secrets for strengthening the body of the nation and even "overpowering" the West despite its technological advantages.

Chen's insistence on the primacy of oral secrets also valorized the centrality of the teacher or adept and helped solidify the hierarchical master-disciple relationship in the practice of inner alchemy. In a practice that had long been institutionally discrete and scattered, the value attached to oral secrets also afforded the adept formidable power over prospective disciples, enabling the adept to dictate the terms of the transmission of oral secrets and to shape the relationship with disciples.

But ironically, Chen's emphasis on the centrality of adepts and their oral secrets may have mirrored their increasing marginalization in the emerging market of mass spiritualism and self-cultivation during the Republican era. As the competition among adepts like Chen Yingning for followers and the spread of inner alchemic knowledge through modern mass media combined to make knowledge of the practice increasingly open and available to the public and the practitioner community alike, the traditional authority of masters and their secrets was diluted and even displaced.

Looking for a Master (fang shi 訪師)

In this scheme of things, an adept was necessary, and the search for such a teacher indispensable. Travels in search of a teacher thus became a vital and routine task for every beginner. In a chapter entitled "A Master Must Be Sought!" ("Shi xu fang ye" 師須訪也!) of his serialized tract *Never Part from It for Even a Second* (*Xuyu mo li* 須臾莫離) in the *Yangshan Biweekly*, Chunqian daoren 純乾道人 advised readers:

Cultivators of immortality must seek out a master. Once an enlightened master is found, one is able to intuit the mysterious and the wondrous (*wutou xuanmiao* 悟透玄妙). Once one has intuited the mysterious and the wondrous, one can then understand the drugs and elixir (*xiao yaowu* 曉藥物), know about refining and cultivating (*zhi duanlian* 知鍛煉), and perfect the sagely embryo of the golden elixir (*cheng jindan shengtai* 成金丹聖胎). But if one follows an unenlightened master who transmits teachings fatuously (*mangshi xiashou* 盲師瞎授), it would just like fishing for a needle in the ocean (*dahai laozhen* 大海撈針).[14]

Here, in line with tradition, the inner alchemic writers of the early twentieth century continued to emphasize the mindset proper for a disciple searching for the transmitting adept. The virtues of humility, reverence, and devotion were considered spiritual and moral prerequisites in a disciple. In his short tract, Chunqian Daoren again cautioned his audience:

> The most important thing for those who want to learn the Way and cultivate immortality is to revere a teacher as a deity. Serve him with sincerity and diligence. Even when laden with a hundred bothers [from the teacher], never feel annoyed. Seek teaching with humility. Whatever comes along, do not fear it beforehand, nor dwell on it afterward. In hardship or comfort, endure and hold fast. If one serves a teacher like this, resolute and unwavering in his heart, he will naturally encounter an enlightened adept and acquire true oral secrets. Otherwise, no matter how one begs, he will not acquire even a shred of the true secrets.[15]

Here Master Chunqian's emphasis on the inner moral and spiritual cultivation of a disciple reflected the perspective of an adept who had apparently served his own master in such an unswerving way. The novice's ultimate reception of alchemic secrets came to be rationalized as the natural outcome of an inner moral and spiritual perfection. Anyone searching for a teacher entered into a moral and spiritual hierarchy in which the traditional values of filial piety, devotion, respect, hard work, and perseverance were valorized as the foundation of the master-disciple relationship.

The personal quest by the late Qing, early Republican adept Fangnei sanren, AKA Wan Ligeng, was a good example. Wan hailed from a literati family in Nanchang, Jiangxi. He attained his *xiucai* degree at the age of twenty and subsequently served in two minor, county-level educational posts in Jiangxi before abandoning Confucian learning in favor of Daoist practice. He then spent the next few decades traveling and sojourning at Daoist and Buddhist monasteries in famous mountains and towns throughout China and built a reputation as an accomplished Daoist inner alchemist adept. He produced several influential writings on inner alchemy and was retained as a personal mentor in Daoist inner alchemic meditation by the late Qing reformer and entrepreneur Zheng Guanying.[16]

The Daoist sobriquet Wan assumed for himself, "Fangnei sanren," means "an unbound rambler of the world." It vividly captures the essence of the rambling life he led in search of Daoist oral secrets and adepts, a search that originated from his childhood experience of a near-fatal illness. Fangnei later recalled that this illness triggered a desire to transcend this world (*you chushi zhizhi* 有出世之志): "Without understanding the Three Teachings (*sanjiao* 三教), it was insufficient to intuit the whole of the great Way." After his hunt for such an understanding in the texts of Buddhism, Confucianism, and Daoism proved unsuccessful, he took to the roads in search of Daoist learning.

According to one of his fellow cultivators, Fangnei spent half of his life traveling about. In his own words, he wanted to "look for a master and seek out friends so as to consummate his life and escape death" (*xunshi fangyou liaosheng tuosi* 尋師訪友了生脫死). So whenever and wherever he encountered any "supreme men and extraordinary personalities" (*gaoren yishi* 高人異士), he humbly sought teachings from them. Through decades of travel, Fangnei claimed to have obtained secrets of both the Northern and the Southern lineages of Daoist inner alchemy and he became one of the most influential inner alchemists of the late nineteenth and early twentieth centuries.[17] Among his many writings on inner alchemic practice was a long poem published in May 1936 entitled "A Ballad on Looking for the Way," in which Fangnei ruminated on his decades of rambling:[18]

> The Great Way circulates and passes on in the world;
> The threads of its Order never end in the universe.
> Longing to transcend life and death, I cultivate the Gold Elixir
> And aspire to fraternize with the Sublime and the Perfected.
> Gone are the Sublime and the Perfected to the Immortals' realm,
> Their absence adds wrinkles daily to my worried face.
> They left tomes on the elixir for us to read.
> But cryptic and obscure are their subtle words and meanings.
> The practice is hard without the guidance of a teacher.
> Yet the bond of transcendence cannot be casual.
> How dare I give up wading the rivers and scaling the mountains?
> The bond is formed by traversing all the peaks and streams.
> Ill at ease is my heart until I find my master.

Practice Makes Perfect

Deviant approaches and false methods rise and rage.
The aberrant kinds may spread due to greed and depravity;
Persist diligently in your practice as if grinding down a brick.
The sagacious will never be swindled.
Peruse the Scriptures, the Ode, the Concordance, and the Treatise.[19]
The road is wider if you know the main schools;
Concealed as it may be, seek the complete truth of heaven.
Sleep exposed to the elements, and eat under the wind;
Ragged and worn may be the clothes and shoes;
But never let the heart turn cold halfway through.

Once upon a time there lived an immortal, the White Jade Toad.
Roaming among clouds his footsteps covered mountains and rivers.
Long he journeyed before he moved Chen the Mud Ball.
Yet still the Mud Ball delayed transmission for three more years.[20]
There was also Master Sanfeng, keen on intuiting the Mystery.
His ramblings led him all the way to Zhongnan Peak.
He had forgotten his age of sixty or seventy,
When he met the Fire Dragon who transmitted the secrets.
So many since time immemorial have learned to be immortals.
Reverent in their heart, they sought guidance from their teachers.
With Heaven silently adjudicating and controlling,
Their conundrum is solved with compassion in due time.
My quest for my master's transmission is truly pitiable.
With utmost sincerity have I beseeched heaven.
Having met my teacher, I was hampered by a lack of means.
Before long my sideburns had turned gray.
Sorrow-stricken at the mirror, I strengthened my resolve in prayer.
Year in and year out I journeyed in search of enlightened worthies
Only to be rewarded by heaven with the fellowship united in *qi*.
Enduring a hundred afflictions I sought the True Lead.

With oral secrets obtained, I returned to try the refining cultivation.
Results instantly shown, I am convinced the Way does not deviate.
Now I know the True differs from the False, as heaven from earth,
And true are the Three Origin methods and the Two Schools.[21]
For those to come who will read my ballad about the search,
Each word herein is a teardrop beyond description.
Worry only about your wavering resolve
And about your unwillingness to spend.
But once the Four Requisites are met,
Your true vessel of salvation is set.

I urge all of you to grab Zu Sheng's staff,[22]
And abandon your mundane passions at once.
Quickly seek the Great Way and intuit the Double Mystery[23]
So as to rub shoulders with Hong Ya the immortal.[24]

In this long ballad, Fangnei, the roamer of the world, showed how such search journeys served several functions in modern inner alchemic practice. First, travel in search of a master was seen as a vehicle that transported the practitioner out of the secular world into the realm of the sacred and eternal. The journey not only physically removed one from the home but also severed one's worldly attachments to family, fame, and fortune and plunged one into a world in which poverty, hardships, solitude, and other tribulations of the body and the spirit were routine. Fangnei's exhortation to let go of worldly attachments to money and mundane passions, as well as his challenge to overcome recurring self-doubt and loneliness and to endure physical suffering, attested to his perception of the search journey as a form of spiritual and moral cultivation.

Second, the search journey was also construed as a learning experience for the practitioner. It took the novice into an enriching milieu and exposed him or her to a variety of styles, methods, personalities, and lineages of practice. In the process, the novice learned to discern and differentiate quackery from true secrets. As alluded to in his ballad, Fangnei spent years searching out many adepts before he understood the true meanings of "the Three Origins and the Two Schools" (*sanyuan liangzong you zhenquan* 三元兩宗有眞筌).

Third, in Fangnei's ballad, undertaking a quest was seen as an act that fulfills the "bond of transcendence" (*chushi yinyuan* 出世因緣). This sense of a predestined bond could only be fulfilled by completing the journey, as attested by these two lines from the poem, "How dare I give up wading the rivers and scaling the mountains?/The bond is formed by traversing all the peaks and streams." Further, as shown in Fangnei's allusions to the stories of the Daoist inner alchemic masters White Jade Toad (Bai Yuchan 白玉蟾, 1194–1229) and Sanfeng (Zhang Sanfeng, fl. 1320s–1410s), setbacks during the quest were construed as part of the expected testing of practitioners' character, which would further prepare them for attaining the goal of immortality. So, in the face of crushing hardships and defeats, perseverance and sheer resolve could lead only to greater merit, which would ultimately cement the predetermined bond of immortality.

Fourth, Fangnei's invocation of legends about early immortals and patriarchs such as Bai Yuchan and Zhang Sanfeng represented another significant aspect of search-related travels in inner alchemic practice. This passage suggests that the travel was more than a journey through the physical landscape. It was also a journey through time and history. Fangnei here invoked the lore and legends of past masters of inner alchemy as the normative standards for his own quest. In emulating these past masters, the rambler's journey became a venue for re-enacting the quintessential search experience encapsulated in stories about the past patriarchs of inner alchemy. The trials and tribulations of the traveler's individual journey were experienced as part of a greater, collective tradition. The inner alchemic past came to life intensely in every moment of physical hardship, mental anguish, and gnawing self-doubt and despair and in the wonderful sense of surprise, joy, and triumph in discoveries and encounters that practitioners like Fangnei experienced in their search.

Further, the search journeys also facilitated the practitioner's encounter with an adept or an immortal, an experience seen as essential to the success of inner alchemic practice. Daoist sacred sites derived their perceived efficacy from the rich lore about past encounters with immortals or previous ascents by perfected patriarchs associated with these sites. For transmitting adepts and novices seeking them, the desire to become part of the history associated with the sites was strong. As is true of Fangnei, it was precisely this desire to relive the sacred experience of transmission at the very site where it occurred that lured both the master and the novice to travel to the mountains, making their journey a spiritual pilgrimage and converting their destinations into meeting grounds for possible new encounters and ascents.

Late in summer 1938, Deng Yucang 鄧雨蒼 (z. Jimin 濟民) undertook a similar journey of search and pilgrimage. Originally from Liancheng 連城 county, Fujian, Deng was a merchant sojourning in

Shanghai. He was also actively involved in a self-cultivation group known as the Hall of Practicing Benevolence (*Xishan tang* 習善堂), which originated in Fujian. Members of the group were believed to be followers of the Way of the Anterior Heaven (*Xiantian dao* 先天道). During the 1930s, a practice group was formed near the Shanghai Railway Station by sojourners from western Fujian like Deng.[25] Their poems on the practice of inner alchemy in the *Immortals' Way Monthly* revealed a vigorous pursuit of inner alchemy practice.

In a poem entitled "With Master Wen on a Trip to Lady Ma Mountain," Deng vividly depicted his journey to Lady Ma Mountain (Magu shan 麻姑山), a sacred site located outside Nancheng county seat in eastern Jiangxi province. At the top of the mountain was an ancient temple believed to be the place where Lady Ma attained the Way.[26] Deng recalled his pilgrimage there with his master:

> I follow my master to verify a predestined bond at the scenic site.[27]
> From seas to mulberry fields, a change wrought in a thousand years![28]
> Only a few chimes of the bell can be heard on this otherworldly path.
> The clouds on the four peaks stand guard for the cavern immortals.
> The waterfall drapes over the top of the pine trees, a chain of silver.
> The numinous pond by the cliff wells forth, a spring of jade.
> Trying in vain to find Cai Jing's house for a visit,
> Long we lingered on the Bridge of Encounters with Immortals.[29]

The encounter theme operates on two levels in the poem. At one level, there is a physical quest for an encounter. Deng and his master journeyed to the site, seeking to confirm an earlier "bond," or encounter, by traversing the mountains. Although not specified, the predestined bond may refer to the master's encounter with his own lineage master on the mountain. The chiming bell, the cloud over the four peaks, the silvery waterfall, and the jade-like water of the spring create an otherworldly ambiance, further enhancing the prospect of an imminent encounter with an immortal at the site.

On another level, there is the imagined or relived encounter. Such encounter is played out by Deng's allusion to Cai Jing 蔡京. According to *Biographies of the Divine Transcendents*, Cai, a resident of Suzhou, was deemed to possess the physiognomy of an immortal. Later Cai was visited at his home by Wang Yuan 王遠 (z. Fangping 方平) the immortal and Lady Ma. During their visit, Lady Ma performed a cleansing ritual for Cai's family and left them some cinnabar drugs. By ingesting the drugs, Cai Jing reportedly attained immortality.[30]

In the poem the legend of the encounter between Lady Ma and Cai Jing is relived when Deng assumed the first-person voice in noting the tectonic changes at the mountain site that had converted vast oceans into mulberry fields. Here Deng repeated or, rather, re-enacted Lady Ma's first remarks as she descended with her master Wang Yuan to visit Cai Jing. In re-enacting Lady Ma's descent, Deng further attempted to locate Cai Jing' house for a visit. This poetic re-enactment continues until the last line of the poem.[31] Indeed Deng's use of the omnipresent first person and his attempt to locate Cai Jing's house for a visit collapse the distance between his own tour of the sacred mountain and Lady Ma's past visit to Cai Jing. In such way, Deng's journey to the site becomes a pilgrimage through the history and myth of the locale. The site's past comes alive in the poem as its legendary encounters are relived through Deng's journey to the mountain. In that sense, Deng's journey also became an encounter with the inner alchemic tradition of the sacred mountain site.

So inwardly such travel to the sacred mountain was experienced by readers and practitioners alike as a personalized enactment of mythic and historical encounters of the past and invigorated their faith in the practice of inner alchemy. At the same time, the actual pilgrimage and its literary representations served to reinforce the perceived potency of the site, adding to its lore of past encounters and ascensions. Meanwhile, the circulation and transmission of such representations of Deng's personal pilgrimage in the *Yangshan Biweekly* also turned private personal experience into a public and shared experience among practitioners and readers.

Forming a Fellowship (ze lü 擇侶)

Next to a teacher and access to the oral secrets, companionship or fellowship constitutes another main prerequisite of the practice. Known by such names as companions (*lü* 侶), companions of the Way (*daolü* 道侶), and friends of the Way (*daoyou* 道友), fellowships formed during search journeys had traditionally been deemed crucial to the pursuit of both inner and outer alchemy. Such fellowships provided companionship, council, guidance, protection, and moral and spiritual support for the advanced practitioner. In his *Rules of Alchemic Chambers* (*Danfang xuzhi* 丹房須知), the Southern Song alchemist Wu Wu 吳悞 discussed the vital role of a trio of companions united in pursuit of the elixir. In such a fellowship of the three "pure cultivators" (*qingxiu zhi shi* 清修之士), each was expected to perform a specific set of functions in reaching their shared goal:

> When refining the elixir, there must be a fellowship of three gentlemen who are pure and modest. They should be of one heart and one aspiration: to perfect the elixir. As they begin work, one must first fast and perform rituals to heaven. While one friend takes charge of replenishing and changing the vessels and cauldrons, the other is in charge of adjusting fire and water in accordance with the alternating cycle of yin and yang. The care exercised by each one of the trio must not allow for even the slightest error.

The close cooperation and teamwork involved in the outer alchemic operation required that the trio be of one heart and share the same aspiration. Wu further stipulated that they must be "internally enlightened with virtues and externally emanating magnanimity and compassion" (*neiming daode waishi huici* 內明道德, 外施惠慈).[32] By the Ming dynasty, the moral and spiritual requirements of fellow cultivators engaged in outer alchemy had been fully integrated into the practice of inner alchemy. The late Ming inner alchemist Wu Shouyang advised his disciples to verify the moral integrity and spirituality of the potential fellow cultivators by checking their speech and conduct before they considered them as being of the "same will" or "comrades" (*tongzhi* 同志).[33]

For an inner alchemist, the emphasis on the moral and spiritual qualifications of a comrade mirrored the practitioners' practical need to be able to trust and depend on their fellow cultivators, especially

Fig. 11 The Triple Rings, late Ming print (*Sanhuan tu*, ca. 1634) (Cao Heng, *Daoyuan yiqi, yuan ji*, 2a).

at the advanced stages of the practice when practitioners entered a profound mental and physical meditative state in seclusion. They remained cut off from the world in a single-minded focus on the final transformation of the self. Any distraction or disturbance to a practitioner in such a sensitive and volatile psychosomatic state was believed to be ruinous, and even possibly fatal. While in this vulnerable state, the practitioner had to rely entirely on companions for daily necessities, for physical security, for emotional and technical support, and, most of all, for moral and spiritual guidance.[34]

The extraordinary mutual trust and dependence involved in such fellowships led the late Ming inner alchemist Cao Heng to characterize it as an interlocking series of "Three Rings" (*san huan* 三環). Having himself formed such a fellowship in pursuit of the elixir, Cao coined a term that vividly captures the profound mutual trust and dependence found within such fellowships. Cao called the main cultivator the "Ring of Death" (*sihuan* 死環) and his two companions who provide spiritual guidance, security, and logistical support, the "Ring of Life" (*huohuan* 活環) and the "Ring of the Cycle" (*xunhuan* 循環) (see Fig. 11).[35]

Selecting a Location (zedi 擇地)

A proper locale or location was another prerequisite for the pursuit of the elixir. Ge Hong, the Eastern Jin alchemist, wrote on the vital importance of a locale to the success of alchemic transformation in *A Master Who Embraces Simplicity* (*Baopuzi* 抱朴子):

> To coalesce the elixir, one must go to a place within the famous mountain where there are no people. Form a companionship of no more than three persons. First observe rituals for one hundred days and bathe in five fragrant herbs to cleanse and purify. Stay clear of the dirty and filthy. Stop all coming and going with mundane people and keep the practice from being known by those who don't believe in the Way and who might slander the deities and the drugs, causing it to fail.

In Ge Hong's writing, famous mountains (*ming shan* 名山) were imagined as part of a physical world in which the *qi* energy condensed or concentrated into various forms of spirits, of which only the Orthodox Deities (*zhengshen* 正神) were considered propitious to the operation of alchemy. Other spirits, known as the Gnomes of the Rock and the Wood (*mushi zhi jing* 木石之精), the Thousand-Year-Old Beings (*qian sui laowu* 千歲老物), and the Blood-Sucking Ghosts (*xueshi zhi gui* 血食之鬼), were viewed as harmful to practitioners. To help alchemists, Ge Hong stipulated a set of rules and criteria for selecting the mountains propitious to the alchemic processes (see Fig. 12).[36]

Ge Hong's speculations on locale became normative for the practitioners of outer alchemy[37] and played a significant role in the development of Daoist sacred geography, which classified the physical landscape into a system of propitious sites given the names Grotto Heavens and Blessed Lands (*dongtian fudi* 洞天福地) by the Tang Daoist Du Guangting 杜光庭 (850–933).[38] His taxonomy of mountains had a great influence on later generations of inner alchemists. By the Yuan dynasty, inner alchemists like Zhao Youqin 趙友欽 (?–1368) had come to imagine a proper locale as a vital prerequisite, or bond (*yuan* 緣), for the success of inner alchemy practice.[39] By the Ming, searching for and securing a propitious locale had become routine. For Wu Shouyang, a "blessed land" not only was a place

Fig. 12   Selecting sites for practice: a view of Mount Huang (Huangshan, ca. 1935) (YS, no. 44 [Apr. 16, 1935]: cover).

protected by the Orthodox Deities but also satisfied certain practical considerations:

A blessed place is simply a locale that is neither beset by the chaos of armed conflicts nor invaded by marauding bandits. It must not be close to any centers of communication and travel. It must not be disrupted by thieves and burglars. Yet it should be near towns or markets where easy access to food and drink is possible. But it must be away from any woods so as to avoid being bothered by the noise of birds and winds.[40]

Another late Ming writer on inner alchemy and medicine, Fu Shan 傅山 (1607–84), offered specific standards for selecting and constructing the practice site. A practitioner himself, Fu had similar concerns for geomantic potency, physical security, and seclusion from the world:

It is suitable to select a secluded and rustic hideaway undisturbed by people. The place should have mountains at the back and a body of water to its front. Its geomantic topography must not contain any evil or fatal elements (*xiongsha zhe* 凶煞者). Build a house made of either bamboo or brick as you wish. Keep the windows and tables clean. Plant bamboo but not trees, lest noisy sparrows and crows nest and squawk.[41]

Because of these concerns for security, seclusion, and geomantic advantages of the site, the journeys undertaken by practitioners fulfilled several functions. On one level, they helped practitioners accomplish the vital task of finding the proper locale for the practice. Travels to mountains also provided practitioners with firsthand knowledge of relationships between the natural environment and the body behind the Daoist geographical system of the Grotto Heavens and the Blessed Lands. Similar to the vital loci and passes in the human body, the mountains and locations consecrated in Daoist sacred geography were believed to be vital nodes and points of the Earth where traces of the atemporal *qi* from the cosmic creation still lingered and were concentrated. This potent residual vitality affected processes both in nature and in the human body. To inner alchemic practitioners, knowledge of the geomantic features of these sacred and potent sites and the ability to pinpoint their locations were indispensable.

In the early twentieth century, modern practitioners like Chen Yingning continued to be preoccupied with the geomantic potency of practice sites. Writing in the 1940s, Chen evinced a similar set of concerns for propitious environs, easy access to practice supplies, security, and relative seclusion from the world:

A proper site for refining cultivation should be close to mountains and woods and far away from cities and towns. There must be spring water running year-round, and trees evergreen in all seasons. The southeastern side of the site must be wide and open so that it will receive optimal sunshine. But to its northwestern side there must be towering ranges and peaks so as to shield it from the cold wind in winter.

The local customs and mores around the site must be simple and pure. Necessities should be easy to purchase. It must be a locale where flora grow and thrive so that they possess the generative *qi* (*sheng qi* 生氣). Ideally it should be covered with pines, firs, and other trees of the same type, for their needle-shaped leaves can emit a particular fragrance. When inhaled, it greatly benefits the body. Such trees must form a forest where their fragrance spreads, permeating all around with a dense and thick scent. Just a few thinly distributed trees would be of no use.[42]

Modern practitioners like Chen also paid great attention to the care and maintenance of the practice buildings:

> In both the rural and forested areas of the southeastern provinces, centipedes, snakes, and other crawlers abound. They often crawl into people's beds. So the building must be kept clean and dry. Its doors and windows must be tightly sealed. Extra care must be taken with the kitchen in order to prevent the spread of noxious qi (du qi 毒氣) to food and drink.
>
> The furnishings inside the building should be sparse and simple. Nondaily necessities must not be stored within the house. The quiet chamber (jing shi 靜室) must have sufficient light and free-flowing air circulation so as to prevent the growth of microbes. But during the practice session, light in the chamber must not be excessively bright. Excessive light makes it difficult to calm and settle the Psyche of the Heart (xinshen nan de anding 心神難得安定). Once inside the chamber, there should be no exposure to the blowing wind, for the wind makes one prone to catching a cold.[43]

Securing Funds (xuncai 尋財)

Financing the searches for alchemic method, fellowship, and locale was another concern of practitioners. Reflecting on the vital importance of money to the practice, the Yuan inner alchemist Chen Zhixu 陳致虛 (1290–?) mused:

> Having the Method without funds, the practice cannot succeed. With both acquired, one attains immortality.[44]

Since its inception around the late Tang period, the practice of inner alchemy had traditionally been supported through two main means. One was the monastery. Quanzhen Daoism, or the Northern Lineage (Beizong 北宗), which arose during the Jin and Yuan periods, adopted the Buddhist monastic tradition and supported the practice with monastic resources. Within the self-sufficient economy of the Quanzhen monasteries, this way of underwriting the practice continued well into the late Qing and early Republican periods.[45]

The other way of supporting the practice was represented by the Southern Lineage (Nanzong), which emerged during the late Song period and was characterized by small groups of individual lay practitioners and enthusiasts.[46] In contrast to clerics in the Quanzhen monasteries, they relied primarily on a combination of personal wealth, patronage, donations, and pooled resources to carry out the practice. Raising funds and finding donors became a familiar element of inner alchemy. In the traditional literature of inner alchemy, devout donors or sponsors were perceived as the guardians of the Law or the Way (*hufa hudao* 護法護道) who devoted their fortune and themselves to the pursuit of the elixir. By forming a fellowship with these rich devotees, one bettered one's chances. The early Yuan adept Zhao Youqin advised:

There are two meanings for funding. Sages come from money. Funding is thus the ladder to attaining the Way. While attaining the Way, one must rely on money. But after the Way is attained, money becomes useless. The ordinary people in the world do not know the subtlety of the different applications of money and the Way.

A poor cultivator living among mountains and woods must indeed rely on virtuous and wealthy families in attaining the Way. This is the dual applications of money and the Way. They aid each other in attaining perfection. On the day of perfection, the constructed alchemic chamber and all its furnishings are left behind without damage. All will be left behind as the practitioner takes his or her departure.[47]

But traditional *neidan* discourse was selective about what constituted appropriate funds for the pursuit of the elixir. Practitioners were urged to distinguish good fortune (*shan cai* 善財) from ill-gotten goods (*nie cai* 孽財) in their search for money. A Ming inner alchemy text attributed to Zhang Sanfeng stipulated a detailed set of criteria for raising money—only properly acquired wealth would aid the practice, and ill-gotten gains would spell disaster.[48]

Whereas their forerunners deliberated over appropriate sources of wealth for the practice, Chen and his fellow modern practitioners had to agonize over its lack. Following the expropriations of monastic properties by the Qing and the Republican governments, Daoist monasteries could seldom support modern lay practitioners. The financial problems were exacerbated by the worsening of political and economic conditions during the 1930s. Given the nature of his audience and his personal ambivalence toward monastic Daoism,

Chen, as well as his followers, had to rely on non-monastic alternatives to secure funding for their practice.

Inner alchemic practice was expensive at all stages. And during the advanced stage, the practitioner would likely incur extra costs for locating and securing a proper locale and for constructing a practice retreat there. In addition, money was needed to sustain the practice in seclusion from the world and to pay for the helpers often needed during this stage. Chen Yingning urged his audience to take steps to ensure proper finances by careful planning and economizing:

Set aside an additional sum of funds, the total of which must be sufficient to support the living expenses of five persons. Although one must eschew extravagant luxuries, one may not be excessively parsimonious, for most people beyond their prime tend to be rather enervated in the body. They often need medicine and drugs to regulate and replenish the body. If they depend only on ordinary food, it simply may not be sufficient to cultivate life. The five persons are the two or three most trustworthy companions of the Way, one or two hired hands (*yonggong* 佣工), and oneself.

Chen further argued that financial reserves were particularly important, especially in light of the central functions the companions of the practitioner performed. Away from home, the practitioner formed a new fellowship, or family, with the practice companions and relied on them for spiritual and emotional support and technical counsel. During the advanced stage of the practice, the companions served as the practitioner's intermediaries to the outside world and ensured the general well-being and security of the practitioner in seclusion.[49] Further, funds had to be raised for other practical needs that arose during the practice. Boredom due to long periods of intensive and isolated practice and the need for relocating the practice to geomantically propitious sites also required more travel and searches, thus incurring additional expenses. Funding for these, too, had to be accumulated in advance.[50]

Additional funds also helped alleviate the social, emotional, and economic impact of the pursuit of inner alchemy on the practitioner's family. As the practice progressed, especially to the advanced stage, its pursuit required periods of seclusion and even separation from family. To properly manage and minimize the social, emotional, and financial disruptions, Chen urged his fellow practitioners to plan and prepare in advance in order to continue to provide and care for the family in the practitioner's absence:

> One must make proper arrangements for one's family's affairs so that family members will have no worries in life (*sheng huo wu you* 生活無憂). If the son is capable of shouldering the responsibility, entrust him with the job. If he is still not yet established, ask a close relative or friend to temporarily assume their care. Or have them live with your brothers' clan. Only then you may extricate yourself from the family.[51]

Such details reveal an unusually practical approach to the economy of the practice, as well as an underlying desire to be in total control of the whole practice experience. Yet, like some of his predecessors, Chen Yingning was also concerned about the moral and spiritual ambivalence of total dependence on donors or sponsors. Chen favored supporting the practice through personal funds as much as possible, or through cooperative finances among dedicated fellow cultivators. This was the case with his early experiments in outer alchemy in Shanghai; he and several other enthusiasts pooled their funds to purchase chemicals, fuel, and other materials needed to conduct the experiments.[52]

It is also significant that in urging his audience to prepare for the practice, Chen insisted that they devise a financial plan based on fiscal discipline and frugality and accumulate resources through persistent saving and careful budgeting. The underlying message of his meticulous financial plan was unmistakable: practitioners must rely on themselves and on their own resources. It was no accident that Chen's message on self-reliance, with its meticulous details about the costs of the practice, was composed in 1945. He had just lost his wife to cancer and was already experiencing frequent moves and changes of patrons. In a sense, Chen's anxiety over financial stability and economic autonomy was mirrored in his call for financial discipline and self-reliance.[53]

But, as we shall see below, with the deterioration of political, economic, and social conditions during the late 1930s and the 1940s, Chen himself and many of his fellow practitioners would rethink the cherished ideal of individual autonomy and self-reliance and adopt innovative alternatives to secure the funds needed for the pursuit of inner alchemy.

Still, in affirming the search for funds as one of the four prerequisites, Chen moralized the issue of money, like his predecessors. The failure to raise the necessary funds and to plan for the practice would generate moral and spiritual anxiety in the prospective practitioner. Acquisition of funds either through saving or profit making became sanctioned. Meticulous planning, fiscal discipline, and, above all, self-reliance became hallmark virtues of the inner alchemic pursuit.

Practice Paths

Once the four prerequisites had been satisfied, the practitioner focused on refining and transforming the body in hope of immortality. The refining practice (*xiulian*) entailed rigorous daily regimens of meditation, accompanied by dietary, sexual, and other bodily adjustments. These regimens and adjustments were aimed at gradually transforming the practitioner's body, converting its postnatal *qi*, or vitalities, into the atemporal energy that purportedly led to immortality. To achieve this goal, the practitioner must learn to properly manage the postnatal bodily processes believed to consume and drain the limited supply of *qi* within the body and find ways to gather and maximize vital energies inside and outside the body.

Timing and locale were essential elements of the practice. Timing the practice to the rhythmic cycles of both the body and the universe enabled the practitioner to optimize the gathering and accumulation of the vitalizing *qi* within his or her body. Selecting locales appropriate to the various stages of the progressive practice ensured a maximal supply of *qi* energies from outside the body.

Although traditional inner alchemy texts prescribed different time frames for the various stages of inner alchemic practice, the duration of the refining practice for each individual practitioner varied according to the practitioner's situation. Chen Yingning proposed a graduated regimen of practice to be completed in five to ten years. During this period, the modern urban practitioner was expected to carry out a daily routine of activities at home or at work and conduct the practice primarily during the night or morning hours. Only as the practice progressed to the advanced stage in the final years of this period was a temporary seclusion or separation from the family required of the practitioner.[54]

Adjusting the Diet (gailiang yinshi 改良飲食)

For Chen and other modern practitioners, a proper dietary regimen was an important component of the practice. An improper diet adversely affected the *qi* equilibrium of the body and hindered one's progress. Food that overstimulated the body's senses upset the tranquility and calm of one's *shen*; this, in turn, led to an increase in desires and dissipation of the body's *élan vital*. Yet, food lacking the proper nutrients failed to nourish the existing *qi* energy of the body. Some inner alchemists preferred a vegetarian diet, but traditional inner alchemy discourse never completely ruled out a nonvegetarian diet. For his part, Chen Yingning held that a proper dietary regimen must not focus solely on the choice between eating vegetarian food (*chi su* 吃素) and eating meat (*chi hun* 吃葷). Rather, it must deal with appropriate ingestion of necessary nutrients (*ying yang* 營養). Understanding the properties and constituents of food was far more important than blindly following a vegetarian diet.[55]

Drawing on modern theories of nutrition, Chen Yingning identified three essential nutritional components for the modern practitioner: carbohydrates (*tanshui huahewu* 碳水化合物), proteins (*danbai zhi* 蛋白質), and fats (*zhi fang* 脂肪). In addition, vitamins (*shenghuo su* 生活素) were also vital nutrients for the body. Chen went on to analyze the main food groups as sources of nutrients and Vitamins A, B, D, and E.[56] He identified nutritional elements such as vitamins as the generative or vitalizing mechanism (*sheng ji* 生機) in food and stressed freshness and proper preparation as the way to preserve and maximize their *qi* nourishing power:

> When eating vegetables, it is essential to wash them clean. But they must not be overcooked. Overcooking diminishes their vitalizing functions. They have no benefits at all when eaten. They must not be too salty. Excessive salt renders the broth of the vegetables impossible to consume. Yet most of the vegetables' vitamins are left in the broth. This is truly regrettable.
>
> Vegetables' vitalizing mechanism is at its fullest when they are just harvested from the field. If vegetables are left for a day or two, or if they are soaked in water, most of their vitamins will inevitably be lost.[57]

Chen also stressed the harmonious interplay of three factors in the dietary regimen: the practitioner's physical constitution (*ti zhi*

體質), the nutritional makeup and properties of the food ingested, and disciplined dietary practice. Chen pointed out that physical constitution of the practitioner differed individually by nationality, region, occupation, and social station. Drawing on Chinese medical tradition, Chen identified two major types of bodily constitution: the cold body (*han ti* 寒體) and the warm body (*re ti* 熱體). Difference in physical constitution determined the type of food best suited to nourishing the *qi* vitality of the body. Further, the practitioner's line of work and status also played a role. A laborer who exerted the body (*laoli zhi ren* 勞力之人) and a writer who used the mind (*laoxin zhi ren* 勞心之人) required different quantities in their daily diets.[58]

Based on categories drawn from the Daoist dietetics, traditional herbalism, and modern nutritional knowledge, Chen divided foods into two large categories according to their properties: cooling (*liang xing* 涼性) and warming (*wen xing* 溫性).[59] Common fresh fruits had cooling properties, for example, whereas dried fruits such as raisins and dates had warming properties. He also tentatively identified the presence of Vitamin C in fresh fruits as the source of their cooling properties. Chen advised his audience that food properties must be properly matched with the physical constitution of the practitioner to maximize the nourishing effect of food on the body:

> Various fruits may be eaten regularly. But they must appropriately accommodate one's own body. The cold body must eat dried fruits (*ganguo* 干果), whereas the hot body should consume fresh fruits (*xianguo* 鮮果). Most fresh fruits are probably of the cooling properties, whereas dried fruits and nuts like red and black dates, walnuts, dried red bayberrys, lychees, longans, cherries, and raisins are mostly of the warming properties.[60]

Following the food restrictions set by earlier Daoist dieticians, Chen discouraged eating food with properties deemed too stimulating or potentially toxic. Fresh bamboo shoots (*sun* 筍) and various edible fungi (*mogu xianjun* 蘑菇鮮菌), which were so bountiful in southeastern China and popular in vegetarian diets, were to be either avoided or consumed minimally.[61] Although never stated explicitly, Chen's proscriptions against these foods followed a long-established Daoist tradition. During the thirteenth century, Li Pengfei 李鵬飛, a Daoist dietician and life cultivator, had written that bamboo shoots were "too disruptive of *qi*" (*dong qi* 動氣), and their excessive consumption would lead to congested "cold lumps" (*leng jia* 冷瘕) in the abdomen. Li had also cautioned against consuming a variety of mushrooms and fungi on the grounds that they tended to bring on such conditions as "cold *qi* (*leng qi* 冷氣), wind and piles (*feng zhi* 風痣), drowsiness (*duo shui* 多睡), and fatigue (*wu li* 無力)."[62]

To prepare and transform the modern practitioner's body, Chen also prescribed a dietary regimen that tapered off in both volume and frequency as the practice progressed:

In the first year, take two meals of food dishes (*fan chai* 飯菜), two of replenishing ingredients (*bu pin* 補品), and a snack of fruits (*guo pin* 果品), for a total of five meals every day.

In the second year, take one meal of food dishes, two meals of replenishing ingredients, and a snack of fruits, for a total of four meals a day.

In the third year, one meal of food dishes, one meal of replenishing ingredients, and one snack of fruits, for a total of three meals a day.

In the fourth year, one meal of food dishes and one of replenishing ingredients or a snack of fruits, for a total of two meals a day.

In the fifth year, alternate between food dishes, replenishing ingredients, and fruits but take only one meal a day.

In the sixth year, all cooked dishes must be given up. Every day, eat only a small portion of fruit. Or have no food at all, or have no food for a few days in a row.[63]

Chen's recommendations reflected both tension and compromise with the modern urban lifestyle and diet. On one hand, this rigorous regimen demanded gradual conformity to a new way of life and diet. Its goal was to reduce food intake and pleasure, and ultimately to liberate the body from its dependency on conventional food sources and on a lifestyle encumbered by the daily routine of work and even social and economic hardship familiar to many of his audience during the late 1930s and the early 1940s. Some even went to extremes by suggesting that Daoist dietary practices be adopted as means of coping with hunger and starvation.[64]

But, on the other hand, the dietary regimen was also meant to accommodate the real social and economic conditions of the urban lay practitioner. It is by no means coincidental that most of the food items identified in the regimen were vegetables, grains, meat, fish, fruits, and other common staples in the daily diet of most urbanites and even inhabitants of rural areas. Their inclusion indicated that Chen intended the diet of modern inner alchemy to be both practical and easily accessible. The concept and consumption of "replenishing ingredients" (*bupin* 補品) in the dietary regimen mirrored both Chen and his fellow practitioners' conformity to the traditional elite ethos of life-cultivation practice, as well as their accommodation to the modern bourgeois concerns for physical health.

In devising the dietary regimen, Chen integrated his knowledge of modern theories of nutrition with his erudition in Daoist dietetics. Modern theories of food and nutrition were adopted as a means of understanding and interpreting the traditional categories of food properties for a modern audience. Thus, the cooling properties of food were associated with the presence of Vitamin C and heating properties with its absence.

More relevantly, however, the dietary regimen proposed by Chen not only served as an auxiliary instrument in the physical transformation of the body, but also became the visible emblem of a body's ongoing self-transformation. A practitioner's ability to reduce consumption and subsist on minimal food confirmed a body in transformation and set the practitioner apart from the mundane world. As a practitioner followed the regimen, food evolved from a source of desire and mortal dependency to a starting point for both physical and spiritual transformation and transcendence. The act of eating ceased to be a mere matter of survival or pleasure and became a practice that promoted self-transformation.

Sexual Relations (nannü zhi shi 男女之事)

Besides food, Chen Yingning and his fellow practitioners also viewed sex and sexual desire as bearing directly on the task of transforming the body. At stake was the postnatal vital *qi*, which was perceived as raw material to be conserved and refined by the practitioner into the atemporal *qi* for sublimation toward immortality. Uncontrolled sexual desire and activity posed serious threats to the body by draining and even depleting its limited endowment of the vital *qi*. Thus, sexual desire and activities had to be properly managed in both men and women. As early as the 1920s, Chen wrote on the importance of cutting off desire (*duanyu* 斷欲):

> The preliminary practice of the immortals lies in reversing dotage by restoring youth. If the *qi* of Essence is depleted or damaged and the muscles and marrow enfeebled, one must apply oneself strictly in practice to repair and replenish them so as to restore them to their original condition, but to achieve this effect, one must cease the bedchamber affairs (*fangshi* 房事). But all that talk by the life-cultivators of ancient and modern times about curtailing desire (*jieyu* 節欲) is by no means the principled teaching of the divine immortals. The emphasis on merely curtailing desires is of no help at all. One must cut off desires completely to achieve success in the practice.[65]

To Chen Yingning, any desire, whether aroused by internal thought (*yunian suo gan* 欲念所感) or stimulated by external sight (*waijing suo she* 外景所攝), had the potential to drain the body's limited supply of primordial vitality. Precisely for that reason, life-cultivation regimens such as the sexual-gathering practices and bedchamber techniques attributed to the legendary sage Patriarch Peng (*Pengzu fangzhong shu* 彭祖房中術) could at best preserve the stock of primordial vitality, but they never augment it or restore it to its original perfection.[66]

Another source of *qi* loss was involuntary emission in men and menstrual periods in women. Many early twentieth-century practitioners saw these as a drain on the body's vitalities. The underlying assumption was that the semen released during coition (*jiaogou zhi jing* 交媾之精), the involuntary emission of semen (*yi xie zhi jing* 遺泄之精), and menstrual flow were degenerated forms of the generative energies that could be refined into *qi* (*hua qi zhi jing* 化氣之精). Uncontrolled leaks and flows of the vital energies in either sex threatened to deplete the limited supply of the essential vitalities, further diminishing the already dwindling stock available for alchemic sublimation. Chen Yingning distinguished two categories of causes of involuntary emissions: physiological (*shengli shang de* 生理上的) and psychological (*xinli shang de* 心理上的). Physiological causes include spontaneous emissions due to over-accretion of semen (*jingman ziyi* 精滿自遺) or excessive production of semen (*shengjing taiduo* 生精太多). Overproduction of semen was seen as resulting from undue stimulation of the nerves (*ciji shenjing* 刺激神經). The physiologically derived emission came from the degeneration of the atemporal *qi* into the temporal turbid semen (*houtian zhuojing* 後天濁精), and proper adjustment of the body through the practice would enable the practitioner to reverse this degeneration.[67]

Mindful of the many sensory seductions available in Shanghai, Chen explained that the psychological factors arose from the stimulants external to the body. As sounds and sights impacted on the senses, they moved the practitioner in the mind. Then their psychological impact manifested itself through the physiology of the body, accelerating the degeneration of the atemporal *qi* into the seedy semen and other bodily fluids, which led to further dissipating emissions. To break this chain of causality, Chen Yingning suggested distance and even abstinence from the sources of psychological stimulants or causes (*qi yin* 起因), including food and drink considered too stimulating to the senses.[68]

Like their predecessors, Chen and modern practitioners of inner alchemy had to confront the fundamental problem of handling sexual desire and drives innate to their postnatal bodies. Over the centuries, inner alchemists devised two major approaches for properly garnering and refining the postnatal vitality to achieve immortality and self-transformation: the Pure and Quiet solo practice (*qingjing gongfu* 清靜功夫), which pursued self-transformation within the confines and available resources of one's own body, and the Yin-Yang paired practice (*yinyang gongfu* 陰陽功夫), which sought to employ the bodily resources of both sexes. In either case, the issue was how mundane sexual energies could properly and morally be tapped for transcendence.

The Yin-Yang Paired Cultivation

The term "paired (or duo) cultivation" has been used in inner alchemy literature since the Song era to denote a special approach to self-cultivation involving women and men. One of the traditional inner alchemy regimens, the practice of Yin-Yang paired cultivation (*yinyang shuangxiu* 陰陽雙修) had long been under attack. To a certain extent, the controversy arose in part from a genuine lack of knowledge about the practice. Critics were all too ready to equate the practice with much eroticized self-cultivation practices such as the bedchamber arts (*fang zhong* 房中) and the sexually exploitative practice of "gathering" (*cai bu* 採補), which typically involved male adepts and pubescent girls. But more fundamentally, the practice was perceived as an affront and threat to the Confucian order of marriage and family. The goal of seeking transcendence, rather than procreation or pleasure, represented a cultural dissent from the Confucian ideals of lineage reproduction and continuation, not to mention familial and marital responsibilities. Further, the practice of engaging females as the means of achieving immortality rendered the practice morally ambiguous in the eyes of critics. Indeed, paired cultivation never quite shed its image as a male-centered practice primarily concerned with the spiritual or physical liberation of man at the expense of the female.[69]

Active in the new atmosphere of anti-tradition and anti-"feudalism" of the post–May Fourth era, Chen and his fellow practitioners were keenly sensitive to the moral ambiguities surrounding the practice. Equally concerned about women's position and rights and the viability of paired cultivation in the modern world, Chen sought to explain the limits and relevance of paired cultivation from a historical perspective:

> The grafting method of the Southern Lineage could indeed be practiced in each of the dynasties prior to the founding of the Republic. But at the present, it is not feasible to promote this kind of learning. First, there is the issue of age (*nianling wenti* 年齡問題). Second, there is the issue of individualhood (*ren'ge wenti* 人格問題). Third, there is the issue of external guardianship (*waihu wenti* 外護問題). Fourth, there is the issue of money (*jingji wenti* 經濟問題). If any single one of these is not properly taken care of, it will turn into a legal problem. I do not know if my fellow cultivators have ever paid attention to this. In my opinion, it is more advisable to promote the Pure and Quiet method of the Northern school. It will spare us many troubles.[70]

What was so elliptically alluded to as the issues of age and individualhood were precisely what had dogged the practice in the past. The alleged use of pubescent girls at their first menses for the purpose of rejuvenating the aging male body problematized any spiritual claims for the practice. The emerging discourse about individual autonomy and rights also raised issues about the use of pubescent girls. Further, the moral character of the practitioner was another decisive factor affecting public perceptions. Lack of moral integrity and spiritual discipline in the practitioner could turn the practice into sexual debauchery, and insensitivity to the spiritual and physical well-being of the female partner could easily lead to her sexual exploitation and even physical injury. Due to the cost and the controversial nature of the practice, paired cultivators had traditionally been advised to seek sponsors who could provide both funding and legal protection. Inner alchemic discourse described financiers and sponsors of the practice as external guardians of the Way, but such support rarely came without expectation of reciprocity or repayment. Reciprocity might take various forms, from spiritual guidance to the divulging of practice secrets. But, like any business transaction, such partnerships were prone to discontent and dispute, which would thus undermine the practice and the parties involved.

Keenly aware of the moral implications of the paired practice in the modern age, Chen sought to dispel the stereotypes of sexual exploitation of women associated with the practice. Following a rationale advocated by earlier duo cultivators, Chen classified the Yin-Yang paired cultivation practice into a scheme of six rankings based on their purported benefit or harm to both parties involved. In this ranking system, the superior practices offered benefits to the partners of both sexes engaged in the practice, or to one party, but caused no harm to the other party. The lower-ranked practices either benefited the male partner exclusively or caused harm to either one or both parties.[71]

In a long reply to a reader published on July 16, 1936, Chen Yingning sought to redefine the tradition of the paired Yin-Yang cultivation in terms of companionate partnership for modern inner alchemy. He reformulated the practice by excavating and reviving what he portrayed as the "ancient way of duo cultivation" (*gufa xiulian* 古法脩煉) from early Daoist legends. At the core of the "ancient way" was the notion of the "Divine Immortal Couple" (*shenxian juanshu* 神仙眷屬).

The ancient way of cultivation is one in which two people, a man and wife (*fufu erren* 夫婦二人), are united in their heart and will (*tongxin heyi* 同心合意). They break off secular passions and engage in paired cultivation for shared confirmation of transcendence for both (*shuangxiu shuangzheng* 雙修雙證). This is radically different from the practice of the Solo Yin and Solitary Yang (*guyin guayang* 孤陰寡陽). Liu Gang and Fan Yunqiao are the most renowned of all man-and-wife paired cultivators (*fufu shuangxiu* 夫婦雙修). Yet among the seven Northern Perfected Ones, Ma Danyang and Sun Bu'er could not but be contaminated by Buddhist customs. With their stress on abandoning family and leaving the spouse, and with the husband and wife apart from each other, the customs and mores of the ancient divine immortals (*gu shenxian fengfan* 古神仙風範) were entirely lost to them.[72]

Key to Chen's reconstruction of the divine immortal couple was that the man and the woman were equal partners in the endeavor. They shared the same aspiration for immortality and transcendence. Chen stressed that both were of one heart and power (*yixin yide* 一心一德) and equally dedicated to the practice. Further, spiritual companionship between man and woman was not just a moral requirement; it was seen as a physiological and technical necessity for the practice. The man and the woman must be evenly or similarly matched in terms of level of proficiency and capabilities. This was deemed essential if both partners were to benefit from the practice. In an unevenly matched couple, the more advanced party would be hampered by the less advanced party. The lesser party would have to make up the deficiency with assistance (*bangzhu* 幫助) from the advanced partner or through intensified solo self-cultivation practice.[73] Additionally, gender equality was manifested in the shared benefits for both man and woman engaged in the paired cultivation. Man was no longer the sole beneficiary of physical and spiritual betterment from the practice. Instead, Chen envisioned the ancient way as enabling both men and women to achieve the goal of immortality.

It is significant that Chen evoked as the embodiment of gender equality the legendary couple of Liu Gang 劉綱 and Fan Yunqiao 樊雲翹 from the Han period. Chen Yingning envisioned paired cultivation as a tradition rooted in China's antiquity, when China was still relatively free of the influence of Buddhism, and when such practice was as "natural" as being Chinese. Chen argued that this ancient way of self-cultivation began to erode with the rising influence of Buddhism, with its prevalent practice of celibacy and monasticism, which had since repressed the companionate couple as the authentic way of self-cultivation:

> In ancient China, there was no such a thing as "leaving the family" (*chujia* 出家). All those who learned the Way and cultivated immortality lived at home together with their spouses (*juanshu tongju* 眷屬同居). Only when Buddhism was introduced to China did the institution of leaving the family begin. So a man who leaves the family is called a monk (*heshang* 和尚), and a woman who leaves the family is known as a nun (*nigu* 尼姑). The original intention of this practice is to get away from the worries of a family so that one may achieve purity and tranquility of the heart and the body. But once enrobed in the *kayasa* (*jiasha* 袈裟), one encounters even more troubles when one's worries still cannot be reduced. The Daoist Quanzhen school was founded following the example of Buddhism. It only arose at a much later time. But it was no longer the ancient way (*bushi gufa* 不是古法).[74]

Chen's rejection of the practices of leaving the family and celibacy as contrary to the authentic ancient traditions of Daoist inner alchemy was clearly evident in his admiration for the legendary Han dynasty couple. The story of Liu Gang and Fan Yunqiao was first told in Ge Hong's *Biographies of Divine Transcendents*. There they were portrayed as a dynamic couple who challenged and complemented each other in their common pursuit of immortality. Their daily relationship was one of friendly competition in wit and magical prowess that honed their alchemic proficiency and ultimately led both to transcendence. In Ge Hong's hagiography, Fan Yunqiao, the wife, was portrayed as possessing a higher and more powerful magic than her husband. She often emerged triumphant in their storied duels of alchemic proficiency and magical prowess. From the Song down to the Ming and Qing periods, stories about Liu and Fan appeared in numerous Daoist hagiographies and in the folk imagination.[75] To Chen Yingning, these Daoist and folk accounts attested to a way of dual cultivation at a point in antiquity when the Daoist paired practice did not involve sexual exploitation of pubescent girls. Women were purportedly the equals, if not the superiors, of men, and man and woman competed as well as collaborated with one another in a practice that benefited both.

As a couple who embodied the "ancient way," Liu and Fan were thus made to represent the new image of the paired cultivation practice for Chen and his fellow modern practitioners. As both competitors and companions in a common quest for immortality, Liu and Fan's intense one-on-one rivalry, so vividly dramatized by their jousts, invoked a loving and dedicated relationship. Their companionate model of paired practice was a dramatic departure from the male-centered imperial model of one male and multiple females long associated with dual cultivation. Thus, in valorizing Liu and Fan as the classic exemplars of the practice, Chen Yingning and his fellow modern inner alchemists also ironically embraced the New Culture ethos of individualism, companionship, compatibility, reciprocal commitment, and dedication as the new model for Yin-Yang paired cultivation practice.

Nature in the form of human physiology constituted the other pillar of Chen Yingning's re-imagined "ancient way." Chen argued that paired cultivation was also based on the natural physiological insufficiency or bias (*pianku* 偏枯) and imperfections (*bu wanquan* 不完全) innate to both sexes:

> In secular terms, a man is lopsided toward yang, whereas a woman inclines toward yin. In terms of the alchemic Way, the man is yang on the outside but yin inside (*waiyang neiyin* 外陽內陰), and the woman is yin on the outside yet yang inside (*waiyin neiyang* 外陰內陽). Yet generally speaking, regardless of gender, each suffers from being lopsided and imperfect. This is the most lamentable imperfection since the birth of humanity. But this is also the one and only mechanism of transmutation between life and death (*shengsi liuzhuan weiyi de dongji* 生死流轉唯一的動機). Take a look at the battery cell. When the positive and the negative charges are linked, a complete circuit is formed. Take another look at a magnet. When the north and the south charges meet, they attract and draw each other. The reason for these phenomena is easily understood. But whereas the yin and the yang of the temporal realm are divided into two, the unitary *qi* of the atemporal realm remains one and whole. Its innate and original nature is not to separate and divide. For those who cultivate the Way, the most valuable thing is to make use of the yin and the yang of the temporal realm so that they may be restored to the unitary *qi* of the atemporal realm. In other words, beginning from the mutated and unnatural state of lopsided deficiency (*pianku bu ziran zhi biantai* 偏枯不自然之變態), move against the transmutation mechanism (*nixing zaohua* 逆行造化), and return and restore to the spontaneous Original Nature of balance and harmony (*zhonghe ziran zhi benxing* 中和自然之本性).[76]

Chen's construction of the alchemic body's physiology here represents a fundamental rethinking of traditional inner alchemy in modern times. Whereas traditional inner alchemic theories recognize the prenatal moment of conception as the origin of human imperfection in both the male and the female bodies, its egalitarian vision had seldom been taken to its logical conclusion due to social factors outside inner alchemy. Instead, the original sexless imperfection was essentialized as a yang deficiency in the body. The anxiety over the yang deficiency in the male body was then externalized as the male's strategic gaze at the female body, objectifying the latter as a potential source and repository of the yang supply in service of sublimating the male body.

Chen, in contrast, emphasized the differentiation and division at conception from the atemporal realm as the original cause of human mortality. This imperfection was therefore truly "original" in the sense that it was equally present in the bodies of both sexes and had nothing to do with their physiological differences. Regardless of their different yin and yang configurations, the male and female bodies were fundamentally equal at the moment of conception, when both were rendered deficient and imperfect by the natural mechanism of transmutation in their respective organisms. Left unchecked, this natural mechanism of transmutation in both men and women would lead ultimately to aging and death.

For Chen Yingning, this congenital deficiency or partiality to either yang or yin was no cause for despair in either sex. Indeed, the very mechanism that afflicted humans with imperfect physiology also offered a path for their ultimate return to the truly natural state of balance and harmony, the state of undifferentiated unity. The Yin-Yang paired cultivation practice was seen as the "True Way" of return. It served as the mechanism for balancing postnatal deficiencies in both sexes and held out the possibility of transcending their respective imperfections. The excesses or deficiencies of yin and yang in both sexes became the ingredients for forging the elixir of perfection and turning the imperfect man and woman into consummate immortals.

Thus, by redefining human imperfection as a deficiency in atemporal vitality rather than valorizing the postnatal yang element in the body, Chen departed from the traditional theory of inner alchemy, which privileged the yang element of the body over its yin counterpart. In the process, he dispelled the long-held but morally ambiguous view that objectified the female body as a resource for male transcendence and immortality.

But Chen never viewed paired dual cultivation as the only viable approach to attaining immortality. To him, paired cultivation was appropriate for husband and wife or mutually devoted partners. Chen's concept of the companionate couple of divine immortals mirrored the social and cultural changes of early twentieth-century China, when concubinage was abolished, oppression of women was challenged, and ideas of gender equality and women's rights were gaining currency. It also represented the efforts of modern adepts and writers of inner alchemy like Chen Yingning to reinvent their tradition and redefine what it meant to be an inner alchemist in a modernizing society.

The Pure and Quiet Solo Cultivation

Although Chen viewed paired cultivation as an efficacious practice, he also pointed to its limits and restrictions. The practice afforded faster alchemic benefits to one or both parties involved, but it was not feasible and practical for those practitioners who could not find dedicated partners in either their spouses or fellow cultivators. Also, it was a preliminary practice susceptible to public misperception and condemnation.

For many, the alternative and more feasible approach was the solo cultivation known as the Pure and Quiet practice. Since the solo practice sought to gather the generative *qi* either by transforming the sexual energies within one's own body or by gathering it from one's environment, it was beyond reproach, and the method was adopted and promoted by Daoist monastic clerics and lay celibate practitioners. Compared with paired practice, the sole approach was believed to be much less complicated and costly and was seen as technically more accessible to practitioners of both sexes. Advising his audience about the limits of dual practice, Chen extolled the virtues of solo practice:

The Pure and Quiet practice and the Yin-Yang paired practice have always been opposite to one another. I think that both approaches are effective. But under the present conditions, it is not convenient to discuss the Yin-Yang practice with my friends of the Way. This is because when the prerequisites of the practice are not fulfilled, the practice will likely create troubles, adding to the karmic deadlock (*mozhang* 魔障). Further, speaking solely of the Yin-Yang practice, it can be implemented only at the beginning stage in which the Essence is refined into *qi* (*lianjing huaqi* 煉精化氣). The practice has little efficacy when the cultivation progresses to the intermediate stage of refining *qi* into the Psyche (*lianqi huashen* 煉氣化神). Practitioners will naturally resort to the way of the Pure and Quiet by then. At the last stage of refining the Psyche to return to the Void (*lianshen huanxu* 煉神還虛), the Pure and Quiet approach is even more indispensable. So from now on, I will discuss exclusively the Pure and Quiet approach.[77]

This pronounced shift in focus of Chen's public discourse on paired and solo practices came in 1945, the year his wife died after a protracted battle with breast cancer. But his endorsement of the solo practice was not a philosophical retreat. Rather, it reconfirmed what Chen had always practiced in his own life: one must adapt the practice to one's situation.

Regimens for Daily Practice

Quiet Sitting

As a concept and practice, quiet sitting (*jingzuo* 靜坐) or quiet practice (*jinggong* 靜功) originated in the writings of early philosophers like Zhuangzi. During the Wei and Jin periods (265–420), quiet sitting as a meditative technique was incorporated in Shangqing Daoist self-transformational regimens. By the Tang, the famous Shangqing Daoist Sima Chengzhen had integrated elements of Buddhist Chan meditative practice into the Daoist sitting regimen, incorporating it as part of the neo-Daoist metaphysics of the Double Mystery Learning (*chongxuan* 重玄). During the Song and Yuan periods, quiet sitting as a meditative regimen spread from Daoist circles into the world of literati, becoming a favored form of self-cultivation and truth-seeking among elite Confucian scholars. By the Ming, quiet sitting was not only a self-cultivation practice for spiritual transcendence but also a popular regimen for health and self-healing.[78]

In the first few decades of the twentieth century, quiet sitting became a public health and spiritual regimen promoted by intellectuals like Jiang Weiqiao and Ding Fubao, among others. It was also the central component of many of the emerging redemptive societies such as the Common Benevolence Society. Chen Yingning began to advocate the practice publicly in the early 1930s as the most convenient and easy approach to self-cultivation. He held that the practice was based on two fundamental inner alchemic perceptions of human mortality. First, the atemporal vitality of life (*xiantian shengmingli* 先天生命力) of the body inherited at the moment of conception was rather limited. Its stock diminished from the time of birth. Second, the temporal powers of life (*houtian shengmingquan* 後天生命權) of the body were seldom restored to their atemporal form after birth. As a result, the body naturally had little hope of rejuvenation. Chen further explained that the temporal energy of the body consists of the beating of the heart and the breathing of the lungs; the atemporal vitality of life was the natural force (*tianran nengli* 天然能力) that made possible the natural functions of the heart and lungs.[79] Quiet sitting with regulated breathing, which purportedly replenished the body with this atemporal vitality, was seen as the key to both health and immortality. Chen Yingning advised his readers:

But what method may be employed to gain control over the atemporal powers of life within the body? That would be the Union of the Psyche and Qi (*shenqi heyi* 神氣合一) by entering the Supreme Quietness and Tranquility (*dajing dading* 大靜大定), a state that one can achieve in which the pulse does not beat, the nose does not inhale or exhale. It is no different from being a dead man, except that the body remains soft and warm and not at all rigid and cold. This is what the Daoist scriptures refer to as "the pulse ceases and the breathing stops; learning to die even before dying" (*maizhu xiting, weisi xian xuesi* 脈住息停, 未死先學死). Yet upon emerging from the state of Stillness, both the pulse and the breathing regain their normal operations. Eating, drinking, speech, and behavior are no different from what they are in a normal person. In this way, the powers of life are brought under one's control and are no longer subject to the rule of Nature. If one wants to die, he dies, without a shred of pain. If he wants to stay alive, he shall have no limit to his days. When the practice reaches this level, it has achieved the preliminary success of the Immortals' Learning.[80]

Postures

To reach this level of practice, one must follow a strict daily regimen, paying close attention to proper posture, the length of daily sessions, and timing and locale of the practice. Based on ancient gymnastics, breathing exercises, and influenced by Buddhist meditative techniques, the postures (*zishi* 姿勢) of inner alchemic meditation covered walking, standing, sitting, and lying down (*xingli zuowo* 行立坐臥). Many of practice postures and gymnastics had been popular since the Ming and Qing periods, as shown in the illustrations from the late Ming inner alchemy text *Xingming shuangxiu wanshen guizhi* 性命雙脩萬神圭旨 (A jade synopsis by a myriad of deities on the dual mind and life cultivation)[81] (see Figs. 5–7 in Chapter 3). According to Chen, each position offered different benefits. Lying prostrate was most efficient for gathering the atemporal *qi* (*shequ xiantian qi* 攝取先天氣), whereas a reclining position was best for uniting the Psyche with *qi*. The sleeping positions were divided into the prostrate position (*yang shui* 仰睡), the half-reclining position (*ban kao shui* 半靠睡), and the side-reclining position (*ce shui* 側睡). These sleeping postures were apparently suitable for elderly practitioners. The sitting posture was the most commonly employed. One might sit with legs tucked in (*pan tui* 盤腿), or hanging (*chui tui* 垂腿), or placed naturally as one pleased (*tingqi zibian* 聽其自便). Chen advised that the key was to find a position that enabled one to persevere in the practice for a long time without agitation (*naijiu budong wei miao* 耐久不動爲妙). For that reason, Chen considered the Buddhist cross-legged sitting position (*jiafu zuo* 跏趺坐), which involved folding one leg atop the other, as ill suited to average practitioners in quiet sitting practice, because prolonged practice in this position could be harmful.[82] In describing how to adjust the body (*tiao shen* 調神) to sit properly, Hong Tai'an 洪太庵 (1877–?), a disciple of Chen's, advised his fellow practitioners:

Upon entering the sitting position, align the ears with the shoulders, and the nose down with the navel. Do not lower the head, nor slouch the back. Tuck in the legs and hold the hands with fingers crossed in front. With both eyes lightly closed and the mouth gently shut, stick the tongue to the upper palate. Anchor all the weight of the body just below the navel.[83]

These instructions on the proper alignment of body parts were aimed at creating a visibly distinct physical space and marking the external parameters of the cultivating body. More important, these bodily postures were also intended as means of priming the body for optimal equilibrium and flow of the postnatal vitalities and thus to facilitate the gathering and refining of *qi* within the body.

These external adjustments of the body were accompanied by internal regulation of the practitioner's Heart (*tiao xin* 調心) and breathing (*tiao xi* 調息). The purpose was to empty the Heart of its ceaseless and spontaneous flow of thoughts so that it became at one with the body and assisted the flow of *qi* within. To help rid the Heart of conscious thoughts, Hong Tai'an recommended two traditional meditative methods: counting of the breaths (*shu xi* 數息) and recitation of the Heart mantra (*song Xinjing* 誦心經):

The method of breath counting is that each breath is made up of one exhalation and one inhalation. Start from one to ten in cycle and count it silently. Count until the Heart and breathing coalesce with each other. Once the thought flow ceases, stop counting.

The method of scriptural recitation is to focus attention on the Top Gate while reciting the Heart Scripture silently. Do not move the mouth and hold the Heart steady. Recite until the Heart and the Psyche are one. Stop reciting once the thought flow ends.[84]

Drawing on an old metaphor from Laozi, Hong likened the regulation of breathing to the workings of the bellows (*tuo yue* 橐籥)[85] and the body of the practitioner to the firing furnace (*huo lu* 火爐):

The Daoist breathing regulation method is just like the operation of a wind bellows. As it is pulled, the wind is pumped into the firing furnace. As it is pushed, the wind is again bellowed into the furnace. The locale of the navel on our body is the firing furnace. So inhalation is drawn upward from below the navel by sucking it in, whereas exhalation is pushed downward by expanding out the navel. These are the workings of a blacksmith's wind bellows as applied to his firing furnace.[86]

Length, Timing, and Place of Practice

In order for the quiet-sitting regimen to produce the desired physical transformation, Chen prescribed a set of standards for the length (*xiulian suiyue* 脩煉歲月) and timing and locale of the practice (*xinggong shijian ji didian* 行功時間及地點). He devised a five-year schedule of graduated practice, with specific criteria for each stage of the practice. Incrementally, the practitioner would reduce and ultimately eliminate the physical need for sleep and would instead engage in quiet-sitting meditation throughout the night, thus further enhancing the visible differences between the cultivating body and the mundane body. At the end of the five-year program, the practitioner would be able to sit for ten hours without moving.[87]

Timing and locale were seen as essential for quiet sitting to achieve optimal results. Timing the practice reflected the traditional inner alchemy belief in a correspondence between the micro-processes of the human body and the macro-cycles of transformative changes in nature. Certain points in the solar and lunar cycles such as the midnight (*zishi* 子時) and the noon (*wushi* 午時) hours were deemed crucial periods when the atemporal yang *qi* (*xiantian qi* 先天氣) of the universe was on the rise and flourishing. Synchronizing the practice to these generative hours enabled the practitioner to gather and absorb the rising atemporal *qi*. During the Song period, a different conception of timing emerged in the inner alchemic writings. It emphasized disengaging the bodily processes of the practitioner from their perceived linkages to the cycles of nature. Indeed, as early as the Five Dynasties period, the inner alchemist Cui Xifang 崔希範 had proposed that inner alchemic practice be conducted independently of nature's cycles: "Within a day, there are the twelve hours. Whenever the Intention wills, the practice can be engaged."[88]

Cui's thinking on spontaneously timing the practice to one's own bodily cycle was continued by the Song inner alchemist writer and practitioner Zhang Boduan 張伯端 (z. Pingshu 平叔, h. Ziyang 紫陽; 987–1082), who saw no connection between the practitioner's internal refining processes and the cosmic cycles.[89] Zhang's argument was interpreted by the Southern Song inner alchemist Huang Ziru 黃自如 (fl. 1241) to mean that the firing moment, when the atemporal *qi* was first thought to rise in the body, did not depend on diurnal rhythms. By the Ming and Qing periods, the idea of a timing mechanism within the practitioner's body and more in tune with the ebb and flow of the vital energies within the body than dependent on external natural processes and seasonal cycles had become encapsulated in the phrase "live (flexible) *zi* and *wu* hours" (*huo ziwu* 活子午). Best represented by *Suoyan xu* 瑣言續, a text transmitted to Min Yide by his master, Shen Taixu 沈太虛, this new conception of a timing mechanism redefined the terms of the body's connection with the macrocosm. It postulated that the body's *qi* had its own rhythm and cycles of change. Rather than timing the body to the external cycles, the practitioner masters the body's internal rhythms and cycles of *qi* in order to gain control of the natural processes of change. The body was conceived as a miniaturized cosmos. The late Qing tract advised its readers that a practitioner who could seize the right moment of the rising *qi* within and cultivate it for the time it took one stick of incense to burn could gain a hundred years of generative transformation in the body (*neng xing zhuxiang, yiduo bainian zaohua* 能行炷香, 已奪百年造化).[90] By the late imperial period, the idea of timing one's practice independently of the external cosmic cycles had become an established alternative to the traditional timing practice.

This flexible, autonomous approach to timing the practice by the practitioner's own bodily cycles was embraced by modern practitioners like Chen Yingning throughout the 1930s and 1940s. In Chen's writings on quiet sitting, the distinction between timing the practice to seasonal changes and natural rhythms and timing it to the cyclical changes of *qi* within the body was much less prominent. Instead, Chen chose to focus on pragmatic considerations; for example, he advised against conducting sessions immediately after eating and suggested that each individual schedule the practice according to his or her daily routine. This latitude reflected a concept of flexible timing dating back to the Song period and embraced by inner alchemists of the late imperial period.[91]

In contrast, situating the practice seemed a greater concern. To maximize the garnering of *qi* from the environment, Chen devised a set of stringent standards for siting the practice in different locales in accordance with the progress of the practice. The practice locale ranged from a quiet chamber in an urban dwelling to a retreat house in the countryside to caves amid the high peaks of the Daoist sacred mountains. In these elaborately explained plans for locating the refining practice, one was expected to match one's level of proficiency with the proper environment in order to benefit from the *qi* energies of the place outside the body. As the practice progressed, the practitioner was expected to conduct secluded sessions (*bi guan* 閉關) of varying lengths and to relocate the practice to places with superior levels of geomantic potency and increasing isolation from the world. The emphasis on situating the practice in places with strong generative *qi* and easy access to daily necessities reflected the persistent connections and interdependence between the practitioner and the environs. Chen advised his audience on the importance of properly locating one's practice:

When people reach middle age, they are often afflicted with an insufficiency of the vitalizing *qi* within the body (*shenzhong sheng qi* 身中生氣) and therefore must rely on the boundless generative *qi* of the external world (*waijie wuxian liang zhi shengqi* 外界無限量之生氣) to foster and replenish their own supply. So they must select a place with dense and thick generative *qi* to conduct the practice so that it is easy to attain efficacy.[92]

The success of the practice ultimately depended on proper coordination of all the factors involved. With perseverance and commitment, the practitioner could hope to attain some preliminary transformation of the body by the end of the fifth year. Chen described the subtle inner change one could expect:

When you look at his appearance, he seems to be engaged in a dead and dull sitting (*si dazuo* 死打坐). But you do not realize that the physiology of his body has already undergone a subtle yet wondrous transformation. Not only is he absolutely different from a real dead man, but also he differs entirely from an ordinary living person. Since his *qi* is supple, he naturally does not crave food. Since his Spirit is sound, he certainly does not think of sleep. His breath and pulse can stop on their own. Having reached this level, he has certainly transcended the mundane even though he may have not attained sagehood (*suifei rusheng queyi chaofan* 雖非入聖, 卻已超凡).[93]

Having advanced the practice from the preliminary stages of "building the foundation" (*zhu ji* 築基) and "gathering the elixir" (*cai yao* 採藥), the practitioner was believed to have accomplished the "gestation of the embryo" (*jie tai* 結胎). This inner transformation was marked externally by a reduced need for food, sleep, and even air.

Becoming Divine Immortals: Techniques of Perfection

The next step in the practice was to advance to the final stage of "parturition of the Yang Spirit" (*chu shen* 出神), which led to the ultimate goal of inner alchemy: becoming a divine immortal (*cheng xian* 成仙). Apparently operating in unexplored territory, Chen Yingning relied heavily on his knowledge of inner alchemy classics as well as Daoist lore about the ascendances of immortals in guiding his audience at this stage of the practice. Chen proposed two approaches: the Rapid Advance (*jijin fa* 急進法) and the Gradual Advance methods (*huanjin fa* 緩進法) to attaining perfection.

The Rapid Advance method was based on the notion that nature, especially the sun, held the atemporal *qi* energies known as the True Solar Fire (*taiyang zhen huoli* 太陽眞火力) that facilitated the final parturition of the Yang Spirit embryo in the body. Chen envisioned the final practice as conducted in a secluded high-mountain grotto and synchronized with propitious hours of the solar cycle:

> Every day, the practitioner waits for the sun to rise, sucking in and absorbing the solar rays via the nostrils and pores into the body. Blend it with his or her Original Qi and the Original Psyche. Mesh and refine them together. Strike them all into a slice (*dacheng yipian* 打成一片). Bind them into one globe (*jiecheng yituan* 結成一團). Begin from the *yin* hours (*yin shi* 寅時) and end the practice at the *wei* hours (*wei shi* 未時).
>
> From the *shen* hours (*shen shi* 申時) to the *chou* hours (*chou shi* 丑時) at night, the practitioner conceals himself or herself within the grotto [to avoid] exposure to light. Devote yourself exclusively to the practice of quieting down in order to absorb and retain the solar *qi* (*yang qi* 陽氣). At the *yin* hours of the next day, practice as before.
>
> Confine yourself to drinking spring water every day and eat no other foods. In no more than three years, the Yang Spirit can break out from the crown of the head (*yangshen ji ke touding erchu* 陽神即可透頂而出). So

even without seeking for the divine efficacy (*shen tong* 神通), such efficacy is bestowed. This is the method whereby the Yang Spirit is born first, and the divine efficacy is attained thereafter.[94]

It is interesting to note the contrast between the dissociation of cosmic synchronization in earlier stages of the practice and the need for it at the final stage of the practice. The disregard for cosmic rhythms prevalent in the late imperial period seemed not so much to confirm the irrelevance of the cosmic process to the inner alchemic transformation as to reflect a realistic accommodation with the out-of-sync nature of the practitioner's temporal body. Indeed, the quiet-sitting practice at earlier stages that disregarded the cosmic cycle in favor of the body's own internal rhythms may well have been an elaborate yet strategic attempt to resensitize and resynchronize the internal processes of the body, so that they would be reattuned to those of the cosmos. Given the strenuous demands on timing the practice to solar cycles, it would be hard to imagine success without a highly attuned body sensitive and responsive to subtle changes in sunlight.

At the final stage of the practice, as the practitioner prepared for the birth of the immortal Yang Spirit, Chen envisioned total seclusion as necessary to ensure success. The practice had to be situated in a locale rich in special geomantic energies known as the Killing Qi (*sha qi* 殺氣). A mortal body would succumb to the otherwise baleful influences of the Killing Qi, but the already transformed body of the advanced practitioner was believed to be impervious to it. Indeed, Chen reasoned that the inhibiting and baleful influences formed a perfect natural defense against disturbance and intrusion by either humans or animals and ensured a safe haven that assisted and protected the birthing of the divine immortal:

The reason why the practice of ascending to the upper realm by flight has to be conducted in a locale with heavy Killing Qi is that humans do not set foot there and there are no poisonous snakes and ferocious beasts. Additionally, the temperature is very low. One can place his or her flesh body in an appropriate place and preserve it for many years without corruption. So he or she can rest assured in engaging boldly in the practice of transcendence (*chaotuo gongfu* 超脫功夫). There is no need for other people to provide protection. Furthermore, since the locale is removed far away from the heavy and densely thick and seedy *qi* of the earth (*zhongzhuo nonghou zhi diqi* 重濁濃厚之地氣) and close to the light, clear, and ethereal *qi* of the empyrean (*qingqing danbo zhi kongqi* 輕清淡泊之空氣), it aids the practice of ascendance.[95]

Since the newborn Yang Spirit is seen as the body outside the body (*shen wai zhi shen* 身外之身), the post-parturition practices are designed to further develop and empower the nascent Yang Spirit while shielding it from loss or harm due to fright or shock. This is especially the case when the newborn Yang Spirit is deemed to be still tainted with *yin* impurities. Indeed the Spirit born with the *yin* impurities is often known as the Yin Spirit (*yin shen* 陰神) and is considered susceptible to temptation and fright on its journeys outside the host body of the practitioner. As such, the Yin Spirit needs more refining to achieve perfection. Chen Yingning had in mind the advice of the late Ming inner alchemist Wu Shouyang when he counseled his modern readers about delicate operations of birthing, nourishing, and training the Yang Spirit as it emerges:

To nurture the Spirit to come out of the carapace (*tiaoshen chuqiao* 調神出殼) is a moment of utmost importance, a moment of grave danger. In the initial stage of inducing it, withdraw it back as soon as it comes out. It is not appropriate to let it stay out for long, or to let it see or hear the distant scenes (*jianwen hu yuanjing* 見聞乎遠境). Having regulated it for a long time, its outings may gradually be prolonged before drawing it back. It may then be allowed to view and hear the distant scenes before retracting it. For without such training, the Spirit may, upon being let out all of a sudden, gallop outward only to stray and lose its own nature. So all the early outings must be carefully regulated.[96]

In contrast to the Rapid Advance method, the Gradual Advance approach placed much less exacting requirements on the locale and cosmic synchronization of the practice. It allowed the practitioner to incrementally transform the body through a process known as "unblocking" (*tong* 通) in which the practitioner employed the guided flow of *qi* to penetrate the various imagined hidden passes or loci in the body and unleashed their latent paranormal powers. Chen advised his audience on the practice details at this stage:

After the preliminary practice is completed, there can be a temporary spell or pause. During this period, practitioners may either tour the mountains or waters to enjoy the leisure and comfort or move to reside in the Grotto Heavens and Blessed Lands to nurture the Numinous Nature (*peiyang xingling* 培養性靈). They may also sit quiet all day long or indulge in long sleep. They may eat or not eat.

If the divine efficacy is sought, one must engage in contemplative visualization (*guan xiang* 觀想).[97] Practice it at any time. Most will first achieve the unblocking of the Celestial Eye (*tianyan tong* 天眼通). Next comes the unblocking of the Celestial Ear (*tianer tong* 天耳通). Then followed by the communion with the Destiny (*suming tong* 宿命通). But it is most difficult to attain the unblocking of the Heart of the Other (*taxin tong* 他心通). As for the unblocking of the Free Will (*ruyi tong* 如意通), it comes after the parturition of the Spirit.[98]

Through such graduated processes, the practitioner was believed to be able to gestate the Yin Spirit, which required further refining cultivation before it could become the superior Yang Spirit.[99] The difference between the two was both practical and important:

The Yang Spirit is capable of manifesting its form (*xianxing* 現形) for all to see. It can speak and gesticulate. But the Yin Spirit possesses only the Numinous Resonance (*linggan* 靈感), but without Form and Substance (*xingzhi* 形質). Although it can see other people, it cannot be seen by them. Whereas the Way is intrinsically without phenomena, the Immortals treasure the Form (*Dao ben wuxiang, xian gui youxing* 道本無相, 仙貴有形). So cultivators have traditionally valued the Yang Spirit over the Yin Spirit.[100]

Chen's insistence on the distinction between the Yang and the Yin Spirits reflected the historical trend toward valorizing the Yang in the inner alchemy discourse of the late imperial period. Yet, whereas the traditional valorization of the Yang Spirit mirrored the entrenched social and cultural discrimination against women, Chen's rhetoric about the primacy of the Yang Spirit reflected the complex cultural turmoil and clashes of his own times. Centered on physicality or corporeality, Chen's valorization of the Yang Spirit signified a rejection of what he perceived to be the Buddhist ideal of perfection rather than an affirmation of the gender bias in traditional inner alchemy. Underlying his notion of the Yang Spirit's supremacy over the Yin Spirit was the belief that the Yang Spirit possessed two potencies that made it superior to the Yin Spirit: a tangible Form and Substance, which were verifiable by our senses and even purportedly by science, and a divinely Numinous Resonance, which would defy and even transcend matter as defined by science. Embedded in this conception of the dual properties of the Yang Spirit was Chen's two-pronged criticism of Buddhism and western materialism, as well as his affirmation of the Immortals' Way. In embracing the Form and Substance of the Yang Spirit over the Yin Spirit's lack of substance and formlessness, Chen asserted his valorization of the physicality and materiality of the body as the foundation for attaining immortality and his dissent from the Buddhist rejection of the flesh body. Yet in his affirmation of the unbound freedom and paranormal powers of the Yang Spirit, modern practitioners like Chen revealed their desire to transcend the materialistic excesses they perceived in western science.

But becoming an immortal during the early decades of the twentieth century was for many a tenuous struggle. In many ways, the normative standards of Chen and his fellow cultivators were revealing of the cultural clashes of the times. Although the need for seclusion from the world may have satisfied the technical requirement of the established tradition in inner alchemy, it was certainly not the only option available to practitioners throughout history. Indeed, paralleling the tradition of secluded practice was another tradition that prided itself on mingling the practice with the secular and sought immortality and transcendence by living amid mundane hustle and bustle. The yearnings for seclusion and security as embodied in the site-selection requirements were just as suggestive of the practice's ideals as they were revealing of the harsh political, economic, social, and personal realities modern urban practitioners like Chen had to face.[101]

— 5 —

The Inner Alchemic Community

Birds chirp in cacophony on this remnant of a late spring.
On falling petals and flying catkins, my thoughts
    woefully linger.
With Jiyun dead and Yaofu far away,[1]
How do I bear to hear again words of departure!

Predestined is our fellowship of a decade long;
A tome of *Cantongqi* attests to your transmission.
My preceptor, your departure leaves me solitary and forlorn;
With whom shall I resume the Lead and Mercury discussion?

Learning the Way did not use to require going into
    the mountains;
But how hard it is nowadays to live hidden in a metropolis!
The Grotto Heavens surely have resting places for
    the transcendents;
But when will be the day we share sesame meals?[2]

Never has it been easy to possess companions and funds both;
Year upon year our talk of buying a mountain has come
    to naught.
But as Junping divined and Han Kang sold herbal drugs,
Come hardships and worries, I'll continue to emulate
    them henceforth.

With these lines, Chen Yingning bade Huang Suizhi farewell on a late spring day in the early 1930s. Huang was one of his closest friends and an influential early twentieth-century writer on and adept of inner alchemy. Like Gao Yaofu and Xie Jiyun, who are mentioned in the poem, Huang and Chen were members of a close circle of inner alchemy adepts and enthusiasts. On weekends during the 1920s, this group of fellow practitioners gathered at Chen's residence near the South Market District, just off the Bund in Shanghai. They spent their time together discussing classics of alchemy such as the *Cantongqi* or engaging in alchemic experiments. Clearly intended for the eye of his friends, the poem would have remained private had Chen not chosen to publish it years later in the New Year's issue of the *Yangshan Biweekly*.

Chen's publication of the poem reflected changes in the social and cultural environment surrounding the practice of inner alchemy. The publication of the biweekly made the discussion and practice of inner alchemy much more open and public in the 1930s. The journal appealed directly to its audience. Soon after Chen published this poem, for example, several fellow cultivators responded by contributing verses commiserating with Chen.[3]

Several themes in Chen's poem resonated with the social, economic, and personal conditions of other cultivators. One was the sense of fellowship among the practitioners of inner alchemy that Chen so touchingly revealed in his poem. For many, such fellowship meant companionship, emotional and technical support, and much-needed material resources. As evident in the poem, Chen regarded Huang, the senior adept, as his own preceptor (*xiansheng* 先生), who had passed on special knowledge of the alchemic classic *Cantongqi* during their decade-long association. Fellowship, in addition to discipleship, constituted a venue for the transmission of alchemic knowledge.

The other theme was the shared sense among many practitioners that the pursuit of the elixir was an arduous journey fraught with hardship and poverty and compounded by the worsening political, economic, and social conditions of the 1930s. Although the specific reasons that led to the breakup of the close-knit Shanghai circle of inner alchemists were not explicitly discussed, the circumstances were insinuated in the line "But how hard it is nowadays to live hidden in a metropolis!" The deteriorating conditions in Shanghai were further highlighted by the reference to bygone days when practitioners did not have to take to the mountains.

The normal difficulties of pursuing inner alchemy were further compounded in the late 1920s and the early 1930s. A life dedicated to the pursuit of inner alchemy became a choice of poverty for many. When Chen vowed to emulate Yan Junping 嚴君平 the diviner and Han Kang 韓康 the herbalist of the Han era, he affirmed his commitment to a life of hardships and struggles familiar to many of his fellow cultivators.[4]

The poem also reveals an unmistakable sense of anxiety over the passage of time and the gradual decay of the body. Every passing minute represented a dwindling away of the precious postnatal energy of bodily *qi* and a lost chance for rejuvenation and transcendence.

Yet such a pervasive sense of loss, yearning for fellowship, and resolve in the face of hardships were by no means unique to Chen Yingning. Other members of the Shanghai group wrote in similar terms about their own lives and practice. Their letters, poems, prefaces, and books afford a rare window into their innermost feelings and daily lives. Their writings also reveal that the early practitioners of inner alchemy came from diverse social and economic backgrounds. There were merchants, doctors, traditional landowning literati, government clerks, politicians, male and female Daoists, Buddhist nuns, widows, and even laborers, from nearly all age groups. A few were wealthy, but the majority such as Ms. Dong were not. They turned to the Daoist practice of inner alchemy for diverse personal, religious, and cultural reasons. Some adopted inner alchemy as a means of healing themselves or as a health regimen. Some pursued the practice as a way of discovering solutions to personal problems. Others embraced the practice for answers to existential questions. Still others saw in the practice a way of creating or maintaining their cultural identity and of finding a spiritual alternative to the Confucian and Buddhist traditions or modern science. Most practitioners probably had a mix of reasons.

For many of them, writing about their shared passion for inner alchemy became an important way of affirming their self-worth, representing their self-identity, and communicating with one another.

Their writings, especially their poems and letters, created a common bond that held them together despite the social, economic, and ideological odds against them.

Although they often wrote in prose, Chen Yingning and his fellow practitioners favored poetry as a medium for reflecting on, discussing, recording, and transmitting their practice of inner alchemy. This choice was no accident. Throughout history, the practice of inner alchemy had been intimately linked with poetry. Many early Daoist scriptures were written in rhymed verse. With its rhythms and imagery, poetry seemed especially well equipped to capture and convey the elusive truths encountered in inner alchemy. Since the Song, poetry has been employed as a mnemonic device and contemplative tool by writers and adepts to record and transmit the teachings of inner alchemy. For Chen and his fellow practitioners, poetry performed several vital functions. Many explored and expressed in their poems their experiences and sense of identity as practitioners of inner alchemy. Some employed poetry as a means of discussing and learning about the practice; others composed verses to inspire and console one another. Still others penned thoughts about their aspirations and their setbacks and triumphs.

By sharing experiences, Chen and his fellow cultivators not only entered into one another's lives but also created a common language about the practice, a way of communication and self-expression in which they imagined and represented their practice to themselves and the reading public. This sharing of experience in a common language established and strengthened their sense of identity and community.

Their published writings, letters, and poems also recorded the collective journey of Chen Yingning and his Shanghai group from the early private circles of friends to a public community of practitioners and advocates. As Chen Yingning and his associates openly and increasingly promoted Daoist inner alchemy as a "public" self-cultivation technique in journals and books between the 1910s and the 1940s, the constituency of the practice gradually shifted from a small elite core group of friends and acquaintances to a large and diverse following drawn from among urban residents with varied political, cultural, economic, educational, and religious backgrounds.

In the process, Daoist inner alchemy practice evolved from a primarily private personal pursuit to an increasingly social and public enterprise among its practitioners in the city and beyond.

The Private Circle of Cultivators in the 1920s

As we have seen, Chen's conceptualization of the alchemic body and the Immortals' Learning first developed among a close circle of elite personal friends who shared an interest in self-cultivation pursuits in Shanghai during the 1910s and the 1920s. Some, such as Lü Bicheng and Huang Chanhua, were western-trained or -influenced reform-minded urban intellectuals and professionals; others belonged to the socially and politically conservative traditional and business elite. Among the latter was a small group of eminent former Qing officials and scholars living in Shanghai who had actively participated in the late Qing reforms between 1880s and 1911. But their conservative bent and politics and their loyalism to the Qing court put them at odds with the Republican revolution. Following the time-honored tradition, many refused to serve the new Republican state. Instead they chose to live out their years in Shanghai after 1912. Given his similar artistic and literary tastes and background, native-place ties, scholarly lineage and patronage relationships, and, not least, shared sense of cultural conservatism, Chen Yingning developed close friendships with leading figures among these retired scholar-officials in Shanghai.

The best-known among Chen's senior friends and patrons was Shen Zengzhi 沈曾植 (z. Zipei 子培, h. Xunzai 巽齋, Yi'an 乙盦, and Meisou 寐叟; 1850–1922). Shen came from a long-established literati family in Wuxing 吳興 in Zhejiang. After attaining his *jinshi* degree in 1880, Shen served with distinction in a host of regional administrative offices in several provinces throughout the Jiangnan region. In Chen's native place of Anqing, Shen served as the provincial educational commissioner from 1906 to 1910. For the last two years of his tenure, until his illness forced him to retire, Shen also served concurrently as the acting provincial finance commissioner.[5] In the late nineteenth century, Shen was widely known as an open-minded and dedicated reformer respected and trusted by Kang Youwei and others at the center of the 1898 reforms. Together with Kang and Liang Qichao, Shen was one of the founders of the reformist Self-Strengthening Society (Qiangxue hui 強學會) in Beijing in 1895, and in 1901 served as the superintendent for Nanyang College 南洋公學 in Shanghai, one of the earliest modern educational institutions in China. Equally well versed in the Classics, law, administration, and economics, Shen was a highly regarded polymath. Like earlier reform-minded thinkers such as Wei Yuan 魏源 (z. Moshen 默深; 1794–1857) and Gong Zizhen 龔自珍 (z. Eryu 爾玉, h. Ding'an 定庵; 1792–1841), Shen combined scholarly erudition with the practical concerns of Confucian statecraft in devising strategies and policies for local administration and frontier defense to confront the Tsarist Russian expansion in the Qing northwestern territories. In addition, Shen was a highly regarded calligrapher whose unique and innovative work was widely sought.

Another prominent patron and friend was Zhu Zumou 朱祖謀 (z. Guwei 古微, Huosheng 藿生, h. Ouyi 漚尹, Qiangcun 疆村; 1853–1931), from Zhejiang. Zhu attained the *jinshi* degree in 1883. Like Shen, Zhu began his career at the Hanlin Academy and subsequently served as an academician of the Grand Secretariat (Neige xueshi 內閣學士). He later served as vice minister of the Board of Personnel (Libu shilang 吏部侍郎) at the Guangxu court before he was transferred to the much-coveted post of educational commissioner in Guangdong. There he served from 1902 till 1905, when he resigned from office due to illness. Zhu was an accomplished poet of *ci* 詞 verse and widely revered as one of the four masters of that genre during the late Qing era. In his scholarship, Zhu combined an interest in Daoism with a passion for poetry. Zhu scoured the Daoist Canon and paid particular attention to poems by the northern Song Daoist inner alchemist Zhang Boduan and the Jin Quanzhen Daoist Qiu Chuji 邱處機 (1148 1227) in his famous compendium of poems from the late imperial dynasties.[6]

After the 1911 Revolution, both Shen and Zhu retreated to Shanghai, where they lived and continued to pursue their literary and other interests in retirement. During this period, Chen Yingning frequently called on them at their residences and engaged them in long and wide-ranging conversations. What attracted Chen to them was not merely their erudition and achievements, their cultural conservatism, and their fierce sense of moral loyalism but their shared interest in Daoist self-cultivation practice. Although few of the late Qing loyalist scholar-officials in Shanghai followed the drastic example of Li Ruiqing 李瑞清 (h. Qingdaoren 清道人; 1873–1935), who defied the new Republican state by assuming a Daoist identity,[7] many—Shen and Zhu among them—did feel an affinity toward Daoism during the great social and political upheavals of this period. For many of them, Daoism offered a cultural and spiritual sanctuary. Historically, becoming a Daoist hermit or recluse pursuing self-cultivation was a legitimate alternative for a loyalist official of an overthrown dynasty. This lifestyle allowed such officials to claim spiritual purity and moral superiority by removing themselves from the political fray and centers of power. For Shen and others living in Shanghai, reclusion allowed them to register their dissent from the new Republican state and their continued cultural allegiance to the traditional moral and cosmic order embodied in the Qing. On a practical level, their interest in Daoist self-cultivation techniques also reflected these aging loyalists' desire for health and vigor.

For these and other reasons, the Daoist self-cultivation techniques of quiet sitting and regulated breathing appealed to loyalists like Shen and Zhu. Others such as Wang Pinsan 王聘三 (n.d.) turned to learning the practice. Wang hailed from Sichuan. Like Shen and Zhu, Wang had been a Hanlin academician. He served as an imperial censor at the Guangxu court in the 1890s and the first decade of the 1900s. After retreating to Shanghai following the 1911 Revolution, Wang took up the study of Daoist meditation practices with Chen Yinging in the late 1910s. His sobriquet "Lurking Daoist" (Qiandaoren 潛道人) reflects his commitment to a Daoist lifestyle. At Wang's request, Chen prepared a practice manual composed of a series of annotations and expository lectures based on the *Yellow Courtyard Scriptures*. In 1921, Wang wrote the preface to Chen's manuscript, discussing the importance of the text for the practice from the perspective of his own experience.[8]

Wang was not alone in this. Daoist self-cultivation practice also became part of the daily health regimen and intellectual discourse among many of Chen's senior patrons in Shanghai. At private social and literary gatherings, they discussed the efficacy of the practice in restoring their health and even saving their lives. Chen Yingning recalled that during a visit to the Shen residence, Shen recounted to his audience a vivid account about how he had come to believe in the validity of the Daoist notion of the Lower Cinnabar Field and its life-sustaining potency through a near-fatal illness:

> The Daoists say that the Root of Life of a human lies within the Lower Cinnabar Field. This is by no means a fallacy. I can attest to it through my past experience. My experience came during a bout of illness, not from any practice. When I was young, I contracted typhoid and was dying. There was no breath through my nose. I could not speak, or see and hear through my eyes and ears. I could hardly move my arms and legs. Lying limp there in bed like that, I could yet still feel a thread of roaming *qi* (*yisi youqi* 一絲游氣), just a few inches in length, moving on and off in my lower abdomen. I felt that several times it attempted to depart my body, but snagged on something. I had no sensations at all in the rest of my body. Nor did I have any conscious ideas rising in my heart. I stayed in this state quite some time before coming to. My family told me that I had been without consciousness for over half a day. My regaining consciousness was totally unexpected. Later, I recovered with drugs and care. I have since kept wondering about this experience. Had it not been for that one thread of life-generating *qi* within my Lower Cinnabar Field, my soul would have long been scattered and lost forever (*hunfei posan* 魂飛魄散)! And I would not have lived to this day! So the Daoist theory [of the body] is definitely not fallacious or fanciful.[9]

Shen's sharing of his personal beliefs with his friends is illustrative of the early social context of Chen Yingning's Immortals' Learning. During the 1910s and 1920s, the practice circle remained primarily private and personal. The practice was learned, taught, and transmitted among a close circle of friends and associates at private gatherings. For some, such as Lü Bicheng in Beijing in 1916, the practice provided an alternative way of creating or exploring spirituality and well-being at a time of rapidly changing social and political realities. For the group of politically marginalized Qing loyalist scholar-officials, the practice became a conduit for recovering and reconnecting with their lost cosmic and moral order and simultaneously retaining or regaining personal physical health and vigor.

The Inner Alchemic Community

Fig. 13   Dr. Zhang Zhuming, publisher of *Yangshan Biweekly* and owner of Yihuatang, ca. 1933 (YS, no. 13 [Jan. 1, 1934]: 218).

In the late 1920s and especially in the early 1930s, Chen's private network of friends and fellow cultivators began to expand, first through his and his wife's professional connections and circles and then from 1933 on by way of Chen's ties with the *Yangshan Biweekly*. This new and expanding inner alchemy community included individuals and groups of far more diverse social, economic, cultural, and religious backgrounds from Shanghai, the provinces, and beyond.

Among this growing community was a group of Chen's colleagues and friends at the *Yangshan Biweekly*. Their common interest in Daoist self-cultivation practice bound them into a close-knit community of practitioners, and their professional roles as writers, editors, and contributors for a public journal helped unleash Daoist inner alchemy. From a coterie of friends and associates, it expanded into the public arena. In the process, the social base of the practice grew from private circles into a community and culture open and accessible to the public at large. Aside from Chen Yingning and Dr. Zhang Zhuming 張竹銘 (1905–2004) (Fig. 13), a physician trained at the prestigious Shanghai Deutsch Medical College (Tongji dewen yixuetang 同濟德文醫學堂) and the publisher of *Yangshan Biweekly*, the most active members of the *Yangshan Biweekly* were Chang Zunxian and Wang Boying 汪伯英 (1907–?).

The Expanding Inner Alchemy Community in Shanghai: Profiles of the Practitioners

Chang Zunxian

Chang's journey in pursuit of the elixir and his entry into the Shanghai inner alchemic community were as circuitous as his early travels, first as a landowning literatus in rural Hunan, then as a political reformer and official in the early Republican regime, and finally as a sojourning medical practitioner, poet, and lay Daoist inner alchemist. Chang was from Xiangyin 湘陰 in Hunan. His Daoist-sounding sobriquet Fisherman of the Xiao and Xiang Rivers (Xiaoxiang yufu 瀟湘漁父) was clearly inspired by the rivers of his hometown (see Fig. 14). Coming from a well-to-do family of considerable means and property, Chang was educated at home in the Classics and poetry. At the age of twelve, while preparing for the official examinations, Chang was exposed to Daoist literature by an elderly tutor. He developed an intense interest in Daoist poems. In the 1930s, he recalled that this tutor always kept a set of the writings of the Daoist patriarch Lü Dongbin on his desk. Fascinated with the lore of the legendary immortal, Chang often questioned his tutor on the meanings of the poems attributed to the immortal. That early exposure to Daoism had an indelible influence on Chang.[10]

During the decade preceding the 1911 Revolution, Hunan, like other parts of southern and central China, was rife with reform ideas and anti-Qing revolutionary activities. Although his primary passion at the time remained poetry, Chang became involved in politics. For several years after what he called the Glorious Restoration (*guang fu* 光復), a term revealing the Han-centric nationalist zeal of his times, Chang, in his own words, "traveled around and worked hard for the newly found state" (*benzou guoshi* 奔走國是) throughout southwestern and southern China as a member of the Republican military establishment in Guangdong.[11] In 1918, Chang was assigned to the

The Inner Alchemic Community

Fig. 14 Mr. Chang Zunxian, ca. 1933
(YS, no. 13 [Jan. 1, 1934]: 204)

strategically vital township of Shaoguan 韶關 in northern Guangdong to assist in establishing the local military governor's administration. The following year, he was transferred to a post in Shantou 汕頭 in eastern Guangdong.[12]

After a decade of political activism and public service, Chang withdrew from politics in 1919 following the death of his father. Chang returned to Xiangyin to look after his family. There, Chang observed his filial duties by living in a hut to attend to his father's tomb (*li lumu* 理廬墓) and spent his time compiling the family genealogy. By the mid-1920s, Hunan, like the rest of southern China, became rife with Communist-led peasant movements. In the ensuing peasant uprisings there, Chang and his family lost all their properties and lands to looting and seizure.[13]

Threatened by armed hostilities in his hometown, Chang, like many of his fellow landed gentry, fled to Shanghai in 1932. There, with endorsements from several friends, Chang began to build a medical practice to support his family. According to his sponsors, Chang was an erudite Confucian scholar (*su ru* 宿儒) with more than four decades of experience in the medical arts of Minister Qi and Emperor Huang (*Qi Huang zhi shu* 歧黃之術). Chang's sponsors attributed his motives for practicing medicine to two factors. First, Chang felt that "the world no longer followed the Way of the ancients" (*shifeng bugu* 世風不古); and second, his wife had passed away (*fenglü diaoling* 鳳侶凋零). Consequently, Chang had withdrawn from the world and devoted himself to practicing the Way of medicine, paying no more attention to worldly affairs.[14]

Chang's sponsors were following custom in promoting his practice, but their description is nonetheless revealing of Chang's approach to medicine. For Chang, his medical practice was not only a way to make a living for himself and his family but also a venue for him to rectify and cure the world of its ills. According to his sponsors, Chang advocated populism (*pingmin zhuyi* 平民主義) in his medical practice, in sharp contrast to the prevalent extravagant and lavish lifestyle of his fellow medical practitioners. He responded promptly to the call of patients whether they were rich or poor. He offered free consultations and medicine to the poor in the city. He was also said to have cured many chronic and severe cases, winning the admiration of many of his colleagues. But despite such flattering claims, Chang's medical practice in Shanghai proved unstable. From July 1933 to February 1934, Chang had to move his clinic three times and halved some of his fees in order to attract and retain clients.[15]

Amid these vicissitudes and difficulties, Chang found in inner alchemy a refuge and a source of emotional stability and strength. By his own account, Chang had engaged in the practice for more than forty years by the summer of 1933. Even before and after 1911, when he was working for the Republican cause, Chang had taken full advantage of his extensive travels in southern China and actively searched for adepts and books on inner alchemy. In 1918, while sojourning in southern Guizhou 貴州, Chang had acquired from a friend a rare version of a well-known Five Dynasties classic of inner alchemy. The following spring, when he was stationed in Shantou in eastern Guangdong, Chang sought out a ninety-three-year-old local adept, from whom he obtained a rare version of a poem often attributed to Lü Dongbin. That same year, Chang spent some time with a fellow practitioner by the Tuo River 沱江 in Shantou in order to disentangle the meaning of this obscure poem on inner alchemy.[16]

While struggling to make a living in Shanghai between 1932 and 1936, Chang devoted his spare time to his inner alchemic practice by developing friendships with other adepts, by engaging in various practice activities, and by reflecting and writing about his inner alchemy practice. Most likely through his medical colleagues, Chang first became acquainted Dr. Zhang Zhuming, the owner of the Yihuatang publishing house in Shanghai. Sometime in 1932, when Dr. Zhang was planning the *Yangshan Biweekly*, Chang met Chen Yingning.

Their initial meeting gradually flowered into a close, lasting fellowship. Their shared literati background and their mutual admiration for one another's erudition, abilities, and dedication drew them together. They meditated together, commiserating with each other's hardships while encouraging the other in his practice. In a poem that celebrated one of their joint nocturnal meditation sessions, Chang comforted a disheartened Chen, who, in his own poem marking the same occasion, had expressed anguish over his advancing age and his dim prospects for alchemic success in a time of great political and social turmoil:

> Grieve not over your half-gray sideburns.
> At this age, Laozi went through the Hangu Pass.[17]
> What mortal affairs of the Dust weigh in the heart of a
>   feathered guest?[18]
> Woeful it is to drift and roam on a forlorn path in times
>   of chaos!
> The Way and your Heart are harmonized with *qi*, thin
>   as silk,
> The Furnace for the Perfected Son is ready for firing.
> Unknown to all, my Master, what a consummate recluse
>   you are!
> In the fall, your Millet Pearl will ripen to fill up the
>   Li hexagram.[19]

Composed as a response to Chen, Chang's poem resonated with his own experiences pursuing the elixir. As an aspiring "feathered traveler" like Chen, Chang also felt the crushing weight of "mortal affairs" that impeded his own progress toward transcendence. Like his friend, Chang was fast approaching the critical age of sixty. He had lost all his family properties and lands in Hunan to the Communist-led peasant insurgencies. He had yet to manage to earn a living from his medical practice in the city.

The disruption and chaos of his private life were deeply embedded in the greater social and political turmoil of the early 1930s, and Chang's sense of forlornness and his drifting sojourn in Shanghai mirrored metaphorically his own alienation from the Daoist practice of self-transformation and the separation of the original *qi* from the original *shen* within his body. In that sense, Chang's encouragement of Chen was also a self-prodding call to himself to engage in the practice of "harmonizing the Way, the Heart, and *qi*" (*dao xin he qi* 道心和氣), so that both could rejuvenate their gray sideburns and mature the Pearl of Millet (*shu zhu* 黍珠), which was believed to lead to an immortal embryo personified as the Perfected Son (*zhen zi* 眞子). By adhering to the personal practice of uniting the *qi* and *shen* in the body, the order and harmony of the external world might also be regained and the Way restored to society. It was this vision of the practice that sustained Chang despite all adversities in his personal life.

From 1933 to 1940, Chang worked alongside Cheng Yingning as one of the handful of special contributing editors for the *Yangshan Biweekly* and its successor, the *Xiandao Monthly*. He published three annotated works on the practice of inner alchemy, two of which were serialized in the *Biweekly*. Chang also wrote many poems about his own practice. Chang's passion for poetry written by early Daoist patriarchs and practitioners of inner alchemy became a venue for him to represent his personal practice and perspective on Daoist inner alchemy. In the summer of 1934, Chang published a set of poems in which he reflected on the various subtle aspects and stages of inner alchemic practice. Dwelling on the subtlety of the firing moment (*huo hou* 火候), a critical time when the practitioner must know and act to capture the rising *qi* within the body for transformation, Chang mused in a poem matching the rhymes of a poem by the Ming master of inner alchemy Cao Huanyang 曹還陽 (1562–?):

> Neither tender nor overdone, when the Great Elixir rises in the furnace;
> The True Mechanism activates to let the Spirit know.

Match the timing by cycling *qi* along the Heavenly Orbit;
Do not let an iota of the Original Yang escape.[20]

While sojourning in Shanghai in the 1930s, Chang continued "roaming" (*lang you* 浪遊) and cultivated an extensive network of friends and fellow practitioners who shared his passion for inner alchemy. Chang managed to find the time and resources to journey to prearranged locations to meet with fellow practitioners and discuss and engage in inner alchemy practice. In 1936, one of Chang's fellow practitioners was a ninety-six-year-old man who went by the sobriquet A Disciple of Mount Heng's Cloud (Hengyun sheng 衡雲生). Early in his life, Hengyun had served as a eunuch at the Qing court. After 1911, he retreated to Mount Heng, where he lived as a recluse. In the fall of 1935 and the following year, during a stay at home in Xiangyin, Chang journeyed twice to Hengyun's retreat deep in the Southern Marchmont (Nanyue 南嶽). There they joined in a rigorous practice of fasting and meditation that lasted for several days. Outside their practice sessions, the two spent their time discussing and exchanging experiences.[21]

Between these mountain retreats, Chang exchanged poems by mail with his fellow practitioners as a means of jointly exploring the practice. Many of these poems were published in the *Yangshan* and *Xiandao* magazines. In one verse, published in the winter of 1938, a mutual friend of Hengyun and Chang from Hunan posited a query to Hengyun about the location of the Yellow Courtyard, the vital center of the body:

> Yearning for restoring the elixir, I ask you the Enlightened;
> Master Hengyun's instruction is like that of a living immortal.
> In the Furnace and Cauldron, boil and refine the waters of
>   the Xiao and Xiang,[22]
> In the Square Inch, sift and purify the Pine and Cypress Spring.[23]
> The Bamboo Post behind your backyard is the place for
>   Pure Cultivation;
> And the humble Penglai Hut is your Supreme Empyrean.
> Using words as means of learning, pray:
> Is the Yellow Courtyard the Upper Cinnabar Field?[24]

Like many among the community of practitioners, Hengyun's friend was concerned about the aging and decay of the body. In his intricate play of poetic images, the Old Man on the Lake (Hushang sou 湖上叟) envisioned his friend Hengyun's body as a small cosmos wherein alchemic processes of self-transformation took place. In this imagined cosmos, Hengyun's body became the refining cauldron where the waters of the Xiao and Xiang rivers were "boiled and refined" and the stream from the Pine and Cypress Spring was "sifted and purified." Even Hengyun's humble mountain residence was imagined as a sanctuary for "pure cultivation" and a sacred space of the "Supreme Empyrean." Seeking instruction from such a living immortal seemed only natural and appropriate.

Deferring to Chang's erudition on inner alchemy, Hengyun turned to his friend for a response on his behalf. Chang offered his own poetic response patterned in rhyme to match the inquiring poem in both wit and imagination:

> Fortuitously, you pass me the query about the Great Way;
> Yet your cherubic face puts even the grotto immortals
>   to shame.
> Purify the Heart so that there will be no more nightmares;
> Sit still till your tongue is moistened with the sweet spring.[25]
> Cycle the River Crafts along the Triple Pass Route without
>   a stop,[26]
> Until an aperture opens to a view of the Hidden Moon Heaven.
> In no time, seek to shelter and nourish the returned elixir
> In the Yellow Court, which is buoyant near the Center
>   Cinnabar Field.

In this reply, Chang likened his friend's youthful complexion to that of a grotto immortal in an advanced state of bodily transformation. Chang also outlined the techniques of the practice that may have lead to Hengyun's unusually youthful appearance and provided a map for properly locating the Yellow Courtyard within the body. He imagined the body as a physical landscape with Three Passes, through which the flow of the cycling *qi*, here vividly embodied as the Triple River Crafts (*san che* 三車), flowed. By persisting in the practice of "sitting still" (*ju heng* 居恆), the practitioner could "purify the heart of its nightmares" and cause the flow of *qi* to rise in the body so as to moisten the tongue. With ceaseless cycling of the *qi* "crafts" through the passes, all the passes and loci within the body would one day be unblocked, and the recycled *qi* could return to the Central Cinnabar Field, here euphemistically called the Hidden Moon Heaven (*yan yue tian* 偃月天). In this central locus, the refined *qi* flow would be "sheltered and nourished" further before the final sublimation and transformation of the body in the sacred locus of the Yellow Courtyard, which was appropriately located nearby.

In the late 1930s when social and political conditions worsened in Shanghai and the rest of the country, Chang left his medical practice in the city and returned to Hunan. From his hometown in Xiangyin, Chang continued working for the *Biweekly*. He regularly contributed poems and articles and persevered in his pursuit of inner alchemy. In a 1937 verse commemorating an excursion to Mount Heng, Chang imaginatively merged the physical landscape of the alchemic body with the natural scenery he encountered on the Southern Marchmont, one of the five major sacred mountains in China:

> At the South Heavenly Gate I linger to gaze at the Divine Realm:[27]
> How many years of human tumult and strife have passed!
> One hundred twenty Gen peaks entwine in attendance;[28]
> Nine Kan streams flow against the current.[29]
> Lovingly, the fragrant mist hangs around the Cypress of Lord Heng.[30]
> Drop by drop, the dew moistens the Scarlet Son's Palace.[31]
> Once in contact with one Grain of Cinnabar in the Grotto,[32]
> No more need to dig for rhizomes on Zhu Rong's Peak.[33]

In this poem, Chang's excursion through the natural landscape of the sacred mountain parallels the internal journey of the *qi* in the body. As Chang began his hike up Mount Heng, he was also embarking on a spiritual journey that was physically embedded in both the natural landscape and his own body. The natural world of Mount Heng was a sacred universe inhabited by immortals and deities like Zhu Rong 祝融, the Fire God, and the Lord of the Southern Marchmont. The occasion of entering such a sacred domain was a sufficiently solemn cause for any mortal to pause and "linger" and even "gaze" back at the human world that he was about to leave behind. Yet as Chang stood at the scenic viewpoint of the South Heavenly Gate, gazing at the world beyond Mount Heng, the Divine Realm (*shenzhou* 神州) of China was hardly divine any more. The vista that came to his mind's eye was one of years of "human tumult and strife" (*renshi fenfen* 人事紛紛), from the collapse of the Qing court, which Chang had worked hard to topple, through the chaos of the post-Republican warlordism, which he loathed, to the outbreak of the rural revolts in Hunan, which drove him from home and brought ruin to his family.

Turning away from the tumultuous world outside, the views to be gained on the mountain assuaged Chang's mind and body. As the vista of the surrounding Gen peaks and the surging Kan streams provided visual relief to the eyes, their names and topography also invoked inner alchemic processes that would replenish and harmonize the *qi* energies of the body. The words *gen zhi* 艮止 in the name of the peak mean literally to "dwell and pause," a term subtly hinting at the inner alchemic meditative technique of Dwelling on the Back (*gen bei* 艮背) popularized by the late Ming syncretist Lin Zhao'en 林兆恩 (1517–98) and the inner alchemist Cao Heng. This meditative method aimed at creating optimal health and balance of *qi* in the body by harmonizing the energies of the Heart and the Kidneys. The image of the Kan streams flowing against the current suggests the practice of "reversing or going against the current" (*ni chaoliu* 逆潮流) in Daoist inner alchemy.

The images of Chang's poem were also reminiscent of the somatic effects of alchemic processes described in the classical literature of inner alchemy, such as the lingering mist and dripping dew, which signified the harmonization between the Kidney Water and the Heart Fire. As discussed in Chapter 2, the mist and dew hovered over or cascaded downward to nourish the viscera within, embodying the reinvigorated flow of the *qi* energies in the body. These classical icons of the cycling *qi* flow were vividly insinuated into the natural scenes that entered Chang's view: the "fragrant mist" hovering around the towering cypress of Lord Heng, which became a visual symbol of the Heart Fire, and the dripping dew moistening the

Scarlet Son's Pavilion, another emblem of the Heart in coition with the Water of the Kidneys.

Next, the coagulation of the elixir resulting from the union between the Heart and the Kidneys, known in inner alchemy as "harmony of Water and Fire" (*shui huo jiji* 水火既濟), was wonderfully transposed onto the natural scenes before Chang's eyes in the poem. Inspired by the name of a cave on the mountain, Chang referred to the coagulated elixir metaphorically as the "one Grain of Cinnabar" (*zhusha yi li* 珠砂一粒) and located it "inside the Grotto" (*dong li* 洞裏), a locale invoking the locus of the Lower Cinnabar Field in the body, where the gestated elixir was further nourished. As the gestated elixir ripened in the body and the practitioner's dependence on food was reduced, he no longer needed to venture out to dig more rhizomes (*zhu* 朮) for food. Thus as the external visual journey reached the apex of the Zhu Rong Peak, so did the alchemic voyage of the *qi* within the body terminate in the Lower Cinnabar Field. By traversing scenic sites on the mountain and the somatic landscape within the body, Chang broke down the dichotomy between the self and the world by enmeshing and harmonizing the two in the poem.

As part of his practice back home in Hunan, Chang also continued to search and prospect for a locale where he hoped to settle down and advance his practice of inner alchemy in the future. He traveled twice to Mount Heng, the Daoist sacred mountain, to seek land on which to build a thatched hut as his own cultivation retreat. In the spring of 1937, Chang wrote Chen Yingning about these excursions:

My dear brother,

I have journeyed twice to Mount Heng but still have not finalized on a good place yet. Although Hengyun has built his own grotto heaven there and insisted on my staying there with him, I still have some family affairs to take care of. But once I get these matters settled, I plan to pay another visit to Hengyun at the Grotto of Cinnabar, where I plan to build a thatched hut for storing rice and rhizomes. It leans against some ancient cypress trees and is thus a true place for cultivating perfection. The lot is quite large. I will tell you more about it in due time.[34]

Wang Boying

Chang's junior colleague at the *Biweekly*, Wang Boying 汪伯英 (1907–?), whose sobriquet Zhizhen 志眞 means "aspiring for perfection," was born in a family of modest means in Wuxi 無錫, in Jiangsu. He managed to receive a rudimentary education in the Classics and learned to write poems. When he was fourteen years old, his family's already strained finances took an even worse turn. In 1921, Wang had to abandon his formal education and become an apprentice at a local herbal medicine shop. A year or two later, Wang developed a condition known as spleen leakage, or splenohorrhea (*pixie* 脾泄), a spleen disorder accompanied by chronic diarrhea. By the time he reached seventeen, Wang's condition improved but only to give way to recurring nocturnal emissions. His doctors diagnosed him as suffering from a terminal exhaustion of both the spleen and the kidneys and beyond medical help (*pishen liangshang, sun xiang yicheng, buke jiuyao* 脾腎兩傷, 損象已成, 不可救藥). Wang abandoned his apprenticeship and turned to the study of the Chinese medical classics in search of a cure. Years later he recalled how he first became aware of Daoist learning in medical classics such as the *Inner Canon*:

> When I read in the *Inner Canon* about the Celestial Perfection of the Primordial Times, about the Invigorating Qi and uniting with Heaven, and about the Four Qi regulating the Spirit, I first came to know the existence of Perfected Men and Consummated Men (*zhiren* 至人), and to understand how to accumulate Essence to solidify *qi* (*jijing quanqi* 積精全氣) and how to conserve and nourish the body according to the change of seasons (*anshi baoquan* 按時保全).[35]

Intrigued by what he read, Wang soon began to experiment with various meditative regimens. He tried the popular quiet-sitting method widely publicized by Jiang Weiqiao. Wang recalled that he was particularly impressed with Jiang's claim that one could practice even without the guidance of an adept. As he followed Jiang's quiet-sitting method in his daily practice, he soon found to his surprise that his chronic syndrome of splenetic emission was "gone." Even the nocturnal emissions abated. Encouraged, Wang felt he was on the right track toward a cure. From 1927 to 1930, Wang devoted himself to the study of Daoist classics of inner alchemy. But because of the difficult and obscure language of these texts, Wang was anxious to find a teacher who could help. But his efforts came to naught. In 1930, at the age of twenty-three, in deference to his father's wishes, Wang got married. But only one year into the marriage, his wife died during labor.

Deeply grieved, Wang took his wife's death as a sign from heaven that he should devote the rest of his life to pursuing transcendence. That same year, he took a vow of celibacy and began to practice vegetarianism. He also started to observe Buddhist rules voluntarily and was particularly keen on the Buddhist practice of "liberating life" (*fang sheng* 放生) by releasing captured animals. Many of his Pure Land Buddhist friends regarded his self-imposed and overtly Buddhist regimen as a sign of his predestined bond with the Buddhist faith and tried to convert him. But displeased with what he perceived to be a Buddhist attack on Daoism, Wang resisted efforts by others to enroll him in the Buddhist sect led by the renowned master Yinguang. Instead, he enrolled in the Common Benevolence Society in his hometown and sought teaching on self-cultivation practice there. But Wang soon discovered that the society's teachings on the body and the practice did not match those he had read in the Daoist classics. Furthermore, his nocturnal emissions did not improve, even though he followed the practice scrupulously. He became doubtful.

In 1933 he learned of the *Yangshan Biweekly*. Wang soon became an avid reader and a contributor. He was particularly impressed with Chen Yingning's articles and books on Daoist inner alchemy, which were published serially in the *Biweekly*. Later he recalled his early reaction to reading some of Chen's writings in the journal:

I am truly graced with Master Yingning's candor and openness. In our very first meeting, he cleared up 70 percent of all the questions I had. Later, after I was formally initiated as one of his disciples, all the questions I had raised were clarified instantly. Ever since that moment, I have come to a true understanding of the saying: "Having intuited the Way at dawn, one does not regret dying at dusk."[36]

In the summer of 1934, Wang was hired by Dr. Zhang Zhuming to serve as a contributing editor to the *Biweekly*. His new position allowed him to work alongside Chen Yingning, from whom he often sought teachings on his practice and the classics of Daoist inner alchemy.[37]

In August 1934, shortly after Wang joined the *Biweekly*, his father died. With a widowed mother and a younger brother to support at home, Wang had to leave his job and return to Wuxi.[38] There Wang faced the pressure of having to support his family while maintaining his own fragile health. In a poem published after his return to Wuxi, Wang reflected on the tribulations of his life and vowed to persevere in the practice in order to achieve immortality:

> Living in the world is like sorting a tangled web of silk.
> The time of liberation is not yet known.
> Although I have known the Being within the Nonbeing,[39]
> I must not depart from it even for an instant.[40]

Unwavering in his convictions, Wang persisted in the practice. In his spare time, Wang wrote profusely on the subject of the practice as one of the regular contributing editors of the *Biweekly*. His writings on the inner alchemic practice, his commentaries on Daoist classics, and his correspondence with readers made him one of the most visible and active members of the inner alchemy community centered on the *Biweekly*.

But the "tangled web" of the world kept getting in the way of Wang's passionate pursuit. The Japanese invasion and his own daily struggle to support his family combined to undermine his practice. As the political and social situation in Wuxi and the Jiangnan region deteriorated under the Japanese occupation in 1941, Wang persevered. He wrote to a fellow practitioner about how he had adapted his practice to the worsened conditions and what he hoped for the future:

> Right now my daily work is very busy. I am no longer paying much attention to any of the practices such as the Greater and the Lesser Orbits of Heaven. At night, I conduct only the practice of Refining the Form in the True Void (*zhenkong lianxing* 眞空煉形) so as to reach the state of Heel Breathing.[41] As for the rest of the techniques, I will have to abandon them for now. I feel that this approach has benefited both my body and mind.

As for the more advanced practice, as soon as the current situation is pacified and my family affairs are taken care of, I will secure a quiet place and practice at full steam. It will not be difficult for me to achieve success.[42]

Expanding the Community of Inner Alchemic Practice: The 1930s and 1940s

With the publication of the *Yangshan Biweekly* in 1933, Chen, Chang, and Wang began to reach beyond the close circles of Daoist inner alchemic practitioners to a much larger audience. Through the journal, their vision of the Immortals' Learning and the practice began to evolve from private pursuit to a public endeavor. Along the way, the social base of the practice also expanded into a diversified community of individuals and groups from different social, cultural, geographical, and religious backgrounds.

The expansion of the inner alchemic network in Shanghai benefited from the location of the *Yangshan Biweekly* in the busiest district of Shanghai. Until the fall of 1938, when the Japanese occupied much of Shanghai, both the business and the editorial offices of the *Biweekly* were headquartered at the Yihuatang Bookstore at No. 18 Yuyuan Road near the City God Temple (Yimiao 邑廟) in the heart of the South Market District. Even after the editorial office of the *Biweekly* was relocated for safety's sake to Haining Road in the French Concession in the fall of 1938, the Yihuatang still maintained its bookstore and business office in the heart of this longtime Chinese business district. The late nineteenth-century economic boom in the International Settlement and French Concession to the north had decreased the commercial importance of the South Market District. But with the demolition of the Chinese city wall in 1914, the district gradually became reintegrated into the fast-paced economic development and expansion of the city.[43] In the early Republican era, even while losing some of its luster as a hub of trade and commerce, the South Market District retained its status as one of the city's main centers of ritual life. It was home to the City God Temple dominated by the Zhengyi Daoist ritual specialists and the White Cloud Monastery, a bastion of the celibate Quanzhen clerics. The area was also home to many merchant guilds, native-place associations, philanthropic and professional organizations, and secret societies such as the Green Gang. Chen and his colleagues on the *Biweekly* thus worked amid one of the busiest centers of commercial, religious, and other forms of human traffic in the city.

In this social and cultural milieu, the Immortals' Learning movement and the community of inner alchemic practitioners grew and flourished in Shanghai during the 1930s and 1940s. As the community expanded, it attracted Republican government officials, urban intellectuals and scholars, sojourning merchants, teachers, doctors, scientists, young college students, landlords, laborers, men and women, Daoist and Buddhist clerics, and lay practitioners belonging to a variety of redemptive societies. Although many worked and lived in the city, a large number of them hailed from geographically diverse urban and rural regions outside Shanghai. These practitioners and institutions became associated with Chen Yingning and his colleagues through their shared interest in Daoist inner alchemy and were bound together through their common experience of reading, discussing, and circulating the *Yangshan* and *Xiandao* journals.

In Shanghai, Chen's association with the members of this community was often initiated by, and then maintained through, personal contacts and common acquaintances. Building on face-to-face meetings, exchanges of letters and poems, mutual visits, shared outings, and other social or personal occasions, an informal fellowship of inner alchemic practice gradually emerged during the late 1930s, connecting many individual lay and monastic self-cultivators both in Shanghai and in other parts of China.

The Hall of Practicing Benevolence: Fujian Merchant Sojourners

Located near the Shanghai Railway Station in the northwestern part of the city, the Hall of Practicing Benevolence was a native-place association that drew its membership from sojourners and merchants from western Fujian. Many of them were paper merchants, tea traders, lawyers, government officials, and other urban professionals from the province.[44] Prominent among the Fujian group were several educated men skilled in the quiet-sitting practice and other self-cultivation techniques: Wu Minzhai 吳敏齋 (z. Jingxu 靜虛), his brother Wu Zhuyuan 吳竹園 (h. Wuyu 無餘), and Deng Yucang, all of whom were natives of the Liancheng region in western Fujian.

Situated in hilly western Fujian adjacent to Jiangxi province to its west, Liancheng was known for its exports of high-quality paper, tea, mushrooms, and other dried foodstuffs derived from the bamboo and pine forests on its mountains. Because the local terrain and soil were ill-suited for agriculture, the region had historically depended on imports of textiles, cooking oils, and other daily necessities.[45] From the mid-nineteenth century, the Liancheng paper trade, which had traditionally supplied the imperial capital of Beijing and overseas markets in southeast Asia, expanded to emerging treaty ports such as Shanghai and Fuzhou, which needed premium paper. To cope with the rising demand, a local cooperative of paper producers was formed in 1874. From the 1870s to the 1920s, total exports of Liancheng paper nearly doubled. This high volume continued throughout the 1930s.[46]

This flourishing trade in paper, tea, and other goods from Liancheng led to the importing of new religious beliefs and practices from the outside world. In the first two decades of the twentieth century, as both new and traditional sectarians cults such as the Common Benevolence Society and the Way of the Anterior Heaven spread to Liancheng, a variety of self-cultivation practices and techniques proliferated among the local populace. In the early 1900s, Li Yunxiang 李雲翔, the head of a local chapter of the Common Benevolence Society and a compatriot of Deng Yuchang from Xinquan 新泉, was among the first to learn the quiet-sitting practice. He became acquainted with quiet sitting in Fuzhou, the provincial capital. In 1919, when Li returned to Liancheng, he transmitted the practice to over one hundred of his followers at the local chapters of the society in Liancheng county. Around the turn of the century, Huang Faqian 黃發千 and Huang Youkuan 黃有寬, two leaders of a local syncretist sect, the Way of the Perfected Void (Zhenkong dao 眞空道), studied quiet sitting in southern Jiangxi, a bastion of the Daoist sect known as the Pure and Bright Way of Loyalty and Filial Piety (Jingming zhongxiao dao 淨明忠孝道) since the thirteenth century. Upon their return to Liancheng in 1920, the two Huangs began to teach the practice in Liancheng and its outlying townships and villages. Thanks to practitioners like Li and the Huangs, quiet sitting soon spread throughout the region.[47]

The practice caught on with many of Liancheng's merchants and literati elite. In Wenheng 文亨, an outlying town south of Liancheng, the two brothers Wu Minzhai and Wu Zhuyuan became devoted practitioners of the quiet-sitting practice associated with the Way of the Anterior Heaven. The Wu brothers came from a family of landowners and merchants, which afforded them a good education in the Classics. In Wenheng, they formed a voluntary practice group known as the Hall of Practicing Benevolence and actively promoted quiet sitting in Liancheng. The local network of self-cultivation practice spread south from Wenheng to the township of Xinquan, where one of Huang Faqian's disciples had actively proselytized their version of Buddho-Daoist quiet sitting in the 1920s. There, both Deng Yuchang and his brother became avid practitioners and teachers of the practice. Deng had previously served in the legal profession, but he was said to have abandoned his official post in favor of self-cultivation in the manner of ancient recluses like Tao Hongjing.[48]

A shared interest in quiet sitting soon brought all these practitioners together. Many regarded Wu Minzhai, the most senior and experienced of the Liancheng group, as their mentor. Toward the late 1920s, the business activities and meditation practices of the Liancheng elite were violently disrupted by the fledgling Communist-led peasant movement in western Fujian and neighboring Jiangxi. In May 1929, Red Army troops under Mao Zedong and Zhu De 朱德 (1886–1976) occupied Xinquan and established a host of local soviets throughout the region. The strategic town of Xinquan became the center of the soviet government in western Fujian.[49] Many of the Liancheng business and professional elite fled for safety to big cities such as Shanghai, where their business and personal networks could provide both moral and material support during their prolonged exile. There, many like the Wu brothers and Deng Yuchang became sojourners. Many were not able to return home until the spring of 1934, when the Nationalist-led military campaigns gradually dislodged and drove the Communist-led Red Army and local guerrilla forces from the region.

As the Wu brothers and other members of the Liancheng merchant and professional elite such as Deng Yuchang resettled in Shanghai during the 1920s and the early 1930s, they introduced their homegrown religious practices to their compatriots in Shanghai. In neighborhoods around the Shanghai Railway Station, where many business sojourners from western Fujian congregated, the Wu brothers and their fellow businessmen revived their Hall of Practicing Benevolence and continued their collective quiet-sitting practice there.

During their unexpectedly long sojourn in Shanghai, Wu, Deng, and many other Fujian sojourners became readers of the *Yangshan Biweekly*, and through it they came to know Chen and his visions of the Immortals' Learning and inner alchemic practice. They became both subscribers and contributors to the journal and were actively involved in supporting a variety of projects aimed at promoting and spreading the Immortals' Learning.

Shanghai's Urban Cultural Elite

Outside the sojourning communities, the Shanghai community of Immortals' Learning advocates and inner alchemic practitioners also spread among other urban cultural, political, business, and religious groups in the city. Huang Chanhua and his wife, who are introduced in Chapter 2, are two examples. While living in Shanghai in the 1910s, Huang and his wife stayed with the Chens at their residence on Minguo Road in the Yu Garden District. On weekends when Chen's fellow self-cultivation practitioners gathered to watch the Chens carrying out alchemical experiments in his makeshift laboratory, Huang and his wife would join the group. The discussions on Daoist alchemy and self-cultivation practice would continue late into the night. As Huang's interest in Daoism and self-cultivation grew, he and Chen even discussed plans to purchase land on a Daoist sacred mountain and build self-cultivation retreats for themselves and their fellow practitioners. In 1919, while vacationing in the summer retreat of Mount Lu, the Chens and the Huangs seriously searched for potential sites. Chen Yingning prolonged his stay on the mountain so that he could conduct further surveys and prospect for the best site for their self-cultivation retreat. He even drew up construction plans and drafted bylaws for the retreat.[50]

Also active in the expanding circle of practitioners were a few prominent intellectuals and scholars, such as the Confucian polymath Ma Yifu 馬一孚 (z. Yifu 一浮, h. Zhanweng 湛翁; 1883–1967). Born in Chengdu, Sichuan, Ma grew up in a learned family. He excelled in Confucian learning as a youth. After achieving the *xiucai* degree in his native town of Shaoxing in 1898, Ma's reputation as a literary virtuoso began to spread among the Zhejiang literary elite. He later studied English, French, and Latin and read widely in western philosophy, literature, and history at the Jiangnan Arsenal's Institute of Foreign Languages in Shanghai. In 1909, Ma, together with Xie Wuliang 謝無量 (1884–1964) and Ma Junwu, began publishing an influential series of translated western classics in Shanghai. He played a pivotal role in introducing western philosophy, literature, history, and science to China. After a brief stint in the Qing embassy in the United States and a study tour in Japan between 1903 and 1905, Ma returned to Hangzhou, where he spent three years immersed in the study of the Chinese classics in the Siku collection at the Buddhist Shengyin Temple scriptorium. This immersion in the classical studies convinced Ma that the Confucian Six Arts (Liu yi 六藝) encompassed the whole range of human knowledge and learning, including western science. Ma's wide literary interests led him to pursue the study of Daoist classics as well, especially *Zhuangzi* and the *Book of Changes*. In his private life, Ma became interested in self-cultivation practice and collected the classic works of Daoist inner alchemy. In the summer of 1935, Ma traveled with Chen Yingning and Dr. Zhang Zhuming to Tiantai Mountain in eastern Zhejiang, where they visited Daoist and Buddhist temples and searched for sites to buy for a practice retreat.[51]

A few examples of urban practitioners will serve to show the diversity of their backgrounds. Gao Guanru 高觀如 (1906–79) was a writer and Buddhologist trained in Japan. He returned to Shanghai in 1930 and thereafter made a living writing books on the history of Buddhism. In his spare time, Gao pursued his interest in Daoist self-cultivation. Shen Linsheng 沈霖生, a mineralogist by training, actively pursued research in early Daoist alchemic practices and gave a lecture to a western audience in Shanghai on the connections between early Daoist alchemic practices and modern chemistry and metallurgic processes. Fang Gongpu 方公溥 was a young and talented practitioner from Yiwu 義烏 county in Zhejiang. A specialist in traditional Chinese medicine, Dr. Fang combined his self-cultivation practice with his medical practice and adopted what he called *qigong* 氣功 healing as a therapeutic tool. Later, in 1938, Dr. Fang published an influential treatise on medical healing *qigong* and established his own clinic in Shanghai.[52]

Many of these urban professionals became practitioners and advocates of Immortals' Learning through their personal and professional connections with Chen Yingning and his wife, Dr. Wu Yizhu. Dr. Wu shared her husband's passion for Daoist self-cultivation, a passion triggered by her childhood fascination with Daoist lore about the elixir and divine immortals. While attending medical college in Shanghai in 1908, she became acquainted with Chen Yingning, in whom Wu found an understanding partner and a knowledgeable adept. Chen's erudition and his passion for the Immortals' Learning deeply impressed her and vindicated her own belief in Daoism. Her marriage to Chen in 1916 further cemented their partnership in the pursuit of Daoist learning and practice. Outside her work from 1916 through the 1930s, Dr. Wu regularly hosted weekend gatherings at their house on Minguo Road, which attracted many of their fellow professionals and became a venue for practitioners in the city over the years.

One of Dr. Wu's colleagues was Dr. Zhu Changya 朱昌亞 (1896–?), an American-trained gynecologist at the Shanghai Renhe Hospital (Shanghai renhe yiyuan 上海人和醫院) during the 1920s. Even though well educated in modern western medicine, Dr. Zhu never felt content. She became one of the frequent participants at the Chens' weekend gatherings and developed a close friendship with Dr. Wu. The two shared an interest in Daoist practice. From 1920 to 1935, they explored the Daoist art of physiognomy and spirit-writing. They also sought instruction from a renowned Daoist diviner at the busy City God Temple in the South Market District. Dr. Zhu was said to have been particularly impressed and influenced by the prognostications this diviner made about her own future.[53] Dr. Wu's and

Dr. Zhu's friendship and shared interests sustained both through difficult times.

In the early fall of 1936, after Dr. Wu was diagnosed with breast cancer, she and Chen Yingning moved to the rural suburbs of western Shanghai to allow her to recuperate. Separated from her colleagues and fellow practitioners, Dr. Wu kept in touch with Dr. Zhu through an exchange of poems. In one poem, Wu recalled their shared days of happiness and friendship and pondered her own illness and its impact on her quest for immortality:[54]

> Since I parted from you, my dear friend,
> The moon is today again full and round.
> Touched I am by your deep friendship
> And your appreciation of me as different from the mundane.
> How we used to join our beds to share joyous dreams;
> And ride in the same car to gain a view of the scenery!
> Caring for my frail body, you took off your coat;
> To quench my parched throat, you shared your drink and food.[55]
> At dusk, my sadness presses, overwhelming;
> As my anguish deepens, the illness does not heal.
> Alas, far and distant is the road to immortality!
> How melancholy is this sky of Shanghai in autumn!
> It's difficult to convey my sense through writing,
> For there is no postman to entrust with the letter.
> With Bai Shi we once consulted on the Mysterious meanings;[56]
> I expect the Muddy Water to turn into a clear stream.[57]
> Where is the place worthy of our retreat?
> We will seek out the famous mountains for retreat.[58]
> Let us look forward to another Double Ninth
> When we shall both ascend to the highest tower, hand in hand.[59]

With renewed resolve, Dr. Wu carried on her practice of female alchemy. But as the Japanese occupation spread from Shanghai to its western suburbs in the fall of 1937, the quiet and semi-secluded life of the Chens came to an end. The couple fled into the safe haven of the French Concession in western Shanghai, leaving all their possessions and valuables behind. As their living conditions worsened in the overcrowded and inflation-ridden concession, Dr. Wu had to resume working at her old hospital. Before long her cancer returned, and she was hospitalized after 1941. Yet she continued with her regimen of female alchemy while in the hospital. In the spring of 1945, Dr. Wu died, almost a decade after she was first diagnosed with cancer.[60]

Wu's passion for Daoist self-cultivation inspired Zhu Changya. In a letter to Chen Yingning, Dr. Zhu deplored the limits of modern medicine because it could not solve the fundamental problem of life and death. She vowed to pursue the learning and practice of the Divine Immortals (*shenxian zhi xueshu* 神仙之學術). Chen Yingning wrote a warm response of encouragement and support.[61]

Dr. Zhu's interest in the practice was fueled by a sense of crisis in her personal life. When she wrote Chen in the fall of 1936 to query him on the practice of female inner alchemy, she had just reached forty and was contemplating new directions in her life and career. In a poem revealingly entitled "Musings to Myself" ("Zi qian" 自遣), she pondered the meaning of life and vowed to pursue her newfound faith in the Immortals' Learning:

> My minor exile into this world of dust has been forty years.
> With the skills of benevolence I have cultivated the heart field.[62]
> But in many a quiet moment I've thought of withdrawal;
> Lost I feel amid the silk curtains and ornate chandeliers.
>
> I sit with Jade Liquid before me, but dare not a sip,[63]
> Lest I become saddened in spirit at its taste.
> An enlightenment in one decade is still not easy;
> Master Bai Shi's poem on immortality exceeds a panacea.[64]
>
> True perfection does not fade away with life or death;
> Wise it is now to end all my present bonds.
> Surely there are women extraordinary in this world,
> Who are resolved to soar to the Nine Heavens.[65]

The poem reveals a woman disillusioned by her present success in life, yet pensive and eager at the prospect of attaining perfection. Although surrounded by luxuries, Dr. Zhu sees her present life as a demotion or exile from an original perfection. Her use of the image of wine shows the depth of her sense of loss and sadness. In inner alchemic parlance, the Jade Liquid (*qiong jiang* 瓊漿) alludes to the coagulated *qi* and *shen* engendered during the inner alchemic process. It is also frequently used to refer to the libation of the perfected. The multiple meanings of the image thus create a subtle yet biting sense of self-irony in the context. Wine was for human consumption, Jade

Liquid the immortals' refreshment. The bouquet of the wine served only to remind her of her rootedness in this world, and the fragrance hinted by the Jade Liquid only highlighted the distance she still had to travel before her return to the immortals' realm.

Further deepening her spiritual crisis was Dr. Zhu's equally painful inner conflict between her resolve to undertake a journey of self-transformation and her lingering sense of both personal and professional obligations. Several decades of practicing the "skills of benevolence" (renshu 仁術) for her patients may have helped cultivate her heart/mind, but that alone was not sufficient for self-transformation of the body. As she came to her painful decision to terminate all her present "bonds," including her medical practice, she was also subtly reminded of the price and dedication required for the final ascent to perfection.

To this end, Dr. Zhu became deeply involved in the Shanghai community of inner alchemic practice and devoted herself to the pursuit of female inner alchemy throughout the 1930s and 1940s. She was actively involved in the activities of the Shanghai Institute of Immortals' Learning (Xianxue yuan 仙學院), which was established in 1937. She regularly attended Chen Yingning's lectures on inner alchemy classics at the institute and remained an active member of the inner alchemy community in Shanghai throughout the 1940s.[66]

Daoist Monastic Communities

Another vital component of the social milieu of the Immortals' Learning and the inner alchemic practice in Shanghai consisted of Daoist monasteries and clerics of both the Quanzhen and the Zhengyi schools in and outside the city. The Daoist monastic presence in Shanghai was the result of the rapid demographic increase and economic expansion that began in the early 1860s. The roots of Daoism in Shanghai could be traced to pre-Song times,[67] but it was during the late Qing period that Daoism expanded rapidly in the city. Before the late nineteenth century, the Daoist community in Shanghai and its suburbs was dominated by ritual specialists and at-home practitioners of the Zhengyi school, which descended from the early Daoist millenarian movements of the second century CE. Although monastic Quanzhen Daoism was introduced to the Shanghai area as early as the fourteenth century, significant growth began only in the aftermath of the Taiping war of the early 1860s, when Quanzhen clerics from Hangzhou began to build branch temples in the city.[68] Both Zhengyi and Quanzhen Daoism developed rapidly during the late nineteenth century, as Shanghai became a major trade and port city. According to a survey based on local gazetteers, there were around 74 Daoist temples and cloisters in the Shanghai area toward the end of the Ming. By 1911, that number had increased to 117. Between 1912 and 1937, the city of Shanghai saw the construction of an additional 14 Daoist temples. By 1949, there were a total of 236 abbeys and cloisters of various sizes housing a total of 3,716 registered Daoist priests and nuns in the city.[69]

Daoist growth in Shanghai was also closely tied to the patterns of demographic expansion in the late nineteenth and early twentieth centuries. With the influx of sojourning merchants from Guangdong, bankers and industrialists from Ningbo, textile workers from eastern Zhejiang and northern Jiangsu,[70] Daoist liturgical specialists and monastic practitioners of both the Zhengyi and Quanzhen sects began to build cloisters, temples, and monasteries in the city to serve their growing constituencies in the city. In most cases, these Daoist cloisters and temples were funded and patronized by their respective immigrant communities and merchant guilds.

The Xinzha Temple of the Great Kings 新閘大王廟, located near Chengdu Road on the south side of the Suzhou River, was one of the city's main Zhengyi temples. It was relocated to its present site in the early nineteenth century at the height of the influx of laborers and sojourners from the surrounding counties of Shanghai. By the early 1920s, this temple offered ritual services and festivals catering specifically to the boat people from Jiangsu.

Zhengyi Daoism historically dominated Shanghai in both numbers and the size of its presence, but Quanzhen Daoism was reintroduced to the city as immigrants from areas dominated by that sect settled in Shanghai during the late nineteenth century. In the Zhabei District, where laborers and textile workers from northern Jiangsu congregated, Quanzhen Daoist temples were established with funding from native-place associations and guilds. The Dutian

Cloister 都天廟, located on Zhongxing Road, for example, was built with donations from the Yangzhou Guild 揚州公所 in 1918. Wang Xinde 王信德, a Quanzhen cleric from northern Jiangsu, served as its abbot from 1918 to 1949. During his tenure, Abbot Wang adopted a dozen orphaned boys uprooted from their famine-stricken hometowns in northern Jiangsu and trained them as Quanzhen novices.

A few years earlier, in 1912, near Hongjiang Bridge 虹江橋 in the Hongkou District, where many sojourning merchants from Guangdong were concentrated, the Guangdong Sojourners Association (Yue lü Hu tongxianghui 粵旅滬同鄉會) paid for the construction of another Daoist abbey and retained He Jisong 何濟松, a Quanzhen cleric from the Shanghai White Cloud Monastery, to manage it. In the main hall of the abbey, Huang Daxian 黃大仙, the most popular Daoist patron god among the Guangdong sojourners, was worshipped. Indeed, this deity was so much in demand among the Guandong sojourning communities in Shanghai that another Quanzhen Daoist priest from Guangdong built a temple for his worship on Hainan Road in the city in 1935.[71]

Since Daoist inner alchemic techniques constituted the foundation of Daoist ritual practice, Daoist clerics, especially Quanzhen priests, often included Daoist self-cultivation practices of quiet-sitting mediation and breathing as part of their daily regimen. This shared interest provided a common ground between Daoist monastic practitioners and Chen Yingning and other promoters of the Immortals' Learning and Daoist inner alchemic practice. Many clerics came to know Chen and his colleagues' writings by reading the *Yangshan Biweekly* and its successor. Some sought Chen's friendship and support for their monastic practice.

Abbot Chen Tiehai 陳鐵海 came from the famous Quanzhen Palace of the Purple Soleil 紫陽宮 on Mount Tiantai in Wenling 溫嶺 in eastern Zhejiang, a region with a history of Quanzhen monasticism dating back to at least the mid-seventeenth century. Better known as the home of the Buddhist Tiantai sect, Mount Tiantai had since the early Tang been known as a Daoist sacred site (*fu di* 福地). It was steeped in a rich Daoist tradition and lore of self-cultivation and the cult of immortals. During the Tang period, Daoist self-cultivation practitioners such as Sima Chengzhen and Du

Guangting pursued meditation, seclusion, and other ascetic practices on Mount Tiantai. The Palace of the Purple Soleil, where Abbot Chen joined the Quanzhen order, was named after Zhang Boduan, the famed Song writer and practitioner of Daoist inner alchemy. Zhang was said to have engaged in the inner alchemic practice that led to his transcendence as an immortal on Mount Tiantai.

When Abbot Chen, a native of Wenling, entered the Quanzhen monastery in his youth in the 1890s, the once-magnificent monastery had fallen into disrepair. As he rose through the monastic ranks to become one of the senior clerics at the monastery, Chen vowed that he would raise funds to renovate it. Beginning in the late nineteenth century, along with its famed local products, eastern Zhejiang's best-known export to Shanghai had been its well-educated young women and men, whose labor and skills were in great demand by the ever-expanding textile industry as well as banks and other emerging businesses in the city.

To maximize fundraising, Abbot Chen and his colleague Cai Qiliang 蔡啓良 decided to follow their sojourning compatriots and potential donors to their new homes in Shanghai. In the summer of 1932, Chen and Cai arrived in Shanghai. With donations raised from their compatriots from eastern Zhejiang, they first settled in a neighborhood known as Huikangli 惠康里 in the northwestern quarter of the city in July of that year. A few months later, in September, Abbot Chen claimed that he received a divine revelation from the Patriarch of the Way (Daozu 道祖) that their cloister must move to another location. In November, Chen and a dozen or so fellow Daoists moved to Dingkangli 鼎康里 near Caojia Ferry (Caojiao du 曹家渡), an area north of the Huangpu River populated mostly by people from eastern Zhejiang. There Abbot Chen and Cai established a branch temple of their famous home monastery. The first few years proved to be especially difficult. The tough competition for lay followers among the city's numerous native-place-bound cloisters and small abbeys made it hard for newcomers like Abbot Chen to survive. In March 1933, when the food supply at the cloister ran out on several occasions, most of Chen's fellow clerics either left for home or joined a more prosperous temple. Abbot Chen alone decided to stay. Eventually his sincerity and tenacity began to pay off.

The cloister gradually flourished. Its following in the neighborhoods of northwestern Shanghai grew rapidly because the divining sticks drawn from the cloister's Shrine to the Patriarch Lü Dongbin were believed by many to be particularly efficacious.

In early February 1935, Wang Lilian 王理蓮 and Guan Lihua 管理化, two female textile workers from Suzhou, joined the cloister. Resolving to expand their cloister, Abbot Chen and his two new acolytes took vows to raise funds through ascetics. The two nuns committed themselves to three years of begging for alms by walking barefoot in the streets of Shanghai, and the abbot entered a three-year-long self-enclosure at the cloister. The three of them persisted in their chosen ascetics, even through the disruptive warfare and subsequent occupation of the city by the Japanese in 1937. Chen Yingning and his colleagues publicized the pious acts of the trio in the *Yangshan Biweekly*. Their story inspired many of their compatriots. For many in Shanghai, the sight of two Daoist nuns walking barefoot throughout the year collecting alms from people in the streets and neighborhoods, and the abbot persisting in meditation in seclusion for three years were reminiscent of the self-sacrifice and piety of the early Quanzhen masters. Some compared the bonds between the nuns and their teacher to that between Sun Bu'er, the Jin patroness of Daoist inner alchemy, and her mentor, Wang Chongyang 王重陽 (1113–70).[72]

This public staging of ascetics proved a great success. A dozen female textile workers joined the cloister as nuns. As the cloister grew beyond its capacity, it had to move again. By 1939, Abbot Chen relocated to a new site in western Shanghai and renamed the nunnery the Palace of the Purple Soleil.[73]

As the *Yangshan Biweekly* publicized the ascetic efforts of Abbot Chen and his female acolytes, they also became aware of Chen Yingning's reputation as a great scholar and practitioner of Daoism. Before long, the abbot and Chen Yingning became friends. They exchanged poems, which were then published in the *Biweekly* and later the *Xiandao Monthly*. At the height of the Japanese siege of Shanghai, Abbot Chen, like many other monastic clerics, invited Chen and his wife to take refuge at his monastery in the city. For their part, Chen Yingning, Dr. Zhang Zhuming, Wang Boying, Shen Linsheng, and others at the *Biweekly* provided both monetary and moral support for the nascent Quanzhen monastery. Chen gave regular lectures at the nunnery on the history, doctrines, and meditative techniques. In February 1941, when the expanded Quanzhen nunnery reopened with repainted statues of the Patriarch Lü and other deities at its new site on Kaina Road in western Shanghai, Chen composed, at the behest of Abbot Chen, the special ritual memorial to commemorate the occasion.[74]

The Shanghai community of inner alchemic practitioners also forged connections with Daoist monastic communities in various parts of the country through the circulation of its journals. Han Sanwu 韓三悟 (h. Sanwu daoren 三悟道人) was a Quanzhen cleric from the White Cloud Monastery in Shanghai. He became an admirer of Chen Yingning after reading Chen's writings in the *Yangshan Biweekly*. Originally from Nanjing, Han had become a Daoist acolyte as a child. In his youth, he entered a Quanzhen cloister at Mount Yunmeng in Shandong. Since then, Han had spent over two decades as a traveling Daoist, sojourning at various major Quanzhen Daoist monasteries in the country.

In 1910, while sojourning at the Dadi Grotto 大滌洞, a Quanzhen Daoist monastery in eastern Zhejiang, Han befriended Abbot Song Zongfu 宋宗富 (h. Qianlong 潛龍), a Quanzhen adept from Weixian 維縣, Shandong. In 1876, Song allegedly attained the *jinshi* degree together with his compatriot Cao Hongxun 曹鴻勳 (z. Zhongming 仲銘, h. Lansheng 蘭生; 1846–1910), a famous scholar-official and calligrapher. But unlike his better-known compatriot, who rose through officialdom to become governor of Shaanxi, Song purportedly became weary of his official career. He then abandoned Confucian learning in favor of Daoist practice (*qi ru ru dao* 棄儒入道) and withdrew to the Dadi Grotto near Hangzhou, where he engaged in Quanzhen ascetics. By the time Han Sanwu befriended Song at the Dadi Grotto, Song was an accomplished adept. Already in his eighties, Song was described as still in his physical prime with a sonorous voice and a sparkle in the eye. He did not adjust his attire to the seasons, a physical ability commonly associated with advanced Daoist adepts and immortals, who were said to be immune to inclement weather. While at the Dadi Grotto, Han studied

Daoist cosmology, divination, and self-cultivation techniques with Song.[75]

In 1936, while sojourning at the White Cloud Monastery in the South Market District, Han first read Chen Yingning's books and articles. He became deeply impressed with Chen, regarding him as superior to all other teachers whom he had encountered in his two decades of travels in search of Daoist secrets. Convinced of Chen's upright character and his erudition, Han wrote a glowing endorsement of Chen for the *Yangshan Biweekly* and called on journal readers interested in pursuing Daoist self-cultivation to regard Chen as their teacher.[76] Han became an active member of the Shanghai inner alchemic circle by contributing his own writings on Daoist inner alchemy to the *Biweekly*. Inspired by Chen's openness in teaching the practice, Han took the unusual step of sharing the full set of oral secrets he had acquired at various stages of his career by publishing them in the *Biweekly* in the winter of 1936.[77]

Chen's vision of the Immortals' Learning also attracted other Daoist monastic practitioners outside Shanghai. Sun Baoci 孫抱慈 was a Daoist adept who specialized in cereal avoidance; he lived at a Daoist cloister in Jinghua, Zhejiang. In the summer of 1935, Sun met Chen Yingning, Dr. Zhang Zhuming, and the renowned scholar Ma Yifu at the Purple Cloud Grotto (Ziyun dong 紫雲洞) on Mount Tiantai in eastern Zhejiang. At the time, Chen was taking Dr. Zhang and Ma on a tour in search of sites to build a self-cultivation retreat. The brief encounter at the Daoist cloister left a deep impression on Sun. He began to read Chen's writings and before long started to correspond with Chen and to contribute articles and poems on the subject of Daoist inner alchemic practice to the *Yangshan Biweekly* and the *Xiandao Monthly*.[78]

The Community of the Immortals' Learning at Large

But the largest constituent of the expanding Daoist inner alchemy community were lay practitioners and groups located in geographically diverse regions outside Shanghai. They were connected primarily through correspondence, travel, and the *Yangshan* and *Xiandao* journals.

Zhou Minde. Zhou Minde 周敏得 (1896–?) was a factory manager and businessman from Huangyan county in eastern Zhejiang. Although he grew up in a poor family, Zhou managed to attend an old-style village school for ten years from the age of five. But when he graduated, his mother passed away, leaving the family finances in shambles. To make a living, Zhou had to give up his chances at further education and apprenticed himself to a local retail store. By twenty, Zhou had completed his apprenticeship and risen to become the store's bookkeeper. At the time, the ferocious demand created by the Great War in Europe drove up prices for daily necessities such as sewing needles and dyes. While his fellow clerks at the store busied themselves in making money, Zhou devoted himself to the pursuit of learning and spent much of his monthly stipend buying new books on science, philosophy, and religion. He was particularly fond of books on physics and chemistry. Like many of his contemporaries, Zhou dreamed about pursuing work and study overseas (*bangong bandu* 半工半讀). Zhou even managed to travel to Japan as a stowaway on a liner. But a lack of money and proper connections in Japan and letters from home pleading for his return brought him back in just a few months. Yet his exposure to the modernized Japan only further whetted Zhou's desire for learning. After his return from Japan, Zhou got married and started a family. He and his business partners at the department store started a factory that produced socks and other textile products in Huangyan. The new business venture took off in the early 1920s. Like many other small and mid-sized textile operations, the Great China Socks Factory (Da Zhonghua wachang 大中華襪廠) developed a branch operation and distribution networks in Shanghai and other cities. Zhou soon found himself traveling frequently between Huangyan and Shanghai.

In February 1935, while in Shanghai, Zhou bought an issue of the *Yangshan Biweekly*. He was so intrigued with the articles on Daoism that he borrowed a dozen issues of the journal from a friend to read. He became particularly interested in books written or edited by Chen Yingning on Daoist inner alchemy practice. Before long, he became a regular subscriber and contributor to the *Biweekly*. In January 1936, Zhou wrote Chen Yingning, expressing a desire to learn the Immortals' Way from Chen. In a long letter to Chen, Zhou wrote that even amid the toils and worries of the business world, he had never lost his desire for spirituality and learning (*ling yu xue* 靈與學). As he reached the age of forty, Zhou felt an urgency to pursue his youthful dreams of self-cultivation.[79]

Zhou Zixiu. Zhou Zixiu 周子秀 (AKA Chuchen daoren 出塵道人), a close friend of Hong Tai'an and a fellow practitioner, was a Fujianese from Xiamen. After a sojourn in Shanghai, Zhou maintained ties with many compatriots among the Fujianese community in the city.[80] Zhou had befriended Chen Yingning through private correspondence and become a regular contributor to the *Yangshan Biweekly*. In his writings, Zhou shared with his audience his own approaches to self-cultivation. In 1936, Zhou sent Chen Yingning a copy of his tract on Daoist self-cultivation and healing practice entitled "How to Be Free of Illnesses Forever" ("Yongmian jibing fa" 永免疾病法). Reflecting his concern and understanding of the difficulties and challenges his fellow merchants might face in their daily practice, Zhou stressed the importance of moral abstinence from prostitution, gambling, drinking, smoking, and overexertion of the mind. In addition, he detailed for his audience a host of daily breathing, dietary, and meditative regimens based on Daoist self-cultivation techniques as a means to health and long life.[81]

Hong Tai'an. Zhou's friend and fellow practitioner Hong Tai'an (h. Wanxin 萬馨), an overseas Chinese merchant sojourning in Manila (see Fig. 15), also became connected with the Shanghai community of inner alchemic practitioners through correspondence and travel. On the eve of the Lunar New Year in 1938, amid exploding firecrackers and beating drums in Manila, Hong wrote the following verse to his master Chen Yingning living in Shanghai:

> Two years have passed to beats of the Pi drum.[82]
> Still I linger on my sojourn in the South China seas.
> From afar I heard the news of the heart-to-heart transmission
>   of the One,[83]
> And I am thrilled to see so many talents in your attendance.
> At my initiation, you anticipated this day;[84]
> Now with scriptures in hand how I yearn to be in
>   your presence.

The Inner Alchemic Community 213

Fig. 15   Mr. Hong Tai'an at practice, ca. 1930s
(Hong Wanxin, *Wuda jiankang xiulian fa*, p. 63).

Alas, when will I fulfill my life's wish: to follow you,
A staff in hand and in straw sandals, as I search for
   Mercury and Lead.[85]

Having learned of the recent lectures Chen gave on the classics of alchemy at the newly established Shanghai Institute of Immortals' Learning, Hong longed to join the other disciples and receive Chen's transmission of the Heart-to-Heart Method of One (*yiguan xinfa* 一貫心法). Invoking the legend of the unwritten esoteric teaching Confucius purportedly passed on to his favorite disciples Yan Hui 顏回 and Min Sun 閔損, Hong used the term to refer specifically to Chen's lectures delivered at the institute on the *Cantongqi*, a text so fundamental and crucial to understanding inner alchemy that it was often extolled as "the scripture of all scriptures on alchemy of all ages" (*wan gu danjing zhi wang* 萬古丹經之王).

For Hong Tai'an, the search for "mercury and lead" he so yearned to undertake with his master had begun more than sixty years earlier in 1877 in his home district of Nan'an county 南安 in Quanzhou in southern Fujian. His family resettled in the Philippines in his youth, where he lived until reaching the age of forty in 1917. That year, Hong moved his family to Fuzhou 福州 and took up residence there. While growing up in the Philippines, Hong received some education and was quite literate, as evidenced by his love of poetry. As a businessman, Hong split his time attending to his commercial interests in the Philippines and living with his family in Fuzhou. He was well traveled and had sojourned for business reasons in Kobe, Japan.[86]

Hong began to be interested in self-cultivation regimens as a result of his weak constitution (*tiruo* 體弱). Disliking ordinary physical exercises, Hong turned his attention to studying self-cultivation (*xiuyang shu zhi yanjiu* 修養術之研究). He was an avid and eclectic reader, and his readings included the classics of inner alchemy and gymnastics, contemporary methods of self-cultivation, and reports on modern physiology and physics.

These readings and his practice experience led Hong to write a tract on Daoist self-cultivation practice, which he completed in the summer of 1928, while staying in a hotel in Kobe on one of his business trips to Japan. Entitled "Five Great Techniques of Health and Self-cultivation" ("Wu da jiankang xiulian fa" 五大健康脩煉法), the tract was based on several decades of personal experience and studies in self-cultivation practice. In this piece, Hong outlined a personal health regimen that combined traditional Daoist gymnastic techniques of "sinew-stretching" (*chang jin* 長筋), "saliva swallowing" (*yan jin* 咽津), and "breath swapping" (*huan qi* 換氣) with the meditative practice of quiet sitting.[87]

Hong's view of the practice was informed by his eclectic readings in inner alchemy and modern sciences. Having read Yan Fu's translation of Huxley's work on Darwinism, Hong believed that competition and natural selection were the fundamental principle of the modern world and human life. But at the same time, Hong was deeply troubled by the implications of such a view of life:

I have also read the *Tianyan lun* 天演論 [(Yan's translation of Huxley's *Evolution and Ethics*)], which sees the evolution of the myriad of beings as stemming from competition. Those who compete and win are called superior (*zheng er sheng zhe wei zhiyou* 爭而勝者謂至優), whereas those who compete and lose are called the inferior (*zheng er bai zhe wei zhilie* 爭而敗者謂至劣). As species compete and Nature selects, the superior wins and the inferior loses. Indeed, this is the universal principle of natural evolution (*tianyan gongli* 天演公理). But although such an argument serves as a sufficient warning to the weak and timid members of a nation to seek occupations and stations appropriate to their own existence, its problems and excesses make it possible for the strong and robust nations to annex and subjugate the weak by engaging in daily competition wherein the strong always eats up the weak (*ruo rou qiang shi* 弱肉強食).

I am very apprehensive about this. I have pondered on it by confining myself in solitude. I now realize that amid the evolution of the myriad of beings, humanity has evolved the most. Human evolution lies in the indestructibility of the soul (*ling hun* 靈魂). Life upon life and generation after generation, it all relies on the cultivation of morality, virtues, and wisdom. Without this, the world will see no true civilization, and there will be no search for human happiness.

Thus, although Hong accepted Darwinian evolution as the governing principle of life, he also saw what he termed the "soul" as the true factor in determining the ultimate course of such evolution. At the individual level, the soul was manifested as Essence and Spirit (*jing shen* 精神), upon which life depended. In the body, Essence and Spirit were embodied as the Heart. For an individual human, it was the careful cultivation and refining of the Heart and of the Essence and Spirit in the body that ultimately determined one's destiny in this world and the next. For Hong Tai'an, cultivation of the Heart also meant a reform of its primary function: the practitioner's way of thinking or consciousness (*si xiang* 思想). Hong saw scientific progress and the power of the West as the results of an incremental progress through generations of change in ways of thinking and consciousness.[88]

By interjecting the soul, Essence, and Spirit into the theory of competition among species, and by stressing the centrality of consciousness in the process of evolution, Hong reached a vitalistic interpretation of evolution that linked individual action and responsibility to the outcome of natural selection. Huxley's scientific proposition about the natural history of the universe was refashioned into a program of action for self-determination. In this way, the personal pursuit of Daoist inner alchemic practice in modern times also became intimately tied to individual health and transcendence and, more important, to the destiny of a nation in an age of ruthless competition for survival.

For several years after he completed the manuscript in 1928, Hong kept it to himself, showing it only to a few friends and enthusiasts. In 1933, at the prodding of his friends, he published it. Again the tract circulated only among a small circle of interested friends and compatriots. By then Hong had become aware of the newly published *Yangshan Biweekly* in Shanghai. He realized that the *Biweekly* was a much better venue for voicing his ideas on self-cultivation. He especially enjoyed reading articles and books by Chen Yingning on the practice of inner alchemy and began corresponding with one of Chen's disciples. In January 1935 at the age of fifty-eight, Hong wrote his first letter to Chen, as he was about to depart for the Philippines. In the letter, Hong expressed great admiration for Chen and anxiously sought an audience with him. After the meeting, which took place later that year, Hong addressed or referred to Chen as "revered master" (*shi zun* 師尊) in all his ensuing correspondence with Chen and others.[89]

As he approached the age of sixty in late 1936, Hong began to doubt the viability of the Pure and Quiet approach, which he had adopted in his own practice. For practitioners like Hong, the age of sixty (*jiazi* 甲子) signified a crucial moment in the evolution of the body. At stake was the dwindling stock of the vitalizing atemporal *qi* in the body. It was believed that such stock, left unchecked, would be exhausted over the natural course of life by the age of sixty-four. After that crucial point, there was little hope of restoring and refining the atemporal *qi* within the body. Distressed by this dim prospect, Hong wrote to one of Chen's disciples, hoping that Chen would teach him the Southern Lineage techniques of paired cultivation, which were considered an effective shortcut to replenishing the vitalizing *qi* within the aging body:

I have come to know the Way too late. I am also too old. I have not been able to totally give up all my mundane obligations. If I do not first try grafting life by "replenishing the oil in the lamp" so that the lost True Lead and True Mercury may be restored, what would I count on to achieve the goal of attaining the Way?[90]

In reply, Chen urged Hong to resist limiting his choices to the sexual "grafting techniques" (*zai jie* 栽接) alone and consider adopting other self-cultivation techniques such as taking drugs (*fu shi* 服食) to achieve his goal. He warned Hong of the potential pitfalls of pursuing the controversial paired cultivation in modern society and assured him that the Pure and Quiet techniques could also help recover and rejuvenate the atemporal *qi* in the body.[91]

When Hong reached the age of sixty-one, he sent a long poem to Chen from the Philippines, reflecting on a life spent in promoting and pursuing health and immortality:

> Ashamed, I've spent my sixty-one years in vain.
> I want to talk not about business, but immortals only.
> While Hong Ya, the immortal, is a kinsman of mine;[92]
> But when will I wrap my arms around you, laughing?[93]
>
> Dogged yet robust, my body is still not old;
> I savor foods simple and delight in clothing coarse.
> Were it not for the extraordinary ideal I hold,
> How could I have remained unsullied in the Dust?[94]
>
> Like an old well, my heart has long been without a ripple;
> What even if there was the Pass of Amorous Attachment![95]
> As long as I can hold on to youth without aging,
> What harm is our shared attachment to this Myriad World?[96]
>
> Lately the Earth and Heaven have been in turmoil.
> To save the world, one must not fear hardship and sufferings.
> Alas, immortals of the past could save only themselves,
> And leave their names in vain among the humans.
>
> Joyful, I hold a mirror only to find my hair no longer young,
> But I resolve to revive the decaying trend with the last of
>   my energy.
> To everyone I meet, I will preach the "art of lengthening
>   the sinew,"
> Which shall be the first practice of my self-cultivation.[97]

Underlying Hong's concern about aging was the fear of a life spent in vain, without proper management and self-cultivation of the body. In Hong's poem, such external signs of physical ruin as white hair were paralleled by the cosmic-political and social disorder of the nation during the late 1930s, here euphemistically alluded to as "heaven and earth in turmoil." Yet for inner alchemists like Hong, the chaos both inside and outside the body was not cause for despair. Rather, it provided opportunity. As Hong believed, the final outcome of both the cosmic process of natural selection and the social process of national competition depended on the combined efforts of each self-cultivating individual doggedly pursuing self-perfection despite the physical, social, or political odds.

By claiming a relationship to Hong Ya, the immortal known for his legendary innovations in music and his engagement with the human realm, and by renouncing the past immortals who abandoned the secular world out of self-interest, Hong reaffirmed his own dedication not only to stemming the tide of natural aging in the body but also to reforming the nation by preaching his art of strengthening the nation.

Women Practitioners in the Inner Alchemy Community

Chen Wuxuan. The extensive network of inner alchemic practitioners outside Shanghai included many women. Chen Wuxuan 陳悟玄 (1889–?), whose name means "intuiting the mystery," became involved with the Shanghai community of practitioners through her correspondence with Chen Yingning. Like many of her male counterparts, Chen's pursuit of inner alchemy was a tumultuous journey. Born in 1889 to a wealthy family in a small town called Forked River (Chahe zheng 岔河鎭) in southeastern Jiangsu province, Chen was the eldest of three children. Her father died when she was still young. Although she never went to school, she learned to read and write by hanging around the desk of her younger brothers and by imitating their reading and reciting of the Classics in secret. As she learned to read, Chen began to browse her family's collection of morality scriptures (*shanshu* 善書) in her spare time. She was particularly impressed with the story about the life and ascendance of a Daoist goddess. She recalled years later that she was so moved by the story that she began to aspire to self-cultivation practice.[98]

The story may well explain Chen Wuxian's fascination with the Daoist goddess. The popular tale recounts the young Lady He's intense yearning for transcendence and her passing of three rigorous tests of her spiritual resolve devised by the legendary immortal Lü Dongbin. Particularly relevant to Chen's own life was perhaps the second test in which Lü urged the young maiden to marry in order to comply with her parents' wish. Completely unaware of the immortal's feigning and true to her own aspiration for transcendence, Lady He resolutely resisted the immortal's attempts to prevail on her, convincing him of her resolve and piety, thus ensuring her future transcendence and immortality.[99]

Indeed, Chen Wuxuan's own life resonated with the trials and tribulations of the goddess. By the time she was sixteen or seventeen, a common age for rural girls to marry, Chen had decided to pursue self-cultivation. She had by then read several major classics of inner alchemy and began to voluntarily observe Daoist precepts (*yuan shou gui jie* 願守規戒). But her widowed mother had different plans for her. She hired a matchmaker to find a husband for her daughter. But Chen told her mother that she would never marry. Refusing to accept the fact, Chen's mother kept interrupting her daily regimen of meditation practice, but to no avail. When her mother finally realized that she could not prevail, she began to inflict all sorts of abuse on Chen (*baiban nuedai* 百般虐待). But Chen Wuxuan refused to budge.

Moved by her resolve and piety, her maternal uncle intervened. He took her from her mother's house and enrolled her at a small Daoist nunnery in the Baoying area as a lay acolyte. There, at the age of seventeen, Chen began her career as a devoted Daoist practitioner of inner alchemy practice. But since the nunnery had little land or properties to support its resident nuns, Chen had to work hard to her earn her keep. She suffered many hardships and barely survived. Two floods in Baoying, one in 1921 and another in 1931, only added to her ordeals at the nunnery. In her own words, the sufferings she had to endure were "beyond description."

Yet, Chen never gave up her dream of transcendence. For more than two decades, amid her daily struggles to survive at the nunnery, Chen kept alive her dream of finding a teacher, funds, practice companions, and a practice location, the prerequisites for engaging in Daoist inner alchemy. She traveled in search of teachers and sought lessons from several adepts. But most of them failed to impress her.

Once, when she did manage to find an adept able to teach her the practice of "slaying the Scarlet Dragon" (zhan chilong 斬赤龍), the master passed away before she could receive the full oral secrets of the practice.[100]

In the absence of a master, Chen Wuxuan read the classics of inner alchemy on her own, and acquired a formidable knowledge of the practice.[101] Her perseverance led to remarkable progress and proficiency in female inner alchemy. In the aftermath of the 1931 floods, Chen persisted in her daily regimen of quiet sitting. She recalled her magical experience of what she regarded as the moment of gestating the elixir within her body for the first time:

> Once, late on a wintry night of the following year, having entered the great stillness (ru ding 入定) and with eyes closed and no longer conscious of my body, I suddenly saw my meditation chamber filled with an effulgence, brighter than daylight. But when I opened my eyes to look, there was nothing there to be seen.[102]

This experience fully convinced her of the viability of the practice. Yet she had to suspend her practice as her nunnery rebuilt after the flood. Anxious to learn more about what she had experienced, Chen journeyed to Nanjing in a vain search for an adept willing and able to teach her. Later that year, after returning from Nanjing, Chen had her hair shaved and joined a local lay Buddhist organization, hoping that the strict Buddhist laws and the more structured monastic life with financial stability would help advance her practice. But deep in her heart, she continued to yearn for the ultimate transcendence, like that of the Daoist immortal Lady He.[103]

Around the same time, Chen befriended a group of fellow self-cultivators in her hometown who supported one another through occasional meetings, mutual visits, and sharing journals and books on the practice. Many also composed and exchanged poems as a means of sharing their practice experience and mutual support. Among Chen's friends in Forked River was Shi Zhihe 石志和 (z. Yunzhong 允中), who began corresponding with Chen Yingning in Shanghai about his own meditation practice in 1934. Like many of his fellow educated practitioners, Shi wrote poems to explore the meaning and experience of Daoist meditation practice. One of Shi's poems on his pursuit of Daoist inner alchemy was so inspiring that Zhou Haixian 周海仙, a fellow self-cultivator, was moved to write a set of four poems rhymed after the original, in which Zhou shared his thoughts on the practice in the *Yangshan Biweekly*.[104]

When Chen Wuxuan decided to advance her practice through ascetic self-enclosure in the spring of 1935, Shi and other local self-cultivators did their best to assist her practice. Employed often by both Quanzhen Daoist and Buddhist practitioners to deepen the self-cultivation of mind and body, the rigorous practice of self-enclosure was traced to the early Daoist mountain hermits of the pre-Qin era. From the mid-twelve century, self-enclosure became part of Quanzhen monastic practice. As a self-transformative technique, the practice spread among lay self-cultivation practitioners in the late imperial period. Lasting from several weeks to several years, self-enclosure aimed at advancing the practitioner's pursuit of self-transformation away from the hubbub of daily life.[105] In secluded practice, the practitioner's contact with the outside world was reduced to the minimum. In Chen's case, her daily routine in the secluded chamber (*guanfang* 關房) consisted of three sessions of quiet sitting during the day and another set of three long sessions throughout the night. A few months into the practice, she reported that she achieved the feat of "slaying the Red Dragon" by suspending her menses, which was considered the first vital stage of female alchemic practice (see Fig. 16). Encouraged by her success, Chen decided to extend her self-enclosure practice from three months to the full three-year term.[106]

While Chen was in her extended self-enclosure, Shi and other friends at Forked River town bolstered her spirits by visiting her and bringing her books and journals to read on Daoist inner alchemy. On one such visit in the summer of 1935, Shi told her about Chen Yinging and his writings on female inner alchemy. Based on her study of Chen's books and the articles that Shi brought to her, Chen Wuxuan became deeply impressed with Chen Yingning's knowledge of inner alchemy and his advocacy of equality of women in the practice. Since she was concerned about preserving and advancing her hard-won progress in "slaying the dragon," Chen began writing letters to Chen Yingning from her enclosure in the fall of 1935.

222   The Inner Alchemic Community

Fig. 16   Women's beginning practice: Beheading the Red Dragon, ca. 1919 (Xi Yukang, *Neiwai gong tushuo jiyao*, p. 204).

Her correspondence with Chen Yingning centered on many issues, ranging from the fundamental principles to the location of key loci in the body to the differences between male and female cultivation practice to the proper meditative techniques and procedures for advancing the practice beyond the preliminary stage of stopping the menses. Chen's ten inquiries demonstrated a remarkable level of knowledge and proficiency and reveal some aspects of the dynamics of the master-disciple relationship in inner alchemy practice during the 1930s.[107]

First, practitioners like Chen Wuxuan who chose to participate in this question-and-answer format were by no means all novices com-

Fig. 17 Female inner alchemy: Women's Self-refining Practice, dates unknown (Fu Jinquan, *Nüdan lianji huandan tushuo*, in He Longxiang, *Nüdan hebian*, p. 1a).

pletely dependent on the teachings of a transmitting adept. Like Chen Wuxuan, they tended to be quite learned and even well versed in the practice. In her queries, Chen revealed her intimate understanding of the fundamental principles of the alchemic body, the location of vital loci, the firing and the timing techniques, and the specific refining methods involved at various stages of the practice.

One of her queries, for example, addressed the critical moment of timing vital to completing the preliminary practice for women practitioners of female inner alchemy. Writers on female alchemy believed that the atemporal *qi* energies within the female body were transformed into Blood (*xue* 血), the vitalizing counterpart to Essence (*jing* 精) in the male body. When the Blood was allowed to dissipate unchecked in the form of menstrual flow, the drain of atemporal *qi* from the female body resulted in her ruin. To stop this natural process of transformation and dissipation, the special regimen known as "slaying the Red Dragon" was introduced in the late Song–Yuan period (see Fig. 17).[108] Although the regimen evolved over time into various different methods, the basic approach involved a daily regimen of breathing, meditation, and timing the practice to the cosmic and bodily cycles. Typically, the regimen involved a daily breathing practice Chen Wuxuan alluded to as the "Wind" (*feng* 風). It aimed at gathering and conserving the rising postnatal energies from the lower abdomen, which Chen called the "Tiger" (*hu* 虎) in the female practitioner's body. When such energies were accumulated in sufficient quantity, a special meditative regimen was employed a few days before the arrival of the menses, which Chen euphemistically labeled the "Rain" (*yu* 雨), so that the downward dissipation of the atemporal *qi* or the "Dragon" (*long* 龍) might gradually be "slain and plucked" (*zhan qu* 斬取) and refined into the elixir within.[109]

In her queries, Chen Wuxuan also showed her intimate understanding of the actual operation of cycling the gathered *qi* along the Heavenly Orbit of the front descent (Yang Fire) and the back ascent (Yin Talisman), of properly locating the key loci (Furnace and Caldron) within the body for refining the gathered energies, and of properly incubating the refined elixir (Congealed or Gestated Elixir).[110] Further, Chen Wuxuan's understanding of alchemic processes and her knowledge of the textual tradition of inner alchemy also made her an extremely perceptive and critical interlocutor. In another of her queries, which dealt with differences between the male and female practice and the lopsided focus on Mercury (*gong* 汞) and Yin elements of the female body in the traditional writings of inner alchemy, she demonstrated her critical sensitivity to the gender-biased construction of the female body in traditional alchemic writings.

Second, the public format of the exchange, which was published in the *Yangshan Biweekly*, also had a mediating effect on the nature of the master-disciple relationship. Although Chen Wuxuan showed deference toward Chen Yingning throughout her queries, the open and public format she chose to field her queries helped dilute the absolute power and authority of the traditional hierarchy of the face-to-face master-disciple relationship. In the end, Chen Yingning's responses were subject to public scrutiny by other adepts and practitioners and, more important, to the specific conditions of the inquiring novice.

Third, a disciple in possession of textual authority and knowledge was also at a great advantage in seeking oral teachings from an adept. A display of knowledge by the disciple probably encouraged the adept to be cautious when dispensing advice. Indeed, on one occasion, Chen Yingning even felt it necessary to assure Chen Wuxuan of the efficacy of the "superior practice" (shangcheng gongfu 上乘功夫) he had taught her.[111] In one of her queries to Chen Yingning, Chen Wuxuan revealed to him that she had tried to ascertain the veracity and superiority of another adept's teachings by comparing them to the teachings of the classics. In so doing, Chen Wuxuan was not simply practicing common sense and caution; she was also following a long-established tradition of "verifying the teacher" (yanshi 驗師) in inner alchemy. Indeed, this was customary practice among many experienced practitioners.[112]

But, more important, Chen Wuxuan's provocative queries enriched and shaped the dialogue, making it an effective and appealing format for disseminating inner alchemic knowledge. Her systematic, well-organized, and well-informed queries highlighted for other female practitioners the critical issues and problems they would encounter in their practice. By raising these issues and eliciting appropriate replies to them, Chen Wuxuan was effectively negotiating and shaping the public dialogue on the practice of female alchemy of her times.

Chen's queries are even more significant in light of the conditions female practitioners had to contend with. Historically, few texts were written on the subject of female inner alchemy, and even fewer of them remained in circulation. The difficulty of accessing these rare texts was a common refrain of complaint among female cultivators. Further, the few available texts were written mostly by male adepts and often in obscure language. Many male adepts lacked a proper understanding of the female body, as their own practice centered primarily on the male body. Together with the obscure language and symbolism, these texts were difficult if not impossible to understand without the guidance of a teacher.

Yet through her study of the classics of inner alchemy and her persistent practice, Chen gained an extraordinary understanding. The psychosomatic phenomena she described in one of her letters to

Chen Yingning conformed perfectly to the classical depiction of the germination of the elixir in the body. In 1936 Chen Wuxuan wrote a letter to Chen Yingning about her experiences in her secluded practice:

> Since I entered seclusion, I have been practicing quiet sitting in six sessions: three during the day and three at night. In the past several months, I have often been hearing wind roaring in my ears. I have been seeing lightning shining in my eyes. Sometimes, I hear the music of strings and flutes, or the twitter and chirrup of the turtledove and insects around. But when I send someone to check outside the house, there are no traces of them.[113]

Chen Yingning responded a few months later, enthusiastically encouraging her to preserve her hard-won progress and to advance her practice further by persisting in the meditative practice of holding to the Center and keeping to the One (*baozhong shouyi* 抱中守一):

> What I can tell you today are only four characters: "embrace the One and hold to the Center." As for embracing the One, it is when the Heart and the breathing rely on one another and when your *shen* and *qi* do not separate. As for holding to the Center, it is to keep to the Supreme Stillness in the Central Palace after achieving the union of *shen* and *qi* so as to restore the undifferentiated state prior to the existence of heaven and earth.
>
> This is the supreme technique of the elixir with all the benefits and no harm at all. Since you have already slain the Red Dragon, it is most suitable that you carry on with this practice. Once you have achieved proficiency at the utmost supreme level, you will be liberated from the Wheel of Karma and transcend any catastrophe, and be coeval with the Saint, the Worthy, the Buddha, and the Immortal.[114]

Chen Wuxuan continued to cultivate her nascent discipleship not only through correspondence but also by travel and meetings. In the spring of 1938, having come out of her enclosure, she traveled to the western suburbs of Shanghai to meet with Chen Yingning in person and seek oral secrets to guide her practice.

Miss Dong. The same yearning and drive to advance the practice also inspired Miss Dong (Dong nüshi 董女士), another woman practitioner in the far-flung network of inner alchemy. She was born into a well-to-do family in Anyang 安陽, in Henan province, in 1912, but her father died when she was young. She grew up with her widowed mother and two other siblings, as the family finances declined. Amid the chaos of her family life and the social and political turmoil in north China in the early 1930s, Miss Dong graduated from the First Women's Normal College of Henan. Soon afterward, Miss Dong recalled that she felt increasingly disillusioned with the "unpredictable vicissitudes of life" (*rensheng moce* 人生莫測) and started to entertain thoughts of "cultivating the Way" (*xiu dao* 修道). She took to studying the classics of inner alchemy.[115] She also subscribed to the *Yangshan Biweekly* and became an avid reader. Impressed with Chen Yingning's learning and expertise on inner alchemy, she resolved to become his disciple. When she first started her correspondence with Chen Yingning in the winter of 1936, Miss Dong was twenty-four years old and had been married for a few years. Yet she was determined to learn and follow the Way with Chen:

Seeing that my Master is so profoundly erudite and virtuous, I hold you in great esteem and worship the ground you walk on. Having gotten to know you recently has deepened my reverence for the Way. Every day I feel so intoxicated and carried away that I forget to eat and sleep. I yearn to be in your presence to listen to you transmit the True Way.

Yet her path to learning the Way proved to be full of obstacles. As a young and vibrant woman still in her twenties and fresh out of college, Miss Dong seemed to everyone poised for marriage and a family. The shock and disbelief her family must have felt about her decision to "cultivate the Way" was reflected by their tenacious efforts to undermine her practice. She was promptly married off to a man twice her age. Luckily, the man shared her passion for self-cultivation. Indeed, the marriage became a legitimate haven for their pursuit of paired cultivation. Both vowed to forgo what Miss Dong called the "mundane passions" (*suqing* 俗情). To focus their energy and resources on their joint practice, Miss Dong and her husband decided not to have any children. But difficulty remained, because of her lack of access to oral secrets and a teacher.[116]

Yet even as she reported that her perseverance in the practice had led to her achieving the feat of "slaying the Red Dragon," she encountered strong objections from her family to her practice. Family objections aside, her own sense of isolation and her yearning for fellowship and a mentor proved almost too overwhelming for her.

What weighed even more heavily in her heart was the sorrow left unspoken in one of her poems: her own sense of filial responsibility to her family put her at odds with her profound yearning for immortality. Indeed, this internal conflict placed serious constraints on her endeavors, causing unbearable pain and anguish to her.[117] Yet she pressed on. In a poem published in May 1937 entitled "Thoughts on Having Slain the Dragon" ("Zhan chilong you gan" 斬赤龍有感), Miss Dong vividly captured the practice that culminated in her success in stopping the menstrual flow during this painful yet critical period in her life:

> First:
> Lower the Curtain, block the Mouth, and focus *shen* within;[118]
> The Sweet Dew circulates and moistens the body.[119]
> I've diligently practiced day and night;
> The sitting practice naturally breaks the meandering
>   Qu River.[120]
>
> Second:
> The practice thereafter concentrates on conserving
>   and holding,[121]
> And ultimately I aspire to transcend this globe of dust.
> All packed and yearning to go to Jiangnan,
> My starting steps are hindered on all sides.
>
> Third:
> I long to seek the methods, funds, companions, and location.
> For the practice is difficult at home as well as away from it.
> Alas, perfection cultivators from far corners on earth,
> When can we unite into a great congregation?
>
> Fourth:
> Entangled in human affairs, a hundred emotions engender
>   within me.
> The old lore about the Blue Bridge calls to mind Yun Ying.[122]
> Convinced I am that my minor exile here is not without
>   divine design,
> Which is to forge immortals' bond for a return to the
>   Jade Capital.

For female practitioners like Miss Dong, the search for the four prerequisites seemed doubly complicated by public expectations of women and their social functions, and by their own sense of themselves as mothers, daughters, and wives. Although Miss Dong had expressed her wish to travel to Shanghai and learn from Chen in one of her earlier letters in 1936, she still found her starting steps "hindered on all sides." It is precisely this sense of being trapped in tangled "human affairs" that blocked her access to the Four Prerequisites and brought to her mind the legendary encounter of the immortals at the Blue Bridge at the end of the poem. In that legend, the encounter between the Daoist Pei Hang 裴航 and the goddess Yun Ying 雲英 at the bridge led to Pei's subsequent ascent to immortality. Although she yearned for such an encounter, Miss Dong's social and familial entanglements only served to deepen her sense of solitude and melancholy.

But the mood of melancholy lifted. Toward the end of her poem and in her real life, Miss Dong reaffirmed the value of her present situation. Like many of her fellow practitioners such as Dr. Zhu and Chang Zunxian, she conceived of her hardship-ridden life as a temporary "minor exile or banishment" (*xiao zhe* 小謫). In so doing, she transformed the obstacles in her life into the motivating forces that inspired her to persevere in her resolve in staging her ascent to the Jade Capital, the abode of the immortals.

Like many of her fellow practitioners, Miss Dong had also come to realize that the demands of modern life and the worsened political and economic conditions of the 1930s had made it difficult, if not impossible, for any individual practitioner to single-handedly achieve a successful practice. In a contribution to the *Yangshan Biweekly* in May 1937, she reflected on the plight of her fellow practitioners:

For any enterprise to succeed, we must rely on collective resources (*zhong li* 眾力). As the Way of the Immortals competes with the Nature itself for control of life, our enterprise is often viewed with suspicion by the mundane, slighted by the pedantic, or defamed by other religions. We must rely even more on joining our collective strength and resources for success. Without a closely organized institution, the assistance of patrons, access to housing, availability of funds and companions, those who rely only on their own resources to conduct the home practice (*zaijia xiulian* 在家脩煉) are bound to become bogged down by household affairs. If they enter mountains for the practice (*rushan xiulian* 入山脩煉), they still lack the resources mentioned above. To expect them to consummate the Way and to attain perfection is a pure fantasy.[123]

Joining an open forum in the *Yangshan Biweekly* that began in November 1936, Miss Dong passionately advocated the establishment of a national practice center. In her proposal, Miss Dong envisioned a cultivation congregation (*xiudao jituan* 修道集團) whose members shared the same aspiration of attaining immortality through joint practice, and whose operation and maintenance were supported by donations and membership dues, rather than by gifts from a handful of patrons and sponsors. As a woman, Miss Dong insisted on gender equality (*nannü pingdeng* 男女平等) among members of the congregation and stressed the need for mutual cooperation and mutual assistance. She argued that only the united congregation would be able to provide the much-needed resources deemed essential to the success of the practice.[124]

6

The Print Culture and Revival of Inner Alchemy

Our principle of learning is inquiry, not worship;
In cultivation, we value practice, not empty talk;
In thinking, we must be active, not apathetic;
In spirit, we aspire for autonomy, not dependence;
For strength, we must unite, not split;
In our endeavors, we prize innovation, not imitation;
For happiness, we treasure the present, not the afterlife;
In creed, we depend on experiment, not scripture;
Living in the world, we strive for long life, not a quick end;
Away from the world, we aim at transcendence, not conversion.

Beginning with the April 16, 1936, issue, these ten mottoes were printed prominently on the cover page of every copy of the *Yangshan Biweekly*. They represented the ideals Chen Yingning and his colleagues envisioned for the twentieth-century version of Daoist inner alchemy. The mottoes were meant to reflect the mission and ethos of the Immortals' Learning and mark the boundaries between it and Buddhism and Confucianism, as well as western science. The emphases on happiness in the present life (*shengqian* 生前) rather than the afterlife (*sihou* 死後), transcendence (*chaotuo* 超脫) over conversion (*guiyi* 皈依), and long life (*changcun* 長存) over death (*suxiu* 速朽) were veiled yet unmistakable criticisms of Buddhist doctrines and practices that valued the mind over the flesh body. Similarly, the valuing of inquiry (*yanjiu* 研究), practice (*shijian* 實踐), and experimentation (*shiyan* 試驗) reflected a commitment to reform and reformulate existing values of Daoist inner alchemy in accordance with the newly ascendant discourse of scientific empiricism. The stress on activism (*jiji* 積極) and innovation (*chuangzao* 創造) was meant to distinguish the Immortals' Learning from the Confucian preference for the status quo, and the emphasis on uniting (*tuanjie* 團結) and autonomy (*zili* 自立) manifested a common yearning for a strong, independent community of inner alchemy practitioners.[1]

These mottoes mirrored the journal editors' need to be innovative and different, to stand out among Shanghai's highly competitive popular magazines and journals. But they also reflected the editors' efforts to capture and present the shared views and values of their fellow practitioners about Daoism and their practice. In that sense, the mottoes and the medium were emblematic of cultural and institutional changes in the vibrant, lay-centered Daoist inner alchemic community in Republican Shanghai. The adoption and implementation of the values embodied in these mottoes by Chen Yingning and his colleagues contributed to the emergence of a thriving inner alchemic culture and community, to novel ideas and approaches to Daoist learning and practice, and to new institutions for organizing self-cultivation practice and the community of practitioners in Shanghai and beyond.

These innovations and institutional developments took place against the background of larger social and historical changes in Republican China. The quickening pace of change since the late nineteenth century had generated both a personal and a cultural sense of urgency. The need for personal and cultural self-definition stimulated an interest in and investigation of China's past. The search for a self-identity was exacerbated by China's external national crisis during the 1930s. The Japanese occupation of northeast China and the subsequent massive invasion of the county led to a full awakening of Chinese nationalism, which had been fermenting for almost a century. This newfound nationalist fervor further fueled and shaped both the personal and the cultural quest for self-definition among various groups in China. Despite this turmoil, material life and technology did improve in China during the early twentieth century, especially in major cities. With the establishment and proliferation of modern railways and steamships, postal services, and modern printing, publishing, and distribution systems, it became increasingly easier to connect with others through both time and space.

The expansion of the modern state, which began during the late nineteenth century, had weakened the traditional monastic institutions of Buddhism and Daoism. To minimize the modern state's assault on their properties and beliefs, Buddhist and Daoist clerics and lay activists began to reorganize themselves at both the local and the national level.[2] From the 1910s to the 1930s, both the Quanzhen and the Zhengyi Daoists in Shanghai made several efforts to form regional and national organizations. As they did in other localities, Daoist clerics and monasteries in Shanghai established elementary and middle schools to provide a rudimentary education to youth in their communities. In addition to the reprinting of the Daoist Canon, other Daoist compendia were published by Daoist clerics and lay patrons. During the economic boom in the early Republican period, Daoist neighborhood temples and cloisters mushroomed in various parts of the city.[3]

It was within this changing social, religious, and cultural environment that the urban and lay-centered renaissance of Daoist inner alchemy took place. Between 1933 and 1941, the publication and circulation of the *Yangshan Biweekly* and *Xiandao Monthly* gave rise to a thriving inner alchemic practice and an emerging community of practitioners centered in Shanghai and marked by intellectual innovation and institutional development. By late 1941, when all of Shanghai was occupied by the Japanese, the lay Daoist inner alchemy practitioners and activists had established a society dedicated to collecting, recarving, and circulating old and rare classics of Daoism. The group reprinted several hundred Daoist scriptures, including many on inner alchemy, and published several popular series of books written by contemporary adepts on the practice for both men and women. They even operated a seminary devoted to the study and practice of Daoist inner alchemy in Shanghai. Most of all, through the active exchange of communications by the readers and supporters of the *Yangshan* and *Xiandao* journals, a community of inner alchemy practitioners emerged and spread to many parts of the country.

The renaissance comprised several key components: a robust print culture consisting of a committed publishing house and a vigorous Daoist nationalist discourse that sought to redefine and reformulate modern Daoism through anti–Pure Land Buddhist polemics and a close engagement with science; an established publication and circulation network dedicated to disseminating Daoist knowledge and practice; and, most of all, a vocal and self-conscious community of lay Daoist reformers who tenaciously experimented and built various new forms and institutions for the practice of inner alchemy in and beyond Shanghai.

The Inner Alchemy Print Culture

The institutional center and driving force behind the inner alchemic print culture in Shanghai was the Yihuatang 翼化堂 publishing house. Initially established in the city in 1857 at the height of the Taiping Rebellion, the publishing house remained in operation until the early 1950s. Its founder, Zhang Weicheng 張韋承 (h. Xuetang 雪堂, 1838–1909), was a wealthy landowner and active philanthropist from Pudong, the western suburb of Shanghai (see Fig. 18). Zhang's original surname was Wei 衛; he came from a prominent literati family descended from a chief councilor at the Southern Song court. Zhang was adopted in childhood by a maternal uncle as a means of continuing the Zhang family line. From his youth he was a devoted vegetarian, and he remained celibate all his life. Zhang carried on his family tradition of public philanthropy and raised funds for famine relief in the Jiangnan and Central Plain regions, acts that earned him commendations both from the Qing court, which made him an honorary prefect with the full third rank, and from local officials.[4]

Like many members of the gentry elite of his generation, Zhang was appalled by the Taipings' extensive destruction of Confucian institutions of learning and Buddhist and Daoist temples. In 1857, Zhang resolved to restore what he called the "Ancient Ways of the Sages" (*shengxian gudao* 聖賢古道) by establishing a printing house

The Print Culture and Revival of Inner Alchemy 235

Fig. 18   Mr. Zhang Xuetang, founder of Yihuatang,
date of image unknown (YS, no. 13 [Jan. 1, 1934]: 216).

dedicated to reprinting and circulating the Confucian classics and Buddhist and Daoist scriptures. His name for the publishing house, Yihua, means "to aid in the transformation." Indeed, assisting in the transformation of individuals and society through the publication of books fittingly expressed Zhang's lifelong goal. Zhang oversaw the operation of the publishing house until his death in 1909. After that, his two adopted sons continued the business. By the early 1920s, when his grandson, Dr. Zhang Zhuming, assumed control of the publishing house from his father and uncle, Yihuatang had been printing and distributing Daoist and other texts for more than half a century and had established itself as one of the major distributors of religious scriptures and classics in East Asia. By then, it had printed and circulated several hundred titles, including many Daoist scriptures and alchemic texts, which had been either given away for free or sold at cost by mail order or in bookstores in major cities and towns throughout the country.⁵

Yihuatang's contributions to the circulation of Daoist scriptures cannot be overemphasized. It continued the private and lay tradition of collecting and distributing Daoist scriptures and was among the few publishing houses dedicated to the collection, production, and distribution of Daoist and Buddhist scriptures free of charge or at cost in the late Qing period. Many Yihuatang titles were reprinted and sold by other presses and publishing houses in Shanghai during the first two decades of the twentieth century. More important, Yihuatang's efforts raised public awareness of Daoism and contributed to the growth of a flourishing inner alchemy print culture in Shanghai by promoting the public pursuit and discussion of the self-cultivation practices and by fostering fellowship and community among the many practitioners and enthusiasts of the practice.

In the late 1920s, when he took charge of Yihuatang, Zhang Zhuming was still in his twenties. He was one of a handful of medical doctors trained at the prestigious German-run Shanghai Deutsch Medical College. He later specialized in radiology and ran a successful practice in Shanghai. Partly inspired by the family tradition and partly stimulated by the booming market for popular journals in the city, Dr. Zhang decided to start a periodical for those who shared his family's vision of promulgating the "Way of the Ancients." One of the first persons he contacted was Chen Yingning. Dr. Zhang had learned of Chen's erudition in Daoism and experiments in outer alchemy through a mutual friend and neighbor of Chen Yingning.⁶

With Chen and other senior adepts as his advisors and editors, Dr. Zhang and his publishing house became even more focused and active in collecting and reprinting Daoist and inner alchemic scriptures. Beginning in 1935, Yihuatang published four series of books devoted to Daoist learning and inner alchemic practice for both men and women. Each collection was presented in the fashionable, modern format of collectanea (*congshu* 叢書). The first series, entitled *The Petite Daoist Learning Series* (*Daoxue xiao congshu* 道學小叢書), contained five carefully chosen titles from the Daoist Canon and was meant as a primer for the general public. Chen Yingning and Chang Zunxian edited the works and supplied introductions on the history and background of each text. The second series, *The Daoist Learning Series* (*Daoxue congshu* 道學叢書), offered two rare texts widely regarded as containing esoteric oral secrets of inner alchemy. These were intended as readings for more advanced practitioners. The audience of the third series is apparent from its title, *Petite Daoist Learning Series for Women* (*Nüzi Daoxue xiao congshu* 女子道學小叢書). It contained five titles on inner alchemy written for and presumably by women during the Qing period. The fourth series, *The Collection of the Immortals' Way* (*Xiandao congshu* 仙道叢書), consisted of two books written by Chen Yingning that addressed historical, philosophical, and technical issues of self-cultivation. By the fall of 1937, when Yihuatang's operations were interrupted by the Japanese siege of Shanghai, all but one of the titles planned for the four series had been published.[7]

Chen and his colleagues carefully edited the titles selected for the series by putting them in their proper historical and praxical contexts and by deleting "superstitious or fantastical" elements. For most of the edited texts, they also provided commentaries and additional information for a modern audience on the history, language, and conceptual and praxical dimensions of these scriptures.

In editing these series, Chen and his associates tried to modernize knowledge about the practice of Daoism by bringing modern ethnographic and historical methods to bear on the scriptures' language, social contexts, and technical dimensions. The scope of their examinations extended beyond traditional textual materials to other Daoist artifacts such as religious paraphernalia, ritual objects and regalia, pictures and photos, and local gazetteers. Two factors were at work here. On one hand, the careful and meticulous textual exegeses, annotations, and commentaries by Chen and his associates reflected their learned background. On the other, their new approach to explicating the scriptures mirrored their desire to present an otherwise esoteric body of knowledge in terms accessible to a modern audience. Their goal was to revitalize the Daoist practice for the modern age.[8]

Besides these series published by Yihuatang, the Shanghai Daoists' shared interest in preserving and promoting their practice also led to joint efforts to collect, reprint, and disseminate hard-to-find or rarely circulated classics of inner alchemy. In the fall of 1935, the Shanghai Metaphysical Study Society (Shanghai xuanxue hui 上海玄學會), a small group of scholars and enthusiasts of Daoism with close ties to Chen and his associates at Yihuatang, published a formal call in the *Yangshan Biweekly*. Addressed to abbots and senior clerics at Daoist monasteries throughout the country, these Shanghai Daoist intellectuals and activists called on them to make available for preservation and circulation written, photographic, and pictorial materials, as well as instruments and artifacts, relating to Daoist cultural relics, temples, lineages, historical and living personages, and historical sites.[9]

Under Dr. Zhang Zhuming's initiative, this group of Daoist scholars, activists, and lay practitioners established the Society for Carving Daoist and Alchemic Scriptures (Dandao kejing hui 丹道刻經會) in 1936. The society counted among its members many of Shanghai's social and cultural elite, as well as several editors of the *Yangshan Biweekly*. In September 1936, Dr. Zhang and his colleagues from the society proposed nine categories of Daoist texts and artifacts to be collected and stipulated six different methods of reproduction for the collected texts. According to the procedures outlined in the announcement, the collected texts were to be examined and authenticated by a special group (*guanli tuan* 管理團) composed of experts like Chen Yingning. Then, the society would negotiate with the owner of each text regarding the means and costs of reproducing it. Next, funds were to be raised among the society's donors and potential buyers for the reproduction and distribution of the selected texts. According to its charter, the society's operating budget was to come primarily from two sources: contributions by sponsors and donors and advance payments from those ordering the books. The charter also stipulated the establishment of a special foundation and strict and open accounting procedures to ensure successful and honest operations. Additionally, the society also appointed book scouts (*jiaoji* 交際) and investigators (*diaocha* 調查) whose jobs were to develop contacts with private book collectors and to follow up and verify leads about books. The society also held regular luncheons or dinner meetings so that members could exchange information and discuss the society's operations.¹⁰

For Chen Yingning, Dr. Zhang, and their close circle of friends, the society's work in collecting and reprinting Daoist and inner alchemic classics represented a cultural enterprise that could lead to national rejuvenation and salvation. In the public announcement, Dr. Zhang and others deplored China's steady and continuous decline and argued forcefully that the best way for the average person to save the country (*jiuguo zhi dao* 救國之道) was to promote Daoist learning and techniques:

May we ask what kind of learning and techniques are best suited to the current times of our country? Some may say science, whereas others may propose Buddhism. Although each may have its own good solution, the two systems of learning will surely clash if they meet. Science is too materialistic, and Buddhism is excessively idealistic. Both are too extreme and are mutually irreconcilable. Only Daoist learning and techniques (*Daojiao xueshu* 道家學術) passed down from ancient times are both subtle and powerful and can harmonize and integrate the ideational and the material. They will neither succumb to the material nor indulge in empty talk about the heart-mind. Practiced by individuals, they protect the body (*bao shen* 保身). Applied to the nation, they can strengthen the race (*qiang zhong* 強種).

Further linking China's decline to the failure to transmit Daoist scriptures, Chen and his associates counted the ancient classics of Daoism and inner alchemy (*danjing daoji* 丹經道籍) among China's national treasures (*Zhonghua guobao* 中華國寶). They thus called on their fellow self-cultivators and the public to raise funds to reprint and circulate the ancient classics to benefit the people and rejuvenate the nation.¹¹

This sense of the mission was shared by many members of the inner alchemy community in- and outside Shanghai. Many volunteered to serve as book scouts and investigators for the society; others donated their time and skills as unpaid clerks and managers in the city. Deng Yucang performed secretarial duties while sojourning in Shanghai, and Shi Zhihe from Baoying in Jiangsu served as a proofreader. Around the same time, Yang Shaochen 楊少臣 from Ji'nan in Shandong and later Beiping, Zhou Minde from Huangyan in Zhejiang, and Cai Dejing 蔡德淨 from Haimen in Jiangsu became book scouts and investigators for the society in their respective regions.[12]

Between 1934 and 1941, the society located and reproduced several important and rare texts on inner alchemy dating from the late Qing period. Their publication resulted from the joint efforts of members of the inner alchemy community both in and outside Shanghai. In 1936, while on a visit to his home in western Fujian, Deng Yucang learned that Mao Fuchu 毛復初, a compatriot and fellow practitioner from Liancheng, owned a bound volume of two rarely seen classics of Daoist inner alchemy: *Discourse on the Aperture of the Way* (*Daoqiao tan* 道竅談) and *Secrets of the Three Crafts* (*Sanche mizhi* 三車秘旨), written by the late Qing inner alchemist Li Xiyue 李西月 (h. Hanxu 涵虛; fl. 1790s–1850s). Deng soon informed Chen Yingning about their existence. Chen had only heard of these works, but he immediately realized their importance for the practice. He made arrangements for Deng to discuss the matter of reprinting them with Dr. Zhang Zhuming and other leading members of the society in Shanghai. Later that year, Deng traveled back to Fujian and persuaded his friend to loan him the two rare classics. Meanwhile in Shanghai, Chen, Zhang, and their colleagues from the society reached an agreement to collectively fund the reprinting of the two rare works and entrusted their editing to Chen once the texts arrived from Fujian. In the fall of 1936, Deng carried the two texts to Shanghai.[13] In less than a year, Chen finished the editing, and the two books were reprinted and published in the spring of 1937 with funds raised from fifteen members of the society, including Wu Minzhai, Fang Gongpu, Zhang Zhuming, Gao Guanru, Chen Yingning, Dr. Wu Yizhu, and Wang Boying. The print run was 900 copies. Support for similar printing projects poured in from the city and beyond. The society's ranks and its board kept expanding as new donors and sponsors joined. By June 1937, more than a dozen self-cultivation advocates, social worthies, and famous scholars in Shanghai and beyond, such as Ma Yifu, Hong Tai'an, Zhang Huasheng, and Xie Qianggong 謝強公, a lay Daoist leader and founder of the martial arts association in Shanghai (Shanghai Zhonghua wushu hui 上海中華武術會), joined as consultants or executive members of the society.¹⁴ After the Japanese siege and occupation of Shanghai in late 1937, the society moved its operations inside the relatively safe haven of the International Settlement. There, it persevered despite adversity and published a few more titles on inner and outer alchemy.¹⁵

Immortals' Learning: A Flourishing Daoist Nationalist Discourse

The thriving Daoist print culture gave rise to a vibrant discourse characterized by lively discussion and sometimes intense polemics in the public space and media. The *Yangshan Biweekly* and *Xiandao Monthly* played an active and vital role in creating and maintaining this discourse in Shanghai's emerging public space.

Sometime after Dr. Zhang Zhuming met and hired Chen to serve as a special contributing editor for the planned *Yangshan Biweekly*, Chang Zunxian, Wang Boying, and half a dozen other lay adepts also joined the journal as editors. Launched in Shanghai on July 1, 1933, the *Yangshan Biweekly* was published on the first and the sixteenth of each month and distributed at cost through the Yihuatang bookstore in the South Market District and at other bookstores in the city. For out-of-town readers, the *Biweekly* was distributed mainly through subscription and mail order. Although its circulation fluctuated from a few hundred to several thousand, the *Biweekly* and its successor reached places as far as Manila and Hong Kong. The subscribers and readers included both clerics at Daoist and Buddhist temples and individual lay practitioners and self-cultivation groups in and outside Shanghai. Its circulation was further expanded through the common practice among readers of sharing their copy with friends and fellow practitioners.¹⁶

Under the editorial guidance of Chen Yingning, Chang Zunxian, and their associates, the *Yangshan Biweekly* focused on promoting the teachings and values of Immortals' Learning to their constituency as well as the general public. These efforts accelerated in early 1935 with a series of published articles and letters by the editors and readers. In their writings, Chen and his colleagues described the Immortals' Learning as embodying the true essence of Daoism, which originated in pre-Zhou antiquity and thus predated both Confucianism and Buddhism:

> The origins of Daoism trace back to the Daoists of the pre-Zhou and Qin periods. The learning of the Daoists originated from the Yellow Emperor, was collected and perfected by Lao Dan, proliferated in the works of Zhuangzi and Liezi, was transformed in the books of Han Fei and Guiguzi, and mutated in the writings of Heguanzi and Huainanzi. The history of Chinese Daoism predates the birth of India's Buddhism by two thousand years. So Daoist Learning is the most ancient and unsurpassed by all other religions and philosophies in the world. . . .
>
> Among the early Daoists were some known as the Refining Self-cultivators. To them, the school of the Divine Immortals traced its origin. The Yellow Emperor studied the Immortals' Learning amid his battles. Laozi further brought the Way of Lengthening Life into greater prominence. So the Immortals' Learning is also part of Daoist Learning.[17]

To Chen and his associates, the core of the ancient learning of the Yellow Emperor was the refining self-cultivation practice (*xiuyang* 修養). Invoking the ancient legend of the Yellow Emperor learning the art of long life from the immortal Guangchengzi 廣成子 as he fought his enemies, Chen and his colleagues conceived of a lineage for their modern inner alchemic practice that predated the emergence of all early Chinese philosophers. By connecting modern Daoist inner alchemy to China's ancient sage-kings, Chen and his associates were attempting to generate cultural legitimacy for inner alchemy as a form of learning distinct from the three later teachings of Confucianism, Buddhism, and religious Daoism.[18]

Yet Chen's classical education also taught him that the most entrenched obstacle to the emerging Immortals' Learning discourse was the established Confucian critique of Daoism typified by the Southern Song scholar Ma Duanlin's comment that "the arts of the Daoists are an indiscriminate and heterogeneous hodgepodge, as confirmed by the abundant comments of many earlier scholars." The influence of Ma's seemingly casual critique was evidenced in the views of the eighteenth-century editors of the imperially sanctioned encyclopedic compendium, the *Siku quanshu* 四庫全書. In their summary of the Daoist Canon, the editors even singled out a long inventory of texts found in the compendium that should, in their opinion, be reclassified as belonging to one of the non-Daoist schools or under such bibliographic categories as geography (*dili* 地理) and daily living (*qiju* 起居).[19]

In an article published in the *Yangshan Biweekly*, Chen Yingning attempted to overcome the Confucian bias toward Daoism by redefining what he termed the "totality of Daoist Learning" (*Daojia xueshu zhi quanti* 道家學術之全體). To Chen Yingning and his followers, the Confucian editors of *Siku quanshu* had erred in ignoring the original intent of the compilers of the Daoist Canon and failed to understand the "natural and intrinsic" linkage between Daoism and other schools of learning. Chen suggested that the reasons that the Daoist Canon appeared to later detractors to be an "inchoate hodgepodge" needed to be understood in two contexts. One was that earlier Daoist compilers operated in a time when foreign religions (*waijiao* 外教) were spreading to China. To resist this cultural invasion, they were compelled to include in the Canon the country's "total culture" (*zhengge wenhua* 整個文化). Second, Chen contended that these compilers truly understood that all philosophical and religious learning of the pre-Qin era originated with Daoists of the pre-Zhou period. Citing the close relationship between the Immortals' Learning of the Yellow Emperor and the various other schools of learning represented by the *Book of Changes* or books on medicine, numerology, law, metaphysics, and strategy and military affairs, Chen argued that Daoist learning should not be reduced to a narrow and tendentious definition centered on the teachings of "pure and quiet nonaction" (*qingjing wuwei* 清靜無為), techniques of drug ingestion and nourishing cultivation, or talismanic and magic rituals. Rather, Daoism was a "total learning" that dealt with all phenomena and united all nine ancient schools of thought of antiquity (*baoluo wanxiang, guanche jiuliu* 包羅萬象, 貫徹九流).[20]

For Chen and his fellow practitioners, Daoism's comprehensiveness and inclusiveness were its strength and gave it the cultural self-sufficiency and confidence to withstand and resist all intellectual and cultural invasions from outside, thus ensuring the survival of both Chinese culture and the Chinese nation in history. Writing in 1936, as China faced escalating encroachment by the Japanese military, Chen argued for the cultural viability of Daoism:

When we speak of Daoism today, we must trace it to the times of the Yellow Emperor and Laozi and connect it to the Hundred Schools. We must affirm that Daoism is the spiritual anchor of the Chinese nation. We must not blindly look down on ourselves by destroying our own jade and pearls only to admire others' broken tiles and gravel. We need to understand that to believe in Daoism is to conserve our body, and to propagate Daoism is to save the country. We should not lead a dependent life by adopting pessimism. We must strive for survival by employing empirical means. Only in this way can our nation hope for a renaissance. A military invasion can at best break up the land of a people and destroy their bodies. The damage is relatively superficial. But a religious and cultural invasion can deprive a people of their thought and enslave their soul. That damage is much more profound. Against those who invade us by military force, we can counter by deploying our military troops. But against a cultural and religious invasion, our military power cannot be deployed successfully. If we fail to use our country's indigenous culture and religion to resist the invasion, all the foundations of our intellectual tradition of several millennia will be shattered one day, and the faith and the core of our four hundred million people will be lost in the end. Can words describe such a catastrophe![21]

Additionally, Chen argued that Daoism's comprehensiveness was further evidence of its learned tradition. He saw its learning as the spirit that had informed Chinese culture and history. In one of his writings, Chen conceived of early Chinese history as the manifestation of the Immortals' Way, which had since propelled the cultural and social development of China:

Our country experienced the five dynasties of Tang, Yu, Xia, Shang, and Zhou (唐虞夏商周) following the reign of the Yellow Emperor. The sage-kings ruled their realms in accordance with the Way. The worthy ministers assisted their rulers in accordance with the Way. During those earlier reigns, governance and education were not separated. One can look at the classics and scriptures and see that all those reigns, without exception, were for the protection of the state and the welfare of the people, and all of them, without a single exception, were the Way of revering Heaven and educating the people.[22]

In Chen's conceptualization of early Chinese history, the key to sage rule was the achievement of self-perfection by the individual sage-kings. The legendary peace and wealth of these early reigns were but external realizations of the inner perfection of the sage-kings, who followed the Way of the Yellow Emperor. By contrast, Chen attributed China's subsequent decline to lack of inner perfection among rulers and the ruled:

Therefore the Great Learning states, "When the heart is rendered straight and the intention sincere, then the body will be refined and the family harmonized; and the state will be governed and the realm pacified." This is a constant and steadfast truth. But people engaged in politics in recent times have neither cultivated their bodies nor harmonized their families, not to mention their hearts and intentions. Yet they persist in empty talk about "governing the state and pacifying the realm." How pitiable!²³

Here, for Chen and his fellow practitioners, lay the significance of Immortals' Learning: the personal pursuit of self-cultivation also had profound meanings for both the self and the nation. When applied outwardly to the realm, the Immortals' Learning manifested itself as sage governance, which could dissolve political disorder and social chaos and bring peace and prosperity to people. When applied inwardly, its cultivation techniques could transform the corruptible and transient self into an immortal who could defy illness, age, and death and be coeval with Heaven and Earth.²⁴ For Chen and his fellow practitioners, the fate of the Chinese nation depended on this learning: "So, as it was once said, without the Yellow Emperor's teachings for even one day, our nation will not have its center; and without Laozi's teachings for one day, our state shall have no future."²⁵

What emerged from Chen's nationalistic interpretations of the past was a new picture of Daoism, one at odds with earlier historiographic traditions. As portrayed by Chen and his associates, Daoism was linked with the legendary divine immortals and synonymous with the epochs of great harmony and peace in China's glorious past. Instead of Confucianism, ancient Daoism became the vehicle and repository for transmitting and preserving the true teachings of the ancient sages. As such, Daoism, not Confucianism, was the spirit informing Chinese culture and the moving force of China's history.

Another significant departure was Chen's rejection of the traditional portrayal of Daoism as a quietist way of life and thinking. Instead, the ancient Immortals' Learning was a robust and assertive tradition capable of repelling foreign cultural invasions, a tradition that had manifested itself in China's past in successive dynasties of sage rule, of conquest and unification, and of great social, political, and cultural triumphs and achievements.

Further, as a self-cultivation tradition aimed at transforming the body and the world, the Immortals' Learning was a robustly proactive (jiji jinqu 積極進取) and empirical (shizheng 實證) approach to life. In contrasting this learning with the Buddhist focus on the mind and the afterlife, Chen and his associates came to depict the Immortals' Learning as a practice that confronted ills and life crises by engaging the flesh body in transformative self-cultivation practice. The emphasis on centering the practice on the body, action, and empirical results was a deliberate break with the quietistic tradition exemplified in Zhuangzi, which Chen Yingning perceived as similar to Buddhism in its emphasis on spiritual enlightenment. At a time when China was experiencing a national crisis, the insistence on action rather than withdrawal or quietism revealed the moral activism and nativistic tendencies present in Chen and many of the Shanghai inner alchemy community. For Chen and many of his readers, such as the Master of the Pure Heart 淨心子, the Immortals' Learning offered a practical and effective regimen for national salvation, a program that would serve to rejuvenate and transform the national spirit through the rigorous individual pursuit of physio-spiritual self-cultivation and ultimately strengthen both the race and the state (qiangmin qiangguo 強民強國).[26]

Engaging This World: Anti-Buddhist Polemics

The nationalist vision of Immortals' Learning reached a height in the late 1930s when Japanese encroachments in China turned into full-fledged invasion and occupation. Chen's and his associates' Daoist nationalism against Japanese cultural and military expansion took the subtle form of an intense anti-Buddhist polemic, especially against Pure Land Buddhism, in Shanghai's popular media throughout the late 1930s and early 1940s. This perceived Japanese Buddhist influence aside, Buddhist ambivalence toward the body and its criticism of the Daoist focus on the flesh body as the vehicle of self-transformation were at the core of the polemics.

The Print Culture and Revival of Inner Alchemy 247

Although the Buddhist critique of the Daoist vision of the body had long been part of the Buddho-Daoist sectarian rift, it acquired a special urgency during the 1930s. By then, the Buddhist revival that began around the turn of the century under the leadership of such prominent lay leaders as Yang Wenhui and eminent monks like Taixu, Yuexia, and Yinguang had achieved tremendous success. Their influence was evident not only in the spiritual and intellectual rigor of a revived Buddhist monastic life but also in the proliferation of Buddhist journals and lay Buddhist self-cultivation societies and clubs throughout the country.

With publications such as the *Buddhist Transformation Monthly* (*Fohua yuekan* 佛化月刊) and *The Tidal Roar*, Buddhist reformers and lay activists achieved unprecedented influence and prestige among religious self-cultivation circles throughout the county. Buddhist dominance of religious discourse in the public sphere inspired a sense of pride among its constituency. In articles and commentaries, many Buddhist lay practitioners strongly asserted sectarian visions of truth and perfection. Some, especially among the lay advocates of Pure Land Buddhism, went even further by calling into question the validity of syncretist doctrines, tendencies, and practices among their own ranks and non-Buddhist communities. They promoted sutra recitation and invocation of the Buddha's name as the supreme, if not the exclusive, way of achieving transcendence or enlightenment. Through an extensive network of local Buddhist lay cultivation centers (*jushi lin*) and several widely circulated journals, many Pure Land Buddhists also evoked the proverbial Buddhist critique of Daoist practices as being "outside the Way" (*waidao* 外道). In these sectarian writings, Buddhists often labeled Daoist inner alchemy practitioners as "corpse-clinging ghosts" (*shoushi gui* 守屍鬼) who could not escape their wretched destiny of repeated and futile rebirths on the Buddhist wheel of karma (*bu mian lunhui* 不免輪回) because of their emphasis on the centrality of the flesh body for the ultimate self-transformation.[27]

These Buddhist jibes often triggered equally strong responses from Chen and his fellow practitioners. In the summer of 1934, Zhang Huasheng, a well-known Buddhist reformer, lay activist, and educator in Wuchang, wrote Chen and his colleagues at the *Yangshan*

Biweekly a sympathetic letter. In his letter, Zhang expressed his objections to Buddhist attacks on Daoism and inner alchemy. In his reply and subsequently serialized comments on a booklet Zhang had written, Chen offered an impassioned analysis of the philosophical and cultural "failings" of Buddhism and western materialism. Echoing themes familiar from the 1920s science vs. metaphysics debate among Chinese intellectuals, Chen faulted Buddhist idealism and western materialism for their respective failures and excesses. He was particularly critical of Buddhism for its perceived inadequacies in dealing with life's daily challenges due to illness, aging, and death.[28]

Chen's response inaugurated an intense anti-Buddhist polemic in the *Yangshan Biweekly*. Many other similar writings by readers of the journal soon followed. A few pro-Buddhist responses were printed, only to provoke more fierce rebuttals. The polemic escalated into an open war of words in early 1936 as pro-Daoist writers and respondents dismissed Buddhism as an outright "fraud and heterodoxy." For those outside and even inside the Buddhist camp, the Pure Land lay activists' sectarian stance was not just misguided, but downright dangerous. In light of China's declining power in the face of Japanese encroachments in Manchuria and north China, the Pure Land sect's close ties with its Japanese colleagues were viewed with deep suspicion, and its teachings on submission and nonviolence were considered irrelevant, if not treasonous.

Daoist nationalism and sectarian resentment fused into a retaliatory polemic against Pure Land Buddhism. In January 1936, the *Yangshan* editors received an essay contributed by a young student and practitioner from Shanghai who claimed that he was studying philosophy in college. In his "Verdict on Immortalology and Buddhism," Qian Xin made a point-by-point comparison of what he perceived to be the weaknesses of Buddhism and the strengths of the Immortals' Learning and indicted Buddhism as a "superstition" that had been destroying the Chinese nation.[29]

Qian's blunt sectarian "judgment" created a stir, even among the *Biweekly*'s editors. Concerned over its outright attack on Buddhist doctrines and practice, they convened a special meeting to decide whether to publish it. Some such as Wang Boying were concerned about the public's reaction, especially from Buddhists, and the essay's possible negative impact on the *Biweekly*'s stated position of fairness. Chen shared some of these concerns and was critical of Qian Xin's sweeping attack on Buddhism as "superstitious." For Chen, who enjoyed friendships with eminent Buddhist monks and lay adepts, the problem was not so much Buddhism per se as Pure Land sectarian zealotry. To Chen, many of these zealots denigrated both the Daoist and the Confucian traditions by rejecting them as inferior to Buddhism. Particularly inflammatory were Buddhist condemnations of the *Yangshan Biweekly*'s articles about Daoist inner alchemy and other self-cultivation practices as being "outside the Way" and of the Daoist self-cultivation practitioners as being doomed to hell permanently (*bumian lunhui* 不免輪回). In the end, Chen and Zhang Zhuming decided to respond to these degrading remarks by publishing Qian Xin's article. They argued that given the current national crisis, the essay could serve as a warning cry to "alert and awaken the nation from its slumbers" (*jingxing guomin zhi mimeng* 警醒國民之迷夢).[30]

At stake in the war of words between the Pure Land Buddhists and the Shanghai inner alchemic practitioners were issues of cultural identity and authenticity. The rebuttals of Buddhist attacks addressed the essential differences between Buddhism and inner alchemy. In affirming the role of the flesh body in the quest for spiritual transcendence and immortality, and in attacking the Buddhist denigration of the body and the present life, Chen and his associates reinforced doctrinal boundaries between Buddhist and Daoist inner alchemic practice, thus forging a stronger sense of identity and community among the practitioners in the Shanghai inner alchemy community.

Further, the anti–Pure Land polemics carried an anti-Japanese nationalist undertone. In characterizing Buddhism as a foreign invasion that was enervating the Chinese nation and Chinese culture, Chen and the other contributors thus impugned the close ties between the Chinese Pure Land sects and their Japanese counterparts as part of Japanese expansionism in China. The traditional Daoist resentment of Buddhism was galvanized by the nationalistic rise in popular antipathy toward Japanese imperialism.

Promoting the Affinity Between Science and the Immortals' Learning

Paralleling their anti-Buddhist polemics of the mid-1930s, Chen and his fellow practitioners also made efforts to accommodate and integrate modern science into Daoist discourse. Indeed, science came to constitute an important component of early twentieth-century Daoism in Shanghai. As with Buddhism, however, Chen and his associates felt ambivalent toward science as a system of knowledge and values. Their understanding of science had been shaped by the perception of western technological superiority as a tool for advancing imperialist interests in China. Yet science and its practical impacts had become permanent fixtures in the daily life of many urban professionals such as Chen Yingning. In addition to a traditional Chinese education, Chen and most of his social peers had also been schooled in western science. Many were trained specialists in the fields of medicine, geology, chemistry, and modern education.[31] But more fundamentally, Chen and his associates envisioned Daoism as congruent with science and tried to uncover Daoist spiritual or intellectual parallels to the scientific spirit (kexue jingshen 科學精神) by exploring the early Daoist legacy of alchemic techniques and processes. Between the early 1910s and the early 1930s, Chen and his fellow alchemists conducted hundreds of experiments, smelting various metals and compounding various chemical ingredients at Chen's residence in the city.[32]

Although their outer alchemy pursuits were twice disrupted by the outbreak of wars in and around Shanghai during the 1920s and early 1930s,[33] Chen and his associates derived from their experiments a strong sense of confidence and pride in the Daoist tradition. In a speech given in English at the invitation of the Shanghai International Mission (Shanghai wanguo zhengdao hui 上海萬國證道會) in the late 1930s, Dr. Shen Linsheng, a mineralogist by training and one of Chen's disciples, described for his western audience the history of Daoist outer and inner alchemy. Based on his years of study of Daoism and his expertise in mineralogy and metallurgy, Shen concluded that Daoist alchemic processes already "contained techniques and methods used in modern chemistry and metallurgy" (bao-

han huaxue he yejin de fangfa 包涵化學和冶金的方法). Shen's lectures were later translated into Chinese by Chen Yingning and published in the *Xiandao Monthly* in 1939. Two years later, in April 1941, Wang Quande 王權德, another member of the Shanghai inner alchemy community, published a critical study of the history of Chinese alchemy written by Obed Johnson of the University of California in 1928.[34]

Indeed, for Chen and many of his fellow practitioners, the core Daoist concept of the interchangeability of various forms of matter qualified Daoist alchemy as the forerunner of modern chemistry. In his preface to a Qing text on outer alchemy published by Yihuatang, Zhang Zhuming informed his modern audience:

The use of lead and mercury and the transmutation of silver and gold are nothing but changes in the [number of] electrons and the nucleus of matter in the most advanced chemistry of modern science. That is why even modern chemists would say that it is possible that nuclei can mutate and why they no longer adhere to the old proposition that matter does not mutate. Yet in fact, this kind of theory had long been developed in the antiquity of our country. Hence the old saying goes, "One ingot can be multiplied into ten thousand pieces, whereas ten thousand pieces can aggregate back into one ingot" (*yiben san wei wanzhu, wanzhu huangui yiben* 一本散爲萬銖, 萬銖還歸一本).

For Zhang, Chen, and their colleagues, their conviction of the affinity between Daoist alchemy and modern science was not only confirmed by the advances in modern chemistry's understanding of the subatomic properties of matter but also validated by western scholarship on Chinese alchemy. Citing the evaluation of the Chinese contribution to chemistry by a Professor E. Williams of the University of California and the study of early Chinese alchemy by Obed S. Johnson, Zhang Zhuming censured his fellow countrymen for their ignorance of their own cultural legacy and their diffidence in the face of criticisms of its viability. To preserve the tradition of outer alchemy, Chen and his colleagues collected and reprinted several Daoist outer alchemic scriptures from the late imperial period.[35]

But, most important, through their alchemic experiments, Chen and his associates were able to relive and reimagine early Daoist outer alchemy and gain for themselves a sense of cultural and spiritual confidence. Their experiences also convinced them that early Daoist outer alchemy experiments were intrinsically similar to those of modern science. They also perceived in the outer alchemy tradition an ethos similar to that of modern science, which valued action over passivity, actual results over blind faith, practice over theorizing, innovation over the status quo, and experiments over empty talk. It was thus no accident that Chen and his associates came to valorize and publicize these core values as the new ethos of the Immortals' Learning in the *Yangshan Biweekly* from 1935 on.

Aside from sharing their outer alchemy experiments and exploring the scientific origins of Daoism, Chen and his associates also tirelessly publicized in the *Yangshan Biweekly* their vision of the affinity between Daoism and science by reinterpreting the alchemic body with concepts borrowed from modern physics, physiology, and cellular biology. Chen Yingning actively promoted his vision of the affinity between inner alchemy and science in his writings. In a letter published in the *Biweekly* in 1936, Chen delivered a scathing criticism of what he perceived to be the Buddhist vision of the body and cosmos as the Void and argued in favor of the Daoist vitalistic vision of the body:

According to my personal cross-verification, the Void is nothing but a hypocritical fraud and empty talk and is completely devoid of reality. Saturating and full, matter fills Heaven and Earth. Where is a place that is void and empty? But because there are myriads of minuscule matter invisible to the eye, they are simply labeled as the Empty Void (*xu kong* 虛空). Ice turns to water. Water then turns to vapor. Vapor further disperses to become the Empty Void. But even if it is called the Empty Void, it is neither empty nor vacuous because the substance of water and ice still exists in the universe. If one thinks that it is empty, vacuous, and nonexistent, isn't one in grave error?

Reasoning in such plain yet compelling language, Chen imparted to his modern audience a materialist view of the world in contrast to the Buddhist cult of the Void. For Chen, the world was made up of matter. The cosmos and the body were undeniably material and physical. Like water, the physical world may take various forms. But regardless how ephemeral and formless it may appear, it exists as solid matter. Chen argued that it was precisely the material nature of life and the world that constituted the basis for the possible integration of Daoism and science.[36]

Others from the Shanghai inner alchemy community also actively promoted the scientific reinterpretation of Daoism. Dr. Shi Yixuan 施毅軒, a medical doctor and a disciple of Chen Yingning, attempted to explain the natural aging process of the body in terms of the shape of brain cells and the number of electrons (*dianzi*) contained in a cell. Trained in Western medicine, Dr. Shi had grown interested in Daoist self-cultivation practice while serving in the Nationalist Army as a field surgeon. His love of the Qing inner alchemist Huang Shang's classic so impressed a colleague that the latter gave him a rare woodblock-print copy of the book from his own collection. Dr. Shi read it avidly to guide his personal practice in Daoist inner alchemy. He even took the book with him on a trip to study tropical medicine in Bombay at the height of World War II in the early 1940s in anticipation of Chinese expeditions against Japanese forces in Burma.[37]

Drawing on studies in cellular biology, physiology, physics, and chemistry, Dr. Shi described the human body as an organism consisting of cells, whose internal dynamics held the key to understanding all human biological and psychological processes and functions. In a 1930 preface to a Daoist self-cultivation tract, Dr. Shi wrote that the interactions among electrons within the cell controlled and directed the mental, physiological, and chemical processes of the body. He further explained that understanding how the cells, especially brain cells, functioned was thus the key to uncovering the mystery of processes within the body:

The structure of the brain cell is similar to that of other cells. The nucleus is in the center surrounded by the cell wall. Its chemical composites are protein, glucose, fat, phosphorus, calcium, and water, among others. Its physics is truly profound and still remains an unsolved mystery in science. But all these chemical ingredients are coalesced together. The interactive attraction and repulsion among the electrons make the cell operate and perform its physiological functions. This has been proven by science.

Citing neurological findings that overused brain cells in the aged tended to be triangular in shape whereas seldom-used brain cells in the young were round, Dr. Shi speculated that the vitality of a brain cell depended on the number of electrons it contained. Since round-shaped brain cells could hold more electrons than the triangular brain cells, the young could grow and thrive with robust *qi* with no physical symptoms of aging and decay. Thus, the key to physical vitality and youth was to maintain and augment the number of electrons in the brain cells. Dr. Shi assured his readers that Daoist practices such as quiet sitting and meditation were the most efficient ways to maintain the electron capacity of the brain cells, and that paired or dual cultivation involving practitioners of both sexes offered the best approach for gathering electrons to rejuvenate the cells of the body. Although solo meditation helped conserve electrons within the body by slowing the metabolism, paired cultivation allowed the male and the female practitioners to gather and exchange electrons in a sexually charged environment that Shi deemed conducive to their generation and absorption.[38]

The "scientizing" efforts reached their height when Chen Yingning circulated his unpublished manuscript, "Learning Immortals Will Surely Succeed," among a close circle of friends in Shanghai in 1945. In his manuscript, Chen systematically incorporated concepts from physics, physiology, and biology to interpret the fundamental notions and processes of Daoist cosmology, as well as the techniques and methods of Daoist inner alchemy practice. Yet, Chen's and his associates' engagement with modern science primarily served their goal of "modernizing" Daoism by reformulating and recasting traditional Daoist inner alchemic discourse in scientific language and concepts accessible to their modern, lay, urban constituencies. They remained keenly aware of the limits of their accommodation with science and never abandoned their own vision of the vitalistic potentials of the alchemic body, potentials that could help transcend the materialistic determinism of science and lead to immortality.[39]

Their yearning for transcendence and immortality through the perfection of both the body and the mind reflected a profound anxiety about bridging the gap between the nihilistic tendencies of Buddhism and the materialistic determinism of modern science. To Chen and his fellow practitioners, the scientific affirmation of the physicality of the body was not a barrier to achieving perfection.

Rather, it was the very means of transforming the body. As the embodiment of the protean continuum, the body's materiality contained the seeds for reversing the natural transformation inherent to the body. This reversal could be effected only by uniting the functional substantive aspects of the Way. This was another important motive behind Chen's efforts at integrating science with traditional inner alchemy.

Chen's and his associates' appropriation of science must not be understood purely in utilitarian or sectarian terms. The open and public discourse about the affinities between science and Daoism reflected a genuine attempt among modern Daoist intellectuals and practitioners to reconstruct an authentic body of the culture and the nation at a historical juncture in modern China. Not only was this reconstruction a metaphysical exercise, but it also carried political and cultural meanings for the public and the practitioners alike. For Chen and his audience, a physical and substantive body was not a mere philosophical subtlety. The material body itself was reason for action and self-cultivation. Contentment with simply being human amounted to a waste of the human potential for perfection. At a time when the survival of the nation was in doubt, a failure to strengthen one's body through self-cultivation was tantamount to dereliction of one's moral duties toward one's self and one's nation.

Expanding the Daoist Cultivation Community

Both the robust public discourse and the flourishing print culture gave rise to significant institutional developments that helped forge and expand the inner alchemy community. The nationwide circulation of the *Yangshan* and *Xiandao* journals transcended the geographic and sociological barriers separating practitioners. The ability to share experiences through writings, letters, travels, and meetings helped forge a sense of fellowship and an imagined community of practitioners.

Sharing one's experience with the public and fellow practitioners was an important means of building this community. In the fall of 1938, when Hong Tai'an, the Fujian merchant and inner alchemy practitioner living in Manila, shared his ruminations over his time-ravaged body and his renewed resolve to pursue the practice in a poem composed on his sixty-first birthday, he triggered a wide sympathetic response among his readers and fellow practitioners at home. Chen Chengkai 陳誠凱, a Quanzhen Daoist cleric at the Purple Ganoderma Monastery (Zizhi guan 紫芝觀) in coastal Yueqing 樂清 county in southern Zhejiang, responded by recalling his own decades of struggles in the pursuit of the practice:[40]

> For years I've admired the name of purity.
> Yet mere talk about the Way leads not to immortality.
> Having obtained the secrets of long life, sir,
> Who can rival you in reaching the bank yonder?
> I stand seven feet tall between earth and heaven;
> But with no one could I discuss the art of refining the elixir
>   and mercury!
>
> Ashamed that I've entered the Order of Mystery when young,
> Still I have yet to detach from the mundane.
> Adrift amid waves of the human sea,
> I have strayed and yet to awaken.
> But how I yearn to intuit and penetrate the Portal of the Dark.
> So that I may soar with the Wind, unfettered and free!
>
> How chaotic and tumultuous are the times!
> But the soldiers on the battlefields shirk not their duties.
> Sacrificing their bodies for the country, their souls rise
>   to heaven,
> And their names linger fragrant in the world to eternity.
> Having perfected the nine-cycled elixir, I will also follow
>   the Jade Boy;[41]
> With the Three Flowers gathered atop, I'll join the
>   Cycled Wind,[42]
> And wait for the day when I soar astride a crane, heaven-bound
> With my fellow immortals to the Purple Palace, hand in hand.

The Daoist cleric's poem was published in September 1939 during the Japanese occupation of the lower Yangtze delta region. Even as Chen spoke admiringly of Hong's acquisition of the oral secrets of longevity, he bemoaned his own ensnarement in the chaos of war. Although the Daoist expressed his regrets at not achieving the same progress as Hong, he also felt inspired by the courage and sacrifice of the resistance fighters. Pledging to renew his own efforts at perfecting "the nine-cycled elixir" (*jiuzhuan dancheng* 九轉丹成), Chen looked forward to joining Hong and other cultivators in attaining immortality and ascending to the Daoist empyrean.

It was precisely this kind of public sharing among practitioners that helped draw them close and forge a sense of fellowship. This form of communication reflected another important change wrought by the modern print culture on the practice of inner alchemy in the twentieth century. As the *Yangshan* and the *Xiandao* journals circulated among an audience separated by geographic as well as socioeconomic barriers, they became a bridge that connected urban lay practitioners and Daoist clerics and monasteries. Further, many practitioners also came to rely on the journals as an alternative or an addition to the traditional sources of inner alchemic learning and support in the practice.

Chen Yingning and his colleagues envisioned the *Yangshan Biweekly* not only as a venue to promote the Immortals' Learning but also as a center of support and communication for their readers and fellow practitioners. To realize this vision, they revamped the *Biweekly* by reorganizing its contents into about twenty different columns to attract and serve the various interests of readers. The new columns addressed issues and interests of concern to the expanding readership. Except for a few syncretist columns dealing with morality, public issues, and the teachings of other religions, the majority of the new columns were devoted to inner alchemy and Daoism.

Under the heading "Correspondences and Answers" ("Tonghan wenda" 通函問答), Chen Yingning and other adepts at the *Biweekly* addressed a multitude of queries on a regular basis. In addition to the published answers and discussions, Chen and his colleagues sometimes corresponded privately with readers on issues such as seminal emissions,[43] somatic or sensory experiences of the practice,[44] and the economy of inner alchemic practice.[45] They also published a host of personal practice diaries, testimonials, and memoirs by members of the Shanghai inner alchemy community.[46]

Chen and his associates encouraged their readers and fellow practitioners to build connections. In their replies, they often referred inquirers to nearby practitioners and adepts as potential teachers or fellow cultivators. The experience of reading an inquiry in the journals from another cultivator in one's hometown or an adjacent region was often the first impetus toward forming a local group of similarly minded devotees.[47] With encouragement from Chen and others at the *Biweekly*, some practitioners sought to form fellowships with other cultivators through personal advertisements. The advertisers would place recruiting notices in the journal, describing in great detail their own methods or approaches to inner alchemy and their level of proficiency, current level of achievement, and goals. In March 1937, for example, Zhao Yinhua 趙隱華, a postal clerk from the port city of Lianyungang 連雲港 in Jiangsu, placed an ad soliciting qualified fellow practitioners (*daoyou*) to join him in the practice. He posited a series of issues designed to elicit responses that would help him gauge the level of knowledge and proficiency of respondents:

Both the Great and the Small Vehicles and the Chan Buddhist approaches are paths for virgins to follow in their cultivation so as to reach the shore of Salvation. But the Great Way of the Golden Elixir is designed specially for adults to pursue cultivation. But both are correct and sanctioned ways. Although their paths differ, their goals remain one and the same.

I hereby seek fellow cultivators who have obtained the oral secrets for the above two paths. Please respond in letters and elaborate on the following questions as the standard. Those who have not received an oral transmission from their masters and would rely on their own wits and imagination in responding need not write so as not to waste our mutual time. I propose the following:

"So the Great Way consists of three elements: the Drug, the Firing Moment, and the Merging of the Elixir."

Please try to explain the procedures involved in each of the three. . . . Please do not equivocate in your response. Do not use technical jargon. You may be circumspect in vernacular language (*baihua* 白話) for the purpose of concealment. Also explain who your transmitting masters are. If your response accords with the Great Way, I am willing to form our fellowship to study the Way so as to reach Penglai together (*gong deng Penglai* 共登蓬萊).[48]

An adequate response to Zhao's ad would require both familiarity with the literature and proficiency in the practice. By placing an ad in a widely circulated journal, practitioners like Zhao hoped to increase their chance of encountering other accomplished practitioners. More remarkably, Zhao's ad was indicative of the lateral connections found among practitioners. As an alternative to the more hierarchically structured traditional model of adept and novice, the lateral ties between fellow practitioners made possible through such ads provided new venues and opportunities for learning, mutual support, and partnership.

Publication of the *Yangshan Biweekly* also fundamentally changed the traditional ways of fulfilling the four cardinal prerequisites of the practice. The modern inner alchemist's search for methods, funds, companionship, and sites became an increasingly public and shared endeavor, a process that was read, imagined, and sometimes joined by many fellow practitioners among the reading public.

The search for practice sites or locations used to be a private act among close associates. Yet when news of such searches was published in public media, they became increasingly public and shared experiences. Chen Yingning and his associates had this development in mind when they first began publishing a column devoted to travelogues and Daoist geography in early 1935. The travelogue column published travel narratives written by both lay and monastic practitioners from various regions of China. In addition to describing the geographical and geomantic conditions of various locales, these narratives also offered accounts of local history and lore that related specifically to Daoism and inner alchemy, as well as detailed information about the current physical, social, and economic conditions of regions where prospective practice sites were located.[49]

Early in the fall of 1933, for example, Zhou Minde, one of Chen Yingning's disciples, wrote about the Grotto of the Treasured Light (Baoguang dong 寶光洞), a Daoist sacred site located in Gaizhu Mountain 蓋竹山 in Yueqing county in southern Zhejiang. Zhou invoked the Tang Daoist Du Guangting's geographical survey of Daoist sacred sites in his narrative, but he also provided information on recent conditions at this sacred site. The publication of Zhou's piece in the *Yangshan Biweekly* informed the practitioners about the current potentials of the site as a cultivation location. More important, both Zhou's personal account of his search and the historical narrative of the sacred grotto became a publicly shared experience as they were read by fellow practitioners and the public.[50]

In the fall of 1939, during the height of the Japanese invasion of the lower Yangtze delta region, experiences of the Treasured Light Grotto came to life through the exchange of poems and information on searches for practice sites by other practitioners. Throughout the 1930s, Ye Xueyu 葉學愚, a Daoist cleric from the Purple Ganoderma Temple, lived and practiced at the grotto in the Gaizhu Mountain. While there, Ye renovated the decrepit mountain grotto and earned a reputation among the local elite and fellow Daoists. Many flocked to the grotto for an audience with the Daoist adept. Some wrote poems expressing admiration of the history of the grotto and its resident adept. These poems were forwarded by Chen Chengkai to the *Yangshan Biweekly* for publication in the winter of 1939. One of the poems celebrated the selection of the site and likened the resident adept to the late Jin Quanzhen patriarch Qiu Chuji:

> A quiet site well chosen for cultivating the Way;
> A life-nourishing method emulating Master Qiu Chuji.
> Three thousand eight hundred merits accomplished,
> You ascend to roam the sky astride a crane.

For readers, travelogues and verses like this served to consecrate the site as an ideal practice location. But more important, their publication turned the private search for a practice location into an experience imagined and enjoyed by the general public. In the same way, Zhou's verse about the grotto inspired public imagination about the site, and the personal pilgrimage depicted in the poem became a public journey and celebration.[51]

The *Yangshan Biweekly*'s open format also made it easier to break down gender barriers between male and female practitioners. The publication of the series of female inner alchemy classics made technical knowledge more accessible to female practitioners. Further, the journal's public and open columns rendered Daoist knowledge and adepts like Chen Yingning equally accessible to both sexes.

Indeed, throughout the 1930s, written correspondence was a common means of learning and inquiry for both women and men. Like many other female practitioners, Zhang Zhide 張志德, a woman practitioner in her forties living in Shanghai, first learned about the practice of "slaying the Scarlet Dragon" through her correspondence with Chen Yingning. From November 1936 to August 1937, Miss Zhang wrote several times to query Chen about the alchemic processes, somatic sensations, and bodily changes during the practice:

Around three o'clock in the morning on June 26, I sat cross-legged for a while before I started to feel the Bottom of the Sea warming up. In no time, I also felt warm in the navel and breasts. Meanwhile, I also felt warm and crawling movements in the forehead and feet. Then, as things quieted down, I entered the Hundun state,[52] but only for a brief while. This repeated itself up to six times. By the seventh round, I suddenly felt my whole body tense and tightening up, as if numb and intoxicated. My breathing felt unnatural. At this time, my head and chest felt very hot, almost perspiring. My Weilü locus and my spine weighed down unbearably heavy.[53] I immediately dealt with it by applying the method of Three Stillnesses.[54] In about twenty minutes, my body gradually loosened up and my breathing returned to normal. The above conditions occurred on the third day after my menses came. It was almost the same as my last report to you. Last time, it also occurred on the third day of my period, except there was perspiration last time whereas there was none this time. Also it lasted longer this time. Attached are my five questions:

1. Every time, before and after my period, I always feel a warm *qi* swelling and pulsating in the Sea of Blood and my privates.[55] I also feel in both legs a sensation of "numbing pleasure."[56] Is this the start of the True Yin? Even as I tried to retrieve it with focused intention, I at times could not quite hold it back. Would you advise me by giving me the oral secrets for retrieving and gathering it so that it wouldn't get lost beyond recovery?[57]

The frankness and straightforwardness with which Miss Zhang discussed her body and bodily processes during the practice was indicative of how comfortable and at ease women practitioners felt in communicating with their adepts. Published correspondences like these opened a unique channel for women as well as men to gain access to Daoist knowledge and inner alchemic masters like Chen Yingning. In a way communicating through letters allowed practitioners to bypass the usual gender and hierarchical complexities of the traditional model of the face-to-face master-disciple relationship.

Correspondence sometimes led to actual travels that completed the quest for a master. In January 1937, soon after she wrote to Chen Yingning, Zhang Zhide visited him at his retreat in the western suburbs of Shanghai. There, with Chen's wife as an intermediary, Zhang queried Chen in person on many more issues relating to women's inner alchemic practice. Zhang later returned to Shanghai, where she rented an apartment and carried on her practice of female inner alchemy entirely on her own means.[58] Indeed, for many, reading the journals was often the beginning of travels in search of a teacher. Whereas a practitioner like Zhang Zhide first established a relationship through correspondence with adepts like Chen, others sought a personal meeting. Many, such as Dr. Hu Haiya 胡海牙, who later became Chen's disciple, even traveled unannounced to Shanghai hoping for a meeting with Chen.[59]

What emerged from published correspondences and inquiries were not only a new model for discussing and transmitting Daoist knowledge and practice but also a vibrant and thriving public space and community. The sense of community and fellowship forged through the public circulation of discussions on inner alchemy gradually gave rise to public expressions of a collective wish for a more institutionalized form of community among practitioners.

A dramatic expression of this interest in developing new forms of organization was a series of published proposals for establishing a national center or group for Daoist inner alchemy practice (*xiudao jituan* 修道集團). The idea of a national organization to promote and coordinate the practice of inner alchemy was initially conceived by Chen Yingning and his associates at the *Yangshan Biweekly* around 1935. Chen and his followers hoped that a national center would help pool scattered financial and material resources to help more lay and monastic practitioners efficiently:

As for the aspirations in my heart, not even one in ten thousand has been realized. An enterprise of such great importance and magnitude cannot be borne solely by individuals. We must get to know more comrades in arms who share the same aspirations, are in spirit willing to sacrifice for all, and possess superior talents and skills. All of us can then establish a congregation (*tuan ti* 團體) to carry out the work. Only then can we have some hope of success.[60]

The Print Culture and Revival of Inner Alchemy 263

In 1937, when at Chen's behest the *Yangshan Biweekly* published a call for proposals, lay and monastic practitioners responded by sending suggestions and plans for such a national organization. Many proposals included detailed bylaws, funding schemes, and rules for operation and membership and even proposed sites for the national headquarters of the organization. The remarkable consensus among the respondents attests to the cohesion among practitioners from around the country. Cai Jimin 蔡積民, a practitioner from Zhejiang proposed:

As for the name of the organization, we can settle on Chinese Institute of Immortals' Learning (Zhonghua xianxue yuan 中華仙學院). Since the Immortals' Learning is a unique national essence exclusive to our nation, we must name it "Chinese." If we call it a temple or monastery, it would easily get tangled up with Buddhist or Daoist habitats. As for such terms as "society" or "club," they sound too much like a kind of social or political organization. Since we students of immortality are always engaged in experiments and practices much like a school, we might as well name it outright the "Academy of Immortals' Learning."

All the internal operations must be made public. Such things as facilities, budget and expenses, membership, progress, daily routines, and others can all be made public for everyone in the public to see. Thus, they will understand our group is a well-organized, orderly, and well-equipped congregation devoted to the Immortals' Learning. Not only will they pay attention and know that we have Immortals' Learning in China, but they will also come to know that it is a viable practice. It is not some religion or philosophy with empty theories. Nor it is a superstition with monotheistic or polytheistic worship.[61]

Cai's emphases on openness, on practice, on cultural and national uniqueness, and on distinction and autonomy from traditional religions reflected a shared desire to bring the practice of inner alchemy up to date with the emerging trends of modernity, science, and nationalism. The choice of the academy or institute as the format for the organization reflected urban elite practitioners' social and educational backgrounds. The insistence on bylaws and rules of operation for the proposed congregation also mirrored these urban elite practitioners' expertise in modern corporate, political, and social organization on one hand and their desire and ability to adapt to the modern state's rigorous regulatory framework for all religious and social organizations on the other.

The format and the method Chen and his associates adopted in planning and preparing for such a national center deserves consideration. Arguably, public consultation, solicitation, and participation in decision making were in part necessitated by the nature and structure of a community held together through the circulation of the *Yangshan Biweekly*. But the implementation of these processes is evidence of how popular and democratic the practice of modern Daoist inner alchemy had become.

The Institute of Immortals' Learning, 1937–41

By the fall of 1937, Japanese forces had taken control of Shanghai, except for the small enclaves within the city controlled by the western powers. As the Japanese siege of the city began earlier in the summer, numerous refugees dislodged from their homes in the suburbs and the surrounding regions sought a safe haven in the International Settlement or the French Concession. Chen Yingning and his wife abandoned their personal belongings and valuable books in their home near Meilong Town 梅龍鎮 in the western suburbs and fled into the French Concession in the western part of the city. From the fall of 1937 to December 1941, when the Japanese overran the foreign concessions, they lived precariously, like many of their fellow inner alchemists, on an isolated island surrounded by Japanese occupation forces.

Yet the occupation did not stop Chen and his colleagues from continuing to promote the Immortals' Learning and pursuing inner alchemy. At the height of the Japanese occupation of greater Shanghai in 1938, Chen Yingning and fellow practitioners who had escaped into the foreign concessions demonstrated their solidarity and common identity by establishing the Shanghai Institute of Immortals' Learning (Shanghai Xianxue yuan 上海仙學院). The institute was the culmination of years of collective effort by Chen and his associates. Founding an institute dedicated to the pursuit of the Immortals' Learning and giving it an unmistakably nationalist name showed Chen and his colleagues' determination to resist the Japanese occupation of the country. The institute was located in a modest building Chen Yingning, Dr. Zhang Zhuming, and a group of close associates had rented in a remote and quiet district in the French Concession. Its members were inner alchemic practitioners from Shanghai.

Chen played a vital role in sustaining the operations of the institute. During the week, the institute doubled as the meditation hall where members could gather to practice quiet sitting and meditation. On weekends, a small congregation of practitioners gathered at the house to listen to lectures by Chen Yingning and others and engage in discussion. From May 1938 to early 1941, Chen delivered a series of lectures on inner alchemy classics at the institute. These lectures proved successful and attracted many Daoists and lay practitioners of inner alchemy throughout the Shanghai region. When news of the institute and Chen's lectures got out, a flood of letters poured into the *Xiandao Monthly*. Many practitioners wrote the editors asking for permission to join the institute and to attend the lectures. Those who could not make it to Shanghai wrote letters requesting that the lectures be made available to them as correspondence courses through the mail.[62]

Although the institute's seminary format reflected the influence of the modern Buddhist educational reforms in which Chen had participated, the Immortals' Learning institute was unprecedented and innovative in its own right. The use of lectures (*jiangyan* 講演) as a means of discoursing and disseminating knowledge of inner alchemy was a far cry from the days of private instruction and secret transmissions. It also suggested that Chen Yingning and his colleagues saw inner alchemy as a public body of knowledge, not unlike other discourses of knowledge that could and should be made available to the public.

While they continued their efforts in organizing and disseminating inner alchemic practice, Chen and his associates also revived the *Yangshan Biweekly* as the *Xiandao Monthly* in January 1939. The *Monthly* carried on the role of supporting individual practitioners, now living in various divided regions of the country. Through the postal services inside the foreign concessions, the *Monthly* managed to keep open its lines of distribution and communication. One of the first tasks of the editors was to publish a notice calling on readers to send in reports about fellow cultivators and local organizations so that contacts with them could be re-established.[63]

But the war and the Japanese occupation exerted considerable pressure on the *Xiandao Monthly* and the community of inner alchemy practitioners. Operating from within the foreign concessions and surrounded and monitored by the Japanese occupation forces, the journal had to be registered with the Police Bureau of the International Settlement. In each issue, the editors felt it necessary to remind readers and contributors of their renunciation of "political discussion" (*butan zhengzhi* 不談政治). In addition, with the flight of some staff and rising production costs, the revived journal could be published only once a month. As the Japanese invasion spread to other parts of the country, many subscribers complained about interrupted or lost mail deliveries. As more refugees from outside Shanghai poured into the foreign concessions, prices of daily necessities and housing rose, inflation soared, and unemployment became rampant. As a result, the *Xiandao Monthly* fell victim to repeated postal rate hikes implemented by the Postal Service of the International Settlement. The editors felt it necessary to publish the new postal fee schedule to inform their readers about the rate hikes. To ensure safe delivery, they also recommended registered mail, which more than doubled delivery costs. In October 1939, the Yihuatang publishing house was forced to raise the prices of its Daoist titles by 20 percent. By August 1940, paper prices had risen tenfold, and the *Xiandao Monthly* had to increase the price by 100 percent.[64]

Yet amid the political chaos and economic hardships in the isolated foreign concessions, the *Xiandao Monthly* editors still hoped for a better future:

We sincerely hope that from today onward, the destiny of our country may turn to the better. May the heart of the people be harmonious and peaceful. May tragic calamity end. May there be a fresh and new beginning, with traffic order restored, prices gradually lowered, and production fulfilled and the economy self-sufficient. May social order be stabilized and famous mountains and sacred sites be unscathed by wars, so that all our fellow pursuers of the Immortals' Way will be able to put their ideals into practice.... But to overcome the present hardships, we must rely on our own courage, wisdom, and forbearance.[65]

But the Japanese occupation authority and its puppet regime in Shanghai soon dealt a severe blow to the community of inner alchemy practitioners. During the height of Japanese occupation between 1937 and 1945, some from the Shanghai Daoist community chose collaboration under pressure and established several regional and national Daoist organizations under the Japanese-controlled puppet regime in the city and Nanjing. The most prominent was a short-lived national organization, the General Daoist Association of China (Zhonghua Daojiao zonghui 中華道教總會). It was established in 1944 at the White Cloud Monastery in Shanghai, with the blessing of the Ministry of Social Welfare (Shehui fuli bu 社會福利部) and the Examination Yuan (Kaoshi yuan 考試院) of the puppet regime in Nanjing. Several prominent Daoist leaders with ties to the Shanghai community of inner alchemy practitioners served on its board of directors.[66] Although their motives were complex and remain poorly understood, some seemed to have based their action on the grounds of sheer convenience and survival.[67]

But many others, including Chen Yingning, adopted the path of passive resistance. In the summer of 1937, when Shanghai was falling to the Japanese, a few Daoist abbots from Sichuan wrote Chen inviting him to move to that province. Chen declined the offer and chose to stay behind with his ailing wife.[68] Yet during the years of the Japanese occupation, some of Chen's fellow cultivators from outside Shanghai wrote to the *Xiandao Monthly* speculating that Chen had given up promoting the Immortals' Way. These conjectures gravely troubled Chen. In a long reply, published in May 1939, Chen explained his thinking on the situation and his solution to the problem the nation confronted:

Having read Mr. Qian Daoji's letter, which you forwarded to me, I am overwhelmed with pity and grief. The situation in East Asia today was not created in one day; it is the result of prolonged processes. To salvage this catastrophe (*haojie* 浩劫), one must first observe the people's heart. If the majority of the people are truly disgusted with the disorder, there will surely be hope for pacification and harmony (*zhiping* 治平). But only a few people [with such hopes] cannot be of great help in the matter. I now follow Confucius' axiom, "When you are not in office, do not execute its duties." I only know how to live up to my personal obligations. This is not about being numb or taking nothing to heart (*moran wudong yuzhong* 寞然無動

於衷). Nor is this simply sitting and waiting for fortune to turn under the pretext that opportunity is not ripe yet. So none of Mr. Qian's speculations fit my way of thinking.

In tracing the origins of the catastrophe, it stems from belligerency in the human heart. Yet the warlike hostility in the human heart is seeded in the Perverse Qi (*liqi* 戾氣). As the Perverse Qi of the cosmos infiltrates the human heart, it intoxicates the populace. They behave as if having drunk caustic medicine, becoming crazed, hateful, avaricious, and totally deprived of reason. For this kind of phenomenon, pray what is the solution to restore it to peace?

Laozi said, "When people fear no death, how can death intimidate them?" So we can see that the conventional belief in employing the measures of either "using killing to stop killing" or "the armed peace" has little efficacy.

I think that in order to stop the catastrophe, we must first rectify the human heart. To rectify the human heart, we must first quell the Perverse Qi. To quell it, we must pay attention to the great method of the Confucian school, "Strive for the central harmony (*zhi zhonghe* 致中和). Heaven and earth will be restored to order, and a myriad of beings will flourish." If things are left as they are for long, there will be no remedy. The Perverse Qi will strengthen daily until the whole world will not be able to escape destruction.

Stranded precariously in occupied Shanghai, Chen perceived the expanding Japanese occupation of China as a result of both cosmic and moral failure on the part of the Japanese. Yet at that juncture, Chen expected little to come from armed resistance to the Japanese, who were already "crazed, hateful, avaricious, and totally deprived of reason." Using killing to stop the killing would amount to succumbing to the dehumanizing influence of the Perverse Qi. Instead, Chen sought the fundamental solution of changing the human heart by advocating the practice of "striving for the central harmony." He argued confidently that the inner alchemic principle of harmonizing all the energies within the body could be extended to the task of quelling the chaos and bringing order to the world:

When a self-cultivator can harmonize the forces within the body, then the body will be without any ills. When the forces of a region can be harmonized, then that region will be free of any calamity. When a whole country can harmonize its forces, the country will enjoy peace and happiness. When the forces in the world are harmonized, peace will prevail.

Keenly aware that others might dismiss his proposition, Chen insisted that he had done his part toward finding a solution. For him, one must still continue to do one's utmost even amid the direst circumstances. He thus challenged others to live up to their own share of responsibility by coming up with a solution.[69]

While living in an isolated corner of the French Concession, Chen continued to promote the Immortals' Learning and Daoism through his writings. He was selective in rendering his services and his reputation as an adept and scholar of inner alchemy to promoting the cause of Daoism. During the early 1920s, Ai Langxuan 艾朗軒, a Daoist cleric from Jiangxi, had built a monastery with the help of a wealthy and generous donor. He named his new cloister the Tongbai Palace (Tongbai gong 桐柏宮) after the Daoist monastery located on Mount Tiantai in Zhejiang where the Song Daoist Zhang Boduan allegedly attained perfection. After Shanghai fell to the Japanese occupation in 1937, Abbot Ai became an active collaborator with the occupation authorities and served as the head of the new Daoist organization endorsed by the puppet regime.[70]

In a subtle yet unmistakable gesture of disapproval of Abbot Ai's collaborationist stance, Chen Yingning chose to lend his pen and renown to promoting a Daoist monastery located on Mount Tiantai, the namesake and now rival to Abbot Ai's prosperous cloister in Shanghai. In a 1941 article published to raise donations for the decrepit ancient temple on Mount Tiantai, Chen affirmed that the original Tongbai Monastery on Mount Tiantai was the genuine sacred site of Daoist inner alchemy and birthplace of the prestigious Southern Lineage.[71]

The Daoist Dining Club (Xuanlü jucan hui 玄侶聚餐會)

The Shanghai inner alchemy community continued to function long after the fall of the city to the Japanese. As the occupation authorities tightened their control over political meetings and press freedom, members of the community devised ingenious ways to continue their social and professional associations. One important means was the informal Daoist Dining Club.

The club started in 1938 when Shanghai's Daoist clerics tried to re-establish contacts and organize. During the 1937 siege and ensuing occupation many Daoists and lay practitioners in the city lost contact with one another. The Japanese occupation authorities' injunction against political gatherings and their censorship made it even more difficult to establish and maintain regular contact. To circumvent the strict occupation rules, some Daoist leaders and practitioners began to meet occasionally at pre-agreed public restaurants. There, over a vegetarian meal, they shared information and discussed their practice. By early 1939, at the behest of Dr. Zhang Zhuming, Chen Yingning, Xie Qianggong, and Wang Boying, among others, these occasional gatherings became a regular event on the first Sunday of each month among Daoist clerics and lay practitioners in Shanghai. Soon others heard of these gatherings and expressed an interest in joining the club by requesting a copy of the flyer containing the group's bylaws. Demand quickly outstripped the supply of flyers, and the organizers had to resort to publishing the bylaws in the Xiandao Monthly.[72] Pledging to avoid discussions of "the state, politics, and secular matters," the club focused on the "teachings of the self-cultivation of the mind and the body" (shengxin xiuyang zhi xue 身心修養之學). The luncheon club's avowed position of passive nonconformity reveals the dilemma faced by Chen and his associates: unwilling to succumb to the political pressure for collaboration yet powerless to change the reality of the occupation.[73]

In the late summer of 1939, the situation in the International Settlement and the French Concession grew even worse. With the Japanese pressuring the International Settlement authorities to tighten their control over the local media, not to mention the soaring inflation and the rising prices of housing and materials throughout the city, the struggling Xiandao Monthly shut down in September 1941, three months before the Japanese took over the foreign concessions in Shanghai.

With the Monthly gone, the last links that had tenuously held together practitioners dispersed in various parts of the country were severed. Just as the community of inner alchemy had first emerged because of the circulation of the two journals throughout the country, it now began to unravel as the Xiandao Monthly ceased publication. For his part, Chen, like many of his associates, withdrew completely from public life. He spent his time caring for his wife at the hospital and writing manuscripts at home. When the *Monthly* closed, Chen also lost a major source of income. With the soaring prices, his strained finances, and his wife's advancing cancer, Chen's life became increasingly difficult. He had to rely on occasional financial support from his nephew Zhang Jiashou 張嘉壽 and Dr. Zhang Zhuming. Yet Chen persisted in his seclusion.[74]

The Post-1945 Years

With the defeat of the Japanese in 1945, Chen resumed his public role as a Daoist scholar and practitioner. But with his wife gone and many of his associates and followers out of contact, Chen was able to revive neither the once-thriving inner alchemy community in Shanghai nor a journal dedicated to the advocacy and dissemination of the Immortals' Learning. Except for meetings with a few close friends and occasional duties as a ghost writer for Shanghai Daoist circles, Chen largely stayed out of the public life. He made a living partly as a private tutor of the classics and medicine and partly as a resident inner alchemy teacher for a few rich clients. In the winter of 1945, Chen was invited to serve as a resident adept of Daoist meditation practice by Mr. Shi Jianguang 史劍光, a nephew of Shi Liangcai 史量才 (1878–1934), the prominent journalist and owner of *Shenbao*. He lived as Shi's special guest at the latter's well-appointed mansion in the old French Concession until the winter of 1949 and the Communist takeover.[75]

Conclusion

The Japanese occupation of all of Shanghai in December 1941 effectively ended the thriving inner alchemic community there, but it did not diminish the historical significance of what Chen Yingning and his fellow practitioners achieved in Republican Shanghai.

Although direct personal or institutional ties are difficult to establish, this urban-based and lay-centered self-cultivation community was tantalizingly evocative of the literati Daoist tradition of late imperial China. Both consisted of well-educated and nonclerical elite practitioners who, although never ordained or formally initiated into a liturgical lineage or monastic order, held Daoist beliefs and pursued Daoist self-cultivation techniques as part of their life goals. Yet until recently, we in the field of Daoist studies have focused largely on the role and agency of the liturgical and monastic Daoist practitioners to understand and explain intellectual, institutional, and political developments in Daoist history. The Immortals' Learning advocated and pursued by Chen and his associates during the 1930s and 1940s shows for the first time how vital a role urban lay intellectuals and practitioners such as Chen Yingning and others played in reshaping the course and configuration of modern Daoism.

Despite similarities or parallels to the early traditions of literati Daoism, the Immortals' Learning was a truly modern response by Chen Yingning and other Daoist intellectuals to the changing personal, social, political, and cultural conditions of modern China.

Drawing on both traditional and their modern scientific educations, as well as their modern professional skills and knowledge, Chen Yingning and other lay Daoist intellectuals refashioned traditional Daoist cosmology and theories of the body to meet the demands of their times. Both the Daoist legacy and the modern ideologies of nationalism, science, and gender were at work in their reformulation of Daoist tradition and inner alchemy. In invoking the alchemic body consecrated in such early texts as *The Yellow Courtyard Scriptures*, Chen Yingning and his colleagues chose to highlight the material and physical dimensions of the classic alchemic body and reject the Buddhist idealistic model of the body, which stressed the primacy of the mind. Reflecting their heightened sensitivity to the gender revolution in Republican China, they also went against traditional inner alchemy by valorizing the gender-neutral duo of *qi* and *shen* (氣, 神) over the male-centered trio of Essence, *qi*, and Psyche (*jing, qi, shen* 精氣神) as the core foundation of the alchemic body for modern practitioners.

Chen and his fellow practitioners actively appropriated concepts and principles from modern physics, biology, and physiology in their reformulation of inner alchemy. Recasting the seemingly intractable duo of *qi* and *shen* in terms of positrons, electrons, and cells, Chen and his associates not only contributed new meanings to Daoist inner alchemy but also gave the traditional practice a new cultural authenticity and currency. Their "scientifically" constructed body repudiated the nihilistic Buddhist insubstantiation of the flesh body and affirmed Daoist notions of long life, rejuvenation, and transformation of the body by appropriating the scientific principles of the indestructibility and transmutability of matter. In "scientizing" inner alchemy, Chen and his associates foreshadowed the approaches adopted by the later *qigong* practitioners and researchers, who would stress the body's fundamental materiality and the "scientific approach" during the 1950s and the 1980s.

The Immortals' Learning also reflects a significant nationalist turn as it emerged amid China's heightened national crisis of the 1930s. As Chen Yingning and his associates sought to construct the alchemic body by connecting it to the Yellow Emperor and by differentiating it from the Buddhist mind-centered body, they envisioned it as the quintessence of Chinese culture and tradition, to be preserved and transmitted through the pursuit of inner alchemy. Thus, they also transformed the individual practice of seeking personal health and transcendence into an enterprise of national survival and renewal.

The elite urban lay Daoist practitioners' utilization of modern mass media shows how inextricably the lay-centered reform movement was tied to Republican Shanghai's thriving public space and popular magazine market. Their innovations were made possible only through the publication and circulation of the *Yangshan Biweekly* and the *Xiandao Monthly*. The two journals and the Yihuatang publishing house had an indelible impact on the practices of modern Daoism. First, the unprecedented use of modern journals to transmit knowledge about the practice of inner alchemy transformed the once largely private and individual practice into an increasingly public experience of self-cultivation and spiritual pursuit. The circulation and innovative editorial management of the journals' content and format helped establish and maintain a public space in which Daoism and inner alchemy became a shared experience for people from geographically, socially, economically, and ideologically diverse backgrounds. As Chen Yingning and his fellow editors dispensed opinions and advice, and as inner alchemists openly discussed with one another the subtleties and hardships of their practices, they helped Daoist inner alchemy move out of the closely guarded sanctums of clerical lineages and monasteries and into the public realm of shared imagination and popular practice. As such, the practice of Daoist inner alchemy ceased to be the exclusive privilege of a few. Rather, it was treated and pursued as a body of knowledge that could and must be shared with the public.

Along with these changes in the perception of Daoist knowledge and practice, a new model of learning and transmitting Daoism emerged as an alternative for many practitioners. The editors and their journals, together with the open flow of correspondence among readers, offered practitioners at large sources of information and authorities on Daoism and inner alchemy outside the Daoist clerical master-disciple lineages and institutions. Although the journals enhanced the prestige and authority of adepts like Chen Yingning, the new relationships that emerged around the journals and the editors did not tend to be institutionally hierarchical. Rather, they were based largely on a sense of fellowship and community among the editors and their audience. Further, the public space created through the journals proved effective in reducing and removing obstacles to female practitioners' access to inner alchemy, since it afforded women, and men, an opportunity to participate in and even shape the experience of learning and transmitting Daoist practice in public.

The Immortals' Learning manifested itself in the vigorous reformulation and dissemination of the cultural, intellectual, and technical legacies of Daoism, in the relentless polemics against the mind-centered Pure Land Buddhist ideology and practice, and in the active appropriation of scientific concepts in reconstituting Daoist cosmology and inner alchemy in the flourishing public arena of Republican Shanghai. Led and inspired by Chen Yingning and other reform-minded urban lay intellectuals and practitioners, it grew from a close circle of friends into a public community and network of both lay and clerical practitioners, culminating in a Daoist renaissance in Republican Shanghai during the 1930s and 1940s.

— Epilogue —

Chen Yingning and Post-1949 Daoism

After 1949, Chen lived with the families of Dr. Zhang Zhuming or his niece for two years before resettling in Hangzhou. There Chen stayed with Dr. Hu Haiya, his disciple and an acupuncturist, who had traveled to Shanghai in the early 1940s to seek to become Chen's disciple. Now living at a residence near the famous West Lake, Chen spent his time tutoring Dr. Hu in the study of the classics of Chinese medicine and acupuncture and in guiding him in his meditative practice.

Although Chen lived in his retirement in Hangzhou, he was not forgotten. In 1953, Chen was recruited by his old friend Ma Yifu to serve as a research fellow at the prestigious Zhejiang Academy of Letters and History (Zhejiang wenshi guan 浙江文史館).

When the *qigong* and self-health movement and the Communist-led reforms of religion began in the early 1950s, Chen Yingning was courted by the state authorities and the advocates of the popular practice, both of whom were impressed by his earlier record in reforming Daoism and his erudition in medicine and meditation. In 1957, while recuperating from a stomach ulcer at the Mount Pingfeng Sanitarium (Pingfengshan liaoyang yuan 屏風山療養院) near Hangzhou, Chen wrote an influential tract on self-healing *qigong* practice and gave lectures and demonstrations to the medical staff and other patients at the sanitarium on how to use quiet sitting for self-healing.[1] In April of that year, when a group of leading Daoists and state officials met in Beijing for the first time since 1949 to discuss plans for reorganizing and reforming Daoism, they called Chen to Beijing for the meeting. There they selected him to serve as the deputy head and secretary general of their new Chinese Daoist Association (Zhongguo Daojiao xiehui 中國道教協會). The following year, Chen left Hangzhou and moved to the White Cloud Monastery in Beijing, where he was in charge of running the new organization. At the second national Daoist congress in 1961, Chen was elected its head.

Chen's tenure first as secretary general and then as head of the Chinese Daoist Association from 1957 to the early 1960s coincided with profound social, political, and cultural transformations in the People's Republic. The land reform of the early 1950s and the subsequent collectivization drive dealt severe blows to the Daoist monastic life and orders. Through a combination of coercion and inducement of employment in cities, or shares of land in their hometowns, many Daoist clerics were forced out of their monasteries and temples and returned to secular life. Those who were allowed to stay in the monasteries could barely survive, since most monastic landholdings were confiscated during the land reform. With the collectivization drives and the Great Leap Forward in the late 1950s, what remained of the monastic Daoist clergy were either organized into agricultural production units or assigned to local rural production teams. Many worked as forest fire monitors and wardens, or factory laborers. These new changes disrupted the rhythm and cycle of traditional Daoist monastic life, traditionally centered on scriptural study, meditation, and ritual practices and services.[2] Daoist monastic life was now organized on the basis of production activities and focused on personal, economic, and political survival. Further, with the proliferation of socialist ideological indoctrination, antisuperstition drives, and campaigns for clerical literacy and science education, Daoism as a system of beliefs and practices fell under increasing state suspicion and scrutiny, as well as self-doubt. Many questioned its viability and survival in the changed social, intellectual, and political conditions of the socialist state.

Yet Chen held firm at the Daoist Association. Under Chen's initiative, the association set up a special research unit to study the culture and history of Daoism. Chen personally directed several research projects and mentored a few key researchers in the research section. He guided them in compiling sourcebooks and primers of Daoism for the public and the Daoist clergy.[3] He wrote several influential studies of the Daoist classics.[4] Chen also began to introduce foreign scholarship on Daoism. Under Chen's tutelage, Ms Yu Zhongjue 余仲珏, a graduate of Peking University and a disciple, translated Joseph Needham's studies of Daoism into Chinese.[5] Later, in September 1962, Chen Yingning hosted Needham and Lu Guizhen during their tour of the White Cloud Monastery and held extended conversations with the two on Daoist history, medicine, alchemy, and the future of Daoism.[6]

Chen also began to promote programs aimed at regaining economic independence and enhancing Daoist clerical literacy and education. Under Chen's initiative, the Daoist Association drew up a special plan in 1961 to train Daoists. Less than a year later, in 1962, a Daoist seminary was established at the White Cloud Monastery to train selected Daoists from monasteries all over the country. The seminary offered intensive courses in the Daoist classics and scriptures as well as modern science and politics. Besides Daoist education, Chen was particularly keen on the idea of converting natural resources, historical sites, cultural relics, and other facilities near monasteries into jobs for the monastic practitioners. He enthusiastically advocated forestry, tourism, gardening, herb cultivation and collection, and the preparation of herbal medicines as means of regaining Daoist monastic economic autonomy.[7]

These measures and programs reflected Chen's efforts to adapt Daoist practices to the drastically changed political, economic, and intellectual environments of post-1949 China. Chen thought that the key to the survival of Daoism in the new society was to strip away what he perceived as magically based liturgical elements and preserve what he saw as the "spirit of Daoism" (*Daojiao de jingshen* 道教的精神). In a speech given at the annual meeting of the National Political Consultative Congress in Beijing in 1962, Chen spoke hopefully about the future of Daoism:

Will our nation's Daoism with its 2,500 years of history (counting from Laozi of the Eastern Zhou dynasty) be doomed to perish? We have to look at two things to answer this question: one is the form of Daoism (*daojiao de xingshi* 道教的形式), and the other is the spirit of Daoism. Such things as leaving home for practice vs. at-home practice, keeping one's hair as opposed to cutting it, vegetarianism vs. meat eating, wearing the Daoist regalia vs. civilian clothes, rituals, prayers, scriptural recitation, and other liturgical elements are nothing but the forms of Daoism. But the *qigong* healing practices (such as the Inhaling and Exhaling Exercise, Regulating Qi, Circulating Qi, Manipulating Qi, Concentrating Qi, Dispersing Qi, the Six-Character Secrets of Qi Exercise, and the Sixteen-Character Secrets of Qi Exercise), the gymnastic regimens (such as *anqiao* 按蹻 and *daoyin* 導引), the Five Animal Play exercise, the Tiger and Dragon practice, the Eight-sectioned Exercise (*baduan jing* 八段錦) and Taiji quan 太極拳, the quiet meditative practices (such as Pausing the Thought, Holding the Consciousness, Keeping to the Center, Hugging the One, Stilling the Gaze, and the Forgetful Sitting), drug ingestion practices (such as preparing various alchemic potions and elixirs and taking various herbs and drugs), and other more profound teachings such as inner alchemy, outer alchemy, and Lao-Zhuang philosophy are the learning of Daoism (*daojiao de xueshu* 道教的學術). The spirit of Daoism is anchored in its learning. As the times change, there is no guarantee that the form of Daoism will remain unchanged forever. But Daoist learning will not only continue and be transmitted forever. It will even gradually thrive and develop because it is what people need. As long as Daoist learning exists, the Daoist spirit will have its grounding. We will have no worry about it![8]

Although Chen suffered and eventually died like many of his fellow Daoist intellectuals during the Cultural Revolution, his teachings on Daoist learning and self-cultivation techniques have endured the political storms of the 1960s and 1970s to regain a vigorous second life in post-Mao China and beyond.

The revival of Chen Yingning's Immortals' Learning began in Taiwan in the 1950s. As Chen lay dying from complications resulting from his old respiratory illness at the height of the Cultural Revolution in 1969, he was unaware that several members of the Shanghai inner alchemic community had taken his writings and books to Taiwan twenty years earlier. There they had rebuilt a small but active community of inner alchemic practice among their newfound audience in Taipei. In a gesture of admiration for Chen Yingning and recognition of the group's historical ties to the once-vibrant Daoist inner alchemic practice in Shanghai, Yuan Jiegui 袁介珪 and Xu Boying 徐伯英, two members of the Taipei group with personal ties to the Shanghai community, inaugurated a journal entitled *Immortals' Learning* (*Xianxue* 仙學) in late 1957. The journal continued publishing well into the 1990s. The publisher of the journal, Song Jinren 宋今人, also claimed personal ties to the Shanghai community of self-cultivation practice of the 1930s and 1940s. From the 1960s to the 1990s, Song and his family in Taipei used their Zhenshanmei Press 眞善美出版社 to republish scores of the Daoist scriptures and inner alchemic titles that Chen Yingning and the Shanghai community of practitioners had first published through the Yihuatang publishing house during the 1930s and 1940s. In 1978, Yuan and Xu co-edited and republished a large compendium of all the major letters, articles, and writings that Chen Yingning and his associates had published in the *Yangshan Biweekly* and the *Xiandao Monthly* decades earlier in Shanghai.[9]

In mainland China, with the new openness and changed political climate, interest in Chen Yingning and his work began to resurface in the early 1980s. Sponsored by Dr. Zhang Zhuming, Yu Zhongjue published the first biographical study of Chen Yingning in 1983. She was soon followed by many others who published commemorative articles in the official Daoist Association journal and other magazines in China. In 1989, based on the compendium published in Taiwan, Li Yangzheng 李養正, a protégé and former colleague at the Daoist Association, published a collection of Chen's articles and writings published in the *Yangshan* and *Xiandao* journals. Compilations of Chen's writings have continued to appear, spawning both scholarly interest and praxis in mainland China and beyond.[10]

Reference Matter

Notes

For complete bibliographic information on the works cited here in short form, see the Bibliography, pp. 339–68. For abbreviations used in the Notes, see p. xiii.

Introduction

1. Eileen Chang 張愛玲, "Zhongguo de riye" 中國的日夜, in idem, *Chuanqi* 傳奇 (Legends) (Shanghai: Shanhe tushu, 1946), pp. 390–91.

2. Chang's sense of nationalist confidence in the city and its people is best evidenced in the poem she composed immediately after her encounter with the Daoist beggar and other ordinary people on her shopping trip (see ibid., pp. 393–94).

3. See Fu Qinjia, *Zhongguo Daojiao shi*; Ren Jiyu, *Zhongguo Daojiao shi*; and Qing Xitai, *Zhongguo Daojiao shi*, vol. 4.

4. See Ma Duanlin, *Wenxian tongkao*, juan 125, pp. 1810–11.

5. See Schipper, *The Taoist Body*, pp. 16–19.

6. See Ren Jiyu, *Zhongguo Daojiao shi*, pp. 737–39. See also Qing Xitai, *Zhongguo Daojiao shi*, pp. 1–13, 217–374. Qing and his collaborators pointed to the lack of doctrinal innovation, the declining clerical order, and weakened social influence as evidence for the Daoist decline during the late imperial period, but they also noted the extensive Daoist integration with local popular cults and practice, a trend they also interpreted as enervating of Daoism as a religion during the period.

7. See Groot, *Sectarianism and Religious Persecution in China*.

8. See Schipper, *The Taoist Body*, pp. 16–19.

9. See Chang Zunxian 常遵先, "Jin bu Li Zhenren Xu'an shi yuan yun er shou" 謹步李眞人虛庵詩原韻二首, *YS*, no. 28 (1934): 4. Li Xu'an 李虛庵 is described by Wu Shouyang 伍守陽 (1552–1640), the great Daoist adept of inner alchemy, as a disciple of the famed Ming Daoist Zhang Jingxu 張靜虛 (b. 1432), sobriquet Zhang the Tiger-skin 虎皮張, who was active during the fifteenth century. According to Wu, Li Xu'an in turn served as the teacher to his own master, Cao Huanyang 曹還陽 (1562–?). See Wu Shouyang, *Tianxian zhengli* 天仙正理, and idem, *Xian Fo hezong yulu* 仙佛合宗語錄 (1622, rev. 1639), in He Longxiang and Peng Hanran, *Daozang jiyao*, vol. *bi* 畢集, *juan* 1–3, 4–5.

10. There has been a boom in reprinting Chen's writings in the past few decades. The most representative of these republications are Yuan Jiegui and Xu Boying, *Zhonghua xianxue*; Li Yangzheng, ed., *Daojiao yu yangsheng*; Hong Jianlin, *Xianxue jiemi*; Chen Zhanqi and Hu Haiya, "Yangshan banyue kan" "Xiandao yuebao" *quanji*; and most recently, Hu Haiya and Wu Guozhong, *Zhonghua xianxue yangsheng quanshu*.

11. See Vincent Goossaert, "Republican Church Engineering: The National Religious Associations in 1912 China," in Mayfair Yang, ed., *Religion, Modernity, and the State in China*.

12. See Schipper, *The Daoist Body*; Bokenkamp, *Early Daoist Scriptures*; Lagerwey, *Taoist Ritual in Chinese Society and History*; Hymes, *Way and Byway*; Kohn, ed., *Daoism Handbook*; Esposito, "The Longmen School and Its Controversial History"; and Goossaert, *The Taoists of Peking*.

13. See Timothy H. Barrett, *Taoism Under the T'ang* (London: Wellsweep Press, 1996). On the Tang poet Li Bai's pursuit of Daoism, see Jiang Jianyuan, "Li Bai yu Daojiao."

14. See Russell Kirkland, *Taoism, the Enduring Tradition* (New York: Routledge, 2004).

15. See Xiao Tianshi, *Daojia yangshengxue gaiyao*, pp. 7–13; and also Robinet, "Original Contribution of Neidan to Taoism and Chinese Thought."

16. For the history of inner alchemy, see Robinet, *Taoism: Growth of a Religion*, pp. 212–56; Lowell Skar and Fabrizio Pregadio, "Inner Alchemy (neidan)," in Kohn, ed., *Daoism Handbook*, pp. 464–98; and, most recently, Fabrizio Pregadio, *Great Clarity: Daoism and Alchemy in Early Medieval China* (Stanford: Stanford University Press, 2006).

17. See Liu Ts'un-yan, "The Penetration of Taoism into the Ming Neo-Confucianist Elite," *T'oung pao* 57 (1971): 31–102.

18. See Zeng Zhaonan, "Daoshi Fu Jinquan sixiang lueshu"; Baldrian-Hussein, "Taoist Beliefs in Literary Circles of the Sung Dynasty"; and Yang Ming, *Daojiao yangshengjia*.

19. See Goossaert, *The Taoists of Peking*.

Chapter 1

1. See Dikotter, *The Discourse of Race in Modern China*, pp. 98–111.

2. Pan Wei's version of the 1771 classic *Shoushi chuanzhen* 壽世傳眞 by Xu Mingfeng 徐鳴峰 was republished in 1881 by Wang Zuyuan 王祖源. The title *An Illustrated Treatise on Inner Practice* was inspired by some illustrations Wang acquired in his youth at the famed Buddhist Shaoling Temple in Henan (see Ma Jiren, *Shiyong yixue qigong cidian*, p. 484). For a historically grounded discussion of the meanings of the term *weisheng*, see Rogaski, *Hygienic Modernity*, pp. 22–47.

3. Yu Muxia 郁慕俠 reprinted the book under the new title (Ma Jiren, *Shiyong yixue qigong cidian*, p. 484).

4. For Zheng's pursuit of Daoist self-cultivation and patronage of Daoism, see his *Shengshi weiyan houbian*. For recent studies of Zheng's religiosity, see Deng Jingbin, "Zheng Guanying de daohao"; Guan Lin, "Zheng Guanying de Daojiao sixiang"; and Fan Chunwu, "Feiluan, xiuzhen yu banshan." In addition to the 1890 compendium on the regimens of "guarding life," Zheng also sponsored the 1915 reprinting and distribution of the rare collection *Fanghu waishi* 方壺外史 written by the renowned Ming adept of inner alchemy Lu Xixing 陸西星 (1520–1606). The rare original was provided by Zheng's adept-friend Huang Suizhi. See Zheng Guanying's preface to Lu Xixing, *Fanghu waishi*, 1915 reprint edition; see also Ma Jiren, *Shiyong yixue qigong cidian*, p. 484.

5. Yan's essay was initially published in *Zhi bao* 直報 of Tianjin in 1895. See Jian Bozan, ed., *Wuxu bianfa* 戊戌變法. See also Yan Fu 嚴復, "Yuanqiang" 原強, in idem, *Houguan Yan shi cong ke* 侯官嚴氏叢刻, reprinted in Shen Yunlong 沈雲龍, ed., *Jindai Zhongguo shiliao congkan xubian di shiba ji* 近代中國史料叢刊續編第十八輯 (Taipei: Wenhai chubanshe, 1975), pp. 113–72.

6. Yan had a profound and palpable influence on members of his generation such as Liang Qichao; see Schwartz, *In Search of Wealth and Power*. Yan's thinking on physical cultivation as a source of national power also inspired such influential figures as Cai E 蔡鍔 (1882–1916) and Mao Zedong 毛澤東 (1893–1976). Both Cai and Mao wrote passionately on physical

education (*tiyu* 體育) and its relevance to national strengthening. See Mao Zedong, "Tiyu zhi yanjiu" 體育之研究 (A study of physical education), in Li Rui, *The Early Revolutionary Activities of Comrade Mao Tse-tung*.

7. The quotation is taken from Yang Suixi 楊燧熙, "Wanguo weishengxue lun" 萬國衛生學論 (On international hygiene), *Shaoxing yiyao xuebao* 59 (1916): 108–9, cited by Andrews, "The Making of Modern Chinese Medicine," p. 62. I have slightly modified her translation of the quotation.

8. See Schram, *The Thought of Mao Tse-tung*, pp. 14–15. I have slightly modified Schram's translation based on my reading of Mao's original. For Mao's pursuit of physical cultivation, see Han Suyin, *The Morning Deluge*, pp. 30–59.

9. See Andrews, "The Making of Modern Chinese Medicine"; and Orliski, "Re-imagining the Domestic Sphere."

10. See Prasenjit Duara, "Knowledge and Power in the Discourse of Modernity: The Campaigns Against Popular Religion in Early Twentieth Century China," *Journal of Asian Studies* 50, no. 1 (1991): 67–83; and idem, *Sovereignty and Authenticity*. The most comprehensive study of the early redemptive societies is Sakai Tadao, *Kindai Shina ni okeru shūkyō kessha*. See also Wang Jianchuan, "Tongshan she zaoqi lishi chutan"; Sakai Tadao, "Daoyuan de yan'ge": and Nedostup, "Religion, Superstition, and Governing Society."

11. See Goossaert, *The Taoists of Peking*, pp. 306–19.

12. Selections of Jiang's extensive correspondence are included in the section entitled "Selected Questions and Answers" 問答選錄 in the 1917 reprint of his book, *Dingzheng Yinshizi jingzuo fa*. Several years after he published his first book, which was based on Daoist inner alchemy practice, Jiang apparently came under pressure from his fellow Buddhists to produce a separate regimen based on Buddhist meditative practice. Liang Shuming 梁漱溟 (1893–1988) attacked his first book as being "saturated with heterodox thoughts" 外道思想. Urged by his fellow Buddhist practitioners, Jiang came out with a sequel to the book, *Yinshizi jingzuo fa xubian*, which he claimed was based on the Buddhist meditation techniques.

13. See Jiang Weiqiao, *Dingzheng Yinshizi jingzuo fa*, pp. 1–2.

14. See ibid., p. 2.

15. See ibid., p. 1. Jiang's original reads: 靜坐法, 即古之所謂內功也. Jiang clearly identified this meditative method he described in the tract as being "Daoist" (*daojia* 道家). He referred to the method described in his tract as being the "Daoist regimen" (*daojia fangfa* 道家方法). Later apparently bowing to sectarian pressure from his Buddhist critics, Jiang described the Daoist regimen as having only limited efficacy in curing illnesses and

lengthening life. He described the Buddhist regimen of self-cultivation he later devised as having superior efficacy in transcending life and death. But the intensity of his sectarian downgrading of his Daoist regimen was ironically diluted by the fact he had achieved his health and physical vitality by initially following his earlier Daoist regimen of quiet sitting (see ibid.).

16. The utopian ideals of social justice, equality, and welfare espoused in the *Book of Rites* (*Li ji* 禮記) are also an integral part of the social and political doctrines that informed early Daoist millenarian movements such as the Five Pecks of Rice sect in Sichuan and the Taiping sects in the Eastern Han of the second century CE. See Wang Ming, *Taiping jing hejiao*; and also Furth, "Intellectual Change."

17. For Hui Dong's annotation of the Daoist classic, see Hui Dong, *Taishang ganying pian jianzhu*, pp. 156–228. For Yu's annotative work on the same classic, see Yu Yue, *Taishang ganying pian zanyi*, pp. 229–67. Yu Yue's evidentiary scholarship on other Daoist classics includes *Zhuangzi ping yi*, *Huainan nei pian ping yi*, and *Liezi ping yi*. For Yu Yue's study of Daoist hagiographies and rituals, see *Chaxiangshi congchao*, vols. 2 and 14; and *Youtai xianguan biji*. For a recent study of Yu Yue's literary writings, see Rania Huntington, "Memory, Mourning, and Genre in the Works of Yu Yue," *Harvard Journal of Asiatic Studies* 67, no. 2 (2007): 253–93.

18. For brief biographies of Yang, see Zhang Ertian, "Yang Renshan jushi biezhuan"; and Shen Zengzhi, "Yang jushi taming." See also Chan, *Religious Trends in Modern China*, pp. 56–68. On Yang Wenhui's life and activities, see also Welch, *Buddhist Revival in Modern China*, pp. 1–22.

19. The four annotated works are *Yinfu jing fayin* 陰符經發隱 (ca. 1896), *Daode jing fayin* 道德經發隱 (1903), *Chongxu jing fayin* 沖虛經發隱 (1904), and *Nanhua jing fayin* 南華經發隱. All were republished in *ZWDS*, 3: 450–58, 459–61, 462–89, and 490–99, respectively.

20. See Yang Wenhui, *Yinfu jing fayin*, 3: 450–58. According to Chen Yingning, who met Yang, Yang had extensive associations with Daoists and possessed formidable learning on Daoism. Chen was especially impressed with Yang's nonsectarian attitude and openmindedness. But Yang's writings on Daoism have received little scholarly attention, and he continues to be seen primarily as a devout Buddhist reformer. See Welch, *Buddhist Revival in Modern China*.

21. Liu Shipei, "Du Daozang ji." Also known by his sobriquet Shenshu 申叔, Liu was from Yizheng 義征 in Jiangsu province. A staunch Han nationalist opponent of the Manchu rule in China, Liu changed his name to Guang Han 光漢 (Restoring the Han). He was a close friend of another Han nationalist intellectual, Zhang Binglin 章炳麟 (1869–1936), and

wrote the famous book *Repelling the Barbarians* (*Rang shu* 攘書) to advocate Han nationalism. He also served as editor of two major anti-Manchu journals: *Warning Bell Daily* (*Jingzhong ribao* 警鐘日報) and *The National Essence Journal* (*Guocui xuebao* 國粹學報). In the aftermath of the Republican revolution, Liu became involved in the restoration activities of Yuan Shikai. He later taught classics and lexicology at Peking University. See Wan Shiguo, *Liu Shipei nianpu*.

22. Some of the Daoist studies completed by the new historians during this period became the object of controversy among Daoists and activists involved in the Daoist revival. Hu Shi's study of Tao Hongjing's 陶弘景 (452–536) *Zhen gao* 眞誥 was severely criticized by one of Chen's close associates for being unappreciative of the Daoist contributions to Chinese learning and for failing to understand the "true meanings of Daoism." So was Fu Qinjia's 1934 work on the history of Daoism. For representative works by these scholars, see Hu Shi, "Hanchu Ru Shi Dao zhi zheng"; idem, "Tao Hongjing de *Zhengao* kao"; Xu Dishan, "Daojia sixiang yu daojiao"; idem, *Daojiao shi*; Chen Yinke, "Tianshi dao yu binhai diyu zhi guanxi"; Chen Yuan, *Daojia jinshi lue gaoben mulu*; idem, "Ji Xu Zuanzeng ke *Taishang ganying pian tushuo*"; and Fu Qinjia, *Zhongguo Daojiao shi*.

23. See Furth, *Ting Wen-chiang*, pp. 94–135; and also Wang Hui, "Differentiation of Knowledge."

24. For the history of the debate, see Furth, *Ting Wenchiang*, pp. 94–135.

25. The mid-seventeenth-century renewal of the Daoist Quanzhen Longmen lineage is a subject that has only recently received scholarly attention. See Chen Bing, "Qingdai Quanzhen Longmen pai de zhongxing"; Qing Xitai, *Zhongguo Daojiao shi*, 4: 77–127; Esposito, "L'Ecole Longmen"; and idem, "Daoism in the Qing." See also Vincent Goossaert, "La Création du Taoïsme moderne: l'order Quanzhen" (Ph.D. diss., Ecole Pratique des Hautes Etudes, Paris, 1997); and idem, "Quanzhen Clergy."

26. Recently there has been an explosion of studies on the roles and functions of Daoist monasteries and clerics in local society and culture in various regions during the Ming and Qing periods. See, e.g., Richard Wang, "Four Steles at the Monastery of Sublime Mystery"; and idem, "Mingdai wanghou yu Daojiao guanxi tanjiu"; Goossaert, *The Taoists of Peking*; Wu Yakui, *Jiangnan Quanzhen Daojiao*; Xun Liu, "Immortals and Patriarchs"; idem, "General Zhang Buries the Bones"; and Lai Chi-tim, *Guangdong difang Daojiao yanjiu*, 2007.

27. Scholars have only recently begun to examine the large body of writings on inner alchemy during the late imperial period. In Western languages, see Wilhelm, *Secret of the Golden Flower*, for a study of Liu Hua-

yang's *Huiming jing* 慧命經. For a translation of Liu Yiming, see Cleary, *Way of Harmony and Balance*. For a pioneering study of the major writings by the mid-Qing inner alchemist Min Yide, see Esposito, "L'Ecole Longmen."

28. On the Daoist influence in Ming and Qing novels, see Liu Ts'un-yan, *Buddhist and Taoist Influence on Chinese Novels*, 1: 254–89. See also Anthony Yu, *Journey to the West*; and Richard Wang, "Daoist Rite of the Yellow Heaven Lu in *Jin Ping Mei*" (paper delivered at the AAS annual meeting, Chicago, 1996). For scholarship on the subject in Chinese, see Zhan Shichuang, *Daojiao wenxue shi*; and also Luo Yonglin, "Baxian gushi xingcheng de shehui lishi yuanyin he yingxiang" 八仙故事形成的社會歷史原因和影響 (The social historical causes and influence of the formulation of the theophanies of the Eight Immortals) and "Fengshen yanyi yu shenxian daojiao sixiang" 封神演義與神仙道教思想 (*Romance of Divine Investiture* and the ideas of immortals and Daoism), in his *Zhongguo xianhua yanjiu*, pp. 199–219 and 230–53, respectively; and, most recently, Philip Clart, trans., *The Story of Han Xiangzi*.

29. For the study of Lu Xixing and his works, see Liu Tsun-yan, *Selected Papers from the Hall of Harmonious Wind*. See also Yang Ming, *Daojiao yangshengjia*. Yang's study represents by far the most comprehensive study of Lu and his writings. On Cao Heng's life and his meditative techniques, see Xun Liu, "Essential Secrets for Conserving Life: Meditative Techniques for Self-healing in the Late Ming" (paper presented at the International Symposium "Medicine in China: Health Techniques and Social History," organized by CNRS, EHESS, Collège de France, and INALCO, June 21–23, 2000). On the life and writings of Fu Jinquan, see Zeng Zhaonan, "Daoshi Fu Jinquan sixiang lueshu," 9: 177–89. On the late Qing Daoist alchemist Li Xiyue (Li Hanxue) and the spread of the Daoist Western lineage, which emerged around the early nineteenth century in Sichuan, see Huang Zhaohan, "Qingdai Daojiao xipai mingming huodong ji daotong kao" 清代道教西派命名活動及道統考 (A study of the naming activities and doctrine of the Western lineage of Daoism), in idem, Huang Zhaohan, *Daojiao yanjiu lunwenji*, pp. 61–91. For writings by Wang Qihuo 汪啟濩, see his *Daotong dacheng* 道統大成 (n.p.: privately printed, 1900). For Wang's life and practice of inner alchemy within the Daoist Western school (*xipai* 西派), see Xu Haiyin, *Tianle ji*.

30. One of the most important developments in Daoism during the late imperial period was undoubtedly the redacting and supplementing of the Ming Daoist Canon during the Qing. For recent research on the subject,

see Esposito, "The Discovery of Jiang Yuting's *Daozang jiyao*"; and Mori Yuria, "Jūkan *Dōzō shūyō*."

31. Abbot Meng Yongcai 孟永才 (?–1881), for instance, was responsible for repairing the Daoist Canon held at the White Cloud Monastery during his tenure in the capital. See Meng Yongcai, "Shoujie bichi." For the efforts of early Republican-era warlords and politicians to reprint the Daoist Canon, see Chen Guofu, *Daozang yuanliu kao*; and Goossaert, "The Taoist Canon in Late Imperial and Modern Peking," in idem, *The Taoists of Peking*, Appendix B, pp. 345–51. See also Ding Fubao, ed., *Daozang jinghua lu*. Additionally, Ding also reprinted a Daoist compilation edited by Min Yide; see Ding Fubao, comp., *Daozang xubian*.

32. For the history of the Buddhist reforms and overseas exchanges with foreign Buddhism, see Welch, *The Practice of Chinese Buddhism*; and idem, *Buddhist Revival in China*.

Chapter 2

1. The expression "Fish and Dragon," *yu long* 魚龍, refers to a mythical animal capable of transforming from a fish to a dragon. The Eastern Han poet Zhang Heng described this protean animal in his famous *Ode to the Western Capital* (*Xijing fu* 西京賦) (Xiao Tong, *Wenxuan*, 2: 48). Here the animal is used figuratively to allude to the alchemic transformation of the body in cultivation.

2. The simian and the crane (*yuan he* 猿鶴) are a metaphor for transformed supernatural beings, especially transformed from well-cultivated gentlemen (*junzi* 君子). Here the expression denotes the transcendent attributes of the perfected self-cultivators.

3. Mount Lu 盧山 in present-day Jiangxi province has long been associated with recluses; indeed, its name derives from a famous ancient recluse.

4. "Empyrean" (*yanluo* 煙羅) refers to the Daoist heaven where the immortals are believed to reside.

5. Chen Yingning, "Song daoyou Hu Yunchang you haidao zhi Yan" 送道友胡允昌由海道之燕, YS 2: 27.

6. During the Spring and Autumn period (770–476 BC), the region was part of the Wan dukedom 皖國. Under the Han dynasties, it became Wan county 皖縣 under Lujiang prefecture 盧江郡. Under the reign of Jin emperor Sima Dezong 司馬德宗 (r. 397–418), Huaining was established as a county and had since been known by its present name. See also Huaining difang zhi bianzuan weiyuanhui, *Huaining xianzhi*, pp. 1–55.

7. Between 1853 and 1862, control of Anqing switched six times between the Qing and the Taiping forces ("Da shi ji" 大事記, in ibid., pp. 14–15).

8. On the Anqing temples, see Shryock, *The Temples of Anking and Their Cults*. See also Zhan Shouzhen (1), "Anqing gexian Daojiao gongguan mingcheng," p. 112.

9. See Zhan Shouzhen (2), "Anqing Daojiao tanzhu ji keshi." In his general survey of the religious temples and cults in Anqing in the 1920s, Shryock (*The Temples of Anking and Their Cults*, p. 88) reported that the Anqing Taoist Association (Daojiao hui 道教會) had 500–600 members, but this number was limited to Huaining county alone.

10. According to Shryock (*Temples of Anking and Their Cults*, pp. 85–94), the two Quanzhen monasteries in Anqing had by then fallen into disrepair, and the Zhengyi hearth ritual masters now dominated local ritual services.

11. See Zhan Shouzhen (1), "Anqing Daoguan de jianzao yu chuanshuo."

12. See Chen Yingning, *Zizhuan*, in Li Yangzheng, ed., *Daojiao yu yangsheng*, pp. 1–5. See also Yu Zhongjue, *Jindai daojia gongfa daoshi*, pp. 1–16.

13. See Chen Yingning, *Zizhuan*, in Li Yangzheng, ed., *Daojiao yu yangsheng*, pp. 1–5. See also Yu Zhongjue, *Jindai daojia gongfa daoshi*, pp. 1–4.

14. The food-processing shop, which is known as Hu Yumei 胡玉美, was first established in 1830. It produced flavoring ingredients enjoyed throughout Anqing and beyond. It is still a best-selling brand today. See *Huaining xianzhi*, pp. 872–73.

15. Hu's major contributions to the studies of *Laozi* and *Zhuangzi* are his *Laozi shuyi* 老子述義 (Nanjing: Zhongshan shuju, 1933) and *Zhuangzi quangu* 莊子詮詁 (Shanghai: Shangwu yinshu guan, 1931). See also *Huaining xianzhi*, pp. 872–73.

16. Chen Yingning, "Da Jiangsu Rugao zhi xing lu" 答江蘇如皋知省廬, YS 91 (1937): 10; Yu Zhongjue, *Jindai daojia gongfa daoshi*, pp. 1–16.

17. See Yu Zhongjue, *Jindai daojia gongfa daoshi*, pp. 1–16; and Chen Zhonglian, "Huainian bofu Chen Yingning," pp. 19–21. In his commemorative essay, Chen Zhonglian recounts some of the Chen clan elders' memories of Chen Yingning. According to Chen, after the chief proctor told Chen's father about Chen Yingning's criticisms of the Qing court, Chen's mother fell sick. Being a dutiful son, Chen assured his mother that he would succeed on his next try at the *xiucai* degree.

18. See Chen Yingning, *Zizhuan*, in Li Yangzheng, ed., *Daojiao yu yangsheng*, pp. 1–5. See also Yu Zhongjue, *Jindai daojia gongfa daoshi*, pp. 1–16.

19. See Chen Zhonglian, "Huainian bofu Chen Yingning," pp. 19–21.
20. See "Da zongshi" 大宗師 in *Zhuangzi*. The original reads: 其爲物, 無不將也, 無不迎也, 無不成也, 其名爲攖寧. 攖寧者也, 攖而後寧.
21. See Chen Yingning, *Zizhuan*, in Li Yangzheng, ed., *Daojiao yu yangsheng*, p. 2. See also Yu Zhongjue, *Jindai daojia gongfa daoshi*, pp. 4–5. For a narrative history of the arsenal as the leading institution that introduced science and technology in China, see Wei Yungong, *Jiangnan zhizao ju ji*. For a more recent study of the arsenal's role and impact on modernization and modernity in China, see Meng Yue, "Hybrid Science Versus Modernity: The Practice of the Jiangnan Arsenal, 1864–1897," in idem, "The Invention of Shanghai," pp. 50–110.
22. See Li Yangzheng, ed., *Daojiao yu yangsheng*, pp. 2 (Chen Yingning's *Zizhuan*), 444–78. Chen may have indeed studied with Yan Fu briefly between 1906 and 1907. We know that some time in late 1906 Yan Fu was invited by then-Anhui governor En-ming to serve as the superintendent of the Anhui Advanced College, but he resigned from the office shortly after En-ming was assassinated by Xu Xilin 徐錫麟 (1873–1907) in the summer of 1907. But it is conceivable that during his brief tenure at the college from 1906 to 1907 Yan Fu may have either lectured or spoken at the Advanced College of Law and Politics. For Yan Fu's appointment at the Anhui college, see Wang Quchang, *Yan Jidao nianpu*. See also Schwartz, *In Search of Wealth and Power*, pp. 212–13; and Wu Yakui, *Shengming de zhuiqiu*, pp. 19–20.
23. Li Yangzheng, ed., *Daojiao yu yangsheng*, p. 2; Yu Zhongjue, *Jindai daojia gongfa daoshi*, p. 5.
24. See Bazhi heshang, *Bazhi toutuo shiwen ji*.
25. Chen Yingning, *Zizhuan*, in Li Yangzheng, ed., *Daojiao yu yangsheng*, p. 2; Yu Zhongjue, *Jindai daojia gongfa daoshi*, pp. 5–6. Chen did, however, acknowledge on one occasion that he had acquired five masters by 1935: two belonged to the Daoist northern school (Beipai 北派), which generally refers to the Quanzhen school of Daoism and stresses solo pure cultivation as means of transcendence; one was a member of the Southern school (Nanpai 南派), which allegedly emphasizes sexual or paired cultivation techniques as means of attaining perfection; one was from the Concealed Immortals school (Yinxian pai 隱仙派); and one from the Confucian school (Rujia 儒家) of self-cultivation. It would seem extremely unlikely that Chen would have acquired all five masters during the two decades between 1912 and 1935. See Chen Yingning, "Dafu Shanghai Nanchezhan Zhangjia long Wang jun xuedao si wen" 答覆上海南車站張家弄王君學道四問, YS 42: 11.

26. See Chen Yaoting, *Shanghai Daojiao shi*, p. 408. See also Yao Shuliang, "Shanghai Baiyun guan shi."

27. For the history of the Daoist Canon and the monastic depository centers throughout the Ming and Qing periods, see Chen Guofu, *Daozang yuanliu kao*; and also Goossaert, "The Taoist Canon in Late Imperial and Modern Beijing," in idem, *The Taoists of Peking*, pp. 345–51. For bibliographic studies of the canon, see Boltz, *A Survey of Taoist Literature*; and, more recently, Schipper and Verellen, *The Taoist Canon*, 3 vols.

28. See Chen Yingning, *Zizhuan*, in Li Yangzheng, ed., *Daojiao yu yangsheng*, pp. 5, 447. Chen claimed that he was one of the few scholars in the late nineteenth and early twentieth centuries in either China or the West to have read the entire canon. Others who did were Wang Guowei 王國維 (1877–1927) and Liu Shipei.

29. See Vincent Goossaert, "Republican Church Engineering: The National Religious Associations in 1912 China," in Mayfair Yang, ed., *Religion, Modernity and the State in China*.

30. On the diffused and discrete nature of Chinese religious organization and practice, see C. K. Yang, *Religion in Chinese Society*.

31. Although unclear about the details, Welch (*Buddhist Revival in China*, pp. 2–15, 295–96) mentioned several early organizations and organizing efforts in the country, particularly the Anhui Provincial Buddhist Association (Anhui sheng Fojiao hui 安徽省佛教會) near Anqing run by the eminent monk Yuexia from 1900 to 1903.

32. For the life and career of Wang Zhen, see Katz, "The Religious Life of a Renowned Shanghai Businessman and Philanthropist."

33. Over his career as a Pure Land practitioner and writer, Gao used several Daoist sobriquets such as Zhongnan shi 終南侍, Yunshan daoren 雲山道人, and Xuanxi daoren 玄溪道人. See Gao Henian, *Mingshan youfang ji*; Huang Changlun, *Fangwai laihong*; and http://www.tznet.cn/Get/wh/ldmx/0562709124878702.htm.

34. See Chen Zixiu 陳子修 (AKA Chen Yingning), "Minguo er nian song Henian jushi chao Wutai" 民國二年送鶴年居士朝五臺, in Gao Henian, *Mingshan youfang ji*, pp. 367–68. See also Chen Yingning, "Song Gao Henian jushi chao Wutai" 送高鶴年居士朝五臺, YS 40: 9–10.

35. According to Chen's account, he became well acquainted with Yuexia at the Buddhist seminary at the Hardoon Gardens. Between 1912 and 1913, Chen served as the lecture assistant to Yuexia, who was hosting the Buddhist Huayan Seminary sponsored by the famous Jewish merchant Simon Hardoon and his Chinese wife. See Chen Yingning, "Dafu Shanghai Gongji tang Xu Rusheng jun xue fo wu wen" 答覆上海公濟堂許如生君學

佛五問, YS 42: 16; and his "Du 'Huasheng xu' de ganxiang" 讀化聲序的感想, YS 52: 1–2.

36. According to Taixu (*Taixu zizhuan*, 1939, p. 43), Mrs. Hardoon initially invited Yuexia to run the Huayan Seminary at her luxurious garden estate in the city in the fall of 1914. But three months later, she allegedly insisted that the Buddhist seminarians perform bows to her. The Buddhist seminarians protested this insult by relocating their seminary to Hangzhou. See also Shi Xuming, *Taixu dashi shengping shiji*.

37. Chen Yingning, *Zizhuan*, in Li Yangzheng, ed., *Daojiao yu yangsheng*, p. 3.

38. In this letter to a reader, Chen used organic images to explain the relationship among the three teachings. He argued that the three teachings were of the same heart and that like the pink lotus flower, the white lotus root, and the emerald lotus leaves, they were of one and the same root. See Chen Yingning, "Dafu Haimen xian Fojiao Jingyehui Cai jun siwen" 答覆海門縣佛教淨業會蔡君四問, YS, 42: 9–10.

39. See Li Yangzheng, ed., *Daojiao yu yangsheng*, p. 447.

40. See Zhongyang Daojiao hui zong jiguan bu, *Daojiao hui diyi ci bugao* (Beijing, 1912).

41. See "Daojiao da gang" 道教大綱, in ibid., n.p. [pp. 19–20].

42. See "Daojiao hui da gang" 道教會大綱, in ibid., p. 10. See also Goossaert, *The Taoists of Peking*, pp. 74–80.

43. For Gao's life and career, see Xun Liu, "Visualizing Perfection"; and Wang Jianchuan, "Qingmo de taijian, Baiyun guan yu Yihe tuan yundong." For Liu Mingrui's writings, see his *Daoyuan jing wei ge* and *Qiao qiao dong zhang*. For Liu's and Zhao's careers as transmitters and practitioners of Quanzhen Daoism in Beijing, see Goossaert, *The Taoists of Peking*, pp. 285–306. For writings by Zhao Bicheng, see also Despeux, *Zhao Bichen*.

44. For the spread of Daode xueshe in Beijing, see Ren Zhen, "Duan Zhengyuan yu Daode xueshe." For the spread of the Common Benevolence Society in Beijing, see Wang Jianchuan, "Tongshan she zaoqi lishi chutan." See also Wang Jianchuan and Fan Chunwu, "Qing mo Min chu Beijing luan tang de ge an yanjiu." For the society's close ties with the early Republican northern warlords and political elite, see also Tan Songlin, *Zhongguo mimi shehui*. For a recent comprehensive study of the redemptive societies in the early Republican era, see Nedostup, "Religion, Superstition, and Governing Society."

45. See Ying Lianzhi, "Lü shi san zimei ji xu," p. 524.

46. See Huang Yanli, "Cong Xu Can dao Lü Bicheng." See also Li Baomin, "Lü Bicheng nianpu" 呂碧城年譜, in idem, ed., *Lü Bicheng ci jian zhu*, pp. 1–20, 566–90.

47. The Void (*xu* 虛) and the Bright (*ming* 明) are ambiguous terms. Here, the Void seems to refer to the realm of the immortals, the supreme state of inner alchemic perfection, and the Bright to the mortal world.

48. See Lü Bicheng, "Fang Yingning daoren kou yi xuanli duo yu bian nan gui hou que ji" 訪攖寧道人叩以玄理多與辨難歸後卻寄, in Li Yangzheng, ed., *Daojiao yu yangsheng*, p. 428.

49. See also Li Baomin, "Lü Bicheng nianpu," in idem, ed., *Lü Bicheng ci jian zhu*, p. 576.

50. See Chen Yingning, "Fu da shi yuan yun" 附答詩原韻, in Li Yangzheng, ed., *Daojiao yu yangsheng*, p. 428.

51. "Mysterious Principles" (*xuanli* 玄理) refers to the learning of inner alchemy.

52. Ban Chao 班超 was a talented female scholar and tutor for the court during the Han dynasty. She authored *Precepts for Women* (*Nüjie* 女誡). For her biography, see Fan Ye 范曄, *Hou Han shu* 後漢書 (The book of the Latter Han dynasty), *juan* 114, in *ESWS*, pp. 1045–46.

53. The Emerald Feathers and the Bright Pearls (*cui yu ming zhu* 翠羽明珠) were purportedly worn by immortals. Here they are metonyms for Lü's previous life as an immortal.

54. The Petal Palace (Rui gong 蕊宮) is an abbreviation for Ruizhu gong 蕊珠宮, one of the Shangqing Daoist heavens. Here Chen again affirmed the divine origin of his disciple. The transformed body (*hua shen* 化身), which can also be understood as the "body in disguise," alludes to her mortal body in contrast to her origin from the Petal Palace.

55. The Celestial Flower (*tian hua* 天花) refers to snowflakes. But in inner alchemic parlance, it alludes to the somatic vision of falling snowflakes, indicating the maturation of elixir and the pending parturition of the Yang Spirit. See Liu Huayang 柳華陽, *Hui ming jing* 慧命經 (1790) in Deng Huiji, *Wu Liu xian zong*, pp. 464, 490–91. Liu stipulated that the sight of the falling Celestial Flowers signified the ripened embryo within the practitioner's body.

In "the Void becomes the Phenomenon" (*kong cheng se* 空成色), the Void refers to the atemporal realm, and Phenomenon (*se* 色) is a Buddhist term denoting the temporal world. There are two possible readings of the line. One is that the atemporal realm is transformed into the temporal world. The other reading, which I endorse, is that once the practitioner experienced the maturation of the inner elixir and saw the somatic vision of the falling Celestial Flowers, the Void or the atemporal realm becomes or extends to the temporal world, transforming it into the atemporal world.

56. The Azure Heaven (qing xiao 青霄) is another reference to the Daoist empyrean or heaven. The Crane (he 鶴) is often associated with the immortality cult. The response by Chen is taken from Li Yangzhen, *Daojiao yu yangsheng*, p. 428. Li, however, provides neither dates nor sources for the two poems.

57. See Chen Yingning, "Da Lü Bicheng nüshi sanshi liu wen" 答呂碧城女士三十六問, YS 86: 1–7. In his commentary on the late Qing scripture Lü had read, Chen also discussed in detail the intense physical or sexual pleasure that female practitioners were supposed to experience at certain stages of the meditative practice. See Chen Yingning, ed., *Nügong shize* 女功十則 (Shanghai: Yihuatang, 1935), pp. 6–7. For the history of female inner alchemy, see Despeux, *Immortelles de la Chine ancienne*; and Valussi, "Beheading the Red Dragon."

58. For the increasing female involvement in religions during the late imperial period, see Zhou Yuqing, "The Heart and the Temple"; and Xun Liu, "Visualizing Perfection."

59. See *Nüdan shize* 女丹十則, in He Longxian, *Nüdan hebian*, 2a, 15b–16b.

60. According to Wu Yizhu, she and Chen became acquainted around 1908 when she was pursuing medical studies, presumably at the Sino-Western Medical School in Shanghai. See Wu's 1938 epilogue to Chen Yingning, *Lingyuan dadao ge baihua zhujie*. Other sources differ on when Chen and Wu met and on the circumstances of the meeting. Yu Zhongjue claimed that Chen and Wu initially met as fellow alchemic cultivators. They had intended to keep their relationship as such. Wary of potential misunderstanding by the public, they went ahead and announced that they were married. See Yu Zhongjue, *Jindai daojia gongfa daoshi*, pp. 6–7. Chen Zhonglian, Chen's nephew, offers an account with details that may allow for an even earlier Chen-Wu acquaintance in 1908; see Chen Zhonglian, "Huainian bofu Chen Yingning," pp. 19–20.

61. See Chen Zhonglian, "Huainian bofu Chen Yingning," p. 20. Chen has so far offered the most detailed information concerning his aunt Wu Yizhu. His account of her is in most parts corroborated by Chen Yingning's own often terse account of her. But Yu Zhongjue (*Jindai daojia gongfa daoshi*, p. 7) offered a slightly different account, claiming that Wu was a returned student from America or England.

62. Li Yangzheng ("Chen Yingning xianxue de tezheng, lilun yu fangfa," pp. 9–17) has also suggested that by the time Chen and Wu were married,

they had been engaged in the dual practice of the yin-yang school of inner alchemy.

63. Chen Yingning, *Zizhuan*, in Li Yangzheng, ed., *Daojiao yu yangsheng*, p. 3.

64. Huang Suizhi (AKA Huang Sui 黃邃), himself an accomplished adept of inner alchemy, described his friends Zheng Dingcheng and Chen Yingning as the most learned and authoritative experts of the practice. See Huang Sui, "Sun Bu'er nüdan jue shizhu Huang xu" 孫不二女丹訣詩注黃序, in Chen Yingning, *Sun Bu'er nüdan shizhu*, 2a–3a.

65. For Huang's association with Zheng Guanying, see Zheng Guanying, "Zhi huaxue Huang jun Suizhi yishi Lü jun Xiantang Foxue yanjiu hui Zhang jun Runsheng shu" 致化學黃君邃之醫士呂君獻堂佛學研究會張君潤生書, in idem, *Shengshi weiyan houbian*, 1: 34b–38b. For Chen Yingning and Huang's friendship, see YS, 49: 17; and also Huang's preface in Chen Yingning, *Sun Bu'er nüdan shizhu*, 2a–3a.

66. Huang made the observation in 1926; see his preface to Chen Yingning, *Sun Bu'er nüdan shizhu*, 2a.

67. Chen probably wrote these comments about the goal and state of outer alchemy as early as 1916 when he first edited *Ten Rules on Female Alchemy* for Lü Bicheng to study. These comments, especially the part about "the loss of the Way" and about foreigners taking the credit for the invention of alchemy were then further revised or added when he re-edited the scripture for publication by Yihuatang in 1935; see Chen Yingning, *Ten Rules on Female Alchemy*, p. 9.

68. The discussion is part of a large debate on the origins of modern chemistry and its origins in ancient alchemy in Egypt, Greece, India, and China. The Japanese historian of chemistry Chikashige Masumi (1870–1941) examined the connections between ancient Chinese alchemy and modern chemistry and metallurgy for twenty years between 1909 and 1929. The history of Chinese alchemy, its Daoist origins, and its relationship to western alchemy were the subject of a doctoral thesis by the American missionary and sinologist Obed Simon Johnson, who later published it in Shanghai in 1928. Around the same time, the same subject was also pursued by the MIT chemistry professor Lenny Davis and his Chinese student Wu Lu-Ch'iang. See Chikashige Masumi, *Tōyō renkinjutsu*. See also Adolph, "The History of Chemistry in China"; and Johnson, *A Study of Chinese Alchemy*. See also Davis and Wu, "Chinese Alchemy."

69. Chen wrote the letter to Huang Canhua in July 1935; see YS, 49: 17. What became of Chen's alchemic experiments remains unclear. In my interviews with several of Chen's disciples and students such as Dr. Zhang

Zhuming, Ms. Yu Zhongjue, and Mr. Li Yangzheng, all asserted that Chen's experiments had indeed yielded knowledge about alchemic transformation. They mentioned that they had seen a small pencil-sized rod of metal alloy with a reddish color at one end and silvery color at the other in Chen's possession.

70. Chen Yingning, "Yuhua gong shishu xianzi jiangtan shi" 玉華宮侍書仙子降壇詩, YS 17: 6.

71. For various divination techniques and practices among both elites and commoners during the Qing period, see Smith, *Fortune-tellers and Philosophers*. For the practice in the early Republican era, see Sakai Tadao, "Minguo shiqi zhi xinxing zongjiao yundong"; and Zhou Yumin, "Minguo shiqi yige wentan juzi jibi xia de lingjie."

72. See Huang Kewu, "Minguo chunian Shanghai de lingxue yanjiu."

73. The Daoist encounter with gods or goddesses is a recurrent trope in Daoist literature and hagiography. The most famous and frequently invoked encounters are the ones between the Queen Mother and King Mu of Zhou and Emperor Wu of Han. See Guo Pu, *Mu Tianzi zhuan*, in DZ, 5: 47–57; and *Han Wudi neizhuan*, in DZ, 5: 58–63.

74. Chen Yingning, "Lushan Xiaotianchi jitan shilu yuanqi" 廬山小天池乩壇實錄緣起, YS 2: 33; idem, "Tianxian Bicheng nüshi jiangtan jilu" 天仙碧城女史降壇紀錄, YS 3: 48–49. In these recollections, Chen offered a rare glimpse into his early experiment with spirit-writing. One of these early séances took place in 1923 in Chen's residence in Shanghai. During this session, a goddess named Bicheng descended to answer a range of questions asked by two female questioners (*wenshi zhe* 問事者). Chen and his wife served as sandbox assistants (*fuji zhe* 扶乩者).

75. The colorful plume here refers to the pen used in the séance.

76. The Jade Rostrum (*yao tai* 瑤臺) is used here to allude to both the sandbox and the celestial residence of the immortals.

77. Chen Yingning, "Yuhua gong shi shu xianzi jiangtan shi," YS 17: 6. The True Fluid (*zhenye* 眞液) refers to the atemporal *qi* in the body, the accumulation and refining of which is believed to lead to the transformation of the body.

78. See Wang Jianchuan, "Tongshan she zaoqi lishi chutan"; Wang Jianchuan and Fan Chunwu, "Qing mo Min chu Beijing luan tang de ge an yanjiu"; Vincent Goossaert, "Taoists in the Modern Self-cultivation Market: The Case of Peking, 1850–1949," paper for the conference "Between Eternity and Modernity: Daoism and Its Reinvention in the 20th Century," Harvard University, June 14–15, 2006; and Li Shiyu, "Tianjin Zaili jiao diaocha yanjiu."

Chapter 3

1. See Chen Yingning, "Sun Bu'er nügong neidan cidi shizhu fanli" 孫不二女功內丹次第詩注凡例," in idem, *Sun Bu'er nüdan shizhu*, p. 6. Ninghai 寧海 was Sun's hometown; it is located in present-day Muping county in Shandong province.
2. The miraculous feat is also known as "soaring dash" (*chongju* 沖舉). Such ascendance is a recurring theme in Daoist hagiographies. The feat symbolizes the highest achievement in self-transformation practice whereby the practitioner is summoned to Heaven by the Supreme One (*Taiyi* 太一), the patron god of inner alchemy (see Wei Boyang 魏伯陽, *Cantongqi* 參同契, in Peng Xiao, *Zhouyi Cantongqi fenzhang tongzhenyi*, in *DZ*, 20: 140).
3. A Buddhist concept in origin, the idea of hard work or "merit" (*gong* 功) as a means to one's salvation or transcendence can be traced to the late Han classic of alchemy *Cantongqi*, which stresses that a practitioner's hard practice is ultimately rewarded with a summons to ascend to the immortals' realm and an investiture in the empyrean (see Wei Boyang, *Cantongqi*, in Peng Xiao, *Zhouyi Cantongqi fenzhang tongzhenyi* in *DZ*, 20: 140; and also Chen Xianwei, *Zhouyi Cantongqi jie*, in *DZ*, 20: 279).
4. Chen Yingning finished revising the practice manual into a manuscript study of the poem in 1926. He then solicited a preface from Huang Sui, who was a close friend and associate in Daoist inner alchemy (see Huang Sui 黃邃 [aka Suizhi 邃之], "Sun Bu'er nüdan jue shizhu Huang xu" 孫不二女丹訣詩注黃序, in Chen Yingning, *Sun Bu'er nüdan shizhu*, pp. 1–3, 6).
5. See "Daojiao hui dagang" 道教會大綱, in *Daojiao hui diyi ci bugao*, p. 10.
6. Dongchu, *Zhongguo Fojiao jindai shi*, p. 238.
7. See Chen Yingning, "Sun Bu'er nügong neidan cidi shizhu," in idem, *Sun Bu'er nüdan shizhu*, pp. 2–3.
8. See ibid., p. 3.
9. See Welch, *The Buddhist Revival in Modern China*, pp. 162–73.
10. At the 1925 East Asian Buddhist Conference, many Chinese Buddhist clerics and lay practitioners openly expressed their suspicion of the real intentions behind Japan's announced policies of friendship and cooperation. They viewed such talk as a mere front for the Japanese goal of expanding its influence in China (ibid., pp. 166–69).
11. Chen Yingning did hold a tender spot in his heart for Hinayana, or Small Vehicle Buddhism (Xiaosheng Fojiao 小乘佛教). To him, the Small Vehicle stresses hard practice that engages the flesh body fully and eschews

the abstruse yet empty talk of metaphysics so characteristic of the Weishi Lineage of Great Vehicle Buddhism (Chen Yingning, "Bian Lengyan jing shizhong xian" 辨楞嚴經十種仙 [Differentiating the ten immortals in the Śūraṅgama sūtra]," YS, no. 96 [1937]: 2–3).

12. Chen Yingning, "Du Huasheng xu de ganxiang: shiyi" (Thoughts on reading Zhang Huasheng's Manifesto), YS, no. 54 (1935): 2.

13. Chen Yingning, "Bian Lengyan jing shizhong xian," YS, no. 96 (1937): 7.

14. Ibid., pp. 2–3.

15. The term "flowing fire" (liuhuo 流火) refers to the Cardiac Constellation (Xinsu 心宿), which consists of three stars; see Hequ zi, Changdao zhenyan, in DZJY, dou ji, 5.30b–32a.

16. Chen Yingning, Sun Bu'er nüdan shizhu, p. 32. Chen seemed to be either quoting or paraphrasing a passage from an inner alchemic scripture of the late imperial period here (see Hequ zi, Changdao zhenyan, juan 2, in DZJHL, 2: 14a).

17. See Chen Yingning, "Fu Nanjing Lifayuan Huang Chanhua xiansheng shu" 覆南京立法院黃懺華先生書, YS, no. 50 (July 16, 1935): 1–2; and also "Hong Tai'an xiansheng xu" 洪太庵先生序 (Preface by Mr. Hong Tai'an) and "Zhu Changya nüshi xu" 朱昌亞女士序 (Preface by Ms Zhu Changya) in Chen Yingning, Lingyuan dadao ge baihua zhujie, pp. 1a–4b and 1a–2b, respectively.

18. See Chen Yingning, Koujue gouxuan lu, YS, no. 86 (1937): 11; no. 36 (1934): 10–11. The immortal's legendary instructions to the Yellow Emperor can be found in Zhuangzi.

19. See ibid., YS, no. 33 (1934): 10.

20. See Leibold, "Competing Narratives of Racial Unity."

21. See Chen Yingning, Sun Bu'er nüdan shizhu, pp. 6, 9.

22. See Tan Qiao, Huashu, in DZ, 23: 592.

23. Chen identified a Song female Daoist, Cao Xiyun 曹希蘊 (h. Daochong 道沖), with the posthumous title Qingxu Wenyi dashi 清虛文逸大師 as the real author of the poem. See "Lingyuan dadao ge benwen" 靈源大道歌本文 and "Wang Dongting xiansheng dui yu Lingyuan dadao ge zhi yijian" 汪東亭先生對於靈源大道歌之意見, in Chen Yingning, Lingyuan dadao ge baihua zhujie, pp. 2a and 25a–26a, respectively.

24. On the meanings of the Divine Fluid, see Chen Yingning, "Yu Jiang Zhuzhuang xiansheng taolun xianhou tian shenshui" 與蔣竹莊先生討論先後天神水, in idem, Lingyuan dadao ge baihua zhujie, pp. 14a–17a, 26a–27b.

25. Chen Yingning, Lingyuan dadao ge baihua zhujie, pp. 6b–7a.

26. Chen Yingning, Sun Bu'er nüdan shizhu, p. 9.

27. Chen Yingning, *Lingyuan dadao ge baihua zhujie*, pp. 26a–27b.
28. Chen Yingning, *Sun Bu'er nüdan shizhu*, pp. 11–12.
29. Ibid., p. 6. The mother-son dynamics is a frequently used metaphor in inner alchemic writings (see Li Daochun, *Zhonghe ji*, juan 2, in DZ, 4: 487–92). In inner alchemy, the natural generative relationship between the maternal Metal and her filial Water is reversed so that the Son, the begotten and the temporal aspect of the body, is transformed to become the begetting Mother, the atemporal aspect of the body. This reversing process is known as the Son begetting the Mother (*zi sheng mu* 子生母; see Liu Yiming, *Wuzhen zhizhi*, in ZWDS, 8: 356).
30. Chen Yingning, *Sun Bu'er nüdan shizhu*, pp. 12–13.
31. Chen Yingning, *Huangting jing jiangyi*, p. 16.
32. Ibid., pp. 3–4.
33. Ibid., p. 3.
34. Chen Yingning, *Sun Bu'er nüdan shizhu*, p. 10.
35. See Chen Yingning, *Huangting jing jiangyi*, p. 7. In this medical body, the Heart is seen as the repository of the Psyche, the Liver as the repository of the Hun soul 魂, the Kidneys as the repository of the Essence 精, the Lungs as the repository of the Po soul 魄, and the Spleen as the repository of the Intent 意. See *Su wen* 素問, in *Huangdi neijing* 黃帝內經, in Chen Menglei, *Yibu quanlu*, juan 93, 4: 1–9. The medical construction of the body was early incorporated into the discourse of self-cultivation and inner alchemy; see Hu Yun, *Huangting neijing wuzang liufu bu xie tu*, in DZ, 6: 686–93. The same viscera-*shen* correlation (*zang shen* 臟神) is also discussed in a Song-era classic on inner alchemy; see Zeng Zao, *Qishen lun*, in DZ, 20: 764.
36. Chen Yingning, *Huangting jing jiangyi*, pp. 17–18.
37. Ibid., pp. 4–5.
38. See ibid., pp. 12–13; Chen Yingning, *Sun Bu'er nüdan shizhu*, p. 29; and idem, *Lingyuan dadao ge baihua zhujie*, p. 10. For the principles of reciprocal benefits of alchemic numerology, see Zhang Boduan, *Jindan sibai zi*, in DZ, 24: 161–64.
39. A Buddhist term in origin, the Root of Life (*ming gen* 命根) clearly alludes to the source of what constitutes life. In the present context, it specifically refers to the revitalizing *qi* of the atemporal realm. Also known as the Bud, or Stalk, of Life (*ming di* 命蒂), it is a classic *neidan* term alluding to the rising True or Original *qi* in the body. See Cao Wenyi, *Lingyuan dadao ge* 靈源大道歌, in Chen Yingning, *Lingyuan dadao ge baihua zhujie*, p. 1. Additionally, the term is also used in inner alchemy literature to refer to the physically generative and vitalistic aspect of life (*ming* 命) in contrast

to the conscious and psychic nature of human existence (*xing* 性). See Chen Zhixu, *Shangyang zi Jin dan da yao*, in *DZ*, 24: 18.

40. Chen Yingning, *Huangting jing jiangyi*, pp. 12–13.

41. Ibid., pp. 11–12.

42. In the male body, it is referred to as the Aperture of Essence (*jing qiao* 精竅), or the Chamber of Essence (*jing shi* 精室). In the female body, the locus is known as the Sea of Blood (*xue hai* 血海), the Sea Bottom (*hai di* 海底), the Sea of Qi (*qi hai* 氣海), the Pond (*tan* 潭), and the Palace of the Sons (*zi gong* 子宮), or the womb. See Chen Yingning, *Huangting jing jiangyi*, pp. 17, 21; and idem, *Sun Bu'er nüdan shizhu*, pp. 14–15.

43. Chen Yingning, *Huangting jing jiangyi*, p. 17.

44. Ibid., p. 18.

45. Ibid., p. 17.

46. See ibid., pp. 18–19. The expression "the Pearl of Son" (*zi zhu* 子珠) has been subject to various interpretations. Annotators since the Song dynasty have tended to define the phrase in terms of inner alchemy. Lu Xixing and others interpreted the Pearl as the nascent elixir formed by the inward focus of the *shen* energies alluded to as "Three Lights" in the previous line. See Qiu Zhao'ao, *Guben Cantongqi jizhu*, in *DZJH*, ser. 13, 1: 137–39.

47. See Chen Yingning, *Huangting jing jiangyi*, p. 14.

48. See Chen Yingning, *Sun Bu'er nüdan shizhu*, pp. 13–14.

49. See Min Yide, *Yin zhenren Liaoyang dian wenda pian*, in *ZWDS*, 10: 384–85. Min described the Jade Pillow as being the smallest of the three passes on the back and hardest to traverse.

50. Chen Yingning, *Huangting jing jiangyi*, p. 15. In other inner alchemic writings, the Dark Bosom locus is situated in the center of the throat (see Wucheng zi, *Taishang huangting waijing jing*, in *DZ*, 22: 90).

51. Chen Yingning, *Huangting jing jiangyi*, pp. 14–15.

52. See ibid., pp. 6–7.

53. See ibid., pp. 5–6.

54. See ibid., p. 28.

55. Ibid., pp. 5–6.

56. See Chen Yingning, "Fu Wuchang Zhang Huasheng xiansheng han" 覆武昌張化聲先生函 (In reply to the letter from Mr. Zhang Huasheng of Wuchang), *YS*, no. 32 (1934): 8–9.

57. Chen Yingning, "Xuexian bicheng," p. 41.

58. Chen Yingning, "Du Huasheng xu de ganxiang" 讀化聲敘的感想 (Reflections on reading Huasheng's manifesto) (11), *YS*, no. 54 (1935): 2–3.

59. Ibid., p. 3.

60. See ibid., p. 2.
61. Chen Yingning, "Xuexian bicheng," pp. 36–38. For the original text of *Laozi*, see Chen Guying, *Laozi zhushi ji pingjie*, p. 232. The translation is my own.
62. Chen Yingning, "Xuexian bicheng," p. 42. In the notes in the upper margin of the manuscript, Chen specifically revised "maternal blood" in the stock phrase of *fujing muxue* 父精母血 to "maternal egg" (*muluan* 母卵).
63. Ibid., p. 42.
64. Ibid., pp. 42–43.
65. Ibid., pp. 41–42; idem, "Bian *Lengyan jing* shizhong xian," YS, no. 98 (1937): 6–7.
66. Chen Yingning, "Du Huasheng xu de ganxiang" (4), YS, no. 41 (1935): 7.

Chapter 4

1. See Miss Dong, "You ju shu zhi" 幽居述志, YS, no. 93 (Mar. 1, 1937), p. 9.
2. See Lin Zuojia, "Qing mo Min chu miaochan xingxue zhi yanjiu"; and Wang Leiquan, "Dui Zhongguo jindai liangci miaochan xingxue fengchao de fansi." For a personal account of Feng's temple-smashing campaign in northern Henan, see Fan Chengdian, "Wode daoshi shengya."
3. See Chen Yingning, "*Xuexian bicheng*," p. 3.
4. Chen Yingning, *Koujue gouxuan lu*, YS, no. 32 (Oct. 16, 1934): 10. Huang Shang (z. Yuanji 元吉) was from Fengcheng in Jiangxi and was active during the late Qing period between the 1840s and 1908, according to Chen Yingning's introduction. Although both books ascribed to Huang seem to have first been published during the late Qing period, their original publication dates remain unclear. *Daodejing jiangyi* 道德經講義 (Lectures on *Daodejing*) seems to be a variant title for *Daodejing zhushi* 道德經注釋 (Annotations on *Daodejing*), which was reprinted in the early twentieth century by Beijing Daode xuehui 北京道德學會. The Beijing Daode xuehui edition was later reprinted in Taipei in 1978 by Zhenshanmei chubanshe. *Leyutang yulu* 樂育堂語錄 appears to have first been printed in 1873, according to the postscript to that edition written by a Long Tengjian 龍騰劍 in 1919. Huang Shang's sobriquet, Yuanji 元吉, seems to have caused many to confuse him with a renowned Daoist from the Yuan period: Huang Yuanji 黃元吉 (1271–1325). For the life and works of the second patriarch of the Pure and Bright Lineage of the Yuan period, see Huang Yuanji et al., *Jingming zhongxiao quanshu*.
5. Chen Yingning, *Koujue gouxuan lu*, YS, no. 36 (Dec. 16, 1934): 10.

6. See Wei Boyang in Peng Xiao, *Zhouyi Cantongqi fenzhang tongzhenyi*, in *DZ*, 20: 142. Wei's famous ponderings about his predicament were also quoted by Chen Yingning in his *Koujue gouxuan lu*, *YS*, no. 37 (Jan. 1, 1935): 4.

7. Chen Yingning, *Koujue gouxuan lu*, *YS*, no. 41 (Mar. 1, 1935): 6.

8. Ibid., *YS*, no. 49 (July 16, 1935): 4.

9. Ibid.; and ibid., no. 50 (July 16, 1935): 4.

10. Ibid., *YS*, no. 49 (July 16, 1935): 4.

11. Ibid.

12. See Chen Yingning, *Zizhuan*, in Li Yangzheng, ed., *Daojiao yu yangsheng*, pp. [1–5].

13. See Chen Yingning, *Koujue gouxuan lu*, in Hong Jianlin, *Xianxue jiemi*, pp. 575–77. This portion of Chen's unfinished manuscript was never published in either the *Yangshan Biweekly* or the *Immortals' Way Monthly*. According to my interviews with Dr. Hu Haiya 胡海牙 in 1994, the editor of this recent compilation relied on the manuscript of the book now in his private possession. Dr. Hu was a disciple of Chen Yingning. He used to teach acupuncture at Beijing Medical University and practiced at its affiliated hospital before his retirement. He now resides in Beijing.

14. See Chunqian daoren, *Xuyu mo li*, *YS*, no. 22 (June 16, 1934): 365.

15. See ibid., pp. 364–65.

16. Fangnei sanren was known among inner alchemists of the late imperial and early Republican periods for his book *Essentials of the Integrated Methods from the Southern and the Northern Lineages* (*Nanbei hecan fayao* 南北合參法要), an attempt to reconcile and integrate the dual-cultivation theory of the Southern Lineage with the solo approach of the Northern Lineage. Fangnei was also the author of several other widely circulated books: *Sanjiao zong zhi* 三教宗旨 (Principles of the Three Teachings), *Xianqing za zhu* 閑情雜著 (Miscellaneous writings in a leisurely mood), *Daoqing shi yong* 道情十詠 (Ten ballads on Daoist contemplation), and *Jibu wenre bingfang* 輯補溫熱病方 (Supplements to the collection of recipes on warm and hot diseases). In 1897 all except the last of these writings were collected into a four-volume compendium by Fangnei's associates and disciples. It took almost six years before the compendium was finally published under a new general title in 1903. See Fangnei sanren, *Tongyizhai sizhong* 通一齋四種.

17. See Fangnei sanren, "Xu" 序 (Preface), in *Nanbei hecan fayao*, 2.1; and also Zhenyi jushi 貞一居士 (Zhao Bencheng 趙本誠), "Xu" (Preface), in Fangnei sanren, *Tongyizai sizhong*, p. 1.

18. The poem was taken from a collection of ten poems called *Daoxue changge shi shou* 道學長歌十首 (Ten long ballads on learning the Way).

This title appears to be a variation of the title of the collection of ballads entitled *Daoqing shiyong* 道情十詠 (Ten ballads on Daoist contemplation), which Fangnei had written on various aspects of his learning and practice in Daoist inner alchemy. These ballads were later handcopied by Fangnei's friend Huang Suizhi and passed on to Chen Yingning, who in early 1936 re-edited the collection of ballads and republished them in a serial column in the *Yangshan Biweekly*. See Fangnei sanren, "Fangdao ge" 訪道歌 (A ballad on searching for the Way), YS, no. 70 (May 16, 1936): 6–7.

19. In the context here, the cluster of abbreviated references is used to denote what Fangnei perceived to be the most important collection of classics of inner alchemy. The Scripture (*jing* 經) most likely refers to either the Shangqing Daoist *Huangting jing* 黃庭經 (Yellow Courtyard scriptures) or another early Daoist classic, *Yinfu jing* 陰符經 (The scripture of the Yin talisman). The referent of the Ode (*ge* 歌) here may be either the famous ballad entitled "Pohuo zhengdao ge" 破惑正道歌 (A ballad to rectify the Way by smashing the conundrum) attributed to the Tang-era Daoist patriarch Zhongli Quan 鍾離權, or the ballad entitled "Qiaoyao ge" 敲爻歌 (A song on meditating on the trigrams) often ascribed to another Daoist patriarch, Lü Dongbin 呂洞賓. The Concordance (*qi* 契) refers to *Cantongqi* 參同契. The referent of the Treatise (*lun* 論) remains unclear to me.

20. White Jade Toad, or Bai Yuchan 白玉蟾 (1194–1229), was the fifth patriarch of the Southern Lineage of inner alchemy from the Southern Song period. His secular name was Ge Changgeng 葛長庚. He followed Chen Nan 陳楠 (h. Niwan 泥丸, ?–1213) for over a decade before receiving the transmission of full secrets from his master, who is also generally regarded as the fourth patriarch of the Southern Lineage.

21. The Three Origins (*san yuan* 三元) method refers to three different approaches to alchemy: the methods of the Heavenly Origin (*tian yuan dan fa* 天元丹法), the Earthly Origin (*di yuan dan fa* 地元丹法), and the Human Origin (*ren yuan dan fa* 人元丹法). The Two Schools (*liang pai* 兩派) refers to the Southern (*nan pai/nan zong* 南派/南宗) and the Northern (*bei pai/bei zong* 北派/北宗) lineages of Daoist inner alchemy traditions.

22. Zu Sheng 祖生 refers to Zu Ti 祖逖 (266–321), the heroic general of the Jin court. Zu was known for his prowess as a warrior using the weapon called *bian* 鞭, which was an iron staff wielded with one hand. Zu Sheng's iron staff 祖生鞭 is a classical allusion to the friendly rivalry between Zu and his friend Liu Kun 劉琨 in serving Emperor Yuan of the Jin dynasty 晉元帝. Upon learning that Zu had been retained by the court, Liu wrote to his relatives that he was so anxious that Zu might be called on ahead of him in leading an expedition that he slept with his dagger-axe every night

waiting for the dawn. For biographies of Zu and Liu, see *Jin shu* 晉書, in *ESWS*, 2: 195–98.

23. "Double Mystery" (*chongxuan* 重玄) refers to the Daoist metaphysics that emerged during the Sui and Tang dynasties. But in the present context, the term is used figuratively to allude to the ultimate secrets of inner alchemic cultivation. For a recent study in Chinese on the schools of Daoist metaphysics from the fifth to the ninth centuries, see Lu Guolong, *Zhongguo chongxuan xue*.

24. Hong Ya 洪崖 is the sobriquet of an early immortal and legendary courtier of the Yellow Emperor by the name of Ling Lun 伶倫. He was allegedly three thousand years old by the times of the sages Yao and Shun. As the more senior of the immortals, Hong Ya, together with Fu Qiu, another immortal from the Yellow Emperor's time, was frequently invoked in the poetry and consciousness of the Han and subsequent periods. The phrase "to pat Hong Ya on the shoulder" 拍洪崖肩 is therefore a metaphor for achieving immortality. The phrase itself seems to have originated with the Jin poet Guo Pu 郭璞 (276–324) when he wrote the memorable couplet 左執浮邱袖,/右拍洪崖肩 (With my left hand, I lead Fu Qiu the Immortal by his sleeve;/and with my right, I pat Hong Ya on the shoulder). See Guo Pu, "You xian shi" 遊仙詩 (The roaming immortal's verses), in Xiao Tong, *Wenxuan*, pp. 620–21.

25. My interview notes with Dr. Zhang Zhuming. Dr. Zhang says that he personally never met Deng Yucang, but he knows that Deng and his associates established a branch temple of their Fujian organization at Chezhan Road in the Lujiabang district of Shanghai during the 1930s.

26. Ma Gu shan, or Lady Ma Mountain, is a sacred Daoist mountain in southeastern China. Located west of Nancheng county seat in Jiangxi province, it is the site where the Eastern Jin Daoist Ge Hong purportedly practiced alchemy, and where the goddess Lady Ma was believed to have attained immortality. See Wu Yufu, *You Magu shan ji*, in *DZJY, zhen ji*, 3.40a–41a.

27. *Qian yuan* 前緣, or "predestined bond," may be a reference to the encounter between the goddess Lady Ma and the Han artisan Cai Jing. That encounter led to Cai Jing's acquisition of alchemic secrets and his ascendance to immortality. See Ge Hong, *Shenxian zhuan*, 7.27b–28a, in *DZJHL*, vol. 2. It is also likely that the bond may be an allusion to Master Wen's own previous and unspecified encounter at the sacred site.

28. "Mulberry Seas" (*sanghai* 桑海) is an abridgment of "immense seas and mulberry fields" (*canghai sangtian* 滄海桑田). The idiomatic phrase refers to the primordial geological transformation in Chinese mythology of the immense oceans into mulberry fields. In this context, it is a parallel

metaphor to the predestined bond of the previous line, alluding to the encounter between Lady Ma and Cai Jing in which Lady Ma announced her arrival by remarking that there had been three cosmic transformations on earth since her last visit. See Ge Hong, *Shenxian zhuan*, 7.27b–28a, in *DZJHL*, vol. 2.

29. *Huixian qiao* 會仙橋 (Bridge of encounters with immortals) is the name of a bridge at the site. The name adds to the tone and theme of the poem.

30. For Lady Ma's exploits and her encounter with Cai Jing, see Ge Hong, *Shenxian zhuan*, 7. 27b–28a, in *DZJHL*, vol. 2.

31. Deng's attempt to visit Cai Jing's house during his tour of Lady Ma Mountain may be misinformed. Cai Jing's house, where he was visited by Lady Ma, was located in Suzhou. However, the line in Deng's poem is ambiguous enough to allow another interpretation: that Deng was merely expressing a wish to visit Cai Jing's house without specifying its location.

32. See Wu Wu, *Danfang xuzhi*, in *DZ*, 19: 57.

33. See Wu Shouyang, *Tianxian zhengli*, pp. 92–100.

34. The vital tasks performed by these partners or fellow cultivators were discussed in great detail by Fu Shan 傅山 (z. Qingzhu 青主; 1607–84) the famous late Ming loyalist writer, calligrapher, and practitioner of inner alchemy. See Fu Shan, *Danting zhenren yangzhen miji*.

35. For an explanation of these unusual names, see Cao Heng, *Daoyuan yiqi*, pp. 107–9.

36. See Ge Hong, *Baopuzi neipian*, in *DZ*, 28: 183, 187–88, 235.

37. See Wu Wu, *Danfang xuzhi*, in *DZ*, 19: 57. Wu stipulated that the locale selected for outer alchemical operation must meet a set of standards for blessings, potency, cleanliness, and purity. Excluded from Wu's category of blessed locales propitious to alchemic operations are places with old tombs, deserted temples, abandoned wells and stoves, locales with constant warfare, and sites of parturition.

38. See Du Guangting, *Dongtian fudi yue du ming shan ji*, in *DZ*, 11: 55–60.

39. See Zhao Youqin, *Xian Fo tongyuan lu*, p. 465. The "Bond of the Locale" (*diyuan* 地緣) is one of the five bonds considered essential by Zhao for the successful practice of inner alchemy.

40. See Wu Shouyang, *Tianxian zhengli*, pp. 85–87.

41. See Fu Shan, *Danting zhenren yangzhen miji*.

42. See Chen Yingning, "Xuexian bicheng," pp. 6–7.

43. See ibid., pp. 7–8.

44. See Fu Jinquan, *Yiguan zhenji yijian lu*, in *ZWDS*, 11: 428.

45. For self-cultivation practice in monastic settings, see Welch, *The Practice of Chinese Buddhism*; and Goossaert, *The Taoists of Peking*, 2007.

46. For the history of the Southern Lineage in inner alchemy, see Skar, "Golden Elixir Alchemy."

47. See Zhao Youqin, *Xian Fo tongyuan lun*, pp. 466–69.

48. See Zhang Sanfeng, *Jindan jieyao*, in *ZWDS*, 11: 339–40. For an English translation, see Wile, *The Art of the Bedchamber*.

49. See Chen Yingning, "Xuexian bicheng," p. 8.

50. See ibid., pp. 5–6.

51. See ibid., p. 5.

52. See Chen Yingning, "Da Nanjing Lifa yuan Huang Chanhua," *YS*, no. 50 (July 16, 1935): 1–2.

53. See Chen Yingning, *Zizhuan*, in Li Yangzheng, ed., *Daojiao yu yangsheng*, pp. 1–5, and also my interview notes and correspondence with Dr. Zhang Zhuming in the summers of 1996 and 1997.

54. See Chen Yingning, "*Xuexian bicheng*," pp. 18–22.

55. See ibid., pp. 8–9.

56. See ibid., pp. 9–11. Chen advised: "Rice and wheat contain the highest content of carbohydrates. Next come legumes. Soybeans, egg yolks, and egg whites contain the highest content of protein. Next come rice and wheat. As for fats, soybeans and egg yolks contain the highest amount, in addition to all kinds of oils. The daily requirement of each of the above three nutrients varies for every individual's body. Only an estimate can be given. Based on the physical constitution (*tizhi* 體質) of the Chinese, each day a person requires about nine ounces (*liang* 兩) of carbohydrates, three ounces of protein, and two and a half ounces of fats. The required amounts of the nutrients for a physical laborer differ from those for a mental laborer."

57. Ibid., pp. 10–13.

58. Ibid., pp. 11–12.

59. Chen never explicitly identified the sources of his dietetics. But given his erudition on Daoist and medical classics, it is quite conceivable that Chen Yingning's categories of food properties drew on the classical *ben cao* 本草 (Materia medica) traditions and Daoist dietetics, especially the sections dealing with the properties of the fruits and grains as medicinal ingredients. For a survey of the Chinese materia medica literature, see Unschuld, *Medicine in China*. For Daoist dietetics and food properties, see Fu Duren, *Xiuzhen milu*, in *DZ*, 18: 522–26; and Li Pengfei, *Sanyuan yanshou zan shu*, in *DZ*, 18: 542–55.

60. Chen Yingning, "*Xuexian bicheng*," pp. 10–13.

61. See ibid., p. 12.
62. See Li Pengfei, *Sanyuan yanshou zan shu*, in *DZ*, 18: 548.
63. Chen Yingning, "Xuexian bicheng," pp. 30–31.
64. See the published Daoist formulas for cereal avoidance and special formulas for famine relief submitted by readers in *YS*, no. 46 (June 1, 1935): 3.
65. See Chen Yingning, *Huangting jing jiangyi*, p. 21.
66. Pengzu 彭祖 was the legendary figure and reputedly the eighth-generation descendent of the Yellow Emperor. He was perceived to be a central figure in the sexual cultivation tradition. For a detailed account, see also Liu Xiang, *Liexian zhuan*, in *DZ*, 5: 66–67. See also Ban Gu, *Qian Hanshu*, in *ESWS*, 1: 85–86. Indeed, Ban Gu's account of Pengzu seems to have been based on Liu's book, which identifies Pengzu as the third great-grandson born of the third wife of Zhuan Xu 顓頊. A later and much more detailed account can be found in Ge Hong, *Shenxian zhuan*, 1.3b–4b, in *DZJHL*, vol. 2.
67. See Chen Yingning, "Xuexian bicheng," pp. 31–33.
68. See ibid., p. 33. There is a certain irony in Chen's advice on abstention. Although Chen advocated total abstinence from drinking and smoking as the ideal approach, he did allow some exceptions. Among the alcoholic beverages, distilled liquors and spirits such as the Chinese distilled *shao jiu* 燒酒, *gaoliang jiu* 高粱酒, and the imported brandies (*bailandi* 白蘭地) were to be avoided, whereas alcoholic beverages such as beer, wine, rice wine from Shaoxing, and sweet rice wines concocted from fermented rice may be indulged in in moderation. A chain smoker himself, Chen exempted premium cigarettes (*shangpin juanyan* 上品卷煙) from the proscription list, which prohibited cigars and shoddy and pungent low-grade brands of cigarettes. See ibid., p. 54.
69. The subject of the bedchamber arts and life-nourishing sexual gathering techniques has been treated by scholars in China and the West. See Ma Jixing, *Mawangdui gu yishu kaoshi*; Song Shugong, *Zhongguo gudai fangshi yangsheng jiyao*; Tanba Yasuyori, *Yixin fang*; and Ye Dehui, *Shuangmei jing an congshu*. For critical scholarship on the practice, see van Gulik, *Sexual Life in Ancient China*; Furth, "Rethinking van Gulik"; and Wile, *The Art of the Bedchamber*.
70. See Chen Yingning's remarks on the potential complication of paired cultivation in "Dao siyuan yuzhou zhong qu" 到四元宇宙中去 (Into the four-dimensional world), *YS*, no. 61 (Jan. 1, 1936): 6–7.

71. See Chen Yingning, "Da Ji'nan Zhang Huiyan jun wen shuangxiu" 答濟南張慧巖君問雙脩 (In reply to questions on paired cultivation by Mr. Zhang Huiyan of Ji'nan), YS, no. 47 (June 1, 1935): 4–5.

72. See Chen Yingning, "Da Suzhou Zhang Daochu jun shiwu wen" 答蘇州張道初君十五問 (In reply to the fifteen questions of Mr. Zhang Daochu of Suzhou), YS, no. 74 (July 16, 1936): 6–9.

73. Chen likened such "mutual help" during paired cultivation practice to financial mutual aid, wherein a person with more money shared his or her wealth with another with less money; see Chen Yingning, "Da fu Henan Anyang mou nüshi" 答覆河南安陽某女士 (In reply to a lady from Anyang of Henan), YS, no. 84 (Dec. 16, 1936): 1.

74. See Chen Yingning, "Da Suzhou Zhang Daochu jun shi wu wen," p. 7.

75. In one such duel, the couple was depicted as being engaged in a game of fire play. To demonstrate his skills, Liu Gang first set a house on fire drawing power from his inventory of magic. To better her husband, Fan cast a spell of her own to douse the raging flames. In another friendly joust, the couple encountered a tiger on their travel to Mount Siming 四明山. To subdue the beast blocking their path, Liu immediately cast a talisman on the tiger. At first the tiger seemed under control. But as soon as Liu tried to move, the tiger threatened to devour him. But as Fan walked forth, the tiger lowered its head to the ground without even daring to look up. Fan then roped the beast and tied it to her bedpost!

But the most dramatic scene of contest comes in the couple's final flight to the empyrean of immortality. In this scene that showcases the ultimate alchemic prowess of the couple, Liu Gang has to climb several dozens of feet up to the top of a honey locust tree before he could take off on his ascending flight. By contrast, the superior Fan needed no such boost. She merely sat on the ground and gradually levitated upward as if a rising cloud mist toward heaven. See Ge Hong, *Shenxian zhuan*, 7.28b, in *DZJHL*, vol. 2. These accounts are also found in Li Fang, *Taiping guangji*, juan 60. The story of the couple also frequently appeared in Daoist hagiographies and popular folklore of the late imperial period. See Wang Jianzhang and Jing Xingshao, *Lidai shenxian shi*. See also Yang Erzeng, *Xin juan Xian yuan ji shi*; and Wang Shizhen, *Youxiang liexian quan zhuan*.

76. See Chen Yingning, "Da Suzhou Zhang Daochu jun shiwu wen," p. 7.

77. See Chen Yingning, "Xuexian bicheng," p. 3.

78. For early Taoist techniques of the practice, see Yamada, "Longevity Techniques and Compilation of the *Lingbao wufu*"; Kohn, "Guarding the One"; idem, "Taoist Insight Meditation"; and Robinet, "Visualization and Ecstatic Flight in Shangqing Taoism." For the role of quiet sitting in late

Ming elite spiritual and religious pursuits, see Berling, *The Syncretic Religion of Lin Chao-en*.

79. See Chen Yingning, "Xuexian bicheng," pp. 15–16.

80. Ibid., pp. 16–17.

81. Many of the practice postures such as the sleeping posture, allegedly developed by the famed Five Dynasties Daoist Chen Tuan 陳摶 (871–989), were widely available in illustrations by alchemist writers during the late imperial period. See *Xingming shuangxiu wanshen guizhi*; Luo Hongxian, *Wanshou xian shu*; and Xi Yukang, *Neiwai gong tushuo jiyao*.

82. See Chen Yingning, "Xuexian bicheng," pp. 18–19.

83. See Hong Wanxin (AKA Hong Tai'an), *Wu da jiankang xiulian fa*.

84. See ibid., pp. 74–75. Breath counting was a long-established meditative technique in both Buddhism and Daoism. One breath consists of an inhalation and an exhalation. See Wang Jianzhang, *Xianshu miku*, juan 2. The Heart Scripture was probably written in the late Tang and had since the late Yuan become part of the Quanzhen Daoist daily scriptural recitations. See *Gaoshang Yuhuang xinyin jing*, in DZ, 1: 749.

85. See Laozi, *Daode jing*, chap. 5, in Chen Guying, *Laozi zhushi ji pingjie* p. 78.

86. See Hong Wanxin, *Wu da jiankang xiulian fa*, pp. 75–76.

87. See Chen Yingning, "Xuexian bicheng," pp. 20–22.

88. See Wang Daoyuan, *Cui gong Ruyao jing zhujie*, in DZ, 2: 885. The original is 一日內, 十二時. 意所到, 皆可為.

89. See Zhang Boduan, *Jindan sibai zi*, in DZ, 24: 164. Zhang's original words are 火候不用時, 冬至不在午 (The firing moment does not use any timing, and the winter solstice is not on the hour of *wu*). In annotating Zhang's words, Huang wrote: 大凡火候非子時冬至午時夏至也 (The firing moment is not at the *zi* hours of the winter solstice, nor the *wu* hours of the summer solstice).

90. See Min Yide, *Suoyan xu*, in ZWDS, 10: 507–19.

91. There are only a few exceptions to this rule. One involves quiet sitting for the sole purpose of ridding oneself of illness and prolonging life (*qubing yanling* 去病延齡). Quiet sitting for this purpose was conducted in the morning before dawn, lasting from a half-hour to two hours, and in the evening from about ten o'clock (*haishi sike* 亥時四刻) to midnight (*zishi sike* 子時四刻). The other case requiring timing involves a more advanced practice, but the rationale for timing the practice has little to do with the traditional schemata of timing and more to do with optimal exposure to the sun for garnishing its vitality of fire (*zhenhuo zhili* 真火之力). See Chen Yingning, "Xuexian bicheng," pp. 19, 21, 25–26, 49.

92. See ibid., pp. 25–30.

93. See ibid., pp. 21–22.

94. The *yin* hours are from approximately three to five hours before the dawn, and the *wei* hours are from one to three hours after the meridian. The *shen* hours are from three to five hours before sundown, and the *chou* hours are from one to three early in the morning. See ibid., pp. 25–28.

95. See ibid., pp. 29–30. The practice of ascendance (*chaotuo gongfu*) here refers to the practices after the gestation and parturition of the Yang Spirit from the body. See Chen Yingning, *Sun Bu'er nüdan shizhu*, pp. 36–42. On the genesis and characteristics of the Yin Spirit, see also Hequ zi, *Chang Dao zhenyan*, in *DZJY*, *dou ji*, 5.32a–b.

96. See Chen Yingning, "Xuexian bicheng," pp. 29–30; and also Wu Shouyang, *Tianxian zhengli*, pp. 75–76.

97. The term *guan xiang* can be read in at least two different ways, denoting several different self-cultivation techniques. One is to read it as an abbreviation of *guan zhao* 觀照 and *cun xiang* 存想, which are two different meditative techniques often associated with the Shangqing Daoist practice. *Guan zhao* refers to the technique of turning the vision inward on the loci inside the body, and *cun xiang* denotes the technique of visualizing or imaging of the bodily loci or orbs and holding on to this visual image during the meditation. For the technique of the inward focus of contemplation, see *Zhuzhen shengtai shenyong jue*, in DZ, 18: 435. For the technique of holding a visualization, see Sima Chengzhen, *Tianyin zi*, in DZ, 21: 700; and Kohn, "Taoist Insight Meditation."

98. The references to the unblocking are apparently derived from a Buddhist term, the Six Divine Powers (*liushen tong* 六神通, also *liu tong* 六通): *shenzu tong* 神足通, *tianyan tong* 天眼通, *tianer tong* 天耳通, *taxin tong* 他心通, *suming tong* 宿命通, and *loujing tong* 漏盡通. The terms denote the discovery and acquisition of extrasensory and psychic powers through physical and mental regimens. These superhuman powers enable the practitioner to move, see, hear, and intuit human affairs and the phenomenal world. The last power, Total Void (*loujing tong*), is said to enable the practitioner to be liberated from the wheel of reincarnation completely. For the Buddhist discussion of the divine powers and their acquisition, see Xuanzhuang, *Apidamo jushe lun bensong*.

Daoist inner alchemic discourse has since incorporated the theory with some modifications. The Six Unblocked Powers are the Unblocked Heart Scene (*xinjing tong* 心境通), the Unblocked Psychic Scene (*shenjing tong* 神境通), the Unblocked Celestial Eye (*tianyan tong*), the Unblocked Celestial Ear (*tianer tong*), the Unblocked Prescience of Destiny (*suxing tong* 宿信通),

and the Unblocked Other Heart (*taxin tong*). See "Lun liu tong jue" 論六通訣 (On the secrets of the Six Unblockings), in Xuanquan zi, *Zhuzhen neidan jiyao*, in DZ, 32: 471–72.

99. See Chen Yingning, "*Xuexian bicheng*," pp. 26–27.

100. See ibid., pp. 33–34.

101. Two wars during the 1930s, one between the warlords around Shanghai and the other a siege of the city by Japan, twice disrupted Chen's outer alchemic experiments and practice. See Chapter 2.

Chapter 5

1. Jiyun refers to Xie Jiyun; Yaofu to Gao Yaofu. Together with Huang Suizhi, both had pursued the practice of alchemy with Chen during the 1920s in Shanghai; see Chen Yingning's notes, YS, no. 85 (Jan. 1, 1937): 12.

2. Sesame (*huma* 胡麻) has long been associated with immortals' lore. It is used in the Daoist diet to lighten the body for the final flight of ascendance. For a description of an immortal by the name of Lu Nüsheng 魯女生 who transformed his body on a diet of sesame seeds, see Ge Hong, *Shenxian zhuan*, 10.44a, in DZJHL, 2.

3. See Chang Zunxian, "He Yingning zi zeng Huang daoyou shi yuanyun" 和攖寧子贈黃道友詩原韻 (Matching the rhymes of Master Yingning's poem to Fellow Cultivator Huang), YS, no. 92 (Apr. 15, 1937): 10; and Xu Dede 許德得, "He shi" 和詩 (A matching poem), XD, no. 4 (Apr. 1939): 4.

4. Both are prominent recluses from the Han period known for their eschewal of fame and devotion to self-cultivation. Yan Junping was a diviner active during the Han. Having made a small profit by practicing divination, Yan closed shop and spent his time lecturing on the teachings of Laozi. Han Kang was an Eastern Han recluse who made a living selling herbs he collected from the mountains outside the capital of Chang'an. He declined the Han emperor's repeated summons to court. See Ban Gu, *Qian Hanshu*, juan 72, in ESWS, 2: 647, 1044.

5. For Shen's career, see Qian Shifu, *Qingdai zhiguan nianbiao*, pp. 1967–69, 2761–64.

6. Zhu included several collections of poems on Daoist practice in his *Qiangcun congshu* 疆村叢書, 40 vols. (Shanghai, 1922). The collection of poems by Zhang Boduan is entitled "Ziyang zhenren ci" 紫陽真人詞 and included in vol. 5 of the compendium. The collection by Qiu Chuji, entitled "Panxi ci" 磻谿詞, can be found in vol. 33. See also Qian Shifu, *Qingdai zhiguan nianbiao*, pp. 723–27, 2757–59.

7. For Li's life and work, see Li Ruiqing, *Qingdaoren yi ji*; and idem, *Qingdaoren ni gu hua ce*. For a different account of Li's turn to Daoism, see Li Li'an 李理安, "Tuoba Chengzhen zhuan" 拓拔誠貞傳 (Biography of Tuoba Chengzhen), in idem, *Changchun guan zhi*, 2.26b.

8. See Wang Pinsan 王聘三, "Huangting jing jiangyi tici" 黃庭經講義題辭, in Chen Yingning, *Huangting jing jiangyi*, p. 1.

9. Chen recalled Shen's testimonial in 1956 in a note he added to his book. See Chen Yingning, "Yingning bu ji" 攖寧補記, in idem, *Huangting jing jiangyi* (1921); reprinted in Hu Haiya, *Zhonghua xianxue yangsheng quanshu*, pp. 76–77.

10. Chang Zunxian, *Lü zu shijie*, p. 1.

11. Chang Zunxian, *Huanghe fu zhenben zhujie*, p. 1. See also the advertisement notice, "Jieshao guoyi Chang Zunxian xiansheng" 介紹國醫常遵先先生 (Introducing Dr. Chang Zunxian), YS, no. 1 (July 1, 1933): 21.

12. See Chang Zunxian, *Lü zu shijie*, p. 1; and idem, *Huanghe fu zhenben zhujie*, pp. 1–2.

13. See Chang Zunxian, *Lü zu shijie*, p. 1.

14. See also the advertisement notice, "Jieshao guoyi Chang Zunxian xiansheng ," YS, no. 1 (July 1, 1933): 21. The introduction reads: 近以世風不古, 鳳侶凋零, 遽不問世事, 專行醫道. In an interview, Zhang Zhuming, the publisher of the *Yangshan Biweekly*, himself a doctor of western medicine and a friend of Chang's, said that Chang was well versed in Chinese medicine and did earn a living in what was a competitive profession in Shanghai.

15. See also the published endorsement, "Jieshao guoyi Chang Zunxian xiansheng," YS, no. 1: (July 1, 1933): 21; no. 2 (July 15, 1933): 3; no. 15 (Feb. 1, 1934): 14. The ads reveal that Chang relocated his clinic several times in less than a year. These frequent moves ultimately landed Chang in the South Market District, where the population was less prosperous but more likely to seek help from a practitioner of traditional medicine. In a summer 1995 interview, Dr. Zhang Zhuming also mentioned that he provided occasional monetary assistance to Chang throughout the 1930s.

16. Chang Zunxian, *Lü zu shijie*, pp. 1, 16–17; idem, *Huanghe fu zhenben zhujie*, pp. 1–3; and idem, *Micang Zhong-Lü chuandao*.

17. The Hangu Pass 函谷關 is located in present-day Lingbao county in Henan province. Here it alludes to the story of Laozi's transmission of Daoist teachings to Yin Xi 尹喜, the superintendent of the pass when Laozi was leaving the Kingdom of Zhou to go to the western regions outside China. See Sima Qian 司馬遷, *Shiji* 史記 (Record of the Historian), in *ESWS*, ser. 1, p. 247.

18. The expression "feathered guest/traveler" (*yuke* 羽客) is a metaphor for a Daoist. It is also used to denote an immortal in classical literature.

19. Chang Zunxian, "He Yingning zi yesu danfang shi yuanyun er shou" 和攖寧子夜宿丹房詩原韻二首 (Matching the rhymes of Master Yingning's two poems "On an Overnight Stay at the Alchemic Chamber"), YS, no. 35 (Feb. 1, 1934): 2. The Millet Pearl 黍珠 is a conventional reference to the refined elixir in the cultivating body of a practitioner.

20. Chang Zunxian, "Jin bu Cao Huanyang zhenren shi yuanyun er shou" 謹步曹還陽眞人詩原韻二首 (Matching the rhymes of the Perfected Man Cao Huanyang's two poems), YS, no. 29 (Sept. 1, 1934): 3. I have translated only the first stanza here. Cao was active during the late Ming period and was allegedly the master of the renowned inner alchemist Wu Shouyang (fl. 1622–39). For Cao's life and his practice, see Wu Shouyang, *Tianxian zhengli*.

21. See Chang Zunxian, "Da Hengyun sheng wen jindan mifa shi shi er shou" 答衡雲生問金丹秘法事詩二首 (In response to Hengyun's two poems of inquiry on the secret methods of the golden elixir), YS, no. 79 (Oct. 1, 1936): 10; idem, "Shu huai ji Yingning zi" 述懷寄攖寧子 (Musings to Master Yingning), YS, no. 89 (Mar. 1, 1937): 10; and idem, "He Yingning zi zeng Huang daoyou shi yuanyun," YS, no. 92 (Apr. 15, 1937): 10.

22. The term Cauldron and Furnace (*ding lu* 鼎爐) is often used in inner alchemy to refer to the cultivator's body, or a locus within the body. In dual cultivation, it was frequently used as a metonym for the body of the female partner. In this context, it clearly refers to the body of Hengyun the recluse cultivator.

23. "Square inch" (*fang cun* 方寸) normally refers to the heart. In inner alchemy, it is associated with the locus of the Central Cinnabar Field, where the alchemic sublimation takes place. See Liangqiu zi, *Huangting neijing yujing zhu*, in DZ, 4: 854.

24. Hushang sou, "Wen dao shi" 問道詩 (A poem in query of the Way), XD, no. 12 (Dec. 1939): 3.

25. "Sweet spring" (*gan quan* 甘泉) is a metaphor for the rising *qi* within the body. Its presence is often signified by the copious secretion of saliva under the tongue. For more details, see Chapter 2.

26. The Triple Passes 三關 are the loci of *Weilü* 尾閭 near the coccyx, *Jiaji* 夾脊 near the kidneys, and *Yuzhen* 玉枕 at the nape of the head. They are located on the Superintendent Channel on the back of the body, which is part of the Heavenly Orbit cycle for the movement of the focused *qi* within the body. See discussion in Chapter 2. "River Crafts" (*heche* 河車) is an established term in inner alchemy for the focused flow of *qi* at various

loci on the ascent channel at the back of the body. They are often represented visually as the Goat Cart (*yang che* 羊車), the Deer Cart (*lu che* 鹿車), and the Ox Cart (*niu che* 牛車). See Cao Heng, *Daoyuan yiqi*, 1.4a.

27. The South Heavenly Gate (Nantian men 南天門), a scenic viewpoint on Mount Heng, is here used to invoke the Southern Gate to Heaven in both popular and Daoist lore. The Divine Realm (*shenzhou* 神州) is China. See Sima Qian, *Shiji*, in *ESWS*, ser. 1, pp. 265–66.

28. "Gen peaks" refers to the Gen Zhi Peaks on Mount Heng. See Chang Zhunxian's notes to this stanza. The word *gen* is also a trigram signifying a mount or hill in the *Book of Changes*. In the parlance of inner alchemy, Gen alludes to the pausing or dwelling meditation known as the Dwelling on the Back (*gen bei* 艮背), which is intended to coagulate the Fire of the Heart and the Water of the Kidneys. See my discussion of this regimen in Chapter 2.

29. "Nine Kan streams" (*jiu tiao Kan shui* 九條坎水) refers to the Kan River 坎江, which Chang reported as a "scenic site" in Mount Heng.

30. The Cypress of Lord Heng (Hengjun bo 衡君柏) refers to the One-Thousand-Year-Old Cypress (Qiannian bo 千年柏), another scenic spot on Mount Heng. Lord Heng 衡君 is Zhu Rong, the patron god of the Southern Marchmont. See *Taishang jiuchi banfu wudi nei zhenjing*, in *DZ*, 33: 518–22.

31. "Scarlet Son's Palace" (*chizi gong* 赤子宮) may refer to a manmade structure on the mountain that commemorates Zhu Xi 朱熹 (1130–1200), the late Song neo-Confucian philosopher. But in the present context, its name insinuates the Scarlet Son's Mansion (*chizi fu* 赤子府), which denotes the vital locus of the Lower Cinnabar Field in inner alchemic parlance. See Wucheng zi, *Shangqing Huangting neijing jing*, in *DZ*, 22: 74.

32. "Grotto" refers to the Grotto of Cinnabar, a natural cave on Mount Heng. But in the present context, the name of the cave had many nuances in inner alchemy. "One Grain of Cinnabar" (*yi dian zhusha* 一點朱砂) is an allusion to the gestated elixir, and the Grotto stands for the Lower Cinnabar Field in the body as the place for refining the elixir.

33. Zhu Rong Peak 祝融峰 is a natural scenic site on Mount Heng. In inner alchemic parlance, it is an allusion to the Upper Cinnabar Field, located in the head. The rhizome (*zhu* 朮) is a common ingredient in Daoist dietetic regimens. Regular ingestion is believed to lead to a light body and prolonged life. See Sun Simiao, *Qian jin yi fang*, p. 43.

34. See Chang Zunxian, "Chongyou Hengyue fang Hengyun laoyou tandao ouzou" 重遊衡嶽訪衡雲老友談道偶作 (A spontaneous poem on my discussion about the Way with my old friend Hengyun upon the occasion of revisiting Mount Heng), *YS*, no. 86 (Jan. 16, 1937): 9; and idem,

"Changsha huai Liu Boxian" 長沙懷劉跛仙 (In memory of the Crippled Immortal Liu of Changsha), YS, no. 89 (Mar. 1, 1937): 10.

35. See Wang Boying 汪伯英, "Dafu Lü Zongyue xiansheng" 答覆呂宗岳先生 (In reply to Mr. Lü Zongyue), XD, no. 27 (Mar. 1941): 3, 8.

36. See ibid., p. 8.

37. For Wang's reflection on his association with Chen Yingning, see his poem "Bu Yingning fuzi Xiao Xiang laoren yuanyun shi si shou" 步攖寧夫子瀟湘老人原韻詩四首 (Matching the rhymes of four poems by Masters Yingning and Xiaoxiang), YS, no. 38 (Jan. 16, 1935): 10.

38. See Wang's letter attached to Chen Yingning, "Dafu Wuxi Wang Boying laihan wendao" 答覆無錫汪伯英來函問道 (In answer to the questions on the Way by Wang Boying of Wuxi), YS, no. 39 (Feb. 1, 1935): 10.

39. The "Being within the Nonbeing" (wu zhong you 無中有) is a term with multiple meanings. In inner alchemy, it refers to the Cinnabar Field, the key locus where the cultivation and refinement of qi take place. See Xingming shuangxiu wanshen guizhi, 3.39a.

40. See Wang Boying, "Bu Yingning fuzi Xiao Xiang Laoren yuanyun shi si shou," YS, no. 38 (Jan. 16, 1935): 10.

41. The method is the last and the highest form of the six techniques of refining the body (lianxing liu men 煉形六門). See Xingming shuangxiu wanshen guizhi, 4.9b–10a. Heel Breathing (zhong xi 踵息) derives from the "Da Zongshi" 大宗師 chapter in Zhuangzi. It describes the unusual way of deep breathing by the Perfected Man (zhen ren 真人). In writings of inner alchemy from the Ming period, "Heel" had come to be interpreted as the locus of the Gate of Life where the breathing is to be centered. As such, it has been equated to the term Fetal Breathing (taixi 胎息). See Zhao Taiding, Mowang, in ZWDS, 9: 622–23.

42. See Wang Boying, "Dafu Lü Zongyue xiansheng," XD, no. 27 (Mar. 1941): 8.

43. See Zhang Zhongli et al., Jindai Shanghai chengshi yanjiu, pp. 127–72.

44. See ibid., p. 159.

45. See Deng Guangying, Liancheng xianzhi, 11.6a–7a.

46. See Liancheng xian difang zhi bianzuan weiyuanhui, Liancheng xianzhi, p. 362.

47. See ibid., p. 775.

48. See Chen Yingning, "Jiling yin gao xu bian xu" 鵝鴿吟稿續編序 (Preface to the draft poems by Master Jiling), XD, no. 15 (Mar. 1940): 3.

49. See "Dashi ji" 大事記 (Great events), in Liancheng xian difang zhi bianzuan weiyuanhui, Liancheng xianzhi, pp. 37–40.

50. See Chen Yingning, "Fu Nanjing Lifayuan Huang Chanhua xiansheng shu," YS, no. 50 (July 16, 1935): 2.

51. See Ma Yifu 馬一孚, "Tiantai shan jiyou shi qi shou" 天台山記遊詩七首 (Seven poems on the tour of Mount Tiantai), YS, no. 83 (Dec. 1, 1936): 9–10.

52. See Fang Gongpu, *Qigong zhiyan lu*. Fang also edited and redacted an earlier anthology of medical cases by famous doctors of the Qing dynasty: Qin Bowei 秦伯未, *Qingdai mingyi yi'an jinghua* 清代名醫醫案精華 (Essential medical cases by famous doctors of the Qing dynasty) (Shanghai: Qinshi yishi, 1947). Fang's own medical practice and theory later became part of the traditional Chinese medical canon; see Wang Wenji, *Fang Gongpu yi'an*.

53. See Chen Yingning, "Tianxian Bicheng nüshi jiangtan jilu" 天仙碧城女史降壇乩錄 (A séance record of the celestial immortal female official Bicheng's descent), YS, no. 25 (July 1, 1934): 48–49; and also Wu Yizhu, "Qiuri xiangju huai Changya" 秋日鄉居懷昌亞 (Thoughts on Changya from my country cottage on an autumn day), YS, no. 82 (Nov. 16, 1936): 11. The name of the Daoist physiognomist they frequently consulted was Bai Shi 白石.

54. See Wu Yizhu, "Qiuri xiangju huai Changya," YS, no. 82 (Nov. 16, 1936): 11.

55. The expressions "took off your coat" and "shared your drink and food" derive from the biography of Han Xin 韓信 in Sima Qian's *Shiji*. Han declined Xiang Yu's proposition that Han declare himself a king, citing his patron Liu Bang's kind and generous acts of taking off his own clothes for Han to wear and offering his own food for Han to eat. The phrases have since come to mean "to care for someone."

56. Bai Shi was the Daoist physiognomist from whom Dr. Wu and Dr. Zhu Changya sought instruction and predictions. See Wu Yizhu, Notes to "Qiuri xiangju huai Changya," YS, no. 82 (Nov. 16, 1936): 11.

57. "Muddy water" (*zhuo shui* 濁水) and "clear stream" (*qing liu* 清流) are two contrastive metaphors, alluding to the physical condition of the female body before and after transformation. In the present context, Wu's reference to the Muddy Water also alludes to menses yet to be stopped and sublimated into pure *qi*.

58. Here the two lines recall the many land purchase plans formulated among Chen Yingning and his fellow practitioners at their weekend gatherings throughout the 1920s. See Chen Yingning, "Fu Nanjing Lifayuan Huang Chanhua xiangsheng shu," YS, no. 50 (July 16, 1935): 1–2.

59. The last two lines describe the ritual practice of climbing high towers or peaks on the occasion of the Double Ninth (Chongyang 重陽) festival. But in Wu's poem, the ending lines also serve as a self-exhortation for advancing the practice of female alchemy to a higher level.

60. See Chen Yingning, "Zizhuan," in Li Yangzhen, *Daojiao yu yangsheng*, pp. 3–4.

61. See Chen Yingning, "Yu Zhu Changya yishi lun xianxue shu" 與朱昌亞醫師論仙學書 (Letter to Dr. Zhu Changya on the Immortals' Learning), YS, no. 86 (Jan. 16, 1937): 7–9.

62. "Skills of benevolence" (*ren shu* 仁術) refers to the medical expertise with which Dr. Zhu had been serving her patients.

63. "Jade Liquid" (*qiong jiang* 瓊漿) is a common metaphor for fine wine.

64. For Master Bai Shi, see note 56 to this chapter. During a visit to Bai Shi, Dr. Zhu and Dr. Wu queried the Daoist concerning their futures. The Daoist's response, presumably in a poem, about their futures was miraculously borne out. Hence Dr. Zhu's line here in praise of Master Bai Shi's unusual prognostication. See Wu Yizhu, Notes to "Qiuri xiangju huai Changya," YS, no. 82 (Nov. 16, 1936): 11.

65. The term Nine Heavens (*jiu tian* 九天) is often used to describe the celestial realm as conceived in Shangqing Daoism. Here it is used as a general metaphor for the celestial realm where the immortals reside.

66. See Zhu Changya, "Zhu Changya nüshi xu" 朱昌亞女士序 (Preface by Ms Zhu Changya), in Chen Yingning, *Lingyuan dadao ge baihua zhujie*, 1b–2b.

67. The origins of some of the Daoist temples in the Shanghai area may be traced to the third century CE. See Chen Yaoting, *Shanghai daojiao shi*, pp. 353–59. See also Ding Changyun, "Shanghai Daojiao de chuanru he fazhan."

68. The first recorded post-Yuan Quanzhen Daoist cloister in Shanghai was built by Abbot Wang Mingzhen 王明眞 as a branch temple of his home Xianzhen Abbey 顯眞觀 in Hangzhou in 1863. The cloister was later moved to a locale near the Shanghai City God Temple in 1882. In 1888, the cloister first established ties with the White Cloud Monastery in Beijing by becoming its branch temple with the identical name in Shanghai. See Ding Changyun, "Shanghai Daojiao de chuanru he fazhan"; and idem, "Hai shang Baiyun guan jinxi."

69. See "Fu er: Sanguo zhi 1949 nian Shanghai jianguan qingkuang biao" 附二：三國至 1949 年上海建觀情況表 (Appendix 2: a survey of Daoist temple constructions from the Three Kingdoms era to 1949), in

Shanghai zongjiao zhi bianzuan weiyuanhui, *Shanghai zongjiao zhi*, p. 215. See also Ding Changyun, "Shanghai Daojiao de chuanru he fazhan," p. 91.

70. See Bergère, "The Shanghai Bankers' Association, 1915–1927." See also Honig, *Sisters and Strangers*; and idem, *Creating Chinese Ethnicity*.

71. See Shanghai zongjiao zhi bianzuan weiyuanhui, *Shanghai zongjiao zhi*, pp. 211–13.

72. See "Ziyang gong daoyuan qishi" 紫陽宮道院啓事 (A public notice about the Daoist Cloister of the Purple Soleil), *XD*, no. 27 (Mar. 1941): 1; and Luo Baoheng 羅寶珩, "Kun Dao Wang Lilian Guan Lihua xing yu mujuan qishi" 坤道王理蓮管理化行木魚募捐啓事 (A notice on the donation drive by nuns Wang Lilian and Guan Lihua), *XD*, no. 28 (Apr. 1941): 1. Luo was a sojourner from Huangyan in Zhejiang and was moved to compose the notice in April 1937, when the two nuns had already been begging for alms for two years. For an overview of the Daoist tradition of alms begging in the late Qing period, see Goossaert, "Starved of Resources."

73. See "Ziyang gong daoyuan qishi," *XD*, no. 27 (Mar. 1941): 1; and Shanghai zongjiao zhi bianzuan weiyuanhui, *Shanghai zongjiao zhi*, pp. 212–13.

74. See "Ziyang gong jiang dao yulu" 紫陽宮講道語錄 (Quotations from the lectures on the Way at Ziyang Cloister), *XD*, no. 29 (May 1941): 4–5; and "Qingzhu kaiguang ping'an yingfu zongtan" 慶祝開光平安迎福宗壇 (In celebration of the opening of the altar for praying for peace and fortune), *XD*, no. 27 (Mar. 1941): 5–7.

75. See Han Sanwu 韓三悟, "Lun Dao zhengli" 論道正理 (On the orthodox principles of the Way), *YS*, no. 76 (Aug. 15, 1936): 12.

76. Han (ibid.) wrote: 以後凡吾修道諸同志可面北師之.

77. Han Sanwu 韓三悟, "Dandao quanbu koujue" 丹道全部口訣 (Complete oral secrets on the Way of Alchemy), *YS*, no. 83 (Feb. 1, 1936): 11–12. Another Daoist priest from Huashan in Shaanxi also shared his secret recipe for cereal avoidance in the *Yangshan Biweekly* in the spring of 1937; see Zhang Wanzhong 張萬鍾, "Xianchuan pigu lingfang" 仙傳辟穀靈方 (Efficacious formulas for cereal avoidance transmitted by the immortals), *YS*, no. 92 (Apr. 15, 1937): 6–7.

78. See "Fu Zhejiang Jinhua Sun Baoci shanren" 覆浙江金華孫抱慈山人 (In reply to the mountain man Sun Baoci of Jinhua in Zhejiang), *YS*, no. 73 (July 1, 1936): 13.

79. See "Jiangsu Huangyan Zhou Minde jun laihan" 江蘇黃巖周敏得君來函 (Letter from Mr. Zhou Minde of Huangyan in Jiangsu), *YS*, no. 62 (Jan. 16, 1936): 5–6.

80. Zhou wrote a preface to his friend Hong Tai'an's tract on self-cultivation practice in 1933; see Zhou Zixiu 周子秀, "Wu da jiankang xiulian fa Zhou xu" 五大健康脩煉法周序 (Zhou's preface to *Five Great Cultivation Methods Toward Health*), YS, no. 93 (May 1, 1937): 5.

81. See Zhou Zixiu 周子秀, "Yongmian jibing fa" 永免疾病法 (How to be free of illnesses forever), YS, no. 92 (Apr. 15, 1937): 5–6.

82. *Pi* is a kind of military drum. Here it is used to refer to the festive drumbeats during the Chinese New Year's Eve celebration.

83. "United in One" (*yi guan* 一貫), a phrase borrowed from the *Lunyu*, meaning a universal principle underlying all matters, is here used as a metaphor for the esoteric secrets of inner alchemy practice that Chen Yingning had purportedly imparted to his other disciples.

84. The term "stroking the top of the head" (*mo ding* 摩頂) refers to the Buddhist initiation ritual in which the top of the novice's head is touched by the initiating adept. The ritual apparently originated from the story told in the *Lotus Sutra* about Shakymuni's transmission of Buddhist Laws to one of his followers.

85. "Mercury and Lead" are terms used in outer alchemy to refer to the chemical compounds. In inner alchemy the terms have several sets of meanings depending on the context. In the current context, the terms are used metaphorically to mean immortality.

86. See Hong Tai'an 洪太庵, "Fulu Hong Tai'an jun yuan laihan si feng" 附錄洪太庵君原來函四封 (Appendix: four letters from Mr. Hong Tai'an), YS, no. 90 (Mar. 16, 1937): 5–7; see also idem, "Wu da jiankang xiulian fa zixu" 五大健康脩煉法自序 (Author's preface to *Five Great Cultivation Methods Toward Health*), YS, no. 93 (May 1, 1937): 6.

87. See Hong Wanxin (Tai'an), *Wu da jiankang xiulian fa*.

88. See ibid., pp. 141–61.

89. See Hong Tai'an, "Fulu Hong Tai'an jun yuan laihan si feng," YS, no. 90 (Mar. 16, 1937): 5–6.

90. See ibid., p. 6. Hong's letter was addressed to Zhang Zhuming and dated Oct. 30, 1936.

91. Chen Yingning, "Da Fuzhou Hong Tai'an jun" 答福州洪太庵君 (In reply to Mr. Hong Tai'an of Fuzhou), YS, no. 90 (Mar. 16, 1937): 4–5.

92. Hong Ya 洪崖 refers to a legendary immortal at the court of the Yellow Emperor. See Zhao Daoyi, *Lishi zhenxian tidao tongjian*, juan 4, in DZ, 5: 125. By the fifth century, Hong Ya had become a celestial immortal with the title of the Perfected One at Mount Qingcheng 青城真人 in the established Shangqing Daoist pantheon, presiding over the sacred mountain of

Qingcheng in Sichuan. See Tao Hongjing, *Dongxuan Lingbao zhenling weiye tu*, in *DZ*, 3: 277.

93. The expression "to slab shoulders or wrap arms" 拍肩 with Hong Ya was a frequently invoked wish by many practitioners of inner alchemy. It came originally from a couplet by Guo Pu, alluding to the legends of Hong Ya's fraternization with other immortals. See Zhao Daoyi, *Lishi zhenxian tidao tongjian, juan* 4, in *DZ*, 5: 125.

94. The Dust (*chen* 塵) is a metonym of Buddhist origin denoting the secular world and emotions.

95. The Pass of Amorous Attachment (*qing guan* 情關) refers to passions or love. Here Hong apparently used the expression to refer to the potential complications involved in his proposed paired cultivation practice.

96. *Suo po* 娑婆 is a Buddhist expression denoting the myriad world of phenomena. Here, it is used to mean the secular realm, which the perfected immortals are not supposed to forsake but rather to intervene in and improve.

97. See Hong Tai'an, "Wuyin qiu liuyi chudu shuhuai" 戊寅秋六一初度述懷 (Thoughts on passing the age of 61 in 1938), *XD*, no. 5 (May 1939): 3.

98. The original text of her letter is incorporated in Chen Yingning's response. See Chen Yingning, "Fu Jiangsu Baoying moumou nüshi" 覆江蘇寶應某某女士 (In reply to Madame X from Baoying county, Jiangsu), *YS*, no. 73 (July 1, 1936): 7–10.

99. See ibid., p. 7. The full title of the scripture is *Lü zu shidu He xiangu yingguo baojuan* 呂祖試渡何仙姑因果寶卷 (A karma sutra of how Patriarch Lü saved Immortal Lady He).

100. See her original letter attached to Chen Yingning's response: "Fu Jiangsu Baoying moumou nüshi," *YS*, no. 73 (July 1, 1936): 7. The transmitting adept was Li Zhongzhou 李中洲.

101. See ibid., p. 8. Most of the classics of inner alchemy Chen Wuxuan read were from the Ming and Qing periods: *Xianfo zhen chuan* 仙佛眞傳 (The true transmission of Buddha and the Immortals), *Xianfo hezong* 仙佛合宗 (An integrated synopsis of the Immortals and Buddhism), and *Tianxian zhengli* 天仙正理.

102. See her letter in Chen Yingning's response: "Fu Jiangsu Baoying moumou nüshi," *YS*, no. 73 (July 1, 1936): 7. Somatic experiences involving sounds and visions have traditionally been documented by many other inner alchemists as confirmatory signs of the *qi* flowing through certain loci of the body, marking the progress of the practice. See related discussion in Chapter 2.

103. See ibid., pp. 7–9.

104. See Chen Yingning, "Dafu Shi Zhihe jun shiwen" 答覆石志和君十問 (In reply to Mr. Shi Zhihe's ten questions), YS, no. 40 (Feb. 16, 1935): 7; and Zhou Haixian 周海仙, "Yu Huaixi Chahe Shi Yunzhong xiansheng shi si shou bing he yuanyun" 與淮西岔河石允中先生詩四首並和原韻 (Matching the rhymes of the four poems by Mr. Shi Yunzhong from west of the River Huai), YS, no. 59 (July 16, 1935): 6.

105. The early Quanzhen practice of enclosure known as *huan du* 圜堵 often took place in the wilderness. But from 1230 on, the practice began to be incorporated into the Quanzhen Daoist monastic practice. As such, it was pursued by both Daoist and Buddhist monastic clerics and even literati practitioners. See Vincent Goossaert, "Quanzhen Dao de huandu kao." For the practice during the Ming period, see Mori Yuria 森由利亞, "Mingdai Quanzhen Dao yu zuobo" 明代全真道與坐缽, in Lu Guolong, ed., *Quanzhen hong dao ji*, pp. 126–42. During the Qing period, the practice of enclosing practitioners in meditation boxes with pointed nails was sometimes employed by both Daoist and Buddhist clerics as a drastic means to collect donations and alms from the public; see Goossaert, "Starved of Resources"; and Xun Liu, "General Zhang Buries the Bones."

106. See her letter in Chen Yingning, "Fu Jiangsu Baoying moumou nüshi," YS, no. 73 (July 1, 1936): 8–9.

107. Chen Wuxuan raised a total of ten questions that were incorporated in Chen Yingning's replies. See Chen Yingning, "Da Baoying Chen Wuxuan nüshi shiwen" 答寶應陳悟玄女士十問 (In reply to the ten queries by Ms Chen Wuxuan from Baoying), YS, no. 82 (Nov. 16, 1936): 3–4.

108. The expression "cutting off or slaying the red dragon" refers to the practice in female inner alchemy that transforms the downward flowing menses into upward moving *qi* by way of breathing exercises. For details on the methods of the practice, see Zhenyi zi 貞一子, *Nüjin dan* 女金丹 (Female gold elixir), in He Longxiang, *Nüdan hebian*; and Despeux, *Immortelles de la Chine ancienne*.

109. See Liu Huayang 柳華陽, *Jinxian zhenglun* 金仙正論; and idem, *Huiming jing* 慧命經 (790), in Deng Huiji, *Wu Liu xianzong*, pp. 604–6, 518. Liu defined the Tiger as the rising warm vitality from the Sea of Qi (*qi hai* 氣海), the equivalent of the Palace of Sons in the female body. See also Chen Yingning, *Sun Bu'er nüdan shizhu*, p. 15.

110. On the meaning of the Yang Fire and the Yin Talisman, and the operation of frontal descent and the back ascent, see Chapter 3.

111. See Chen Yingning, "Da Baoying Chahe zhen Chen Wuxuan nüshi" 答寶應岔河鎮陳悟玄女士 (In reply to Ms Chen Wuxuan of Chahe township of Baoying county), YS, no. 87 (Feb. 1, 1937): 6.

112. See Chen Yingning, "Fu Jiangsu Baoying moumou nüshi," YS, no. 73 (July 1, 1936): 7. In her query, Chen Wuxuan mentioned that she had studied female alchemy practice with a former teacher only after she had ascertained that "his words on the practice were coherent with the classics." The famous late Ming dual cultivator Sun Ruzhong recalled that his father Sun Jiaoluan did not fully commit his loyalty to a newfound teacher of dual cultivation until he withdrew to verify that the oral instructions he just received fully concurred with all the classics of inner alchemy. See Sun Ruzhong, *Jindan zhenchuan*, in ZWDS, 11: 860.

113. The original text of her letter is incorporated in Chen Yingning's response: "Fu Jiangsu Baoying moumou nüshi," YS, no. 73 (July 1, 1936): 7–10.

114. Chen Yingning, "Da Baoying Chen Wuxuan nüshi shiwen," YS, no. 82 (Dec. 12, 1936): 4–5.

115. See her letter attached to Chen Yingning, "Dafu Henan Anyang mou nüshi" 答覆河南安陽某女士 (In reply to Miss So-and-So from Anyang in Henan), YS, no. 84 (Dec. 12, 1936): 1–2. The inner alchemy classics she read included *Lü zu quanshu* 呂祖全書 (The complete writings of Patriarch Lü), *Tianxian zhengli*, *Xianfo hezong*, and *Daotong dacheng* 道統大成.

116. See her letter attached to ibid., pp. 1–2.

117. See Dong nüshi 董女士, "Youju shuzhi" 幽居述志 (My aspirations in solitude), YS, no. 92 (Apr. 15, 1937): 11.

118. The word "curtain" (*lian* 簾) refers to the half-closed eyelids. *Shen* is a term with multiple meanings in inner alchemy. Here it refers to the focal awareness one must keep during inner alchemy practice.

119. The expression "Sweet Dew" (*gan lu* 甘露) refers to the coagulation of *qi*, *jing*, and *shen*, which occurs during the meditative practice when the process of microcosmic movement is conducted along the tracts within the body. See Chapter 3.

120. According to Chen Yingning's commentary on the poem, the "Qu River" is another name for the River Zhe, which meanders through Zhejiang. Hence the name Qu (twisted). Chen interprets it quite appropriately as an allusion to the menstrual flow. See Chen's comments attached to Miss Dong, "Zhanlong gong bi you gan" 斬龍功畢有感 (Thoughts on having slain the Dragon), YS, no. 93 (May 15, 1937): 12.

121. The expression "conserving and holding" (*bao shou* 保守) refers to the incubation practice that begins after the regular menstrual or seminal emissions are stopped.

122. The Blue Bridge (Lan qiao 藍橋) is the name of the bridge where Pei Hang, the Dao seeker of the Tang dynasty, met and married the goddess

Yun Ying. Pei later went with her into the Yufeng mountain, where he achieved immortality by taking an alchemic formula known as Scarlet Snow and Orange Essence. See Li Fang, *Taiping guangji*, pp. 7–11.

123. See Miss Dong, "Wei xiudao jituan shi yuanjin churao zhiyan" 爲修道集團事願進芻蕘之言 (My preliminary thoughts on the proposed self-cultivation congregation), YS, no. 93 (May 1, 1937): 10–11.

124. The first editorial call for public discussion and proposal appeared in the mid-November issue of the *Biweekly* in 1936. See "Wei xiudao jituan shi zhengqiu tongzhi zhu jun zhi yijian" 爲修道集團事征求同志諸君之意見 (Seeking fellow practitioners' suggestions and opinions on the proposed self-cultivation congregation), YS, no. 82 (Nov. 16, 1936): 2. For her proposal, see Miss Dong, "Wei xiudao jituan shi yuan jin churao zhiyan," YS, no. 93 (May 1, 1937): 10–11.

Chapter 6

1. These mottoes first appeared on the cover page of issue no. 68 (Apr. 16, 1936) and on every issue thereafter. They were introduced as part of the editorial reorganization of the *Biweekly* in early 1935 under Chen Yingning's direction.

2. For succinct summaries of the modern state's campaigns against religions, see Duara, *Rescuing History from the Nation*, pp. 85–113; and Welch, *Buddhist Revival in China*.

3. See Chen Yaoting, *Shanghai daojiao shi*, pp. 420–35.

4. See Yao Wennan 姚文枏, "Zhang jun Xuetang mu zhi ming" 張君雪堂墓誌銘 (Epitaph for Mr. Zhang Xuetang), YS, no. 13 (Jan. 1, 1934): 217.

5. See Zhang Zhuming, "Yihuatang shan shuju zhi chuangshe ji benkan faxing zhi yuanyin" 翼化堂善書局之創設及本刊發行之原因 (On the history of the establishment of the morality books bureau of Yihuatang and the origins for the publication of this biweekly), YS, no. 12 (Jan. 1, 1934): 217–18; and Wu Yakui, "Lun *Yangshan banyuekan*" 論揚善半月刊 (On the *Yangshan Biweekly*), *Daojiao wenhua yanjiu*, no. 9 (1996): 462–65.

6. Zhang Zhuming, "Yihuatang shan shuju zhi chuangshe ji benkan faxing zhi yuanyin," p. 218. Dr. Zhang recalled that they met for the first time on a rainy day in the late 1920s. He was so impressed with Chen's learning and personality that he soon agreed to sponsor the publication of *Lectures on the Yellow Courtyard Scriptures*, one of Chen's early writings on Daoist inner alchemy (interview with Zhang Zhuming, Orange, California, 1995).

7. The first series contains *Tianyin zi* 天隱子, *Zuowang lun* 坐忘論, *Wuxi zhizhi* 五息直指, *Pangmen xiaoshu lu* 旁門小術錄, and *Jinhuo danjue* 金火丹訣. The second series consists of *Jinsi baolü* 金笥寶籙 and *Lü zu si jie* 呂祖

詩解. The former is a variant of the late imperial inner alchemic scripture entitled *Yu qing jin si qing hua mi wen jin bao nei lian dan jue* 玉清金笥青華秘文金寶內煉丹訣, often ascribed to Zhang Boduan. The third series contains *Kunning jing* 坤寧經, *Nügong zhengfa* 女功正法, *Nüdan shize* 女丹十則, *Nannü dangong yitong bian* 男女丹功異同辨, and *Nüdan shiji* 女丹詩集, all of which were selected from He Longxiang's *Nüdan hebian* 女丹合編 (1906). The fourth series contains Chen Yingning's *Lectures on the Yellow Courtyard Scriptures* (1933) and *Annotations on Sun Bu'er's Poem on Female Alchemy* (1934).

8. See (Chen Yingning), "Yihuatang daoxue xiao congshu bianji dayi" 翼化堂道學小叢書編輯大意 (Editors' goals for the petite series on Daoist learning by Yihuatang), YS, no. 39 (Mar. 16, 1935): 3; and "Nüzi daoxue xiao congshu bianji dayi" 女子道學小叢書編輯大意 (Editors' goals for the petite series on Daoist learning for women), YS, no. 40 (Apr. 1, 1935): 5.

9. See the society's notices in YS, no. 42 (Mar. 16, 1935): 1; and YS, no. 56 (Oct. 16, 1935): cover page. The history of the Metaphysical Study Society is still not clear. Its membership included many personnel of the YS staff, and it had very close ties with the *Biweekly*.

10. See "Dandao kejing hui gongqi" 丹道刻經會公啓 (Public notice by the Society for Carving Daoist and Alchemic Scriptures), YS, no. 77 (Sept. 1, 1936): 1–2; and also the society's luncheon report in YS, no. 94 (May 16, 1937): inside cover.

11. See "Dandao kejing hui gongqi," YS, no. 77 (Sept. 1, 1936): 1–2.

12. See "Dandao kejing hui qishi" 丹道刻經會啓事 (Notice by the Society for Carving Daoist and Alchemic Scriptures), YS, no. 95 (June 1, 1937): inside cover, 12.

13. See the notices by the society in YS, no. 97 (July 1, 1937): front page; no. 98 (July 16, 1937): front page; and no. 99 (Feb. 1, 1937): front page.

14. See Chen Yingning's editorial notes to *Sanche mizhi* and *Daoqiao tan*, YS, no. 84: 2–4; no. 92: 8–9; and no. 94: inside cover, 12–13. The complete list as of June 1937 comprised the following: 石鎮之、林品三、吳彝珠、洪太庵、胡漸逵、馬一浮、孫抱慈、高堯夫、高觀如、張化聲、梁南鏘、常遵先、陳攖寧、溫雲臺、彭遜之、華文敏、黃監周、黃忏華、劉仁航、劉宗漢、劉繼賢、謝強公、韓國卿、顧拱辰、歐陽德三.

15. The two books funded by the society were *Qin huo chong guang* 琴火重光 (1939), an extremely rare book from the late imperial period, and Chen Yingning's *Vernacular Annotations to the "Ode to Great Dao of the Numinous Origin"* (1938). See Zhang Zhuming, "Wai dan zhuan ji *Qinhuo chong guang* xu" 外丹專籍琴火重光序 (Preface to the outer alchemic treatise *Double Brilliance of the Zither Fire*), in XD, no. 1 (Jan. 1939): 4. See also

Chen Yingning, *Lingyuan dadao ge baihua zhujie*. The society's two other publication projects did not succeed. One was the planned reproduction of a Buddhist Diamond Sutra text in 1937. It was canceled due to the fact that the owner fled Shanghai when the Japanese laid siege to the city in the fall of 1937. See the society's notice in *XD*, no. 3 (Mar. 1939): 1. The other was a planned compendium on inner alchemy by the famous contemporary Daoist adept Xu Haiyin, which was aborted due to the author's inability to provide sufficient funding. By summer of 1937, the society requested that either two-thirds or one-half of the estimated production costs be paid by the party or person(s) interested in having the text printed. See the notice in *YS*, no. 95 (June 16, 1937): 12. See also Xu Haiyin, Epilogue to *Tian le ji* 天樂集.

16. In interviews, Dr. Zhang also pointed out that the way the *Biweekly* was passed from reader to reader may have limited the growth of subscriptions. Many also chose to handcopy what they considered relevant to their own practice from a borrowed copy of the *Biweekly*.

17. See the editor's note, *YS*, no. 40 (Feb. 16, 1935): 3. For Guiguzi 鬼谷子, see *Guiguzi*, in *DZ*, 21: 669–98. For Heguanzi 鶡冠子, see Song Dianjie, *Heguanzi*, in *DZ*, 203: 202–28; and Defoort, *The Pheasant Cap Master*. The legend of the Yellow Emperor learning the immortals' longevity techniques began with Zhuangzi, who described a meeting the Yellow Emperor sought with the legendary immortal Guangchengzi. See Guo Xiang, *Nanhua zhenjing zhushu*; and also Zhao Heng, *Ji Zhenzong huangdi yu zhi xiantian ji*.

18. Chen Yingning was critical of the syncretism of the three teachings. See his notes on Fangnei sanren's "Daoxue changge" 道學長歌 (Long ballad on Daoism), *YS*, no. 66 (Mar. 16, 1936): 4–5.

19. The massive compendium was the result of collective efforts led by Yong Rong 永瑢 and Ji Yun 紀昀 (1724–1805) and is regarded as an influential work in Chinese bibliography and an important part of the Qing evidential learning. See Chen Yingning, "Lun *Siku tiyao* bu shi Daojia xueshu zhi quan ti" 論四庫提要不識道家學術之全體 (On the *Siku Compendium Abstract*'s ignorance of the totality of Daoist learning), *YS*, no. 68 (Apr. 16, 1936): 1–2.

20. See ibid., *YS*, no. 69 (May 1, 1936): 1–2; no. 70 (May 16, 1936): 1–2.

21. See ibid., *YS*, no. 70 (May 16, 1936): 1–2.

22. See Chen Yingning, "Zhongguo Daojiao yuanliu gailun" 中國道教源流概論 (A brief discourse on the origins of Daoism in China), *YS*, no. 14 (Jan. 16, 1934): 1.

23. See ibid.

24. Ibid. See also Chen Yingning, "Dafu Beiping xueyuan hutong Qian Daoji xiansheng" 答覆北平學院胡同錢道極先生 (In response to Mr. Qian Daoji of College Lane in Beiping), YS, no. 49 (July 1, 1935): 6; and idem, "Lun *Siku tiyao* bu shi Daojia xueshu zhi quanti," YS, no. 68 (Apr. 16, 1936): 1–2; no. 69 (May 1, 1936): 1–2; no. 70 (May 16, 1936): 1–2.

25. Chen Yingning, "Zhonghua quanguo Daojiao hui yuanqi" 中華全國道教會緣起 (Origins of the Chinese National Daoist Association), YS, no. 67 (Apr. 1, 1936): 1–2.

26. See Jingxin zi 淨心子, "Xianxue shi qiangguo de weiyi miaofa lun" 仙學是強國的惟一妙法論 (The Immortals' Learning is the only efficacious method for strengthening the nation), YS, no. 59 (Dec. 1, 1935): 1–2. See also Qian Xin 錢心, "Xian Fo panjue shu" 仙佛判決書 (A verdict on the Immortals' Learning and Buddhism), YS, no. 63 (Feb. 1, 1936): 1–3.

27. See Qian Xin, "Xian Fo panjue shu," YS, no. 63 (Feb. 1, 1936): 3.

28. See Chen Yingning, "Fu Zhang Huasheng xiansheng han" 覆張化聲先生函 (In response to Mr. Zhang Huasheng), YS, no. 32 (Oct. 16, 1934): 8–9; and idem, "Du Huasheng xu de ganxiang," YS, no. 37 (Jan. 1, 1935): 8–9; no. 39 (Feb. 1, 1935): 8. See also Zhang Huasheng, "Bo mo jushi shu" 駁某居士書 (In refutation of a certain lay practitioner's letter), YS, no. 43 (Apr. 1, 1935): 1–2.

29. See Qian Xin, "Xian Fo panjue shu," YS, no. 63 (Feb. 1, 1936): 1–3.

30. See Chen's comments appended to ibid.

31. See Chunyi zi 純一子, "Fojing Xiandao yu kexue zhi yanjiu" 佛經仙道與科學之研究 (Buddhist scriptures, the Immortals' Way, and scientific studies), YS, no. 54 (Sept. 16, 1935): 5–7; no. 55 (Oct. 1, 1935): 5–8; no. 57 (Nov. 1, 1935): 1–3. See also Jingxin zi 淨心子, "Kexue yinggai he Xianxue hezuo shuo" 科學應該和仙學合作說 (On "Science must cooperate with the Immortals' Learning"), YS, no. 58 (Nov. 16, 1935): 4–6. See Chen Yingning's marginal notes on his *Lingyuan dadao ge baihua zhujie* and his "*Xuexian bicheng.*"

32. See Chen Yingning, "Fu Nanjing Lifayuan Huang Chanhua xiansheng shu," YS, no. 50 (July 16, 1936): 1–2. Huang was also a friend of Chen. A devotee and a scholar of Buddhism, Huang was at the time a member of the Legislative Yuan. Huang was keen on inner alchemic self-cultivation. At the time of his writing, he had sought transmission of oral secrets from Chen on the practice; see ibid., p. 2.

33. Chen never identified the dates of these two wars. But the first was most likely the 1924 scuffle over the control of Shanghai between the Hebei Army under Qi Xieyuan 齊燮元 (1879–1946) and the Anhui Army commanded by Lu Yongxiang 盧永祥 (1867–1933); and the subsequent

war between Lu and the Hebei Army general Sun Chuanfang 孫傳芳 (1885–1935) in the same year. The second war probably referred to the Japanese siege of Shanghai in early 1932.

34. Chen Yingning, trans., "Sanyuan yiguan danfa yingwen yanjiang lu zhiyi" 三元一貫丹法英文演講錄直譯 (A direct translation of my notes on the English speech on the Unitary Alchemic Methods of the Three Origins), XD, no. 7 (July 1939): 2; and no. 8 (Aug. 1939): 2. Although Chen did not reveal the identity of the speaker, Dr. Zhang Zhuming assured me in my 1995 interview that his friend Dr. Shen Linsheng authored and delivered the lecture to the Shanghai International Mission congregation. For Wang's critical study of Johnson's monograph on Chinese alchemy, see his "Du *Zhongguo liandan shu kao* suibi" 讀中國煉丹術考隨筆 (Notes on *A Study of Chinese Alchemy*), XD, no. 28 (Apr. 1941): 3–5; no. 29 (May 1941): 3–4.

35. See Zhang Zhuming, "Waidan zhuanji Qinhuo chongguang xu" (A preface to the outer alchemic treatise *Double Brilliance of the Zither Fire*), XD, no. 1 (Jan. 1939): 4. The identity of Professor E. William remains unclear to me. Obed S. Johnson's *Study of Chinese Alchemy* was published in Shanghai in 1928. Aside from *Qinhuo chongguang*, one of the most important Daoist outer alchemic compendia reprinted by Yihuatang, Chen and his colleagues also collected and published another Qing collection entitled *A Great Compendium of the Golden Fire* (*Jinhuo dacheng* 金火大成), edited by the Qing alchemist Li Baoqian 李保乾 and published originally in 1874.

36. See Chen Yingning, "Du Huasheng xu de ganxiang (11)," YS, no. 54 (Sept. 16, 1936): 3.

37. Dr. Shi gave an account of the ordeals of his treasured copy of the book in his preface to Huang Yuanji, *Daodejing zhujie* 道德經注解 (Taipei: Zhenshanmei chubanshe, 1978), pp. 5–7.

38. See Shi Yixuan's preface to Yin Quan, *Xiuzhen busi fang*, pp. 7–11. Dr. Shi enthusiastically endorsed Master Yin Quan's openly sexual approach to inner alchemy.

39. Chen Yingning, "Bian *Lengyan jing* shizhong xian," YS, no. 98 (July 16, 1937): 6–7.

40. See Chen Chengkai 陳誠凱, "Fenghe Fuzhou Hong Tai'an xiansheng shuhuai yuanyun" 奉和福州洪太庵先生述懷原韻 (Matching the rhymes of a poem of rumination by Mr. Hong Tai'an), XD, no. 9 (July 1939): 3. There were five other response poems from Zhejiang and Fujian. See Ye Xueyu 葉學愚, "Gonghe Hong Tai'an xiansheng shuhuai wu shou" 恭和洪太庵先生述懷五首 (Respectfully matching the rhymes of Mr. Hong Tai'an's "Self-musings" in five stanzas), XD, no. 7 (July 1939): 3; and Wu Xinpeng 吳信蓬, "Gonghe Fuzhou Hong Tai'an xiansheng shuhuai

yuanyun" 恭和福州洪太庵先生述懷原韻 (Respectfully matching the rhymes of "Self-musings" by Mr. Hong Tai'an of Fuzhou), XD, no. 9 (Sept. 1939): 2; and Shi Zhaoyu 施召愚, "Fenghe Hong Tai'an jun liuyi chudu shuhuai shi sanzhang" 奉和洪太庵君六一初度述懷詩三章 (Respectfully matching the rhymes of "Self-musings" in three stanzas by Mr. Hong Tai'an on passing his sixty-first birthday), YS, no. 13 (Jan. 1940): 4.

41. "The nine-cycled elixir" (jiuzhuan dancheng 九轉丹成) refers in outer alchemy to the multiple alchemical processes that yield the elixir of immortality; see *Huangdi jiu ding shen dan jing jue*. The term "Jade Boy" (yu tong 玉童) appears to be a variant of the inner alchemic term "jade embryo" (yu tai 玉胎), which refers to the gestated embryo or elixir within the body of the cultivator; see Zhang Junfang, *Yunji qiqian*, in DZ, 22: 211–14.

42. The expression "Three Flowers gathered atop" (sanhua juding 三花聚頂) is an inner alchemic term alluding to the integration of the Original Essence, Qi, and the Spirit at the elusive Aperture of the Mysterious within the body. This assembly is believed to lead to the gestation of the potent inner elixir. The term "Cycled [or "Recycled"] Wind" (hui feng 回風) refers to the somatic condition for the congregation of the trio. See Xiao Tingzhi, *Jindan dacheng ji*, in DZ, 4: 637–42, 653–56.

43. See Chen Yingning, "Da Jiangsu Juegang Yang Fengqi xiansheng lai han" 答江蘇掘港楊逢啓先生來函 (In answer to Yang Fengqi of Juegang, Jiangsu), YS, no. 62 (Jan. 16, 1936): 2–3. Also Chen Yingning, "Du Hong Tai'an xiansheng *Wuda jiankang xiulian fa*" 讀洪太庵五大健康脩煉法 (On reading Mr. Hong Tai'an's [tract] *Five Great Cultivation Methods Toward Health*), YS, no. 62 (Jan. 16, 1936): 3–4. See also Wang Huazhen 汪化眞 (AKA Wang Boying), "Yijing de wojian" 遺精的我見 (My view on emission), XD, no. 4 (Apr. 1939): 3.

44. Chen also wrote detailed commentaries on one of the testimonies, offering his own judgment on the appropriateness of the methods and the confirmatory physical signs and psychic visions offered in the testimony. See Puyi zi 溥一子, "Puyi zi Neigong riji" 溥一子內功日記 (Master Puyi's diary on inner practice), YS, no. 89 (Mar. 1, 1937): 11–12; and "Yu zhi qiudao jingguo" 余之求道經過 (My experience of seeking the Way), XD, no. 23 (Nov. 1940): 1–2; no. 24 (Dec. 1940): 1; no. 25 (Jan. 1941): 1–2; no. 27 (Mar. 1941): 2; no. 28 (Apr. 1941): 2–5; no. 29 (May 1941): 2.

45. Having experienced the pinch of money in his practice, Chen tried to offer practical advice. For those who were old and poor, Chen advised them to concentrate on preserving and improving their current physical condition and keep to their present practice. Chen consoled them by arguing that as long as they kept up their current practice, they could hope to

advance their practice when money and other resources became available to them. For those who had some means at their disposal, Chen gave them advice on how to better utilize their available funds. He pointed to the interregional and urban-country differentials in the cost of living and suggested that they relocate their practice to places where they could benefit from these differentials. See Chen Yingning, "Da Xiamen Zhou Zixiu" 答廈門周子秀 (In reply to Zhou Zixiu of Xiamen), YS, no. 90 (Mar. 16, 1937): 7–8.

46. Several practice diaries and testimonials were published in serial format with detailed comments by Chen Yingning; see, e.g., Chen Yingning, "Qian Anhui shifan xuesheng Li Chaorui zhi qi jiaoshou Hu Yuanru jun yanjiu neidan xin shisan han" 前安徽師範學生李朝瑞致其教授胡淵如君研究內丹信十三函 (Thirteen letters on the practice of inner alchemy from Li Chaorui, a former normal school student, to his professor Hu Yuanru), YS, no. 67 (Apr. 1, 1936): 4; no. 68 (Apr. 16, 1936): 6–7; no. 69 (May 1, 1936): 6–7; no. 71 (June 1, 1936): 5–7; no. 72 (June 16, 1936): 5–7; no. 76 (Aug. 15, 1936): 5–7; no. 79 (Oct. 1, 1936): 4–5; no. 81 (Nov. 1, 1936): 6–7; no. 85 (Jan. 1, 1937): 4–6. See also "Puyi zi neigong riji," YS, no. 89 (Mar. 1, 1937): 11–12; no. 95 (June 1, 1937): 7–10; and Cheng Yuanru 程淵如, "Puyi zi Huizhou Cheng Yuanru jun sinian jian gongfu zhi jinbu" 溥一子徽州程淵如君四年間工夫之進步 (The progress of Master Puyi's [AKA Cheng Yuanru of Huizhou] practice in the last four years), YS, no. 94 (May 16, 1937): 8–9. Lastly, see also "Yu zhi qiudao jingguo," XD, no. 23 (Nov. 1940): 1–2; no. 24 (Dec. 1940): 1; no. 25 (Jan. 1941): 1–2; no. 27 (Mar. 1941): 2; no. 28 (Apr. 1941): 2; no. 29 (May 1941): 2–3; no. 30 (June 1941): 2–3.

47. For example, Chen Yingning, in his reply to Chen Wuxuan, the Daoist nun from Baoying in Jiangsu, on post-amenorrhea practice, discussed the case of another female practitioner residing in Shanghai and urged the nun to contact her. Later, the two began a correspondence. See Chen Yingning, "Da Baoying Chen Wuxuan nüshi shiwen" 答寶應陳悟玄女士十問 (In answer to the ten questions of Ms. Chen Wuxuan of Baoying), YS, no. 87 (Feb. 1, 1937): 6; and idem, "Da Jiangsu Haimen moumou jun" 答江蘇海門某某君 (In answer to so-and-so of Haimen in Jiangsu), YS, no. 87 (Feb. 1, 1937): 8–9.

48. See Zhao Yinhua 趙隱華, "Zhengqiu daoyou" 征求道友 (Looking for Dao companions), YS, no. 90 (Mar. 16, 1937): 1.

49. A good example is Fang Songshan 方嵩山, "Mao Shan kan di ji" 茅山勘地記 (A record of surveying land on Mount Mao), YS, no. 86 (Jan. 16, 1937): 10–11.

50. See Zhou Minde 周敏得, "Dongtian fudi kao" 洞天福地考 (A survey of grottoes and blessed sites), YS, no. 6 (Sept. 16, 1933): 94.

51. See Yi Sou 逸叟, "Gaizhu shan Baoguang dong changhe shi" 蓋竹山寶光洞唱和詩 (A poetic dialogue at the Grotto of the Treasured Light on Mount Gaozhu), YS, no. 11 (Nov. 1939): 2.

52. The Hundun 混沌 state refers to the undifferentiated state before the creation of the universe. In this context, it refers to the special meditative state of great stillness in which the practitioner breaks down the distinction between the self and the world.

53. The Weilü 尾閭 locus is generally located right below the end of the spinal column. In inner alchemy, it is considered the first of the Three Passes on the Superintendent Channel at the back of the body. See Chapter 3 for details.

54. The exact content of the method of Three Stillnesses (*san bu dong fa* 三不動法) remains unclear to me. But in this context, it appears to be a special meditative technique Chen had taught Zhang. In classical inner alchemy, the Three Stillnesses/Non-movements are the Stillness of the Body (*shen bu dong* 身不動), of the Heart (*xin bu dong* 心不動), and of the Intent (*yi bu dong* 意不動). The Three Stillnesses were considered essential to the generation and transformation of the Essential Qi in the body. See Li Daochun, *Zhong he ji*, *juan* 3, in DZ, 4: 493–502.

55. The Sea of Qi is a locus in the lower abdomen; see Chapter 3. The privates 陰部 are the female genitalia in this context.

56. *Suanma* 酸麻 is a term often used in inner alchemy to denote a somatic sensation or pleasure in the body associated with a certain deep meditative state. Literally translated, it means "sore, or languid, and numbing," an expression often associated with pleasant languor after physical exertion or sexual climax.

57. See "Shanghai mou nüshi laihan" 上海某女士來函 (A letter from a lady from Shanghai), YS, no. 99 (Aug. 1, 1937): 8. Chen Yingning revealed that the anonymous lady was Zhang Zhide. See his "Da Jiangsu Haimen mou xiansheng" 答江蘇海門某先生 (In reply to Mr. X from Haimen, Jiangsu), YS, no. 87 (Feb. 1, 1937): 9.

58. See Chen Yingning, "Da Baoying Chahe zhen Chen Wuxuan nüshi" 答寶應岔河鎮陳悟玄女士 (In reply to Ms Chen Wuxuan of Chahe township in Baoying county), YS, no. 87 (Feb. 1, 1937): 6.

59. See the published letters and responses in YS, no. 42 (Mar. 16, 1934): 9–14. Chen Yingning himself was often the object of these search tours. In a November 1994 interview in Beijing, Dr. Hu revealed to me that he, like

many others, traveled to Shanghai to see Chen unannounced and asked to be his disciple in the early 1940s.

60. See "Wei xiudao jituan shi zhengqiu tongzhi zhu jun zhi yijian" 爲修道集團事征求同志諸君之意見 (An invitation for opinions and proposals from comrades on the matter of Daoist practice clubs), YS, no. 88 (Feb. 16, 1937): 2; and also Chen Yingning, "Dafu Wuxi Wang Boying laihan wendao" 答覆無錫汪伯英來函問道 (In reply to the inquiry on the Way by Wang Boying of Wuxi), YS, no. 39 (Feb. 1, 1935): 10.

61. See the six proposals; and also Cai Jiming 蔡積民, "Da guikan xiudao jituan zhengqiu yijian ge wen" 答貴刊修道集團征求意見各問 (In answer to the questions in your journal's call for proposals on a cultivation group), YS, no. 89 (Mar. 1, 1937): 1–7.

62. See Chen Yingning, "Dafu Fujian Fuqing xian Lin Daomin jun" 答覆福建福清縣林道民君 (In reply to Mr. Lin Daomin of Fuqing county, Fujian), XD, no. 5 (May 1939): 2; and idem, "Dafu Tiantai Chichengshan Zhang Huikun nüshi" 答覆天台赤城山張慧坤女士 (In reply to Ms Zhang Huikun of Chichengshan in Tiantai), XD, no. 6 (June 1939): 2. See also Wang Hongyi 王弘毅 and Xu Qianguang 徐乾光, "Zhi benshe Zhang Zhuming xiansheng han" 致本社張竹銘先生函 (A letter to Mr. Zhang Zhuming of this society), XD, no. 6 (June 1939): 2.

63. See the notice by the editorial staff in XD, no. 5 (May 1939): 1. Addressed to readers at large, the notice called for the names and addresses of self-cultivation practitioners and organizations so as to establish mutual contact and exchange. Clearly another purpose of the notice was also to reestablish and expand the subscription base of the new monthly.

64. See the editors' notice by Zhizhen 志眞 (AKA Wang Boying 汪伯英), "Fakan ci" 發刊辭 (A publication notice), XD, no. 1 (Jan. 1939): 1. The regular mail rate was 3 cents, whereas the registered mail rate was 8 cents. The price per issue was 5 cents in early 1939. By July 1941, it had risen to 10 cents per copy. See the Yihuatang rate increase notice and the editorial notice in XD, no. 10 (Oct. 1939): 1; no. 21 (Aug. 1940): 4; and no. 32 (July 1940): 4. Soaring paper prices forced many of Shanghai's small newspapers and magazines to shut down. See also Ma Guangren, *Shanghai xinwen shi*, pp. 980–84.

65. See the editorial "Jinnian de xin yuanwang" 今年的新願望 (This year's new wishes), XD, no. 25 (Jan. 1941): 1.

66. Several Daoist regional organizations were established during the Japanese occupation. One was the Pudong Daoist Association of Shanghai Special Municipality (Shanghai tebie shi Pudong Daojiao tongren lianyi hui 上海特別市浦東道教同仁聯誼會), established in 1942. Its member-

ship consisted mainly of Zhengyi Daoists from Shanghai and its suburbs. The other was the Shanghai Daoist Society (Shanghai tebie shi Daojiao hui 上海特別市道教會), established by Zhengyi Daoists in the Pudong district in 1943. The two prominent Daoist leaders with extensive connections to the emerging inner alchemy community were Xie Qianggong 謝強公, the former secretary general of the Chinese National Daoist Society 中華道教會, established in Shanghai in the 1930s, and Abbot Chen Tiehai of the Daoist Palace of the Purple Soleil in Shanghai; both served as directors for the short-lived General Daoist Association of China (Zhonghua Daojiao zonghui). See Chen Yaoting, *Shanghai Daojiao shi*, pp. 431–33.

67. Poshek Fu examines the evolution of the "peace movement" led by Wang Jingwei from its origins in a dissenting minority of intellectuals who aimed for national salvation through self-sacrifice and accommodation in the 1930s to the full-blown puppet government and total cultural anachronism during the Japanese occupation in the 1940s. Understanding the Daoist motives for collaboration is an even more complicated task and remains to be undertaken. One complicating factor was intra-sectarian rivalry. The Daoists in Shanghai had long been plagued by rifts defined by sectarian competition between the Zhengyi and the Quanzhen sects, and by regional rivalries among the local Shanghai indigenous monasteries (*benbang* 本幫) and those built and run by non-Shanghai (*waidi* 外地) Daoists from the Suzhou, Wuxi, Ningbo, and Guangdong regions. Safe passage through the numerous Japanese checkpoints throughout the city was a big concern for many ordinary residents of Shanghai during the occupation. Chen Yaoting reported that members of the collaborative Pudong Daoist Association were issued special ID passes and badges that ensured their safe passage and immunity from searches of their ritual paraphernalia by the Japanese sentries as they traveled in and out of the occupied city. See Poshek Fu, *Passivity, Resistance, and Collaboration*, pp. 110–54; and Chen Yaoting, *Shanghai Daojiao shi*, pp. 420–33.

68. See Chen Yingning, "Zhi Sichuan Guan xian Qingchengshan Yi daoren shu" 致四川灌縣青城山易道人書 (To Master Yi of Mount Blue Citadel of Guan county in Sichuan), *XD*, no. 9 (Sept. 1939): 2. Yi Xinying 易心瑩, the abbot at the famous Daoist monastery on Mount Qingcheng outside Chengdu, together with several of his fellow abbots wrote Chen in the summer of 1937, urging him to move to Sichuan.

69. See Chen Yingning, "Zhi benshe han" 致本社函 (A letter to the editors), *XD*, no. 5 (May 1939): 2.

70. Abbot Ai's cloister became the most prosperous Daoist temple in Shanghai largely because of his collaboration with the puppet regime. With

the wealth generated from his cloister, Abbot Ai was said to have led a lavish and libertine life during the occupation. See Chen Yaoting, *Shanghai Daojiao shi*, p. 425.

71. See Chen Yingning, "Muxiu Tiantaishan Tongbai gong shengji yuanqi" 募修天台山桐柏宮勝跡緣起 (On the origins of the donation drive for repairing the sacred sites at the Tongbai Monastery on Mount Tiantai), *XD*, no. 25 (Jan. 1941): 3.

72. The luncheon club gathering was formalized at a meeting held at the Quanzhen Abbey of the Purple Soleil in April 1941. See "Xuanlü jucan hui choubei chengli" 玄侶聚餐會籌備成立 (On the preparation and establishing of the Daoist Dining Club), *XD*, no. 29 (May 1941): 8; "Xuanlü jucan hui yuanqi" 玄侶聚餐會緣起 (On the origins of the Daoist Dining Club), and "Xuanlü jucan hui jianzhang" 玄侶聚餐會簡章 (The charter of the Daoist Dining Club), *XD*, no. 32 (Aug. 1941): 5–6.

73. See the published notice and the club charter in *XD*, no. 29 (May 1941): 8; and no. 32 (Aug. 1941): 5–6.

74. See Poshek Fu, *Passivity, Resistance, and Collaboration*; and Chen Yingning, *Zizhuan*, in Li Yangzheng, *Daojiao yu yangsheng*.

75. Chen Yingning, *Zizhuan*, in Li Yangzheng, *Daojiao yu yangsheng*, pp. 1–5.

Epilogue

1. See Chen Yingning, *Shenjing shuairuo jinggong liaoyang fa wenda*.

2. For a detailed description of the Quanzhen monastic daily routine, see Yoshioka Yoshitoyo, "Taoist Monastic Life," in Welch and Seidel, *Facets of Taoism*, pp. 229–52.

3. See, e.g., "Daojiao zhishi leibian chuji" 道教知識類編初集 (A categorical compilation of Daoist knowledge), chaps. 1–2, *DXHK*, no. 2 (Mar. 1963): 1–25; chap. 3, *DXHK*, no. 3 (Oct. 1963): 29–62; and chap. 4, *DXHK*, no. 4 (Oct. 1964): 23–48. For a complete list of the research projects completed by the research section, see Li Yangzheng, *Dangdai Zhongguo Daojiao*, pp. 120–21.

4. See Chen Yingning, "*Shiji* Laozi zhuan wenti kaozheng" 史記老子傳問題考證 (A study of the biography of Laozi in *Shiji*), *DXHK*, no. 1 (Aug. 1962): 41–49; idem, "Taiping jing de qianyin yu houguo" 太平經的前因與後果 (The precursors and consequences of the Taiping Scriptures), *DXHK*, no. 1 (Aug. 1962): 50–79; idem, "Nanhua neiwai pian fengzhang biao zhi" 南華內外篇分章標旨 (A sectional annotative commentary on the Inner and Outer chapters of the *Nanhua Scripture*), *DXHK*, no. 4

(Oct. 1964): 1–13; and idem, "*Laozi* di wushi zhang yanjiu" 老子第五十章研究 (A study of Chapter 50 of *Laozi*), *DXHK*, no. 4 (Oct. 1964): 14–22.

  5. See Yu Zhongjue, "Daojia yu daojiao" 道家與道教 (Daoist schools and Daoist religion), 3 pts., *DXHK*, no. 2 (Mar. 1963): 56–97; no. 3 (Oct. 1969): 71–112; no. 4 (Oct. 1964): 49–113.

  6. See Li Yangzheng, *Dangdai Zhongguo Daojiao*, pp. 135–37. According to Li, Needham came to visit China at the invitation of Guo Moruo 郭沫若, then-head of the Chinese Academy of Sciences. Mr. Li claimed to have been present at the meeting and provided a detailed account of the meeting and conversations between Chen and Needham. In December 1994, I was able to interview the late Yu Zhongjue, the translator of Needham's work on Daoism, and confirm some of the details of Li's account.

  7. Chen Yingning, "Fenxi Daojiao jie jinxi butong de qingkuang" 分析道教界今昔不同的情況 (An analysis of present and past conditions among Daoist circles), *DXHK*, no. 1 (Aug. 1962): 83–84. See also Li Yangzheng, *Dangdai Zhongguo daojiao*, pp. 99–100.

  8. Chen Yingning, "Fenxi Daojiao jie jinxi butong de qingkuan," *DXHK*, no. 1 (Aug. 1962): 80–85.

  9. See Yuan Jiegui and Xu Boying, *Zhonghua xianxue*.

  10. See Hong Jianlin, *Xianxue jiemi*. For the most recent compendium of Chen Yingning's writings, see Hu Haiya and Wu Guozhong, *Zhonghua xianxue yangsheng quanshu*. See also Hu Haiya and Wu Guozhong, "*Yangshan banyue kan*" "*Xiandao yuebao*" *quanji*.

Selected Bibliography

For the abbreviations used here, see p. xiii.

Primary Sources

Periodicals

Daoxie huikan 道協會刊 (Journal of the Chinese Daoist Association). 24 issues. Internal publication. Beijing: Zhongguo Daojiao xiehui, 1962–86.

Xiandao yuebao 仙道月報 (Immortals' way monthly). 32 issues. Shanghai: Yihuatang, 1939–41. Copy at Baiyun guan scriptorium in Beijing.

Yangshan banyuekan 揚善半月刊 (Promulgate the good semimonthly). 99 issues. Shanghai: Yihuatang, 1933–38. Issues 1–98 held at Shanghai Library; issue 99 held at the library of the Chinese Academy of Social Science in Beijing.

Interview Notes

Li Yangzheng 李養正. 1994. Interview by the author, Dec. 14, 1994. Beijing. Interview notes in my collection.

Lü Zongyue 呂宗岳. 1994. Interview by the author, Dec. 10, 1994. Shanghai. Interview notes in my collection.

Yu Zhongjue 余仲玨. 1994. Interview by the author, Dec. 15, 1994. Beijing. Interview notes in my collection.

Zhang Zhuming 張竹銘. 1995. Interview by the author, July 16, 1995. Orange, CA. Interview notes in my collection.

———. 1996. Interview by the author, Aug. 7, 1996. Santa Ana, CA. Interview notes in my collection.

———. 1997. Interview by the author, July 25, 1997. Orange, CA. Interview notes in my collection.

Books and Journal Articles

Cao Heng 曹珩. *Daoyuan yiqi* 道元一氣 (The Unitary Qi of the origin of the Way). N.p., 1634. Copy held at Bibliothèque Nationale de France. Reprinted—Beijing: Beijing shifan daxue chubanshe, 1990.

Chang Zunxian 常遵先. *Huanghe fu zhenben zhujie* 黃鶴賦眞本注解 (Annotations to an authentic version of the *Ode to the Yellow Crane*). Shanghai: Yihuatang, 1935. Reprinted—Taipei: Zhenshanmei chubanshe, 1970.

———. *Lü zu shi jie* 呂祖詩解 (Explications of Patriarch Lü's poem). Shanghai: Yihuatang, n.d.

———. *Micang Zhong-Lü chuandao ji* 秘藏鍾呂傳道集 (Annotations to the secretly held version of the *Collection of Patriarchs Zhongli and Lü's Transmission of the Way*). Shanghai: Yihuatang, n.d.

Chen Xianwei 陳顯微. *Zhouyi Cantongqi jie* 周易參同契解 (Expositions on *Zhouyi Cantongqi*). 3 juan. In *DZ*, 20: 271–97.

Chen Yingning 陳攖寧. *Huangting jing jiangyi* 黃庭經講義 (Lectures on the *Yellow Courtyard Scriptures*). Shanghai: Yihuatang, 1933.

———. *Koujue gouxuan lu* 口訣鉤玄錄 (Explorations in oral secrets). Serialized in *YS*, nos. 32–37, 40–41, 49–51, 80, and 86 (1934–35).

———. *Lingyuan dadao ge baihua zhujie* 靈源大道歌白話注解 (Vernacular annotations on the *Ode to the Great Way of the Numinous Origin*). Shanghai: Shanghai dandao kejinghui, 1939.

———. *Pangmen xiaoshu lu* 旁門小術錄 (Collection of side-door and minor techniques and practices). Shanghai: Yihuatang, 1935.

———. *Shenjing shuairuo jinggong liaoyang fa wenda* 神經衰弱靜功療養法問答 (Questions and answers on the quiet practice healing method for neurasthenia). 1957. *DXHK* 3 (Oct. 1963). Reprinted—Taipei: Zhenshanmei chubanshe, 1967.

———. *Sun Bu'er nüdan shizhu* 孫不二女丹詩注 (Annotations to Sun Bu'er's poem on female alchemy). Shanghai: Yihuatang, 1934.

———. "Xuexian bicheng" 學仙必成 (Learning immortals will surely succeed). 1945. Unpublished manuscript held in a private collection at the White Cloud Monastery, Beijing.

Chen Zhanqi 陳湛琦 and Hu Haiya 胡海牙, comps. "Yangshan banyue kan" "Xiandao yuebao" quanji 揚善半月刊仙道月報全集 (A compendium of the *Yangshang Biweekly* and the *Xiandao Monthly*). 9 vols. Beijing: Quanguan tushu guan wenxian shuowei fuzhi zhongxin, 2005.

Chen Zhixu 陳致虛. *Shangyang zi Jindan da ya* 上陽子金丹大要 (Master Shangyang's great essentials of the Golden Elixir). 16 *juan*. In *DZ*, 24: 1–80.

Daojiao hui diyi ci bugao 道教會第一次布告 (The Daoist Association's first announcement). Beijing: Baiyun guan, 1902.

Daozang 道藏 (The Daoist canon). N.p., 1444 and 1607. Ed. Hu Daojing 胡道靜 et al. Reprinted—Shanghai: Shanghai shudian; Beijing: Wenwu chubanshe; Tianjin: Tianjin guji chubanshe, 1988. 36 vols.

Deng Guangying 鄧光瀛. *Liancheng xianzhi* 連城縣志 (Liancheng county gazetteer). Liancheng: Weixin shuju, 1939.

Deng Huiji 鄧徽積, comp. *Wu Liu xianzong* 伍柳仙宗 (Masters Wu's and Liu's immortal lineages). Reprinted—Zhengzhou: Henan renmin chubanshe, 1987.

Ding Fubao 丁福寶 (h. Shouyi zi 守一子), ed. *Daozang jinghua lu* 道藏精華錄 (An essential collection from the Daoist canon). Shanghai: Yixue shuju, n.d. Reprinted—Hangzhou: Zhejiang guji chubanshe, 1989. 2 vols.

Ding Fubao, comp. *Daozang xubian* 道藏續編 (A supplementary compilation to the Daoist Canon). Shanghai: Yixue shuju, n.d.

Du Guangting 杜光庭. *Dongtian fudi yue du ming shan ji* 洞天福地嶽瀆名山記 (A record of the heavenly grottoes, blessed places, marchmonts, rivers, and famous mountains). 901. In *DZ*, 11: 55–60.

Fan Chengdian 范誠滇. "Wode daoshi shengya" 我的道士生涯 (My life as a Daoist). *Henan wenshi ziliao* 河南文史資料, no. 79 (2001): 211–24.

Fang Gongpu 方公溥. *Qigong zhiyan lu* 氣功治驗錄 (A record of efficacious healing through *qigong*). Shanghai: n.p., 1938.

Fangnei sanren 方內散人 (AKA Wan Ligeng 萬立賡, z. Ganchen 干臣, h. Qiyingzi 啓英子,1848–?). *Nanbei hecan fayao* 南北合參法要 (Essentials of the integrated methods from the southern and the northern lineages). *DZJH*, ser. 3, no. 7.

———. *Tongyizhai sizhong* 通一齋四種 (Four selections from the Studio of Intuiting the One). Shanghai: Zundetang, 1903.

Fu Duren 符度仁. *Xiuzhen milu* 修眞秘錄 (Secret notes on cultivating perfection). In *DZ*, 18: 522–26.

Fu Jinquan 傅金銓, comp. *Jiyi zi daoshu shiqi zhong* 濟一子道書十七種 (Master Jiyi's seventeen Daoist classics). In *ZWDS*, 11: 1–743.

———. *Jiyi zi dingpi daoshu sizhong* 濟一子頂批道書四種 (Four Daoist scriptures with marginal annotations by Master Jiyi zi). In *ZWDS*, 11: 744–888.

———. *Yiguan zhenji yijian lu* 一貫眞機易簡錄 (A simple and brief record of the true mechanism for intuiting unity). 12 vols. 1814. In his *Jiyi zi daoshu shiqi zhong* (q.v.), in *ZWDS*, 11: 395–541.

Fu Shan 傅山. *Danting zhenren yangzhen miji* 丹亭眞人養眞秘笈 (Danting the perfected man's secret collectania on cultivating perfection). In Xiao Tianshi 蕭天石, ed., *Shangcheng xiudao mishu sizhong* 上乘修道秘書四種 (Four superior secret books on cultivating the Way). In *DZJH*, ser. 12, 2: 122–248.

Gao Henian 高鶴年. *Mingshan youfang ji* 名山遊訪記 (Travels to famous mountains). 1913. Reprinted—Beijing: Zongjiao wenhua chubanshe, 2000.

Gaoshang Yuhuang xinyin jing 高上玉皇心印經 (Heart Sutra of the Supreme Jade Emperor). In *DZ*, 1: 749.

Ge Hong 葛洪. *Baopuzi neipian* 抱朴子内篇 (A master who embraces simplicity: inner chapters). In *DZ*, 28: 171–251.

———. *Shenxian zhuan* 神仙傳 (Biographies of the divine transcendents). 10 *juan*. In *DZJHL*, vol. 2, 1a–44b.

He Longxiang 賀龍驤. *Nüdan hebian* 女丹合編 (Compilation on female inner alchemy). Chengdu: Erxian an, 1905. Reprinted—Chengdu: Qingyang gong, n.d.

He Longxiang 賀龍驤 and Peng Hanran 彭瀚然, eds. *Daozang jiyao* 道藏輯要 (Essential collection from the Daoist Canon). Chengdu: Erxian an, 1906. Reprinted—Chengdu: Qingyang gong, 1985.

Hequ zi 鶡臞子. *Changdao zhenyan* 唱道眞言 (True words in praise of the Way). 5 vols. In *DZJY, dou ji* 斗集, 5: 1a–83a.

———. *Changdao zhenyan* 唱道眞言. 5 vols. In *DZJHL*, 2: 1a–37b.

Hong Wanxin 洪萬馨 (h. Tai'an 太庵). *Wu da jiankang xiulian fa* 五大健康脩練法 (Five great cultivation methods toward health). Shanghai: privately printed, 1933. Reprinted—Taipei: Zhenshanmei chubanshe, 1963.

Hu Daojing 胡道靜 et al., eds. *Zangwai daoshu* 藏外道書 (Daoist books outside the Daoist canon). 36 vols. Chengdu: Bashu chubanshe, 1992–94.

Hu Yun 胡愠. *Huangting neijing wuzang liufu bu xie tu* 黃庭内景五臟六腑補瀉圖 (An illustration of the replenishing and leaking of the Yellow Courtyard's Inner Vision of the Five Viscera and Six Orifices). In *DZ*, 6: 686–93.

Huang Chang 黃裳 (z. Yuanji 元吉). *Daodejing zhujie* 道德經注解 (Annotations to *Daodejing*). N.p., n.d. Reprinted—Taipei: Zhenshanmei chubanshe, 1978.

———. *Daomen yuyao* 道門語要 (Essential quotations of the Daoist lineage). N.p., n.d. Reprinted—Taipei: Zhenshanmei chubanshe, 1971.

———. *Leyutang yulu* 樂育堂語錄 (Quotations from the Hall of Joyful Cultivation). Reprinted—Shanghai: Shanghai guji chubanshe, 1990.

Huang Yuanji 黃元吉 (1271–1325) et al., comps. *Jingming zhongxiao quanshu* 淨明忠孝全書 (A complete book of the pure, bright, loyal, and filial Way). 6 vols. In *DZ*, 24: 620–53.

Huangdi jiu ding shen dan jing jue 黃帝九鼎神丹經訣 (The oral secrets of the Yellow Emperor's *Scripture of the Nine Cauldrons of Divine Elixir*). In *DZ*, 18: 795–859.

Jiang Weiqiao 蔣維喬. *Dingzheng Yinshizi jingzuo fa* 訂正因是子靜坐法 (Revised edition of *Quiet Sitting Method* by Master Yinshizi). Beiping: privately printed, 1914–17.

———. *Yinshizi jingzuo fa xu bian* 因是子靜坐法續編 (Supplement to *Quiet Sitting Method* by Master Yinshizi). Beijing: Shangwu yinshu guan, 1922.

Li Daochun 李道純. *Zhonghe ji* 中和集 (A compendium of central harmony). 6 *juan*. In *DZ*, 4: 482–524.

Li Fang 李昉 et al. *Taiping guangji* 太平廣記 (A comprehensive record of the Great Peace era). 978. Reprinted—Shanghai: Shanghai guji chubanshe, 1990. 4 vols.

———. *Taiping yulan* 太平禦覽 (An imperial review of the Great Peace era). 977. Reprinted—Beijing: Zhonghua shuju, 1960. 4 vols.

Li Hanxu 李涵虛. *Daoqiao tan Sanche mizhi* 道竅談三車秘旨 (A discourse on the aperture of the Way and Esoteric precepts on the triple crafts). In *DZJH*, ser. 2, no. 5.

Li Li'an 李理安. *Changchun guan zhi* 長春觀志 (Gazetteer of the Monastery of Eternal Spring). Wuchang: privately printed, 1936. Copy at Shanghai Library.

Li Pengfei 李鵬飛. *Sanyuan yanshou zan shu* 三元延壽贊書 (A laudatory book for lengthening life by the three primordials). 1291. 5 *juan*. In *DZ*, 18: 526–57.

Li Ruiqing 李瑞清. *Qingdaoren ni gu hua ce* 清道人擬古畫冊 (An album of paintings in the style of the ancients by Qingdaoren). Shanghai: Wangping jie youzheng shuju, n.d.

———. *Qingdaoren yi ji* 清道人遺集 (A collection of works by Qingdaoren). Linchuan: Li shi, 1939.

Liancheng xian difang zhi bianzuan weiyuanhui 連城縣地方志編纂委員會. *Liancheng xianzhi* 連城縣志 (Liancheng county gazetteer). Beijing: Qunzhong chubanshe, 1993.

Liangqiu zi 梁丘子, annot. *Huangting neijing yujing zhu* 黃庭內景玉經注 (Annotations to the jade scripture of the inner vista of the Yellow

Courtyard). In *Xiuzhen shishu* 修真十書 (Ten compendia for Cultivating Perfection). In *DZ*, 4: 854–69.

Liu Mingrui 劉明瑞. *Daoyuan jing wei ge* 道源精微歌 (An ode on the refined and subtle origin of the Way). Beijing, 1889. Reprinted—Taipei: Zhenshanmei chubanshe, 1965.

———. *Qiao qiao dong zhang* 敲蹻洞章 (A luminous treatise on knocking on the Qiao aperture). Beijing, 1892. Reprinted—Taipei: Zhenshanmei chubanshe, 1965.

Liu Tishu 劉體恕, ed. *Lü zu quanshu* 呂祖全書 (The complete writings of Patriarch Lü). 1742. Reprinted—Taipei: Zhenshanmei chubanshe, 1980.

Liu Xiang 劉向. *Liexian zhuan* 列仙傳 (Biographies of all the immortals). 2 juan. In *DZ*, 5: 64–76.

Liu Yiming 劉一明. *Wuzhen zhizhi* 悟真直指. 1799. In *ZWDS*, 8: 327–402.

Lu Xixing 陸西星. *Fanghu waishi* 方壺外史. 1564–80. Reprinted—Shanghai, 1915. Reprinted in Hu Daojing et al. eds., *Zangwai daoshu* (q.v.), 5: 208–377.

Meng Yongcai 孟永才. "Shoujie bichi" 受戒必持 (Precepts for those receiving ordination). In *Renwu tan dengzhen lu* 壬午壇登真錄 (Ordination register of the 1885 altar). Beijing, 1882. Copy held at Peking University Library.

Min Yide 閔一得. *Suoyan xu* 瑣言續 (Supplements to verbose sayings). 1846. In *ZWDS*, 10: 507–19.

———. *Yin zhenren Liaoyang dian wenda pian* 尹真人寥陽殿問答篇 (Dialogues with Yin the Perfected Man at Liaoyang Shrine). In *ZWDS*, 10: 384–85.

Peng Xiao 彭曉. *Zhouyi Cantongqi fenzhang tongzhenyi* 周易參同契分章通真義 (Expositions of true meanings of the chapters of *Cantongqi*). 3 juan. In *DZ*, 20: 131–57.

Qiu Zhao'ao 仇兆鰲. *Guben Cantongqi jizhu* 古本參同契集注 (A collection of ancient annotated texts of *Cantongqi*). In *DZJH*, ser. 13, 1: 137–39.

Shanghai guji chubanshe 上海古籍出版社, ed. *Ershiwu shi* 二十五史 (Histories of the twenty-five dynasties). Shanghai: Shanghai guji chubanshe, 1986.

Sima Chengzhen 司馬承禎. *Tianyin zi* 天隱子 (Master Celestial Hermit). In *DZ*, 21: 699–700.

Sun Ruzhong 孫汝忠. *Jindan zhenchuan* 金丹真傳 (True transmission on the Golden Elixir). 1615. In Fu Jinquan, *Jiyi zi dingpi daoshu sizhong* (q.v.), in *ZWDS*, 11: 860–76.

Taishang jiuchi banfu wudi nei zhenjing 太上九赤班符五帝內真經 (The Superior Lord's nine vermilion-striped talisman for the *Five Emperors' True Internal Scripture*). In *DZ*, 33: 518–22.

Tan Qiao 譚峭. *Huashu* 化書 (The book of metamorphosis). 6 *juan*. In *DZ*, 23: 589–604.

Tanba Yasuyori 丹波康賴. *Yixin fang* (J. *Ishimpō*) 醫心方 (Formula for treating the heart). 984. Reprinted—Beijing: Renmin weisheng chubanshe, 1955.

Tao Hongjing 陶弘景. *Dongxuan Lingbao zhenling weiye tu* 洞玄靈寶真靈位業圖. In *DZ*, 3: 272–82.

Tianji miwen 天笈秘文 (Esoteric scriptures from the celestial bookcase). Manuscript copy from Chongfu Monastery. Reprinted—Taipei: Zhenshanmei chubanshe, 1966.

Wang Daoyuan 王道淵 (h. Hunran zi 混然子), annot. *Cui gong Ruyao jing zhujie* 崔公入藥鏡注解 (Annotations to Lord Cui's *Mirror for Ingesting the Drug*). In *DZ*, 2: 881–86.

Wang Qihuo 汪啓穫. *Dao tong dacheng* 道統大成 (A great compilation of the order of the Way). Shanghai, 1900. Reprinted—Taipei: Xin wen feng, 1975.

Wu Shouyang 伍守陽. *Tianxian zhengli zhilun qianshuo* 天仙正理直論淺說 (A synopsis to the direct discourse on the orthodox theory of the celestial immortals). 1639. In Deng Huiji, *Wu Liu xianzong* 伍柳仙宗 (q.v.).

Wu Wu 吳誤. *Danfang xuzhi* 丹房須知 (Rules for the alchemic chamber). 1163. In *DZ*, 19: 57–61.

Wucheng zi 務成子, annot. *Taishang huangting waijing jing* 太上黃庭外景經 (The Supreme Lord's *Yellow Courtyard Scripture of the Outer Vista*). In Zhang Junfang, *Yunji qiqian* (q.v.), in *DZ*, 22: 89–100.

Xi Yukang 席裕康, ed. *Neiwai gong tushuo jiyao* 內外功圖說輯要 (An essential collection of illustrated inner and outer practices). 2 vols. Shanghai, 1919. Reprinted in *Yangsheng changshou mijue jicheng xuji* 養生長壽秘訣集成續集 (Supplement to the *Compendium of Life Nourishing and Longevity Secrets*), ed. Xiao Tianshi 蕭天石, ser. 2, no. 10. Taipei: Ziyou chubanshe, 1962.

Xiao Tianshi 蕭天石, ed. *Daozang jinghua* 道藏精華 (Quintessence of the Daoist canon). 17 series. Taipei: Ziyou chubanshe, 1955–75.

———. *Jingzuo fa jiyao* 靜坐法輯要 (A collection of essentials on quiet sitting regimens). Reprinted in *Yangsheng changshou mijue jicheng xuji* 養生長壽秘訣集成續集 (Supplement to the *Compendium of Life Nourishing and Longevity Secrets*), ed. Xiao Tianshi, ser. 2, no. 12. Taipei: Ziyou chubanshe, 1962.

Xiao Tingzhi 蕭廷芝. *Jindan dacheng ji* 金丹大成集 (Great compendium of the Golden Elixir). 13 *juan*. In *DZ*, 4: 633–56.

Xingming shuangxiu wanshen guizhi 性命雙修萬神圭旨 (A jade synopsis by ten thousand deities on the dual cultivation of the mind and life). 1615.

Copies in Stanford University Library and the Harvard-Yenching Library.

Xu Haiyin 徐海印 (h. Haiyin shanren 海印山人 and Xuanjing 玄靜). *Tianle ji* 天樂集 (An anthology of celestial joy). 8 vols. Shanghai: privately printed, 1942.

Xuanquan zi 玄全子, comp. *Zhuzhen neidan jiyao* 諸眞内丹集要 (Essential collections of inner alchemy by perfected ones). 3 juan. In *DZ*, 32: 458–72.

Yang Erzeng 楊爾曾. *Xin juan Xian yuan ji shi* 新鐫仙媛記事 (Chronicles of immortal ladies). 1602. Reprinted—Taipei: Xuesheng shuju, 1989.

Yang Jizhou 楊繼洲. *Zhenjiu dacheng* 針灸大成 (Complete collection on acupuncture). 1601. Reprinted—Taipei: Liming wenhua shiye gongsi, 1974.

Yang Qingli 楊青藜, ed. *Dacheng jiejing* 大成捷徑 (A shortcut to great perfection). Taipei: Zhenshanmei chubanshe, 1964.

Yang Wenhui 楊文會. *Chongxu jing fayin* 沖虛經發隱. 1904. Reprinted in Hu Daojing et al., eds., *Zangwai daoshu* (q.v.), vol. 3.

———. *Dao de jing fayin* 道德經發隱. 1903. Reprinted in Hu Daojing et al., eds., *Zangwai daoshu* (q.v.), vol. 3.

———. *Nanhua jing fayin* 南華經發隱. 1904. Reprinted in Hu Daojing et al., eds., *Zangwai daoshu* (q.v.), vol. 3.

———. *Yin fu jing fayin* 陰符經發隱. Ca. 1896. Reprinted in Hu Daojing et al., eds., *Zangwai daoshu* (q.v.), vol. 3.

Ye Dehui 葉德輝. *Shuangmei jing an congshu* 雙梅景闇叢書 (A compendium from the Studio of the Double Plums in Shaded View). Changsha, 1914.

Yin Quan 印權 (h. Daoyi zi 道一子). *Xiuzhen busi fang* 修眞不死方 (A regimen for cultivating perfection and immortality). 1929. Reprinted—Taipei: Zhenshanmei chubanshe, 1967.

Yu Yue 俞樾. *Chaxiangshi congchao* 茶香室叢鈔 (Collections from the Studio of Tea Fragrance). 4 vols. Shanghai: Shanghai guji chubanshe, 1995–99.

———. *Huainan nei pian ping yi* 淮南内篇評議 (A critical commentary on the inner chapters of *Huainanzi*). Reprinted in Hu Daojing et al., eds., *Zangwai daoshu* (q.v.), vol. 3.

———. *Liezi ping yi* 列子評議 (A critical commentary on *Liezi*). Reprinted in Hu Daojing et al., eds., *Zangwai daoshu* (q.v.), vol. 3.

———. *Taishang ganying pian zanyi* 太上感應篇讚義 (A laudatory exposition of the *Taishang ganying*). 1877. Reprinted in Hu Daojing et al., eds., *Zangwai daoshu* (q.v.), vol. 12.

---. *Youtai xianguan biji* 右臺仙館筆記 (Written notes from the Right Altar of the Immortal's Studio). Ji'nan: Qilu shushe, 1986.

---. *Zhuangzi ping yi* 莊子評議 (A critical commentary on *Zhuangzi*). Reprinted in Hu Daojing et al., eds., *Zangwai daoshu* (q.v.), vol. 3.

Yuan Jiegui 袁介珪 and Xu Boying 徐伯英, eds. *Zhonghua xianxue* 中華仙學 (Chinese Immortals' Learning). Taipei: Zhenshanmei chubanshe, 1978.

Zhang Boduan 張伯端. *Jindan sibai zi* 金丹四百字 (Four hundred words on the Golden Elixir). Annot. Huang Ziru 黃自如. In *DZ*, 24: 161–64.

Zhang Junfang 張君房, comp. *Yunji qiqian* 雲笈七籤 (Seven tomes from the Cloud Bookcase). 122 *juan*. In *DZ*, 22: 1–850.

Zhang Sanfeng 張三丰. *Jindan jieyao* 金丹節要 (Essentials of the Golden Elixir). In *Sanfeng danjue* 三丰丹訣 (Master Sanfeng's alchemical secrets). In Fu Jinquan, *Jiyi zi daoshu shiqi zhong* (q.v.). In *ZWDS*, 11: 322–52.

---. *Zhang Sanfeng ji* 張三豐集 (Collected works of Zhang Sanfeng). Ed. Wang Xiling 汪希齡 and Li Hanxu 李涵虛. 1844. Reprinted—Yangzhou: Jiangsu guangli guji keyinshe, 1993.

Zhang Zhuming 張竹銘. *Waidan zhuanji Qinhuo chong guang* 外丹專籍琴火重光 (The outer alchemic treatise *Double Brilliance of the Zither Fire*). Shanghai: Yihuatang, 1938.

Zhao Daoyi 趙道一. *Lishi zhenxian tidao tongjian* 歷世眞仙體道通鑑 (A concordant mirror of the perfected immortals' understanding of the Way of all dynasties). 53 *juan*. In *DZ*, 5: 99–414.

Zhao Youqin 趙友欽. *Xian Fo tongyuan lun* 仙佛同源論 (A treatise on the shared origins of immortals and Buddhas). In Zhu Zaiwei 朱載瑋, ed., *Zhuzhen xuan ao jicheng* 諸眞玄奧集成 (A collection of subtle teachings by the perfected ones). Republished in Songyue zhuren 嵩嶽主人, comp., *Daoshu quanji* 道書全集 (A compendium of Daoist books). 1538. Reprinted—Beijing: Zhongguo shudian, 1990.

Zeng Zao 曾慥. *Qishen lun* 七神論 (Treatise on seven deities). In *Dao shu* 道樞 (The nexus of the Way). 30 *juan*. In *DZ*, 20: 764.

Zhuzhen shengtai shenyong jue 諸眞聖胎神用訣 (Numinous secrets by the perfected men on the divine embryo). In *DZ*, 18: 433–37.

Secondary Sources

Adler, Joseph S. *Yoga in Modern India: The Body Between Science and Philosophy*. Princeton: Princeton University Press, 2004.

Adolph, William Henry. "The History of Chemistry in China." *Scientific Monthly* 14, no. 5 (May 1922): 441–46.

Anderson, Benedict. "The Goodness of Nations." In Peter van der Veer and Hartmut Lebmann, eds., *Nation and Religion: Perspectives on Europe and Asia*. Princeton: Princeton University Press, 1999, pp. 197–204.

———. *Imagined Communities: Reflections on the Origin and Spread of Nationalism*. London: Verso, 1991 (1983).

Andrews, Bridie J. "The Making of Modern Chinese Medicine, 1895–1937." Ph.D. diss., Gonville & Caius College, Cambridge University, 1996.

Baldrian-Hussein, Farzeen. "Inner Alchemy: Notes on the Origin and Use of the Term *neidan*." *Cahiers d'Extrême-Asie* 5 (1989–90): 163–90.

———. "Taoist Beliefs in Literary Circles of the Sung Dynasty—Su Shi (1037–1101) and His Techniques of Survival." *Cahiers d'Extrême-Asie* 9 (1996–97): 15–53.

Ban Gu 班固. *Qian Hanshu* 前漢書 (The book of the Former Han). 100 juan. In *ESWS*, 1: 365–760.

Bazhi heshang 八指和尚 (AKA Jing'an 敬安, 1851–1912). *Bazhi toutuo shiwen ji* 八指頭陀詩文集 (A collection of poems and essays by the Eight-Fingered Monk). Changsha: Yuelu shuyuan, 1984.

Bergère, Marie-Claire. "The Shanghai Bankers' Association, 1915–1927: Modernization and the Institutionalization of Local Solidarities." In Frederic Wakeman, Jr., and Wen-hsin Yeh, eds., *Shanghai Sojourners*. Berkeley: Institute of East Asian Studies, University of California, 1992, pp. 15–34, 305–42.

Berling, Judith A. *A Pilgrim in Chinese Culture: Negotiating Religious Diversity*. Maryknoll, NY: Orbis Books, 1997.

———. *The Syncretic Religion of Lin Chao-en*. New York: Columbia University Press, 1980.

Bokenkamp, Stephen. *Early Daoist Scriptures*. Berkeley: University of California Press, 1997.

Boltz, Judith. *A Survey of Taoist Literature: Tenth to Seventeenth Centuries*. China Research Monograph of Center for Chinese Studies at Institute of East Asian Studies. Berkeley: Institute of East Asian Studies, 1987.

Bray, Francesca. *Technology and Gender: Fabrics of Power in Late Imperial China*. Berkeley: University of California Press, 1997.

Cahill, Suzanne E. *Transcendence and Divine Passion: The Queen Mother of the West in Medieval China*. Stanford: Stanford University Press, 1993.

Chan, Wing-tsit. *Religious Trends in Modern China*. New York: Octagon Books, 1969.

Chen Bing 陳兵. "Qingdai Quanzhen Longmen pai de zhongxing" 清代全真龍門派的中興 (The renaissance of the Longmen lineage of Complete

Perfection Daoism during the Qing dynasty). *Shijie zongjiao yanjiu* 2 (1988): 84–96.

Chen Guofu 陳國符. *Daozang yuanliu kao* 道藏源流考 (A study of the origins and evolution of the Daoist Canon). 2 vols. Beijing: Zhonghua shuju, 1963.

Chen Guying 陳鼓應. *Laozi zhushi ji pingjie* 老子注釋及評介 (Annotations and commentaries on *Laozi*). Beijing: Zhonghua shuju, 1984.

Chen Guying 陳鼓應, ed. *Daojia wenhua yanjiu* 道教文化研究 (Studies of Daoist culture). 17 vols. Shanghai: Shanghai guji chubanshe, 1991–99.

Chen, Kenneth K. S. *Buddhism in China: A Historical Survey.* Princeton: Princeton University Press, 1954.

Chen Menglei 陳夢雷, comp. *Yibu quanlu* 醫部全錄 (A complete compendium of medical classics). 1725. Reprinted—Beijing: Renmin weisheng chubanshe, 1991.

Chen, Nancy. *Breathing Spaces: Qigong, Psychiatry, and Healing in China.* New York: Columbia University Press, 2003.

———. "Cultivating Qi and the Body Politic." *Harvard Asia Pacific Review* 4, no. 1 (2000): 45–49.

Chen Xing 陳星. *Yinshi ruzong Ma Yifu* 隱士儒宗馬一孚 (Ma Yifu: a recluse and a Confucian master). Ji'nan: Shandong huabao chubanshe, 1996.

Chen Yaoting 陳耀庭. *Shanghai Daojiao shi* 上海道教史 (History of Daoism in Shanghai). In Ruan Renze 阮仁澤 and Gao Zengnong 高振農, eds., *Shanghai zongjiao shi* 上海宗教史 (History of religions in Shanghai). Shanghai: Shanghai renmin chubanshe, 1992.

Chen Yinke 陳寅恪. "Tianshi Dao yu binhai diyu zhi guanxi" 天師道與濱海地域之關係 (Celestial Master Daoism and its relation to the coastal regions). *Guoli zhongyang yanjiuyuan, Lishi yuyan yanjiusuo jikan* 國立中央研究院歷史語言研究所集刊 3, no. 4 (1934): 439–66.

Chen Yuan 陳垣. *Daojia jinshi lue gaoben mulu* 道家金石略稿本目錄 (Table of contents for the draft of the *Daoist Stelae and Epigraphical Materials*). N.p.: Ligeng shuwu 勵耕書屋, ca. 1912.

———. "Ji Xu Zuanzeng ke *Taishang ganying pian tushuo*" 記許纘曾刻太上感應篇圖説 (On Illustrated Tract of Taishang on Action and Response carved by Xu Zuanzeng). *Dagong bao tushu fukkan* 大公報圖書副刊, Oct. 22, 1936, p. 153.

Chen Zhonglian 陳仲䋲. "Huainian bofu Chen Yingning" 懷念伯父陳攖寧 (Remembering my uncle Chen Yingning). *Zhongguo Daojiao* 中國道教 2 (May 1989): 19–21.

Chikashige Masumi 近重眞澄. *Tōyō renkinjutsu* 東洋鍊金術 (Alchemy of the Orient). Tokyo: Uchida Rokakuho, 1929.

Clart, Philip, trans. *The Story of Han Xiangzi: The Alchemical Adventures of a Daoist Immortal.* Seattle: University of Washington Press, 2007.
Cleary, Thomas, trans. *Immortal Sisters: Secrets of Taoist Women.* Boston: Shambhala, 1989.
———. *The Way of Harmony and Balance.* Boston: Shambhala, 1996.
Creel, Herrlee G. *What Is Taoism? And Other Studies in Chinese Cultural History.* Chicago: University of Chicago Press, 1970.
Davis, Edward L. *Society and the Supernatural in Song China.* Honolulu: University of Hawai'i Press, 2001.
Davis, Lenny L., and Wu Lu-Ch'iang. "Chinese Alchemy." *Scientific Monthly* 31, no. 3 (Sept. 1930): 225–35.
Dean, Kenneth. *Taoist Ritual and Popular Cults of Southeast China.* Princeton: Princeton University Press, 1993.
Defoort, Carine. *The Pheasant Cap Master: A Rhetorical Reading.* Stonybrook, NY: SUNY Press, 1997.
Deng Jingbin 鄧景濱. "Zheng Guanying de daohao ji xuedao shi nian kao" 鄭觀應的道號及學道始年考 (A study of Zheng Guanying's Daoist sobriquets and his first years of Daoist studies). *Xueshu yanjiu* 學術研究 5 (1996): 71–72.
Despeux, Catherine. *Immortelles de la Chine ancienne: Taoïsme et alchimie féminine.* Paris: Pardès, 1990.
———. *Taoïsme et corps humain: Le Xiuzhen Tu.* Paris: Guy Trédaniel, 1994.
———. *Zhao Bichen: traite d'alchimie et de physiologie Taoïste.* Paris: Les Deux Oceans, 1979.
Dikotter, Frank. *The Discourse of Race in Modern China.* London: Hurst & Co., 1992.
Ding Changyun 丁常雲. "Hai shang Baiyun guan jinxi" 海上白雲觀今昔 (The White Cloud Monastery of Shanghai). *Shanghai wenshi ziliao*, no. 81 (1996): 91, 102–10.
———. "Shanghai Daojiao de chuanru he fazhan" 上海道教的傳入和發展 (The transmission and development of Daoism in Shanghai). *Shanghai wenshi ziliao*, no. 81 (1996): 90–95.
Dongchu 東初. *Zhongguo Fojiao jindai shi* 中國佛教近代史 (A history of modern Chinese Buddhism). Taipei: Zhongguo Fojiao wenhua guan, 1976.
Duara, Prasenjit. *Culture, Power, and the State: Rural North China, 1900–1942.* Stanford: Stanford University Press, 1988.
———. *Rescuing History from the Nation: Questioning Narratives of Modern China.* Chicago: University of Chicago Press, 1995.
———. *Sovereignty and Authenticity: Manchukuo and the East Asian Modern.* Lanham, MD: Rowman & Littlefield, 2003.

Ebrey, Patricia Buckley. *The Inner Quarters: Marriage and the Lives of Chinese Women in the Sung Period*. Berkeley: University of California Press, 1993.
Ebrey, Patricia Buckley, and Peter N. Gregory, eds. *Religion and Society in T'ang and Sung China*. Honolulu: University of Haiwai'i Press, 1993.
Eliade, Mircea. *Yoga: Immortality and Freedom*. 2nd ed. Princeton: Princeton University Press, 1970.
Eskildsen, Stephen. *Asceticism in Early Taoist Religion*. Albany: SUNY Press, 1998.
Esposito, Monica. "Daoism in the Qing." In Livia Kohn, ed., *Daoism Handbook*. Leiden: Brill, 2000, pp. 623–58.
———. "The Discovery of Jiang Yuting's *Daozang jiyao* in Jiangnan: A Presentation of the Daoist Canon of the Qing Dynasty." In Mugitani Kunio 麥谷邦夫, ed., *Kōnan Dōkyō no kenkyū* 江南道教の研究 (Research on Daoism in Jiangnan). Kyoto: Jinbun kagaku kenkyūjo, 2007, pp. 79–110.
———. "L'Ecole Longmen du Mont Jin-gai et ses practiques alchimiques d'après le *Daozang xubian*." Ph.D. diss., University of Paris 7, 1993.
———. "The Longmen School and Its Controversial History During the Qing History." In John Lagerwey, ed., *Religion and Chinese Society*. 2 vols. Hong Kong: Chinese University of Hong Kong Press, 2004, pp. 621–98.
Fan Chunwu 范純武. "Feiluan, xiuzhen yu banshan: Zheng Guanying yu Shanghai de zongjiao shijie" 飛鸞, 修眞與辦善: 鄭觀應與上海的宗教世界 (Flying Pheonix, self-cultivation and philanthropy: Zheng Guanying and the religious world of Shanghai). Paper presented at the International Conference "The City and Chinese Modernity," Academia Sinica, Taipei, 2007.
Fan Lizhu 范麗珠. "Popular Religion in Contemporary China." *Social Compass* 50 (2003): 449–57.
Faure, Bernard. *The Red Thread: Buddhist Approaches to Sexuality*. Princeton: Princeton University Press, 1998.
Feuchtwang, Stephan. *Popular Religion in China: The Imperial Metaphor*. Richmond, Eng.: Curzon Press, 2001.
Fu, Poshek. *Passivity, Resistance, and Collaboration: Intellectual Choices in Occupied Shanghai, 1937–1945*. Stanford: Stanford University Press, 1993.
Fu Qinjia 傅勤家. *Zhongguo Daojiao shi* 中國道教史 (History of Chinese Daoism). Shanghai: Shangwu chubanshe, 1937.
Furth, Charlotte. *A Flourishing Yin: Gender in China's Medical History, 960–1665*. Berkeley: University of California Press, 1999.
———. "Intellectual Change from the Reform Movement to the May Fourth Movement, 1895–1920." In John King Fairbank, ed., *Cambridge*

History of China, vol. 12, Part 1, *Repubican China*. London: Cambridge University Press, 1983, pp. 322–405.

———. "Rethinking van Gulik: Sexuality and Reproduction in Traditional Chinese Medicine." In Christina K. Gilmartin and Gail Hershatter, eds., *Engendering China: Women, Culture and the State*. Cambridge: Harvard University Press, 1994, pp. 125–46.

———. *Ting Wen-chiang: Science and China's New Culture*. Cambridge: Harvard University Press, 1970.

Gernet, Jacques. *Buddhism in Chinese Society: An Economic History from the Fifth to the Tenth Centuries*. Trans. Franciscus Verellen. New York: Columbia University Press, 1995.

Goossaert, Vincent. "Bureaucratic Charisma: The Zhang Heavenly Masters Institution and Court Taoists in Late Qing China." *Asia Major* 17, no. 2 (2004): 121–59.

———. "Counting the Monks: The 1736–1739 Census of the Chinese Clergy." *Late Imperial China* 21, no. 2 (2000): 40–85.

———. "1898: The Beginning of the End for Chinese Religion?" *Journal of Asian Studies* 65, no. 2 (2006): 307–36.

———. "The Quanzhen Clergy, 1700–1950." In John Lagerwey, ed., *Religion and Chinese Society*. 2 vols. Hong Kong: University of Hong Kong Press, 2004, pp. 699–771.

———. "Quanzhen Dao de huandu kao" 全真道的圜堵考 (A study of the practice of seclusion in Quanzhen Daoism). In Lu Guolong 盧國龍, ed., *Quanzhen hongdao ji* 全真弘道集 (An anthology of Quanzhen Daoist proliferation). Hong Kong: Qingsong chubanshe, 2004, pp. 143–56.

———. "Starved of Resources: Clerical Hunger and Enclosures in Nineteenth-Century China." *Harvard Journal of Asiatic Studies* 62, no. 1 (2002): 77–133.

———. *The Taoists of Peking, 1800–1949: A Social History of Urban Clerics*. Cambridge: Harvard University Asia Center, 2007.

Groot, J. J. M. de. *Sectarianism and Religious Persecution in China*. Amsterdam: Johannes Müller, 1904.

Guan Lin 管林. "Zheng Guanying de Daojiao sixiang jiqi yangsheng zhi dao" 鄭觀應的道教思想及其養生之道 (Zheng Guanying's Daoist thought and way of life-cultivation). *Lingnan wenshi* 嶺南文史 2002, no. 4: 5–8.

Guo Pu 郭璞, ed. *Mu Tianzi zhuan* 穆天子傳 (A biography of Sovereign Mu). In *DZ*, 5: 45–47.

Guo Wu 郭武. *Daojiao jiaoyi yu xiandai shehui: Guoji xueshu yantao hui lunwen ji* 道教教義與現代社會：國際學術研討會論文集 (Daoist doctrine and modern society: international symposium proceedings). Shanghai: Shanghai guji chubanshe, 2003.

———. "Lun Chen Yingning zai Daojiao shi shang de diwei" 論陳攖寧在道教史上的地位 (On Chen Yingning's position in Daoist history). *Shanghai Daojiao* 上海道教 1994, no. 15: 1–4.

Guo Xiang 郭向, annot. *Nanhua zhenjing zhushu* 南華眞經注疏 (Annotations to *Nanhua zhenjing*). In *DZ*, 16: 414–23.

Hahn, Thomas. "Chen Yingning: ershi shiji Daojiao dashi" 陳攖寧: 二十世紀道教大師 (Chen Yingning: a Daoist master of the twentieth century). Paper presented at International Symposium on Daoist Liturgy and Music, Hong Kong, 1985.

Han Suyin. *The Morning Deluge: Mao Tsetung and the Chinese Revolution (1893–1954)*. Boston: Little Brown, 1972.

Han Wudi neizhuan 漢武帝內傳 (An inner biography of Emperor Wudi of the Han). In *DZ*, 5: 47–63.

He Jianming 何建明. "Chen Yingning de jipian zhongyao yiwen jiqi sixiang" 陳攖寧的幾篇重要佚文及其思想 (A few important lost essays by Chen Yingning and their thinking). *Zhongguo Daojiao* 中國道教 2008, no. 2: 23–27.

Herrou, Adeline. *La vie entre soi: les moines taoïstes aujourd'hui en Chine*. Nanterre: Société d'Ethnologie, 2005.

Hong Jianlin 洪建林, ed. *Xianxue jiemi: Daojia yangsheng miku* 仙學解秘: 道家養生秘庫 (Unlocking the secrets of immortals' learning: a secret treasure of Daoist life-cultivation). Dalian: Dalian chubanshe, 1991.

Honig, Emily. *Creating Chinese Ethnicity: Subei People in Shanghai, 1850–1980*. New Haven: Yale University Press, 1992.

———. *Sisters and Strangers: Women in the Shanghai Cotton Mills, 1919–1949*. Stanford: Stanford University Press, 1986.

Hou Jie 侯傑. "Jindai Daojiao xianxue de kaituo zhe: Chen Yingning" 近代道教仙學的開拓者—陳攖寧 (Chen Yingning: a trailblazer in modern Daoist Immortals' Learning). *Hongdao* 宏道 2001, no. 1: 17–20.

Hou Jie 侯傑 and Qin Fang 秦方. *Nannü xingbie de shuangchong bianzou: yi Chen Yingning he Lü Bicheng weili* 男女性別的雙重變奏: 以陳攖寧和呂碧城爲例 (An alternating duet of gender: the case of Chen Yingning and Lü Bicheng). *Shanxi shifan daxue xuebao* 山西師範大學學報 30, no. 3 (July 2003): 118–22.

———. "Zheng Guanying yu jindai Daojiao chuyi" 鄭觀應與近代道教芻議 (A preliminary discussion of Zheng Guanying and modern Daoism). *Hongdao* 宏道 2004, no. 18: 14–19.

Hu Fuchen 胡孚琛. *Wei Jin shenxian Daojiao* 魏晉神仙道教 (Divine immortals' Daoism of the Wei-Jin era). Beijing: Renmin chubanshe, 1991.

———. *Wei Jin shenxian Daojiao: "Baopu zi neipian" yanjiu* 魏晉神仙道教: 抱樸子內篇研究 (Daoism of the divine immortals during the Wei-Jin period: a study of the inner treatise of the Master Who Embraces Simplicity). Beijing: Renmin chubanshe, 1989.

Hu Haiya 胡海牙. "Chen Yingning xiansheng xianxue lilun chutan" 陳攖寧先生仙學理論初探 (Preliminary explorations into the theories of Master Chen Yingning's Immortals' Learning). 3 pts. *Shanghai Daojiao* 上海道教 2000, no. 2: 24–25; no. 3: 12–15; and no. 3: 23–25.

———. "Mianhuai laoshi Chen Yingning" 緬懷老師陳攖寧 (In memory of my teacher Chen Yingning). *Zhongguo Daojiao* 中國道教 1989, no. 4 (1989): 8–10.

———. "Mianhuai xianshi Chen Yingning" 緬懷先師陳攖寧 (In memory of my late teacher Chen Yingning). Unpublished manuscript, 1994.

Hu Haiya 胡海牙, ed. *Xianxue zhinan: Chen Yingning xianxue xilie congshu* 仙學指南:陳攖寧仙學系列叢書 (A guide to Immortals' Learning: a series of Chen Yingning's Immortals' Learning). Beijing: Zhongyi guji chubanshe, 1998.

Hu Haiya 胡海牙 and Wu Guozhong 武國忠. "Yangshan banyue kan" "Xiandao yuebao" quanji 揚善半月刊仙道月報全集 (Complete collection of *Yangshan Biweekly* and *Xiandao Monthly*). Beijing: Quanguo tushuguan weisuo fuzhi zhongxin, 2006.

———. *Zhonghua xianxue yangsheng quanshu: Chen Yingning xiansheng dui jiankang changshou xueshuo de dute gongxian* 中華仙學養生全書:陳攖寧先生對健康長壽學説的獨特貢獻 (A complete collection of Chinese immortals' learning: Master Chen Yingning's unique contribution to the scholarly learning of health and longevity). 3 vols. Beijing: Huaxia chubanshe, 2006.

Hu Shi 胡適. "Hanchu Ru Shi Dao zhi zheng" 漢初儒釋道之爭 (Contentions among the Ruists, Buddhists, and Daoists in the early Han dynasty). 1925. Reprinted in idem, *Hu Shi wencun sanji* 胡適文存三集 (Writings by Hu Shi, vol. 3); and in *Minguo congshu, diyi bian* 民國叢書第一編 (Compendia of Republican books, ser. 1), vol. 95. Shanghai: Shanghai shudian, 1989, pp. 879–83.

———. "Tao Hongjing de *Zhengao* kao" 陶弘景的眞誥考 (A study of Tao Hongjing's *True Memorials*). 1933. Reprinted in idem, *Hu Shi lunxue jin zhu* 胡適論學近著 (Recent works on scholarship by Hu Shi); and in *Minguo congshu, di yi bian* 民國叢書第一編 (Compendia of Republican books, ser. 1), vol. 96. Shanghai: Shanghai shudian, 1989, pp. 155–76.

Huaining difang zhi bianzuan weiyuanhui 懷寧地方誌編纂委員會, comp. *Huaining xianzhi* 懷寧縣志. Hefei: Huangshan shushe, 1996.

Huang Changlun 黃常倫. *Fangwai laihong: jinxiandai gaoseng zhi Gao Henian jushi shuxin shouji* 方外來鴻:近現代高僧致高鶴年居士書信手跡 (Geese from outside the world: handwritten notes and letters addressed to the lay practitioner Gao Henian by contemporary senior Buddhist masters). Beijing: Zongjiao wenhua chubanshe, 2002.

Huang Kewu 黃克武. "Minguo chunian Shanghai de lingxue yanjiu: yi 'Shanghai lingxue' hui weili" 民國初年上海的靈學研究: 以"上海靈學會"爲例 (The psychical science studies of early Republican Shanghai: the case of the Shanghai Psychical Research Society). *Zhongyang yanjiu yuan Jindaishi yanjiusuo jikan* 中央研究院近代史研究所集刊 2007, no. 55: 99–136.

Huang Yanli 黃嫣梨. "Cong Xu Can dao Lü Bicheng: Qingdai funü sixiang yu diwei de zhuanbian" 從徐燦到呂碧城: 清代婦女思想與地位的轉變 (From Xu Can to Lü Bicheng: the transformation in thought and status of the late Qing women). *Lishi yu wenhua* 歷史與文化 1998, no. 1: 33–43.

Huang Zhaohan 黃兆漢. *Daojiao yanjiu lunwenji* 道教研究論文集 (A collection of research essays on Daoism). Hong Kong: Hong Kong Chinese University Press, 1988.

Hui Dong 惠棟. *Taishang ganying pian jianzhu* 太上感應篇簡注 (A brief annotation to *Tract of Taishang on Action and Response*). 1750. Reprinted in Hu Daojing et al., eds., *Zangwai daoshu* 藏外道書 (q.v.), vol. 12.

Hymes, Robert. *Way and Byway: Taoism, Local Religion, and Models of Divinity in Sung and Modern China.* Berkeley: University of California Press, 2002.

Jian Bozhan 翦伯贊, ed. *Wuxu bianfa* 戊戌變法 (The 1898 Reform Movement). Zhongguo jindai shi ziliao congkan 中國近代史資料叢刊 (Collection of materials on modern Chinese history). Shanghai: Shanghai renmin chubanshe, 1953.

Jiang Jianyuan 蔣見元. "Li Bai yu Daojiao" 李白與道教 (Li Bai and Daoism). In Chen Guying, *Daojia wenhua yanjiu* (q.v.), vol. 4 (1994).

Jin Zhengyao 金正耀. *Daojiao yu kexue* 道教與科學 (Daoism and science). Beijing: Zhongguo shehui kexueyuan chubanshe, 1990.

Johnson, Obed Simon. *A Study of Chinese Alchemy.* Shanghai: Commercial Press, 1928.

Kaltenmark, Max. *Lao Tzu and Taoism.* Trans. Roger Greaves. Stanford: Stanford University Press, 1969.

Katz, Paul. *Images of the Immortal: The Cult of Lü Dongbin at the Palace of Eternal Joy.* Honolulu: University of Hawai'i Press, 1999.

———. "The Religious Life of a Renowned Shanghai Businessman and Philanthropist: Wang Yiting 王一亭." Paper presented at the international conference "The City and Chinese Modernity." Taipei: Academia Sinica, 2007.

Katz, Paul, and Murray A. Rubinstein, eds. *Religion and the Formation of Taiwanese Identities.* New York: Palgrave Macmillan, 2003.

Kieschnick, John. *The Eminent Monk: Buddhist Ideals in Medieval Chinese Hagiography*. Studies in East Asian Buddhism, 10. Honolulu: University of Hawai'i Press, 1997.
Kohn, Livia. "Guarding the One: Concentrative Meditation in Taoism." In idem, ed., *Taoist Meditation and Longevity Techniques* (q.v.), pp. 125–58.
———. "Taoist Insight Meditation: The Tang Practice of Neiguan." In idem, ed., *Taoist Meditation and Longevity Techniques* (q.v.), pp. 193–224.
Kohn, Livia, ed. *Daoism Handbook*. Leiden: Brill, 2000.
———. *The Taoist Experience: An Anthology*. Albany, New York: SUNY Press, 1993.
———. *Taoist Meditation and Longevity Techniques*. Michigan Monographs in Chinese Studies, vol. 61. Ann Arbor: Center for Chinese Studies, University of Michigan, 1989.
Kuriyama Shigehisa. *The Expressiveness of the Body and the Divergence of Greek and Chinese Medicine*. New York: Zone Books, 1999.
Lagerwey, John. *Taoist Ritual in Chinese Society and History*. New York: Macmillan, 1987.
Lagerwey, John, ed. *Religion and Chinese Society*, vol. 2, *Taoism and Local Religion in Modern China*. Hong Kong: Chinese University of Hong Kong Press, 2004.
Lai Chi-tim 黎志添. *Guangdong difang Daojiao yanjiu: Daoguan, Daoshi ji keyi* 廣東地方道教研究: 道觀, 道士及科儀 (Guangdong local Daoism: Daoist temples, masters, and ritual). Shatin, Hong Kong: Chinese University of Hong Kong Press, 2007.
Lai Chi-tim 黎志添, ed. *Daojiao yanjiu yu Zhongguo zongjiao wenhua* 道教研究與中國宗教文化 (Daoist studies and Chinese religious culture). Hong Kong: Zhonghua shuju, 2003.
Leibold, James. "Competing Narratives of Racial Unity: From the Yellow Emperor to Peking Man." *Modern China* 32, no. 2 (Apr. 2006): 181–220.
Li Baomin 李保民, ed. *Lü Bicheng ci jian zhu* 呂碧城詞箋注 (Annotations to the rhymed verses by Lü Bicheng). Shanghai: Shanghai guji chubanshe, 2001.
Li Rui 李銳. *The Early Revolutionary Activities of Comrade Mao Tse-tung*. 1957. Trans. Anthony W. Sariti. White Plains, NY: M. E. Sharpe, 1977.
Li Shiyu 李世瑜. "Tianjin Zaili jiao diaocha yanjiu" 天津在理教調查研究 (Researches on Zaili sect of Tianjin). *Minjian zongjiao* 民間宗教 1996, no. 2: 169–210.
Li Yangzheng 李養正. "Chen Yingning xianxue de tezheng, lilun he fangfa" 陳攖寧仙學的特徵, 理論和方法 (The characteristics, theory and methods of Chen Yingning's Immortals' Learning). *Zhongguo Daojiao* 中國道教 1989, no. 3: 9–17.

———. "Lun Chen Yingning ji suo tichang Xianxue 論陳攖寧及所提倡仙學 (On Chen Yingning and his promotion of Immortals' Learning). In idem, ed., Daojiao yu yangsheng (q.v.), pp. 444–78.
Li Yangzheng, ed. Dangdai Daojiao 當代道教 (Contemporary Daoism). Beijing: Dongfang chubanshe, 2000.
———. Dangdai Zhongguo Daojiao, 1949–1992 當代中國道教 1949–1992 (Daoism in contemporary China). Beijing: Zhongguo shehui kexue chubanshe, 1993.
———. Daojiao yu yangsheng 道教與養生 (Daoism and life-cultivation). Beijing: Huawen chubanshe, 1989.
———. Xinbian Beijing Baiyun guan zhi 新編北京白雲觀志 (New gazetteer of the White Cloud Monastery in Beijing. Beijing: Zongjiao wenhua chubanshe, 2003.
Li Zhiyong 李志庸. Zhongguo qigong shi 中國氣功史 (History of Chinese qigong). Zhengzhou: Henan kexue jishu chubanshe, 1988.
Lin Zuojia 林作嘉. "Qing mo Min chu miaochan xingxue zhi yanjiu" 清末民初廟產興學之研究 (A study of the expropriation of temple properties for establishing schools in the late Qing and early Republican periods). M.A. thesis, Tunghai University, Taichung, 2000.
Liu Shipei 劉師培. "Du Daozang ji" 讀道藏記 (Notes on reading the Daoist Canon). In DZJHL.
Liu Ts'un-yan 柳存仁. Buddhist and Taoist Influence on Chinese Novels, vol. 1. Wiesbaden: Otto Harrassowitz, 1962.
———. Daojiao shi tanyuan 道教史探源 (Explorations in the history of Daoism). Beijing: Beijing daxue chubanshe, 2000.
———. Daojia yu Daoshu: Hefengtang wenji xubian 道家與道教：和風堂文集續編 (Daoism and Daoist techniques: supplement to Papers from the Hall of Harmonious Wind). Shanghai: Shanghai guji chubanshe, 1999.
———. Selected Papers from the Hall of Harmonious Wind. Leiden: E. J. Brill, 1976.
Liu, Xun 劉迅. "Cultivating the Self and Saving the Nation: Lay Urban Practice, Print Culture, Community of Daoist Inner Alchemy in Early Republican Shanghai." Bulletin of the Institute of Modern History, forthcoming.
———. "Immortals and Patriarchs: The Daoist World of a Manchu Official and His Family in Nineteenth Century China." Asia Major 17, no. 2 (2004): 161–218.
———. "General Zhang Buries the Bones: Early Qing Reconstruction and Quanzhen Collaboration in Mid-Seventeenth Century Nanyang." Late Imperial China 27, no. 2 (2006): 67–98.

———. "Scientizing the Body for the Nation: Chen Yingning and the Reinvention of Daoist inner alchemy in 1930s Shanghai." In David Palmer and Xun Liu, eds., *Daoism in the Twentieth Century: Between Eternity and Modernity*, forthcoming.

———. "Visualizing Perfection: Daoist Paintings, Court Patronage, and Elite Female Piety in the Late Qing." *Harvard Journal of Asiatic Studies* 64, no. 1 (2004): 57–115.

Liu Yan'gang 劉延剛. "Chen Yingning xianxue sixiang de xiandai xing tedian" 陳攖寧仙學思想的現代性特點 (The characteristics of the modernity of Chen Yingning's Immortals' Learning thought). *Shehui kexue yanjiu* 社會科學研究 2004, no. 3: 70–72.

———. *Chen Yingning yu Daojiao wenhua de xiandai zhuanxing* 陳攖寧與道教文化的現代轉型 (Chen Yingning and the modern transformation of the Daoist culture). Chengdu: Bashu shushe, 2006.

Loewe, Michael. *Ways to Paradise: The Chinese Quest for Immortality*. Boston: George Allen & Unwin, 1979.

Lu Guolong 盧國龍. *Zhongguo chongxuan xue* 中國重玄學 (The "Double Mystery" in China). Beijing: Renmin Zhongguo chubanshe, 1993.

Lu Guolong 盧國龍, ed. *Quanzhen hong dao ji: Quanzhen dao: Chuancheng yu kaichuang guoji xueshu yantaohui lunwen ji* 全真弘道集. 全真道: 傳承與開創國際學術研討會論文集 (A collection of Complete Perfection for promulgating the Way. Complete Perfection Daoism: tradition, transmission, and innovation: international symposium proceedings). Hong Kong: Qingsong chubanshe, 2004.

Luo Hongxian 羅洪仙. *Wanshou xian shu* 萬壽仙書 (Immortals' book for longevity of ten thousand years). Reprinted—Beijing: Zhongyi guji chubanshe, 1993.

Luo Weiguo 羅偉國. *Fozang yu Daozang* 佛藏與道藏 (The Buddhist and Daoist canons). Shanghai: Shanghai shudian, 2001.

Luo Yonglin 羅詠麟. *Zhongguo xianhua yanjiu* 中國仙話研究 (Studies in Chinese immortal lore). Shanghai: Shanghai wenyi chubanshe, 1993.

Ma Duanlin 馬端臨. *Wenxian tongkao* 文獻通考 (A concordance of literature). Vol. 125 in *Shi tong* 十通 (The ten concordances). Reprinted—Taipei: Shangwu yinshu guan, 1987.

Ma Guangren 馬廣仁, ed. *Shanghai xinwen shi* 上海新聞史, 1850–1949 (A history of newspapers in Shanghai, 1850–1949). Shanghai: Fudan daxue chubanshe, 1996.

Ma Jingquan 馬鏡泉, ed. *Ma Yifu ji* 馬一孚集 (An anthology of Ma Yifu's works). 3 vols. Hangzhou: Zhejiang guji chubanshe, 1996.

Ma Jiren 馬繼人. *Shiyong yixue qigong cidian* 實用醫學氣功辭典 (A practical dictionary of medicine and *qigong*). Shanghai: Shanghai kexue jishu chubanshe, 1989.
Ma Jixing 馬繼興. *Mawangdui gu yishu kaoshi* 馬王堆古醫書考釋 (An expository study of the ancient medical books from Mawangdui). Changsha: Hunan keji chubanshe, 1992.
Mann, Susan. *Precious Records: Women in China's Long Eighteenth Century.* Stanford: Stanford University Press, 1997.
Meng Naichang 孟乃昌. "*Zhouyi Cantongqi*" kaobian 周易參同契考辨 (Investigative studies of *Zhouyi Cantongqi*). Shanghai: Shanghai guji chubanshe, 1993.
Meng Yue. "The Invention of Shanghai: Cultural Passages and Their Transformation, 1860–1920." Ph.D. diss., University of California, Los Angeles, 2000.
Mori Yuria 森由利亞. "Jūkan *Dōzō shūyō* to Shinchō Shisen chiiki no shūkyō" 重刊『道藏輯要』と清朝四川地域の宗教 (The republication of *Daozang jiyao* and religion in the Sichuan region during the Qing dynasty). In Okazaki Yumi 岡崎由美, ed., *Chūgoku koseki ryūtsūgaku no kakuritsu: ryūtsū suru koseki, ryūtsū suru bunka* 中國古籍流通學の確立: 流通する古籍・流通する文化 (The establishment of the studies of ancient Chinese classical texts: ancient texts and culture in circulation). Tokyo: Yuzankaku, 2007, pp. 339–401.
Naquin, Susan. *Millenarian Rebellion in China: The Eight Trigrams Uprising of 1813.* New Haven: Yale University Press, 1976.
———. *Peking: Temples and City Life, 1400–1900.* Berkeley: University of California Press, 2000.
———. *Shantung Rebellion: The Wang Lun Uprising of 1774.* New Haven: Yale University Press, 1981.
Naquin, Susan, and Yü Chün-fang. *Pilgrims and Sacred Sites in China.* Berkeley: University of California Press, 1992.
Nedostup, Rebecca A. "Religion, Superstition, and Governing Society in Nationalist China." Ph.D. diss., Columbia University, 2001.
Needham, Joseph. *Chemistry and Chemical Technology. Spagyrical Discovery and Invention: Historical Survey, from Cinnabar Elixir to Synthetic Insulin.* In idem, ed., *Science and Civilisation in China*, vol. 5, pt. 3. London: Cambridge University Press, 1976.
———. *Chemistry and Chemical Technology. Spagyrical Discovery and Invention: Magisteries of Gold and Immortality.* In idem, ed., *Science and Civilisation in China*, vol. 5, pt. 2. London: Cambridge University Press, 1974.

———. *Chemistry and Chemical Technology. Spagyrical Discovery and Invention: Physiological Alchemy*. In idem, ed., *Science and Civilisation in China*, vol. 5, pt. 5. London: Cambridge University Press, 1983.

Orliski, Constance. "Re-imagining the Domestic Sphere: Bourgeois Nationalism and Gender in Shanghai, 1904–1918." Ph.D. diss, University of Southern California, 1999.

Overmyer, Daniel L. "From 'Feudal Superstition' to 'Popular Beliefs': New Directions in Mainland Chinese Studies of Chinese Popular Religion." *Cahiers d'Extrême-Asie* 12 (2001): 103–26.

Palmer, David A. *Qigong Fever: Body, Science, and Utopia in China*. New York: Columbia University Press, 2007.

———. "Tao and Nation: Li Yujie's Appropriation of Huashan Taoism." Paper presented at the International Symposium "Between Eternity and Modernity: Taoist Tradition and Transformation in Twentieth Century China," Harvard University, 2006.

Pan Xianlian 潘先連. "Zhuming Daojiao xuezhe Chen Yingning yishi" 著名道教學者陳攖寧軼事 (Stories about the famous Daoist scholar Chen Yingning). *Jianghuai wenshi* 江淮文史 1995, no 5: 87–89.

Qian Shifu 錢實甫. *Qingdai zhiguan nianbiao* 清代職官年表 (Chronology of Qing officials). 4 vols. Beijing: Zhonghua shuju, 1980.

Qing Xitai 卿希泰, ed. *Zhongguo Daojiao shi* 中國道教史 (History of Chinese Daoism). 4 vols. Chengdu: Sichuan renmin chubanshe, 1988–95.

Ren Jiyu 任繼愈, ed. *Zhongguo Daojiao shi* 中國道教史 (History of Daoism in China). Shanghai: Shanghai renmin chubanshe, 1989.

Ren Zhen 任真. "Duan Zhengyuan yu Daode xueshe" 段正元與道德學社 (Duan Zhengyuan and the Morality Learning Institute). In Yang Zibin 楊子彬, ed., *Guoxue lunheng* 國學論衡 (Forum on national learning). Lanzhou: Dunhuang chubanshe, 1998.

Renmin tiyu chubanshe 人民體育出版社, ed. *Qigong jingxuan* 氣功精選 (Essential selections on *qigong*). Beijing: Renmin tiyu chubanshe, 1984.

Robinet, Isabelle. "Original Contribution of Neidan to Taoism and Chinese Thought." In Kohn, ed., *Taoist Meditation and Longevity Techniques* (q.v,), pp. 297–331.

———. "Recherche sur l'alchimie intérieure (*neidan*): l'école Zhenyuan." *Cahiers d'Extrême-Asie* 5 (1989–90): 141–62.

———. *Taoism: Growth of a Religion*. Stanford: Stanford University Press, 1997.

———. *Taoist Meditation: The Mao-shan Tradition of Great Purity*. Albany: SUNY Press, 1993.

Rogaski, Ruth. *Hygienic Modernity: Meanings of Health and Disease in Treaty-Port China*. Berkeley: University of California Press, 2007.

Sakai Tadao 酒井忠夫. "Daoyuan de yan'ge" 道院的沿革 (The evolution of the morality centers). *Minjian zongjiao* 民間宗教 1997, no. 3: 93–150.

———. *Kindai Shina ni okeru shūkyō kessha no kenkyū* 近代支那に於ける宗教結社の研究 (Studies on popular religious societies in modern China). Tokyo: Tōa kenkyūjo, 1944.

———. "Minguo shiqi zhi xinxing zongjiao yundong yu xin shidai chaoliu" 民國時期之新興宗教運動與新時代潮流 (The new religious movements and new epoch currents of the Republican era). *Minjian zongjiao* 民間宗教 1995, no. 1: 1–36.

Schafer, Edward H. *The Divine Woman: Dragon Ladies and Rain Maidens in T'ang Literature*. San Francisco: North Point Press, 1980.

Schipper, Kristofer. *The Taoist Body*. Trans. Karen C. Duval. Berkeley: University of California Press, 1993.

Schipper, Kristofer, and Franciscus Verellen, eds. *The Taoist Canon: A Historical Companion to the Daozang*. 3 vols. Chicago: University of Chicago Press, 2005.

Schram, Stuart. *The Thought of Mao Tse-tung*. Cambridge: Cambridge University Press, 1989.

Schwartz, Benjamin. *In Search of Wealth and Power*. Cambridge: Belknap Press of Harvard University Press, 1964.

Seaman, Gary. *Journey to the North: An Ethno-historical Analysis and Annotated Translation of the Chinese Folk Novel "Pei-yu chi."* Berkeley: University of California Press, 1987.

Seidel, Anna. "Chronicle of Taoist Studies in the West, 1950–1990." *Cahiers d'Extrême-Asie* 5 (1989–90): 223–347.

Shanghai zongjiao zhi bianzuan weiyuanhui 上海宗教志編纂委員會, ed. *Shanghai zongjiao zhi* 上海宗教志 (Gazetteer of religions in Shanghai). Shanghai: Shanghai shehui kexue yuan chubanshe, 2001.

Shaw, Miranda. *Passionate Enlightenment: Women in Tantric Buddhism*. Princeton: Princeton University Press, 1994.

Shen Zengzhi 沈增植. "Yang jushi taming" 楊居士塔銘 (An inscription to the stupa of Lay Master Yang). In Min Erchang 閔爾昌, comp., *Beizhuanji bu* 碑傳集補 (Supplements to the *Collection of Steles and Inscriptions*). Reprinted in Shen Yunlong 沈雲龍, ed., *Jindai Zhongguo shiliao congkan* 近代中國史料叢刊 (Compendia of modern Chinese historical materials). Series 100. Taipei: Wenhai chubanshe, 1966, pp. 2052–55.

Shi Xuming 釋續明. *Taixu dashi shengping shiji* 太虛大師生平事跡 (Life and career of Grand Master Taixu). Taipei: Haichaoyin yuekan she, 1957.

Shryock, John. *The Temples of Anking and Their Cults: A Study of Modern Chinese Religion*. Paris: Librairie Orientaliste Paul Geuthner, 1931.

Sibu congkan chubian jibu 四部叢刊初編集部 (A compendium of the four treasures, ser. 1, collectania). Reprinted—Shanghai: Shangwu yinshu guan, 1965.

Skar, Lowell. "Golden Elixir Alchemy: The Formation of the Southern Lineage of Taoism and the Transformation in Medieval China." Ph.D. diss., University of Pennsylvania, 2003.

Smith, Richard J. *Fortune-tellers and Philosophers: Divination in Traditional Chinese Society*. Boulder, CO: Westview Press, 1991.

Song Shugong 宋書功, comp. *Zhongguo gudai fangshi yangsheng jiyao* 中國古代房室養生輯要 (An anthology of essentials on life-cultivation in the bedchamber in ancient China). Beijing: Zhongguo yiyao keji chubanshe, 1991.

Sun Simiao 孫思邈. *Qian jin yi fang* 千金翼方 (Supplementary formulas worth a thousand gold). 682. Reprinted—Shanghai: Shanghai guji chubanshe, 1999.

Taixu 太虛. *Taixu zizhuan* 太虛自傳 (Autobiography of Taixu). 1939. Reprinted—Singapore: Nanyang foxue shuju, 1971.

Tan Songlin 譚松林, ed. *Zhongguo mimi shehui* 中國秘密社會 (Chinese secret societies). Fuzhou: Fujian renmin chubanshe, 2002.

Tian Chengyang 田誠陽. "Chen Yingning xianxue xiulian fayao" 陳攖寧仙學脩鍊法要 (Essentials of Chen Yingning's Immortals' Learning cultivation methods). 19 pts. *Wuhun* 武魂 1996, nos. 6–12; 1997, nos. 1–12.

Tian Chengyang 田誠陽, ed. *Xianxue xiangshu: Zhonghua Daojia xiulian zhushu xilie zhiyi* 仙學詳述:中華道家脩鍊著述系列之一 (Expositions of Immortals' Learning: Chinese Daoist writings on self-cultivation, no. 1). Beijing: Zongjiao wenhua chubanshe, 1999.

Tsui, Bartholomew Pui Ming. *Taoist Tradition and Change: The Story of the Complete Perfection Sect in Hong Kong*. Hong Kong: Christian Study Center on Chinese Religion and Culture, 1991.

Unschuld, Paul U. *Medicine in China: A History of Pharmaceutics*. Berkeley: University of California Press, 1986.

Valussi, Elena. "Beheading the Red Dragon: A History of Female Alchemy in China." Ph.D. diss., School of Oriental and African Studies, University of London, 2002.

van der Veer, Peter. *Religious Nationalism: Hindus and Muslims in India*. Berkeley: University of California Press, 1994.

van der Veer, Peter, and Hartmut Lehmann, eds. *Nation and Religion: Perspectives on Europe and Asia*. Princeton: Princeton University Press, 1999.

van Gulik, R. H. *Erotic Colour Prints of the Ming Period with an Essay on Chinese Sex Life from the Han to the Ch'ing Dynasty, B.C. 206–A.D. 1622*. Leiden: E. J. Brill, 1951.

―――. *Sexual Life in Ancient China*. Leiden: E. J. Brill, 1961.
Wan Shiguo 萬仕國. *Liu Shipei nianpu* 劉師培年譜. Yangzhou: Guangling shushe, 2003.
Wang Hui. "Differentiation of Knowledge, Reform of Education and the Study of Metaphysics: A Re-examination of Zhang Junmai and the Debate on 'Science and Outlook of Life.'" University of California, Los Angeles, conference paper, 1994.
Wang Jianchuan 王見川. "Qingmo de taijian, Baiyun guan yu Yihe tuan yundong" 清末的太監, 白雲觀與義和團運動 (Eunuchs, the White Cloud Monastery, and the Boxer movement in the late Qing). *Taiwan zongjiao yanjiu tongxun* 台灣宗教研究通訊 7 (2005): 123–56.
―――. "Tongshan she zaoqi lishi chutan" 同善社早期歷史初探 (A preliminary study of the early history of the Common Benevolence Society). *Minjian zongjiao* 民間宗教 1995, no. 1: 57–81.
Wang Jianchuan 王見川 and Fan Chunwu 范純武. "Qing mo Min chu Beijing luan tang de ge an yanjiu: Qingyun tan ji qi lishi" 清末民初北京鸞堂的個案研究: 青雲壇及其歷史 (A case study of the spirit-writing altar in late Qing and early Republican Beijing: the Azure Cloud Altar and its history). *Minjian zongjiao* 民間宗教 1996, no. 2: 261–80.
Wang Jianzhang 王建章 (z. Kentang 肯堂; 1645–1718). *Xianshu miku* 仙術秘庫 (A secret storehouse of immortals' techniques), *juan* 2, in *DZJH*, ser. 4, no. 4.
Wang Jianzhang 王建章 and Jing Xingshao 景星杓. *Lidai shenxian shi* 歷代神仙史 (A history of divine immortals of all the dynasties). 1693. Reprinted—Shanghai: Jiangyou shulin, 1920.
Wang Jiayou 王家祐. *Daojiao lun gao* 道家論稿 (Essays on Daoism). Chengdu: Bashu chubanshe, 1987.
Wang Leiquan 王雷泉. "Dui Zhongguo jindai liangci miaochan xingxue fengchao de fansi" 对中国近代两次庙产兴学风潮的反思 (Reflections on the two waves of expropriating temple properties to establish schools in modern China). *Fayin* 法音 1994, no. 12: 14–19.
Wang Ming 王明. *Taiping jing hejiao* 太平經合校 (The Great Peace Scriptures, joint collation). Beijing: Zhonghua shuju, 1992 (1960).
Wang Mu 王沐. *Wuzhen pian qian jie* 悟眞篇淺解 (An easy exposition of *Treatise on Intuiting Perfection*). Beijing: Zhonghua shuju, 1990.
Wang Quchang 王蘧常. *Yan Jidao nianpu* 嚴幾道年譜 (A biographic chronology of Yan Jidao). 1935. Reprinted in Shen Yunlong 沈雲龍, ed., *Jindai Zhongguo shiliao congkan xubian di shiba ji fu* 近代中國史料叢刊續編第十八輯附 (Supplements to *Compendia of Modern Chinese Historical Materials*, ser. 18). Taipei: Wenhai chubanshe, 1975, pp. 1–138.

Wang, Richard (Wang Gang 王崗). "Four Steles at the Monastery of Sublime Mystery (Xuanmiao guan): A Case Study of Daoism and Society on the Ming Frontier." *Asia Major* 13, no. 2 (2000): 37–82.

———. "Mingdai wanghou yu Daojiao guanxi tanjiu: yi Lanzhou he Kunming weili" 明代王侯與道教關係探究：以蘭州和昆明爲例 (A study of the relationship between the Ming princes and Daoism: the cases of Lanzhou and Kunming). In Lai Chi-tim, ed., *Daojiao yanjiu yu Zhongguo zongjiao wenhua* (q.v.), pp. 125–212.

Wang Shizhen 王世貞 (1526–90). *Youxiang liexian quan zhuan* 有像列仙全傳 (Illustrated complete biographies of all the immortals). 1590. Reprinted—Taipei: Xuesheng shuju, 1989.

Wang Wenji 王文濟. *Fang Gongpu yi'an* 方公溥醫案 (Medical cases by Fang Gongpu). Shanghai: n.p., n.d.

Wang Zhizhong 王志忠. *Ming Qing Quanzhen jiao lun gao* 明清全眞教論稿 (Collection of essays on Quanzhen Daoism of the Ming and Qing eras). Chengdu: Bashu shushe, 2000.

Wang Zuyuan 王祖源, ed. *Nei gong tu shuo* 內功圖説 (An illustrated treatise on Inner Practice). N.p.: privately printed, 1881.

Weber, Max. *From Max Weber: Essays in Sociology*. Ed. and trans. H. H. Gerth and C. Wright Mills. New York: Oxford University Press, 1946.

Wei Yungong 魏允恭. *Jiangnan zhizao ju ji* 江南制造局記 (A record of the Jiangnan Arsenal). Shanghai: Wenbao shuju, 1905.

Welch, Holmes. *The Buddhist Revival in Modern China*. Cambridge: Harvard University Press, 1968.

———. *The Practice of Chinese Buddhism*. Cambridge: Harvard University Press, 1967.

———. *Taoism: The Parting of the Way*. Boston: Beacon Press, 1957.

Welch, Holmes, and Anna Seidel, eds. *Facets of Taoism: Essays in Chinese Religion*. New Haven: Yale University Press, 1979.

Weller, Robert P. *Unities and Diversities in Chinese Religion*. Seattle: University of Washington Press, 1987.

Weller, Robert, and Meir Shahar, eds. *Unruly Gods: Divinity and Society in China*. Honolulu: University of Haiwai'i Press, 1996.

Wile, Douglas, trans. *The Art of the Bedchamber: The Chinese Sexual Yoga Classics Including Women's Solo Meditation Texts*. Albany: State University of New York Press, 1992.

Wilhelm, Richard, trans. *The Secret of the Golden Flower*. 1931. Reprinted—San Diego: Harcourt Brace Jovanovich Publishers, 1962.

Wu Dazhen 吳大振. "Chen Yingning de nüdan xiuxian sixiang chutan" 陳攖寧的女丹修仙思想初探 (A preliminary study of Chen Yingning's thinking on female alchemic self-cultivation). *Hunan keji xueyuan xuebao* 27, no. 4 (2006): 131–33.

Wu Yakui 吳亞魁. "Chen Yingning de Daojia guan" 陳攖寧的道家觀 (Chen Yingning's perspective on Daoist philosophers). In Chen Guying, ed., *Daojia wenhua yanjiu* (q.v.), vol. 20 (2003): 519–27.

———. "Chen Yingning de shengping he sixiang" 陳攖寧的生平和思想 (Chen Yingning's life and thoughts). *Dangdai zongjiao yanjiu* 當代宗教研究 1990, no. 2: 20–27.

———. "Chen Yingning yu jindai Daojiao" 陳攖寧與近代道教 (Chen Yingning and Modern Daoism). *Shanghai Daojiao* 上海道教 1996, no. 4: 7–9.

———. *Jiangnan Quanzhen Daojiao* 江南全真道教 (Quanzhen Daoism in Jiangnan). Hong Kong: Zhonghua shuju, 2006.

———. "Lun Yangshan banyue kan" 論揚善半月刊. In Chen Guying, ed., *Daojia wenhua yanjiu* (q.v.), no. 19 (1996): 462–76.

———. *Shengming de zhuiqiu: Chen Yingning yu jin xiandai Zhongguo Daojiao* 生命的追求：陳攖寧與近現代中國道教 (In search of life: Chen Yingning and Daoism in modern China). Shanghai: Shanghai cishu chubanshe, 2005.

Wu, Yao-yü. *The Taoist Tradition in Chinese Thought*. Trans. Laurence G. Thompson and Gary Seaman. Los Angeles: Enthnographics Press, Center for Visual Anthropology, University of Southern California, 1991.

Wu Yufu 伍餘福. *You Magu shan ji* 游麻姑山記 (Travelogue of Lady Ma Mountain). In Wu Qiushi 吳秋士, ed., *Tianxia mingshan ji* 天下名山記 (A record of famous mountains in the realm), in *DZJY*, *zhen ji* 軫集, 3.40a–41a.

Xiao Tianshi 蕭天石. *Daojia yangshengxue gaiyao* 道家養生學概要 (Essentials of Daoist life-cultivation learning). Taipei: Ziyou chubanshe, 1963.

Xiao Tong 蕭統 (Zhaoming taizi 昭明太子). *Wenxuan* 文選 (Selections of literary classics). Ca. 689. Annot. Li Shan 李善. Reprinted—Beijing: Zhonghua shuju, 1977.

Xu Dishan 許地山. *Daojiao shi shangbian* 道教史上編 (History of Daoism, vol. 1). Shanghai: Shangwu yinshu guan, 1934.

———. "Daojia sixiang yu Daojiao" 道家思想與道教 (Daoist thought and Daoist religion). *Yanjing xuebao* 燕京學報 2 (Feb. 1927): 249–82.

Xuanzhuang 玄奘, trans. *Apidamo jushe lun bensong* 阿比達摩俱舍論本頌. Harvard-Yenching Library.

Yamada, Toshiaki 山田利明. "Longevity Techniques and Compilation of the *Lingbao wufu*." In Kohn, ed., *Taoist Meditation and Longevity Techniques* (q.v.), pp. 99–124.

Yang, C. K. *Religion in Chinese Society*. Berkeley: University of California, 1961.

Yang, Mayfair, ed. *Religion, Modernity and the State in China*. Berkeley: University of California Press, forthcoming.

Yang Ming 陽明. *Daojiao yangshengjia: Lu Xixing yu tade Fanghu waishi* 道教養生家: 陸西星與他的方壺外史 (Daoist life-cultivator: Lu Xixing and his *Fanghu waishi*). Chengdu: Sichuan daxue chubanshe, 1995.

Yao Shuliang 姚樹良. "Shanghai Baiyun guan shi" 上海白雲觀史 (A history of the White Cloud Monastery in Shanghai). In Shanghai shi Daojiao xiehui 上海市道教協會, ed., *Shanghai Daojiao wenhua tansuo* 上海道教文化探索 (Explorations into the Daoist culture of Shanghai). Shanghai: Shanghai Daojiao xiehui, 2001, pp. 223–39.

Ye Xiaoqing. *The Dianshizhai Pictorial: Shanghai Urban Life, 1884–1898*. Ann Arbor: Center for Chinese Studies, University of Michigan, 2003.

Yin Zhihua 尹志華. "Chen Yingning de xianxue sixiang" 陳攖寧的仙學思想 (Chen Yingning's thoughts on Immortals' Learning). *Zongjiao xue yanjiu* 宗教學研究 2000, no. 1: 21–24, 130.

Ying Lianzhi 英斂之. "Lü shi san zimei ji xu" 呂氏三姊妹集序 (Preface to the Three Lü sisters' compendium). In Li Baomin, ed., *Lü Bicheng ci jian zhu* (q.v.), p. 524.

Yu, Anthony, trans. *Journey to the West*. Chicago: University of Chicago, 1977.

Yü Chün-fang. *Kuan-yin: The Chinese Transformation of Avalokiteśvara*. New York: Columbia University Press: 2001.

Yu Zhongjue 余仲珏. *Jindai Daojia gongfa daoshi: Chen Yingning xiansheng zhuanlue* 近代道家功法導師: 陳攖寧先生傳略 (A brief biography of Chen Yingning, a great master of modern Daoist practices). Shanghai: Yihuatang, 1988.

Zeng Zhaonan 曾召南. "Daoshi Fu Jinquan sixiang shulue" 道士傅金銓思想述略 (A brief account of Daoshi Fu Jinquan's thought). In Chen Guying, ed., *Daojia wenhua yanjiu* (q.v.), vol. 9 (1996): 177–89.

———. "Lun Daoshi Fu Jinquan" 論道士傅金銓 (On the Daoist Fu Jinquan). Paper presented at International Symposium on Daoism and Daoist Culture, Chengdu, 1994.

Zhan Shichuang 詹石窗. *Daojiao wenxue shi* 道教文學史 (A history of Daoist literature). Shanghai: Shanghai wenyi chubanshe, 1992.

Zhan Shouzhen 詹壽禎 (1). "Anqing Daoguan de jianzao yu chuanshuo" 安慶道觀的建造與傳說 (Anqing Daoist temples: their construction and legends). *Anqing wenshi zhiliao* 安慶文史資料, no. 25 (Aug. 1994): 108–10.

———. "Anqing gexian Daojiao gongguan mingcheng" 安慶各縣道教宮觀名稱 (Names of the Daoist temples in various counties of Anqing). *Anqing wenshi ziliao* 安慶文史資料, no. 25 (Aug. 1994): 112.

Zhan Shouzhen 詹守真 (2). "Anqing Daojiao tanzhu ji keshi" 安慶道教壇主及客師 (Daoist altar masters and their assistants in Anqing). *Anqing wenshi ziliao* 安慶文史資料, no. 25 (Aug. 1994): 116–18.

Zhang Ertian 張爾田. "Yang Renshan jushi biezhuan" 楊仁山居士別傳 (A biography of lay master Yang Renshan). In Min Erchang 閔爾昌, comp., *Beizhuanji bu* 碑傳集補 (Supplements to the *Collection of Steles and Inscriptions*). Reprinted in Shen Yunlong 沈雲龍, ed., *Jindai Zhongguo shiliao congkan* 近代中國史料叢刊 (Compendia of modern Chinese historical materials), series 100. Taipei: Wenhai chubanshe, pp. 2045–52.

Zhang Guangbao 張廣保. "Ming Qing neidan sichao yu Chen Yingning xuepai de xianxue" 明清內丹思潮與陳攖寧學派的仙學 (Intellectual currents in inner alchemy of the Ming and Qing periods and the Immortals' Learning of the Chen Yingning school). *Zongjiao xue yanjiu* 宗教學研究 1997, no. 4: 21–29.

Zhang Heng 張衡. *Xijing fu* 西京賦 (Ode to the Western Capital). In Xiao Tong 蕭統 comp., *Wenxuan* 文選 (Selections from literary classics), vol. 2. Shanghai: Shanghai guji chubanshe, 1986.

Zhang Wenjiang 張文江 and Chang Jin 常近, eds. *Zhongguo chuantong qigong xue cidian* 中國傳統氣功學辭典 (A dictionary of Chinese traditional *qigong*). Taiyuan: Shanxi renmin chubanshe, 1989.

Zhang Zhongli 張仲禮 et al. *Jindai Shanghai chengshi yanjiu* 近代上海城市研究 (Studies of modern urban Shanghai). Shanghai: Shanghai renmin chubanshe, 1990.

Zhao Heng 趙恒. *Ji Zhenzong huangdi yu zhi xiantian ji* 紀真宗皇帝禦製先天紀敘 (An imperially prepared narrative record of the Primordial Heaven). In *DZ*, 22: 674–84.

Zhao Shiyu 趙世瑜. *Kuanghuan yu richang: Ming Qing yilai de miaohui yu minjian shehui* 狂歡與日常：明清以來的廟會與民間社會 (Carnivals and the quotidian: temple fairs and local society since the Ming and Qing). Beijing: Sanlian shudian, 2002.

Zhao Taiding 趙臺鼎. *Mowang* 脈望 (A gaze at the meridians). 8 vols. In *ZWDS*, 9: 603–720.

Zheng Guanying 鄭觀應. *Shengshi weiyan houbian* 盛世危言後編 (Alarming words for prosperous times). 3 vols. Reprinted in Li Yushu 李毓澍, ed., *Jindai shiliao congshu huibian diyi ji* 近代史料叢書彙編第一輯 (Collections of modern historical materials, ser. 1). Taipei: Datong shuju, 1968, pp. 1–244.

Zhongguo shehui kexue yuan, Daojiao yanjiu shi 中國社會科學院道教研究室 (Section of Daoist Research, Chinese Academy of Social Sciences), ed. *Zhongguo Daojiao yanjiu luncong* 中國道教研究論叢 (Collected papers on Chinese Daoist studies). Beijing: Zhongguo shehui kexue yuan chubanshe, 1993.

Zhou Yumin 周育民. "Minguo shiqi yige wentan juzi jibi xia de lingjie" 民國時期一個文壇巨子乩筆下的靈界 (The divine realm under the spirit-writing pen of a literary giant of the Republican era). *Minjian zongjiao* 民間宗教 1995, no. 1: 37–56.

Zhou Yuqing. "The Heart and the Temple: Mapping Female Religiosity in Late Imperial China, 1550–1900." *Late Imperial China* 24, no. 2 (2003): 109–55.

Zito, Angela, and Tani E. Barlow, eds. *Body, Subject and Power in China*. Chicago: University of Chicago Press, 1994.

Index

Ai Langxuan 艾朗軒, 269, 336n
Alcazar of Darkness (xuan que 玄闕), 103
altar (tan 壇), 42–43, 322n
altar master (tan zhu 壇主), 43
Ancient Ways of the Sages (shengxian gudao 聖賢古道), 234
Anhui Advanced College (Anhui gaodeng xuetang 安徽高等學堂), 45, 294n
Anhui Provincial Advanced College of Law and Politics (Anhui gaodeng fazheng xuetang 安徽高等法政學堂), 48, 294n
Annotations to Sun Bu'er's Poem on Female Alchemy (Sun Bu'er nüdan shizhu 孫不二女丹詩注), 87–88, 91, 112, 299n, 301–4n, 314n, 325n, 328n
anqiao 按蹻, 280
Anqing 安慶, 41–46, 48, 67, 74, 177, 293n, 295n
anshi baoquan 按時保全, 192
Anyang 安陽, 122, 226, 312n, 326n

Aperture of Essence (jing qiao 精竅), 304n
application of the Way (dao zhi yong 道之用), 120
application(s) (yong 用), 33, 116, 119, 144
atemporal (xiantian 先天), 63, 91–96, 98, 110, 112, 118–19, 142, 147, 151, 153, 158–59, 162–68 passim, 217, 223–24, 297–98n, 300n, 303n
atemporal qi (xiantian qi 先天氣), 63, 91–93, 95, 118, 142, 151, 153, 163–68 passim, 216–17, 223–24, 300n
at-home or hearth Daoist ritual specialists (huoju daoshi 火居道士), 42–43, 195, 204, 293n

baduan jin 八段錦, 280
Bai Shi 白石, 202, 320–21n
baihui 百會 (Hundred Convergences), 112
bairi feisheng 白日飛升, 77
bai yuan 白元 (White Origin), 101

Bai Yuchan, or White Jade Toad 白玉蟾, 45, 133–35, 307n
Baiyun guan 白雲觀, see White Cloud Monastery
Ban Chao 班超, 63, 297n
bangong bandu 半工半讀, 211
Baoguang dong 寶光洞, 259, 334n
bao shen 保身, 239
baozhong shouyi 抱中守一, 226
ba su 八素, see Eight Pure Ones
bedchamber arts or techniques (fangzhong shu 房中術), 13, 152, 154, 311n
Beijing 北京, 15, 30, 35, 37, 51, 56–62 passim, 65, 67, 70, 75, 78, 81, 88, 178, 180, 197, 278–79, 295–96n, 300n, 305–6n, 321n, 334n
Beizong 北宗, 143, 307n. See also (Daoist) Northern School; Northern Lineage
bian 變, 29
Bian Que 扁鵲, 28
biguan 閉關, see self-enclosure
Biographies of the Divine Transcendents (Shenxian zhuan 神仙傳), 45, 137, 157, 308–9n, 311–12n, 315n
biqian 鄙淺, 4
Biweekly to Promote the Good (Yangshan banyue kan 揚善半月刊), 7–8, 16, 275, 281, 286n, 304–7n, 311–12n, 316n, 318–35n passim, 338n; links to body cultures, 81, 84, 87, 90; involvement in inner alchemic practice, 122, 124, 130, 137; roles in building inner alchemic self-cultivation community, 174, 181–82, 185–87, 189, 192–96, 199, 206, 208–12, 216, 221, 224, 229–30, 257–65 passim; Daoist print culture, 231, 233, 238; ties to Immortals' Learning, Buddhism, and science, 241, 243, 247–49, 252
Blood-sucking Ghosts (xueshi zhi gui 血食之鬼), 140
Body of Phenomena (seshen 色身), 85
Book of Changes (Zhouyi 周易), 13, 200, 243, 318n
Book of Metamorphosis (Huashu 化書), 92, 302n
Boxer Uprising or Rebellion, 5, 21
Brain Marrow (naosui 腦髓), 111–13
Bridge of Encounters with Immortals (Huixian qiao 會仙橋), 136, 309n
Bright Hall (ming tang 明堂), 109–10
Bud, or Stalk, of Life (ming di 命蒂), 303n
Buddhist Canon (Da zangjing 大藏經), 30, 55
Buddhist Monthly, The (Foxue yuebao 佛學月報), 80
Buddhist Study Society (Foxue yanjiuhui 佛學研究會), 30
Buddhist Transformation Monthly (Fohua yuekan 佛化月刊), 247
building the foundation (zhu ji 築基), 168
bu mian lunhui 不免輪回, 247
bu pin 補品, 150. See also replenishing ingredients

cai bu 採補, 154. See also sexual-gathering practices
Cai Dejing 蔡德淨, 240

Cai E 蔡鍔, 287n
Cai Jimin 蔡積民, 263, 335n
Cai Jing 蔡京, 136–37, 308–9n
Cai Qiliang 蔡啓良, 207
cai yao 採藥, 168
canchan 參禪, 84
Canon on Problematic Cases (*Nanjing* 難經), 46
Cantongqi 參同契, 101, 104, 126, 173–74, 213, 301n, 304n, 307n
Cao Heng 曹珩, 36, 139, 190, 291n, 309n, 318n
Cao Hongxun 曹鴻勳, 209
Cao Huanyang 曹還陽, 186, 286n, 317n
Cao Wenyi 曹文逸, 92–93, 303n
Cao Xiyun 曹希蘊 (h. Daochong 道沖), 302n
Cauldron and Furnace (*dinglu* 鼎爐), 187, 224, 317n
Ceasing the gaze (*zhi guan* 止觀), 79
Celestial Masters (Tianshi 天師), 11, 290n
Center (or Central) Cinnabar Field (*zhong dantian* 中丹田), 188–89, 317n
Central Daoist Association (Zhongyang Daojiao hui 中央道教會), 56, 79–80, 296n
Chamber of Essence (*jing shi* 精室), 304n
Chan 禪, 82, 161, 258, 289n
Chang, Eileen 張愛玲, 2, 3, 6, 10, 285n
Chang Zunxian 常遵先 (h. Xiaoxiang yufu 瀟湘漁父), 7–8, 10, 14, 286n, 315–18n, 328n; early travels, 182–84; *Yangshan* and *Xiandao* journals, 185–86; roaming and poem exchanging, 187–91; cultivation community, 192, 195, 229; print culture, 237, 241
changcun 長存, 231
chang jin 長筋, 214
Changping 昌平, 58
chaofan rusheng 超凡入聖, 31
chaoren zhexue 超人哲學, *see* Transcendents' or Supermen's philosophy (*chaoren zhexue* 超人哲學)
chaotuo 超脱, 231
chaotuo gongfu 超脱功夫, 169, 314n
Chen Chengkai 陳誠凱, 256, 260, 331n
Chen Jingbo 陳鏡波, 44
Chen Mingbin 陳明霦, 56–57
Chen Nan 陳楠, 307n
Chen Qubing 陳去病, 70
Chen Tiehai 陳鐵海, 206–9, 336n
Chen Tuan 陳摶, 313n
Chen Wuxuan 陳悟玄, 218–19, 220–26, 324–26n, 333–34n
Chen Yingning 陳攖寧, 1, 6, 8–10, 14–19, 21, 23, 39–40; early life and career, 41–48; Buddhist reforms, 48–49, 51, 53–57; on female inner alchemy, 59–67; marriage to Wu Yizhu, 67–68; outer alchemy and spirit writing, 70–76; on body, antiquity, nationalism, and science, 77–121 *passim*; on practice techniques, 122–30, 142–72 *passim*; inner alchemic community, 173–81, 185–86, 191, 193–96, 199–210 *passim*; personal correspondences on self-cultivation, 210–29 *passim*, 256–65, 267–71;

editorial work and role in inner alchemic print culture, 231–32, 236–40; defining and promoting the Immortals' Learning, 241–55, 273–81, 286n, 289–90n, 293–338n passim
Chen Yinke 陳寅恪, 31, 290n
Chen Yuan 陳垣, 31, 290n
Chen Zhixu 陳致虛, 143, 304
Cheng Xuanying 成玄英, 12
Cheng Yuanru 程淵如 (h. Puyi zi 溥一子), 332–33n
cheng jindan shengtai 成金丹聖胎, 130
cheng xian 成仙, 168
chi hun 吃葷, 148
Chinese Academy of Immortals' Learning (Zhonghua xianxue yuan 中華仙學院), 263
Chinese Daoist Association (Zhongguo Daojiao xiehui 中國道教協會), 278–79, 281
Chinese National Daoist Association (Zhonghua quanguo Daojiao hui 中華全國道教會), 330n, 336n
chi su 吃素, 148
chi zhou 持咒, 84
chongxuan 重玄, 161, 308n. See also Double Mystery
chuangzao 創造, 232
chujia 出家, 157
Chunqian daoren 純乾道人, 130–31, 306n
Chunyang daoyuan 純陽道院, 43
chu shen 出神, 168. See also Parturition of the Yang Spirit
chushi yinyuan 出世因緣, 134
ciji shenjing 刺激神經, 152

City God Temple (Yimiao 邑廟), 70, 195, 201, 321n
Clear Stream (qing liu 清流), 202, 320n
Collection of the Immortals' Way, The (Xiandao congshu 仙道叢書), 237
Common Benevolence Society (Tongshan she 同善社), 26, 58, 65, 75, 80, 162, 193, 197, 296n
Complete Perfection (Quanzhen 全眞), see Quanzhen (Daoism)
Concealed Immortals school (Yinxian pai 隱仙派), 294n
Conception Channel (renmai 任脈), 106–7, 109
conglin 叢林, 50
Contemplative (Chan 禪) school, 82
Converging Yin (huiyin 會陰), 107
Crimson Palace (jiang gong 絳宮), 109
Cui Xifan 崔希範, 165
cun xiang 存想, 111, 314n. See also visualization or visualizing

dacheng yipian 打成一片, 168
Dadi Grotto (Dadi dong 大滌洞), 209
Dagong bao 大公報, 59–60
dahai laozhen 大海撈針, 130
dai du 待度, 66
dajing dading 大靜大定, 162
danbai zhi 蛋白質, 148. See also diet or diets
Dandao kejing hui 丹道刻經會, 238, 328n
Dao ben wuxiang 道本無相, 171

Daodejing 道德經, 118, 124, 289n, 305n, 313n, 331n. See also *Laozi* 老子
Daode xueshe 道德學社, 26, 296n
Daoist Canon (Daozang 道藏), 29, 31, 36–37, 49–51, 55, 72, 125, 178, 233, 236, 242–43, 291–92n, 295n
Daoist Dining Club (Xuanlü jucan hui 玄侶聚餐會), 269, 337n
Daoist Learning (*Daojiao zhi xueshu* 道教之學術, 道學), 16, 19, 30, 37, 44–45, 63, 67, 72, 129, 132, 192, 201, 232, 236, 239, 242–43, 280, 328n
Daoist Learning of the Yellow Emperor and Laozi (*Huang Lao zhi xue* 黃老之學), 44
Daoist Learning Series, The (*Daoxue congshu* 道學叢書), 237
(Daoist) Northern school (Beipai 北派), 154, 294n
(Daoist) Southern school (Nanpai 南派), 294n
Daoist technologies (*Dao shu* 道術), 23
Daoist Western school or lineage (Xipai 西派), 15, 291n
Daojia 道家, 90, 288n, 338n
Daojiao 道教, 90, 338n
Daojiao de jingshen 道教的精神, 279
Daojiao de xingshi 道教的形式, 280
Daojiao de xueshu 道教的學術, 280
Daojiao yu yangsheng 道教與養生, 286n, 293–99n, 306n, 310n, 321n, 337n
Daojiao zhi xueshu 道教之學術, 19
Daojia wenhua 道家文化, 114
Daojia xueshu 道家學術, 239

Daojia xueshu zhi quanti 道家學術之全體, 243
daolü 道侶, 68, 138
daoshi 道士, 8
Daotong dacheng 道統大成, 291n, 326n
Dao xin he qi 道心和氣, 186
Daoxue congshu 道學叢書, 237
Daoxue xiao congshu 道學小叢書, 236, 328n
daoyin 導引, 4, 280
daoyou 道友, 138, 258, 292n, 315n, 317n, 333n
daoyuan 道院, 26, 288n, 322n
Daozang 道藏, see Daoist Canon
Daozang jiyao 道藏輯要, 286n, 292n
Dao zhi jingjie 道之境界, 119
Dao zhi ti 道之體, 120
Dao zhi yong 道之用, 120
Daozu 道祖, 207
Dark Bosom (*xuan ying* 玄膺), 109–10, 304n
Dark Nether (*xuan ming* 玄冥), 104
Da zangjing 大藏經, 30. See also Buddhist Canon
Dead and dull sitting (*si dazuo* 死打坐), 167
Deluded beliefs (*mixin* 迷信), 4, 52
Deng Yucang 鄧雨蒼 (z. Jimin 濟民), 135–37, 197–99, 239–40, 308–9n
Deutsch Medical College (Tongji dewen yixuetang 同濟德文醫學堂), 181–82, 236
dianzi 電子, 117, 253
diaocha 調查, 238, 300n
dideng dongwu 低等動物, 118
diet or diets, 46, 148–51, 315n; dietary (regimen), 25, 124, 147–

51, 212; dietetics, 149, 151, 310n, 318n
Ding Fubao 丁福寶 (h. Shouyi zi 守一子), 37, 162, 292n
Ding Wenjiang 丁文江, 33
Discourse on the Aperture of the Way (*Daoqiao tan* 道竅談), 240, 328n
Divine Efficacy (*shen tong* 神通), 43, 169, 171
Divine Effulgence (*shen guang* 神光), 104
Divine Fire, 106
Divine Fluid (*shen shui* 神水), 92–93, 302n
Divine Immortals (*shenxian* 神仙), 4, 89–90, 98, 116, 152, 156, 160, 168, 201, 203, 242, 245
Divine Realm (*shenzhou* 神州), 75, 189–90, 318n
Divine Transcendents (*shenxian jia* 神仙家), 66, 89, 91, 94
di yuan 地元, 70, 307n. See also Three Origins
Di yuan zhenjue 地元眞訣, 45
Dong nüshi 董女士, see Miss Dong
dongtian fudi 洞天福地, 140, 309n, 334n. See also Grotto Heavens and Blessed Lands
Double Mystery (*chongxuan* 重玄), 134, 161, 308n
Double Pass (*shuang guan* 雙關), 108
Drug ingestion, or taking drugs (*fushi* 服食), 4, 137, 217, 243, 280
Dual Lords of Water (*liangbu shuizhu* 兩部水主), 103
duanyu 斷欲, 152
Du Guangting 杜光庭, 140, 206–7, 259, 309n
dumai 督脈, 106

duoluo jingjie 墮落境界, 119
duo shui 多睡, 150
du qi 毒氣, 143. See also noxious *qi*
Dutian Cloister (Dutian miao 都天廟), 205

Eight-Fingered monk (Bazhi heshang 八指和尚, Jing'an 敬安), 49
Eight Pure Ones (*ba su* 八素), 111
Embryonic breathing (*taixi* 胎息), 102. See also Fetal breathing
Empty Void (*xu kong* 虛空), 115, 252
Essence (*jing* 精), 86–87, 92, 96, 152, 161, 192, 215, 223, 303n, 327n
Essence and Psyche, 102
Essence and Spirit, 215
Essence, *qi*, and the Psyche (*jing qi shen* 精氣神), 86–87, 115, 274
Explorations in Oral Secrets (*Koujue gouxuan lu* 口訣鉤玄錄), 87, 124, 302n, 305–6n

fajie 法界, 85
Fan Yunqiao 樊雲翹, 156–58, 312n
Fan Zengxiang 樊增祥, 60
fang cun 方寸, 102, 317n
Fang Gongpu 方公溥, 201, 240, 320n
Fangnei sanren 方内散人 (AKA Wan Ligeng 萬立賡), 23, 70, 131–32, 134–35, 306–7n, 329n
fang sheng 放生, 193
fangshi 房事, 152
fangyu 方語, 31
fang zhong 房中, 154
fangzhong shu 房中術, 13
feibu zhi gong 肺部之宮, 101

fei zhenshi 非真實, 84–85
fellow cultivators (of the Way) or companions of the Way (*daolü* 道侶), 68, 126, 132, 138, 145–46, 154, 160, 172, 174–76, 181, 258, 266–67, 309n
female inner alchemy, 61, 65, 128, 203–4, 220–21, 223, 225, 260, 262, 298n, 325n
Feng Yuxiang 馮玉祥, 123
feng zhi 風痣, 150
fenzi 分子, 117
fetal breathing (*taixi* 胎息), 98, 319n
Fire of the Heart (*xinhuo* 心火), 103–4, 106, 318n
Firing (moment) (*huo hou* 火候), 86, 112, 165, 185–86, 223, 258, 313n
Firing Furnace (*huo lu* 火爐), 164
Five Classics (*Wujing* 五經), 44
Five Great Techniques of Health and Self-cultivation or *Five Great Cultivation Methods Toward Health* (*Wu da jiankang xiulian fa* 五大健康修煉法), 213–14, 313n, 323n, 332n
Five Orifices (*wu qiao* 五竅), 104
Five Peck of Rice sect, 289n
Five Phases (*wuxing* 五行), 13, 97, 100–101, 103
Five Viscera and (or) Six Orbs (*wuzang liufu* 五臟六腑), 98–101, 103
Form and Substance (*xingzhi* 形質), 171–72
Four Books (*Sishu* 四書), 44
Foxue yanjiuhui 佛學研究會, 30
Foxue yuan 佛學院, 37

Frontal descent and (the) back ascent (*qianjiang housheng* 前降後升), 106, 325n; Front descent (Yang Fire) and the back ascent (Yin Talisman), 224
fufu shuangxiu 夫婦雙修, 156
fu jing mu luan 父精母卵, 118
Fu Jinquan 傅金銓, 36, 223, 287n, 291n, 309n
Fu Qinjia 傅勤家, 31, 285n, 290n
Fu Qiu 浮邱, 308n
Fu Shan 傅山, 141, 309n
fulu 符籙, 4
funds (*cai* 財), 122, 124, 143–47, 173, 207–8, 219, 228–29, 234, 238–40, 259, 333n
fu shi 服食, 4, 217

gai liang yinshi 改良飲食, 148
Gaizhu Mountain 蓋竹山, 259, 334n
ganguo 干果, 149
ganliang zhi jinye 甘涼之津液, 106
Gao Guanru 高觀如, 200, 240, 328n
Gao Henian 高鶴年 (z. Yeren 野人, h. Yinshi 隱士), 54–55, 295n
Gao Rentong 高仁峒, 58
Gao Yaofu 高堯夫, 70, 173–74, 315n, 328n
gaodeng dongwu 高等動物, 118
gaoren yishi 高人異士, 132
Gate of Life (*mingmen* 命門), 97, 108, 319n
Gate of Nativity (*shenmen* 神門), 96–97, 103
gathering the elixir (*cai yao* 採藥), 40, 168
Ge Hong 葛洪, 12, 45, 140, 157, 308–9n, 311–12n, 315n

gen bei 艮背, 190, 318n
gen zhi 艮止, 190, 318n
General Daoist Association of China (Zhonghua Daojiao zonghui 中華道教總會), 267, 336n
generative qi (sheng qi 生氣), 104, 142, 160, 167
gestation of the embryo (jie tai 結胎), 168
Gnomes of the Rock and the Wood (mushi zhi jing 木石之精), 140
Golden Elixir (jindan 金丹), 71, 130, 258, 310n, 317n
gong 汞, 224
Gong Zizhen 龔自珍, 178
gongde 功德, 67
gong deng Penglai 共登蓬萊, 258
Grafting techniques (zai jie 栽接), 217
Gradual Advance method(s) or approach (huanjin fa 緩進法), 168, 170
Great Compendium of the Golden Fire, A (Jinhuo dacheng 金火大成), 331n
Grotto Heavens and Blessed Lands, or Grottoes and Blessed Sites (dongtian fudi 洞天福地), 140, 142, 171, 173, 191, 334n
gu 骨, 98
gudao 孤島, 9
gu shenxian fengfan 古神仙風範, 156
guan 關, 107. See also Passes
Guan Lihua 管理化, 208, 322n
Guangcheng zi 廣成子, 89, 242, 329n

guanli tuan 管理團, 238
guanyuan 關元, 96
guardians of the Law or the Way (hufa hudao 護法護道), 144, 155
guest adepts (ke shi 客師), 43
gufa xiulian 古法脩煉, 155
guiyi 皈依, 231
Guo Pu 郭璞, 300n, 308n, 324n
guomin genxing 國民根性, 27
guyin guayang 孤陰寡陽, 156
gymnastics (daoyin 導引), 4, 13, 163, 214

haishi sike 亥時四刻, 313n
Haiyan Temple (Haiyan si 海嚴寺), 55
Hall of Practicing Benevolence (Xishan tang 習善堂), 136, 196, 198–99
Han Kang 韓康, 173, 175, 315n
Han Sanwu 韓三悟 (h. Sanwu daoren 三悟道人), 209–10, 322n
han ti 寒體, 149. See also ti zhi
haojie 浩劫, 267
Hardoon Gardens 哈同花園, 54–55, 295n
He Jisong 何濟松, 206
He Longxiang 賀龍驤, 223, 286n, 298n, 325n, 328n
Heart Deity (xinshen 心神), 96, 99, 100–101. See also Psyche of the Heart
Heart Fire (xin huo 心火), 190
Heart-to-Heart Method of One (yiguan xinfa 一貫心法), 213
Heel Breathing (zhong xi 踵息), 194, 319n

Hengyun sheng 衡雲生 (A Disciple of Mount Heng's Cloud), 187–88, 191, 317–18n
Hidden Moon Heaven (yan yue tian 偃月天), 188–89
Higashi Honganji 東本願寺, 38, 83
Hinayana or Small Vehicle Buddhism (Xiaosheng Fojiao 小乘佛教), 301n
Holding to the Center and Keeping to the One (baozhong shouyi 抱中守一), 226
Hong Tai'an 洪太庵 (h. Wanxin 萬馨), 302n, 313n, 323–24n, 328n, 331–32n; quiet sitting, 163–64; journey of search, 212–15, 255–57; correspondences, 216–18; print culture, 240
Hong Ya 洪崖, 134, 217–18, 308n, 323–24n
Hongzhen township (Hongzhen xiang 洪鎮鄉), 41
houtian 後天, 91. See also temporal or postnatal
houtian qi 後天氣, 95
houtian shengming quan 後天生命權, 162
houtian zhuojing 後天濁精, 153
Hu Chun 胡椿, 44
Hu Haiya 胡海牙, 262, 277, 286n, 306n, 316n, 334n, 338n
Hu Shi 胡適, 31, 290n
Hu Yuanjun 胡遠濬 (z. Yuanru 淵如, h. Tianfang sanren 天放散人), 44–45, 48, 333n
Hu Yunchang 胡允昌, 40, 292n
hua fu 畫符, 45
hua gai 華蓋, 101

Huang Chanhua 黃懺華 (z. Canhua 燦華), 299n, 302n, 310n, 320n, 328n, 330n; outer alchemy, 69–70, 72; cultivation community, 177, 199
Huang Daxian 黃大仙, 206
Huang Faqian 黃發千, 197–98
Huang Lao zhi xue 黃老之學, 44
Huang Shang 黃裳 (z. Yuanji 元吉), 124–25, 253, 305n
Huang Suizhi 黃邃之 (AKA Huang Sui 黃邃), 23, 287n, 299n, 301n, 307n, 315n; outer alchemy, 70, 173–74
Huang Youkuan 黃有寬, 197–98
Huang Ziru 黃自如, 165
Huangdi neijing 黃帝內經, 46, 303n
huangting 黃庭, 96. See also Yellow Courtyard
Huangting jing jiangyi 黃庭經講義, see Lectures on the Yellow Courtyard Scriptures
huanjin fa 緩進法, 168
huanjing bunao 還精補腦, 112
huan qi 換氣, 214
huan wang 幻妄, 114
hua qi zhi jing 化氣之精, 152
Huayan Seminary (Huayan daxue 華嚴大學), 55–56, 65, 295–96n
hufa hudao 護法護道, 144
Hui Dong 惠棟, 30, 289n
huiyin 會陰, see Converging Yin
Hundred Convergences (baihui 百會), 112
hunling 魂靈, 96
huo hou 火候, 186. See also Firing (moment)
huohuan 活環, 139. See also san huan

huoju daoshi 火居道士, *see* at-home or hearth Daoist specialists
huo ziwu 活子午, 166
Hushang sou 湖上叟 (Old Man on the Lake), 188, 317n
huxi 呼吸, 13

Immortals' Learning, or Transcendents' Learning (*xianxue* 仙學), 4, 8, 16, 18–19, 72, 273–74, 276, 280–81, 321n, 330n; body cultures, 87, 89–90, 113, 116, 119–20; quiet sitting, 163; cultivation community, 177, 180, 195–96, 199, 201, 203–4, 206, 210, 213, 257, 263–64, 269, 271; print culture, 231–32; Immortals' Learning, Buddhism, and science, 241–52 *passim*
Immortal's raft (*xian cha* 仙槎), 55
Immortals' techniques (*xianshu* 仙術), 129
Immortals' Way (*xiandao* 仙道), 68, 102, 122, 172, 211, 229, 244, 266–67, 330n
Immortals' Way Monthly, or *Xiandao Monthly* (*Xiandao yuebao* 仙道月報), 8–9, 16, 275, 281, 286n, 306n, 315n, 317n, 319n, 322n, 324n, 328–29n, 331–33n, 335–38n; body cultures, 87, 136, 186–87; inner alchemy community, 196, 208, 210, 251, 255, 257, 265–67, 270–71; print culture, 233, 241
inner alchemist(s), 36, 88–89, 94, 100, 115, 124, 131–32, 138–40, 143, 148, 153, 158, 160, 165–66, 170, 174, 178, 182, 190, 218, 240, 253, 259, 264, 275, 291n, 306n, 317n, 324n
inner alchemy (*neidan* 內丹), 1, 6–21 *passim*, 35–36, 39–41, 57, 70, 72, 286n, 288n, 290–91n, 298–99n, 301n, 303–4n, 307n, 309–10n, 317–19n, 323–26n, 329n, 331n, 333n; female inner alchemy, 61, 64–66; body cultures, 78–79, 87, 89–90, 94–97, 106–7, 113–14, 116, 121; method, funds, fellowship, and locale, 122–26, 128–32, 135–46 *passim*; practice paths, 147–48, 151–60 *passim*, 163, 165, 168, 171–72; cultivation community, 174–77, 181, 184–96 *passim*, 200, 203–4, 207–8, 210–27 *passim*, 255–71 *passim*; print culture, 231–41 *passim*; Immortals' Learning, Buddhism, and science, 242, 246–55 *passim*, 274–76
Inner Canon of the Yellow Emperor, The (*Huangdi neijing* 黃帝內經), 46, 98, 192, 303n
inner cultivation, 28
inner practice (*neigong* 內功), 22, 28, 287n, 332–33n
Institute of Buddhist Learning (Neixue yuan 內學院), 30
Intelligent Psyche (*shishen* 識神), 112, 119
Iron Wall (*tie bi* 鐵壁), 109

Jade Liquid (*qiong jiang* 瓊漿), 203–4, 321n
Jade Manor (*yu que* 玉闕), 101
Jade Pillow (*yu zhen* 玉枕), 108–9, 304n, 317n
Jade Pond (*yuchi* 玉池), 109

jiafu zuo 跏趺坐, 163
jia ji 夾脊, see Narrow Bluff
Jiang Weiqiao 蔣維喬 (h. Yinshizi 因是子), 26–28, 58–59, 61, 65, 88, 162, 192, 288n
Jiang Zhuzhuang 蔣竹莊 (AKA Jiang Weiqiao), 302n
jiang gong 絳宮, 101, 109. See also Crimson Palace; Purple Palace
Jiangnan Arsenal (Jiangnan zhizao ju 江南製造局), 48, 294n; Institute of Foreign Language, 200
jiang shuo 講說, 57
jiankang 健康, 22
Jiankang zhi lu 健康之路 (The path to health), 22
jiaogou zhi jing 交媾之精, 152
jiaoji 交際, 238
jiecheng yituan 結成一團, 168
jie tai 結胎, 168
jiji 積極, 232
jiji jinqu 積極進取, 246
jijin fa 急進法, 168
jijing quanqi 積精全氣, 192
jin 筋, 98
jing 精, 86, 223. See also Essence
Jingde 旌德, 59
jing gong 靜功, 161. See also quiet sitting
jingji wenti 經濟問題, 154
jingman ziyi 精滿自遺, 152
Jingming zhongxiao dao 淨明忠孝道, 197, 305n. See also Pure and Bright Way of Loyalty and Filial Piety
jing qi shen 精氣神, 115, 274. See also Essence, *qi*, and the Psyche
jingshen 精神, 24, 121
jing shi 精室, 304n

jing shi 靜室, 143. See also quiet chamber
Jingtu 淨土, 82. See also Pure Land
Jingxinzi 淨心子 (Master of the Pure Heart), 246, 330n
Jinling Scripture Carving Bureau (Jinling kejing chu 金陵刻經處), 30
jin yanghuo 進陽火, 106
jin ye 津液, 103
jiuguo zhi dao 救國之道, 239
Jiuhua Mountain 九華山, 49
jiuzhuan dancheng 九轉丹成, 257, 332n
Journal of the Enlightenment Society, The (*Jueshe congkan* 覺社叢刊), 80–81
jushi lin 居士林, 53, 247
juanshu tongju 眷屬同居, 157
jue 訣, 125
jue 覺, 84

Kang Youwei 康有為, 29, 51, 54, 178
Kaoshi yuan 考試院, 267
kaozheng 考證, 29, 337n
kexue jingshen 科學精神, 250
kexue yu rensheng guan 科學與人生觀 (science and the outlook on life), 32
kexue yu xuanxue 科學與玄學 (science and metaphysics), 32
Kidney Water, or Water of the Kidneys (*shenshui* 腎水), 103–4, 190–91, 318n
killing *qi* (*sha qi* 殺氣), 169
koujue 口訣, see oral secrets
Koujue gouxuan lu 口訣鉤玄錄, see Explorations in Oral Secrets

380   Index

Lady He (He Xiangu 何仙姑), 218–20, 324n
Lady Ma (Ma Gu 麻姑), 136–37, 308–9n
Lady Mud Ball (niwan furen 泥丸夫人), 110
lang you 浪遊, 187
laoli zhi ren 勞力之人, 149
laoxin laoli 勞心勞力, 95
laoxin zhi ren 勞心之人, 149
Laozi 老子 or Lao Dan 老聃, 4, 11, 44, 90, 164, 185, 242, 244–45, 268, 280, 313n, 315–16n, 337n
Laozi 老子, 45, 117, 293n, 305n, 338n. See also Daodejing 道德經
learning and practice of the Divine Immortals (shenxian zhi xueshu 神仙之學術), 203
Learning Immortals Will Surely Succeed (Xuexian bicheng 學仙必成), 87, 108, 116, 126, 254, 304–5n, 309–15n, 330n
Lectures on Daodejing (Daodejing jiangyi 道德經講義), 124, 305n
Lectures on the Vimalakīrti Sūtra (Weimo jing jiangyi 維摩經講義), 55
Lectures on the Yellow Courtyard Scriptures (Huangting jing jiangyi 黃庭經講義), 87–88, 96, 102, 303–4n, 307n, 311n, 316n, 327–28n
leng jia 冷瘕, 150
leng qi 冷氣, 150
Li Bai 李白, 12, 286n
Li Baoqian 李保乾, 331n
Li Pengfei 李鵬飛, 149–50, 310–11n
Li Ruiqing 李瑞清 (h. Qingdaoren 清道人), 179, 316n

Li Xiyue 李西月 (h. Hanxu 涵虛), 36, 240, 291n
Li Xu'an 李虛庵, 286n
Li Yangzheng 李養正, 281, 286n, 293–300n, 306n, 310n, 321n, 337–38n
Li Yunxiang 李雲翔, 197–98
Liang Qichao 梁啓超, 178, 287n
liangbu shuizhu 兩部水主, 103
liang xing 涼性, 149
lianjing huaqi 煉精化氣, 115, 161
lianqi huashen 煉氣化神, 115, 161
lianshen huanxu 煉神還虛, 115, 161
lianxu hedao 煉虛和道, 115, 161
lianyang 煉養, 4
Lianyun gang 連雲港, 258
li chan 禮懺, 57
Life-Centered Vitalism (shengben zhuyi 生本主義), 114
Life Force of the body (ming 命), 86
Lin Daomin 林道民, 335n
Lin Zhao'en 林兆恩, 190
linghun 靈魂, 120, 215
lingfu 靈府, 96
linggan 靈感, 171
Lingyuan dadao ge baihua zhujie 靈源大道歌白話注解, see Vernacular Annotation on the Ode to the Great Way of the Numinous Origin
lingzhi 靈質, 111
liqi 戾氣, 268
Literati Daoism (wenren Daojiao 文人道教), 10, 12–14, 273
Literati Daoists, 10, 12–15, 21
Liu Gang 劉綱, 156–58, 312n
Liu Huayang 柳華陽, 36, 290–91n, 297n, 325n
Liu Mingrui 劉名瑞, 58, 296n

Liu Shipei 劉師培, 31, 289–90n, 295n
Liu Yazi 柳亞子, 70
Liu Yiming 劉一明, 36, 291n, 303n
liu chen 六塵, 94
liufu jiuqiao 六腑九竅, 103
liushen tong 六神通, 314n
liu yi 六藝, 200
Longmen (sect, school, or lineage), 35, 58, 286n, 290n
Longmen Daoist, 50
Lower Cinnabar Field (*xia dantian* 下丹田), 101, 103, 106, 109–10, 180, 191, 318n
Lower Magpie Bridge (*xia queqiao* 下鵲橋), 107
Lu Xixing 陸西星, 36, 287n, 291n, 304n
Lü Bicheng 呂碧城, 297–99n; early activities, 59–61; pursuit of female alchemy, 61–67, 70, 79, 88, 180; cultivation community, 177
Lü Dongbin 呂洞賓 or Patriarch Lü (Lüzu 呂祖), 43, 56, 182, 184, 208–9, 219, 307n, 324n, 326n
Lü Fengqi 呂鳳歧, 59
Lü Zongyue 呂宗岳, 319n
Lüzu ge 呂祖閣, 56
Luo Baoheng 羅寶珩, 322n

Ma Danyang 馬丹陽, 156
Ma Duanlin 馬端臨, 4, 242, 285n
Ma Gu 麻姑, see Lady Ma
Ma Junwu 馬君武, 70, 200
Ma Yifu 馬一孚 (z. Yifu 一浮), 200, 210, 240, 277, 320n, 328n

Mahayana Buddhism or Great Vehicle Buddhism (Dacheng Fojiao 大乘佛教), 84–85, 302n
mai 脈, 98
mangshi xiashou 盲師瞎授, 130
Mao Fuchu 毛復初, 240
Mao Zedong (Mao Tse-tung) 毛澤東, 24–25, 198, 287–88n
martial arts, 25, 240
Master Dixian 諦閒法師, 49
Master Who Embraces Simplicity, A (*Baopuzi* 抱樸子), 140, 309n
Master Yinshizi's Method for Quiet Sitting (*Yinshizi jingzuo fa* 因是子靜坐法), 26, 59, 288n
Master Yuexia 月霞法師, 49, 53–56, 247, 295–96n
materialism (*wuben zhuyi* 物本主義), 32, 114, 121, 172, 248
medical arts of Minister Qi and Emperor Huang (*Qi Huang zhi shu* 岐黃之術), 183
Meng Yongcai 孟永才, 292n
Method, Funds, Fellowship, and Locale (*fa cai lü di* 法財侶地), 122
method of Three Stillness/Nonmovements (*san bu dong fa* 三不動法), 261, 334n; Stillness of the Body (*shen bu dong* 身不動), of the Heart (*xin bu dong* 心不動), and of the Intent (*yi bu dong* 意不動), 334n
mihu 密户, 97
Millet Pearl or Pearl of Millet (*shu zhu* 黍珠), 185–86, 317n
Min Sun 閔損, 213
Min Yide 閔一得, 36, 166, 291–92n, 304n, 313n

Mind-Centered Idealism (*xinben zhuyi* 心本主義), 114, 121
mind-nature (*xin xing* 心性), 49, 86
ming 命, 86
ming gen 命根, 102, 303n
mingmen 命門, 97
ming shan 名山, 140, 295n, 309n
ming tang 明堂, 109
miscellaneous learning (*zaxue* 雜學), 31
Miss Dong (Dong nüshi 董女士), 122–24, 175, 220, 226–30, 305n, 326–27n
mixin 迷信, 4
Monastery of the Sage Guardian (Yousheng guan 祐聖觀), 43
Monk Yekai 冶開和尚, 49
Morality Learning Institute (Daode xueshe 道德學社), 26, 58, 296n
Mountain Root (*shan gen* 山根), 109
Mount Jin'gai 金蓋山, 49
Mount Lao 崂山, 49, 55
Mount Mao 茅山, 49, 333n
Mount Pingfeng Sanitarium (Pingfengshan liaoyang yuan 屏風山療養院), 277
Mount Wudang 武當山, 49
Mount Wutai 五臺山, 54
mozhang 魔障, 161
mu pin zhi xiang 牡牝之相, 101
Mud Ball (*ni wan* 泥丸), 7, 107, 109–13, 133
muddy water (*zhuo shui* 濁水), 202, 320n
mundane passions (*suqing* 俗情), 134, 227
"Musings to Myself" or "Self-musings" ("Zi qian" 自遣), 203, 331–32n

Nanjing 難經, 46
nannü pingdeng 男女平等, 230
nannü zhi shi 男女之事, 151
Nanshe 南社 (Southern Society), 70
Nanyang College (Nanyang gongxue 南洋公學), 178
Nanyue 南嶽 (Southern Marchmont), 187
Nanzong 南宗, 143, 307n. *See also* Daoist Southern School; Southern Lineage
naosui 腦髓, 111
Narrow Bluff (*jia ji* 夾脊), 108
national character (*guomin genxing* 國民根性), 27–28
national religion (*guojiao* 國教), 56, 80
Nature of the Heart (*xin xing* 心性), 86
neidan 內丹, 1, 144, 286n, 303n, 315n, 333n. *See also* inner alchemy
neigong 內功, 28, 332–33n. *See also* inner practice
Neigong tushuo 內功圖說 (An illustrated treatise on inner practice), 22
neiming daode 內明道德, 138
Neixue yuan 內學院, 30
nengli 能力, 119, 162
Neo-Confucian, 3–5, 11, 318n
nianling wenti 年齡問題, 154
ni chaoliu 逆潮流, 190
nie cai 孽財, 144. *See also* funds
niwan 泥丸, *see* Mud Ball
niwan baijie jie you shen 泥丸百節皆有神, 111
niwan furen 泥丸夫人, *see* Lady Mud Ball

nixing zaohua 逆行造化, 158
nize chengxian 逆則成仙, 120
nizhuan zaohua 逆轉造化, 95
North China Women's College (Beiyang nüzi gongxue 北洋女子公學), 60
Northern Lineage (Beizong/Beipai 北宗/北派), 143, 306–7n
nourishing life (*yangsheng* 養生), 13, 22
noxious *qi* (*du qi* 毒氣), 143
Numinous Mansion (*lingfu* 靈府), 96
Numinous Marrow, 112–13
Numinous Matter, 113
Numinous Nature (*xingling* 性靈), 171
Numinous Resonance (*linggan* 靈感), 171–72
Numinous Soul (*hunling* 魂靈), 96–97, 99

Opium War, 21
oral secrets (*kou jue* 口訣) or alchemic instruction (*dan jue* 丹訣), 90, 98, 123–33, 138, 210, 220, 226–27, 237, 256, 258, 261, 322n, 330n
Orbits of Heaven or Heavenly Orbits (*zhoutian* 周天), 106–7, 110, 112, 187, 224, 317n; Greater and Lesser Orbits of Heaven, 194
Original Essence (*yuan jing* 元精), 110, 332n
Original Qi (*yuan qi* 元氣), 24, 102, 110–12, 168, 186, 303n
Original or True Vitality (*yuan qi* 元氣, *zhen qi* 眞氣), 92
Original or True Psyche (*yuan shen* 元神, *zhen shen* 眞神), 92, 110, 112, 168
Original Trio (*san yuan* 三元), 110
Original Yang, 187
origin of the earth (*di yuan* 地元), 70. See also Three Origins
Orthodox Deities (*zhengshen* 正神), 140–41
Orthodox One (Zhengyi 正一), see Zhengyi (Daoism) 正一
Ouhua 歐化, 114
outer (or laboratory) alchemy (*waidan* 外丹), 13, 70–72, 75, 114–15, 138, 140, 146, 236, 241, 250–52, 280, 299n, 323n, 332n
Ouyang Xiu 歐陽修, 4

Palace of the Purple Soleil (Ziyang gong 紫陽宮), 206–8, 322n, 336–37n
Palace of the Sons (*zi gong* 子宮), 304n, 325n
Pan Wei 潘蔚, 22, 287n
parturition of the Yang Spirit (*chu shen* 出神), 168, 297n, 314n
passes (*guan* 關), 107, 132, 142, 170, 189
Passions and Lust, or Lustful Passions (*qingyu* 情欲), 117, 119
Pass of Amorous Attachment (*qing guan* 情關), 217, 324n
Pass of Origin (*guanyuan* 關元), 96–97
Patriarch of the Way (Daozu 道祖), 207
Pearl of Son (*zi zhu* 子珠), 104, 304n
Pei Hang 裴航, 229, 326–27n

Peng Hanran 彭瀚然, 286n
Peng Xiao 彭曉, 301n, 306n
Pengzu 彭祖, 152, 311n
Pengzu fangzhong shu 彭祖房中術, 152
Perfected Man (*zhen ren* 眞人), 317n, 319n
Perfected Son (*zhen zi* 眞子), 185–86
Perverse Qi (*liqi* 戾氣), 268
Petite Daoist Learning Series, The (*Daoxue xiao congshu* 道學小叢書), 236, 328n
Petite Daoist Learning Series for Women, The (*Nüzi Daoxue xiao congshu* 女子道學小叢書), 237, 328n
pi 皮, 98
pianku 偏枯, 158
pianku bu ziran zhi biantai 偏枯不自然之變態, 158
pian zhong xin xing 偏重心性, 49
ping kong 憑空, 119
ping liang 評量, 63
pingmin zhuyi 平民主義, 184
Pinjia Hermitage (Pinjia jingshe 頻迦精舍), 54
pishen liangshang 脾腎兩傷, 192
pixie 脾泄, 192
Poem on Female Alchemy by Sun Bu'er, A (*Sun Bu'er nüdan shi* 孫不二女丹詩), 64
popular religion, 12, 288n
postures (*zishi* 姿勢), 163–64, 313n
Precepts for Women (*Nüjie* 女誡), 297n
"Proposals on Managing Religions" ("Guanli zongjiao yijian shu" 管理宗教意見書), 52–53, 56

Psyche (*shen* 神), 303n; locus and functions, 86–87, 91–93, 100, 102, 105, 110, 115; relations to the heart, 162–64; Essence and qi, 274. *See also shen* 神
Psyche of the Heart (*xinshen* 心神), 105, 143
Pudong Daoist Association of Shanghai (Shanghai tebie shi Pudong Daojiao tongren lianyi hui 上海特別市浦東道教同仁聯誼會), 335n
Pure and Bright Way of Loyalty and Filial Piety (Jingming zhongxiao dao 淨明忠孝道), 197, 305n
pure and quiet nonaction (*qingjing wuwei* 清靜無爲), 243
Pure and Quiet (solo) practice (or approach, techniques) (*qingjing gongfu* 清靜功夫), 153, 160–61, 216–17
Pure Land (Jingtu 淨土) (sect, school, of Buddhism), 15, 38, 54–55, 82–84, 193, 234, 246–49, 276, 295n
Pure Void (*qingxu* 清虛), 117, 119
Purple Ganoderma Monastery or Temple (Zizhi guan 紫芝觀), 256, 260
Purple Palace (*jiang gong* 絳宮), 101, 256

qi 氣, 86. *See also particular types of* qi *by name*
Qian Daoji 錢道極, 267–68, 330n
Qian Xin 錢心, 248–49, 330n
qiangguo qiangzhong 強國強種, 25
qiangmin qiangguo 強民強國, 245
qiang zhong 強種, 239

qianjiang housheng 前降後升, 106
qian sui laowu 千歲老物, 140
Qiao Zhongshan 喬仲珊, 49, 51
qidong wei zhi shen 氣動謂之神, 100
qigong 氣功, 9–10, 16, 19, 201, 274, 277, 280, 320n
qi hai 氣海, see Sea of Qi
Qi Huang zhi shu 歧黃之術, 183
qijing wei zhi xin 氣靜謂之心, 100
Qin Bowei 秦伯未, 320n
qingjing gongfu 清靜功夫, 153. See also Pure and Quiet (solo) practice
qingjing wuwei 清靜無爲, 4, 243. See also pure and quiet non-action
qing ju 輕裾, 63
qingxiu zhi shi 清修之士, 138
qingxu 清虛, see Pure Void; Void
qingyu 情欲, 117, 119
qiong jiang 瓊漿, 203, 321n
Qionglongshan daoyuan 穹窿山道院, 54
qishu 奇書, 30
Qiu Chuji 邱處機, 178, 260, 315n
Qiu Jin 秋瑾, 61
Qiu Zhao'ao 仇兆鰲, 36, 304n
Qiyuan zhi zi 七元之子, 101
Quanzhen (Daoism) 全眞, 11, 35–36, 43, 45, 50–51, 55–58, 80, 143–44, 157, 178, 195, 204–9, 221, 233, 256, 260, 290n, 293–94n, 296n, 313n, 321n, 325n, 336–37n
quiet chamber (*jing shi* 靜室), 143, 167
quiet practice (*jinggong* 靜功), 161. See also quiet sitting

quiet sitting (*jingzuo* 靜坐), 26–28, 59, 61, 65, 88, 161–63, 165–66, 169, 179, 192, 196–99, 206, 214, 220–21, 226, 254, 265, 278, 289n, 312–13n
Quotations from the Hall of Joyful Cultivation (*Leyutang yulu* 樂育堂語錄), 124, 305n
"Quotations from the Lectures on the Way at Ziyang Cloister" ("*Ziyang gong jiang dao yulu*" 紫陽宮講道語錄), 322n

Rapid Advance method(s) (*jijin fa* 急進法), 168, 170
Realm of the Dharma (*fajie* 法界), 85
Refining the Form in the True Void (*zhenkong lianxing* 眞空煉形), 194
religious Daoism (*daojiao* 道教), 90, 242
ren'ge wenti 人格問題, 154
Renhe Advanced School of Obstetrics (Renhe fuchan gaoji xuexiao 仁和婦產高級學校), 68
renmai 任脈, 106
renshu 仁術, 204
ren zhong 人種, 24
replenishing ingredients (*bu pin* 補品), 150–51
re ti 熱體, 149. See also *ti zhi* 體質
roaming (*lang you* 浪遊), 77, 133, 180, 187, 308n
Root of Life (*ming gen* 命根), 102, 180, 303n
rou shen 肉身, 49
routi 肉體, 115
ru ding 入定, 220

Rujia 儒家 (Confucians or Confucian school), 90, 294n
Rules of Alchemic Chambers (Danfang xuzhi 丹房須知), 138, 309n
ruo rou qiang shi 弱肉強食, 215
rushan xiulian 入山脩煉, 229
ruyi tong 如意通, 171

san cun 三寸, 94
san guang 三光, 104, 304n
san huan 三環, 139. See also huohuan; sihuan; xunhuan
sanjiao 三教, 132, 306n
sanqian gong man 三千功滿, 77
schools of the Daoist philosophers (daojia 道家), 90
Scribe of the Jade Flower Palace (Yuhua gong shishu xianzi 玉華宮侍書仙子), 74, 300n
Scripture of the Yin talisman (Yinfu jing 陰符經), 30–31, 307n
Sea Bottom (hai di 海底), 304n
Sea of Blood (xue hai 血海), 261, 304n
Sea of Qi (qi hai 氣海), 107, 110, 304n, 325n, 334n
secluded chamber (guanfang 關房), 221
Secret Door (mihu 密戶), 96–97
Secrets of the Three Crafts (Sanche mizhi 三車秘旨), 240, 328n
se jie 色界, 77
self-cultivation (xiulian 脩煉), 1, 8–17 passim, 22–28 passim, 37, 41, 43, 47–49, 56–62 passim, 65–88 passim, 114, 123, 130, 136, 153, 156–57, 161–62, 176–77, 179, 181, 193, 197–201, 203, 206, 210–21 passim, 227, 232, 236–42 passim, 245–47,
249, 253, 255, 270, 273, 275, 280–81, 287n, 289n, 294n, 300n, 303n, 310n, 314–15n, 327n, 330n, 335n
self-enclosure (biguan 閉關), 208, 221
self-meditation, 58
Self-Strengthening Society (Qiangxue hui 強學會), 178
self-transformation, 12, 54, 77, 83, 114, 151, 153, 186, 188, 221, 246–47, 301n
seshen 色身, 85
sexual-gathering practices (cai bu 採補), 152, 154, 311n
shan cai 善財, 144. See also funds
shan gen 山根, see Mountain Root
Shanghai 上海, 1–3, 6, 8–9, 14–19, 21, 30, 39–40, 42, 46–56 passim, 59, 67–75 passim, 78, 81–83, 88, 116, 124, 136, 146, 153, 174–87, 189, 195–213 passim, 216, 218, 220, 226, 229, 232–41 passim, 246–54 passim, 257, 261–77 passim, 280–81, 285n, 294–95n, 298–300n, 308n, 315–16n, 319n, 321–22n, 327n, 329–31n, 333–37n
Shanghai Daoist Association (Shanghai tebie shi Daojiao hui 上海特別市道教會), 336n
Shanghai Institute of Immortals' Learning (Shanghai xianxue yuan 上海仙學院), 204, 213, 264–65
Shanghai International Mission (Shanghai wanguo zhengdao hui 上海萬國證道會), 250, 331n

Index 387

Shanghai Metaphysical Study Society (Shanghai xuanxue hui 上海玄學會), 238, 328n
Shanghai Psychical Research Society (Shanghai lingxue hui 上海靈學會), 73
Shanghai Renhe Hospital (Shanghai renhe yiyuan 上海人和醫院), 201
Shanghai Zhonghua wushu hui 上海中華武術會, 240
Shanghan lun 傷寒論, 46
Shangqing (Daoist or Daoism) 上清, 96, 103, 110–11, 113, 128, 161, 297n, 307n, 312n, 314n, 321n, 323n
shang queqiao 上鵲橋, see Upper Magpie Bridge
Shangxian Hospital (Shangxian yiyuan 尚賢醫院), 68
shangyan 上炎, 104
shanshu 善書, 218
sha qi 殺氣, 169
Shehui fuli bu 社會福利部, 267
sheli 舍利 (relic bones), 86
shen 神, 17; locus and functions in the alchemic body, 86, 91–106 passim, 111–12, 148, 186, 203, 226, 228, 274, 304n, 326n. See also Psyche
Shen Linsheng 沈霖生, 200, 208, 250–51, 331n
Shen Taixu 沈太虛, 166
Shen Zengzhi 沈曾植, 177–80, 289n
Shenbao 申報, 52, 80, 271
shenbu zhi gong 腎部之宮, 103
shengben zhuyi 生本主義, see Life-Centered Vitalism

shenghuo su 生活素 (vitamins), 148. See also diet
sheng ji 生機, 148
shengjin zhi qiao 生津之竅, 109
shengjing taiduo 生精太多, 152
sheng lao bing si 生老病死, 82
sheng qi 生氣, 142. See also generative qi
shengqian 生前, 231
Shengshi weiyan 盛世危言 (Alarming words for prosperous times), 23
shen guang 神光, 104
shengxian gudao 聖賢古道, 234
she nian 攝念, 79
shenjing tong 神境通, 314n
shenmen 神門, 97
shenqi heyi 神氣合一, 162
shen shui 神水, 93
shenshui 腎水, 104
shen tong 神通, 169, 314n. See also unblocking
shen wai zhi shen 身外之身, 170
shen wei zhuzai 神為主宰, 100
shenxian 神仙, 4, 291n. See also Divine Immortals
shenxian jia 神仙家, 89. See also Divine Transcendents
shenxian juanshu 神仙眷屬, 155
shenxian zhi xueshu 神仙之學術, 203
Shenxian zhuan 神仙傳, see Biographies of the Divine Transcendents
shenxin xiuyang zhi xue 身心修養之學, 270
shenzhong sheng qi 身中生氣, 167
Shenzhou 神州, 190, 318n
Shi Jianguang 史劍光, 271
Shi Liangcai 史量才, 271

Shi Yixuan 施毅軒, 253–54, 331n
Shi Zhaoyu 施召愚, 332n
Shi Zhihe 石志和 (z. Yunzhong 允中), 220–21, 239, 325n
shi'er chonglou 十二重樓, 109
shijian 實踐, 232
Shingon (Zhenyan 眞言) school, 82–83
shishen 識神, see Intelligent Psyche
shiyan 試驗, 232
shizheng 實證, 246
Shoushi chuanzhen 壽世傳眞, 287n
shoushi gui 守屍鬼, 247
shuang guan 雙關, see Double Pass
shuangxiu shuangzheng 雙修雙證, 156. See also Yin-Yang paired (or duo, dual) cultivation
shui huo jiji 水火既濟, 191
Shunde 順德, 69
shun ze cheng ren 順則成人, 94
shu zhu 黍珠, 186
sihou 死後, 231
sihuan 死環, 139. See also san huan
Siku quanshu 四庫全書 or Siku 四庫, 200, 242–43
Sima Chengzhen 司馬承禎, 12, 161, 206, 314n
Sino-Occidental Medical College or Sino-Western Medical School (Zhongxi yixue yuan 中西醫學院), 67, 298n
site selection or selecting sites (zedi 擇地), 141, 172
Six Dusts (liu chen 六塵), 94
Six Mansions and Nine Apertures (liufu jiuqiao 六府九竅), 103
slaying the Scarlet (or Red) Dragon (zhan chilong 斬赤龍), 220–21, 223, 226–28, 261, 325–26n

smash temples (da miao 打廟) campaign, 123
social Darwinist or Darwinism, 22, 24, 214
Society for Carving Daoist and Alchemic Scriptures (Dandao kejing hui 丹道刻經會), 238, 328n
Society of the Way and Its Virtues, see Morality Learning Institute
solo (pure) cultivation, 160, 294n
Solo Yin and Solitary Yang (guyin guayang 孤陰寡陽), 156
Song Jinren 宋今人, 281
Song Zongfu 宋宗富 (h. Qianlong 潛龍), 209–10
songjing 誦經, 84
Southern Lineage (Nanzong/Nanpai 南宗/南派), 132, 143, 154, 216, 269, 306–7n, 310n
South Market District (Nanshi 南市), 7, 50, 68–69, 72, 174, 195, 201, 210, 241, 316n
spirit-writing (jixian 乩仙, fuji 扶乩, or fuluan 扶鸞), 70, 73–75, 201, 300n
Square Inch (fang cun 方寸), 102, 187, 317n
Su Manshu 蘇曼殊, 70
substance (ti 體), 71, 92, 252; function and, 111–20 passim; forms and, 170–72
substance of the Way (dao zhi ti 道之體), 116–17, 119–20
suming tong 宿命通, 171, 314n
Sun Baoci 孫抱慈, 210, 322n, 328n
Sun Bu'er 孫不二, 64, 70, 77–78, 91, 93–95, 156, 208

Sun Bu'er nüdan shizhu 孫不二女丹詩注, see Annotations to Sun Bu'er's Poem on Female Alchemy
Suoyan xu 瑣言續, 166, 313n
suqing 俗情, 227
Superintendent Channel (*dumai* 督脈), 106, 317n, 334n
Supreme Quietness and Tranquility (*dajing dading* 大靜大定), 162
suxiu 速朽, 231
Sweet (Cool) Saliva (*ganliang zhi jinye* 甘涼之津液), 106, 109–10

Taiji quan 太極拳, 280
Tailgate locus (*wei lü* 尾閭), 106–7, 317n, 334n
Taiping sects, 289n
Taiping Uprising (or Rebellion), 21–22, 41, 234
taixi 胎息, 98, 319n
Taixu 太虛, 53, 80, 247, 296n
talismans (*fulu* 符籙), 4, 57, 74; talisman writing (*hua fu* 畫符), 45; talismanic writing, 74–75
Tan Qiao 譚峭, 92–93, 302n
Tan Sitong 譚嗣同, 29
Tang Yu Xia Shang Zhou 唐虞夏商周, 244
tan shui huahe wu 碳水化合物, 148. See also diet
Tao Hongjing 陶弘景, 198, 290n, 324n
Tao Susi 陶素耜, 36
taxin tong 他心通, 171, 314n
temporal or postnatal (*houtian* 後天), 3, 91–95, 98, 112, 119, 153, 158, 162, 169, 297–98n, 303n

Ten Rules on Female Alchemy (*Nüdan shize* 女丹十則), 64, 66, 71, 298–99n, 328n
Thousand-Year-Old Beings (*qiansui laowu* 千歲老物), 140
Three Origins (*sanyuan* 三元), 133–34, 307n, 331n; methods of the Heavenly Origin (*tian yuan dan fa* 天元丹法), the Earthly Origin (*di yuan dan fa* 地元丹法), and the Human Origin (*ren yuan dan fa* 人元丹法), 307n
Three Passes or Triple Passes (*san guan* 三關), 188, 304n, 317n, 334n
Three Rings (*san huan* 三環): Ring of Death (*sihuan* 死環), Ring of Life (*huohuan* 活環), and Ring of the Cycle (*xunhuan* 循環), 139
Three Teachings (*sanjiao* 三教), 55, 132, 296n, 306n, 329n
ti 體, 114. See also Substance
tianer tong 天耳通, 171, 314n
Tianshi 天師, 11, 290n
Tiantai 天台 school, 82, 206
Tianxian zhengli 天仙正理, 286n, 309n, 314n, 317n, 324n, 326n
tianyan gongli 天演公理, 215
Tianyan lun 天演論, 214
tianyan tong 天眼通, 171, 314n
Tianyin zi 天隱子, 314n, 327n
tianzhu fohua 天竺佛化, 114
tiao shen 調神, 163
tiaoshen chuqiao 調神出殼, 170
tiao xi 調息, 164
tiao xin 調心, 164
Tidal Roar, The (*Haichao yin* 海潮音), 81, 247

tie bi 鐵壁, see Iron Wall
tipo qiangjian 體魄強健, 23
ti yong 體用, 33
ti zhi 體質, 148–49. See also *han ti*; *re ti*
tong 通, see unblocking
Tongbai Palace (Tongbai gong 桐柏宮), 269, 337n
Tongshan she 同善社, see Common Benevolence Society
tongzhi 同志, 138, 327n, 335n
tongzi lao 童子癆 (pupils' consumption), 46
Tract of Taishang on Action and Response (*Taishang ganying pian* 太上感應篇), 30, 289–90n
Transcendents' or Supermen's philosophy (*chaoren zhexue* 超人哲學), 88
Treatise on Cold Damage Disorders, The (*Shanghan lun* 傷寒論), 46
Treatise on the Mysterious Essential, A (*Xuanyao pian* 玄要篇), 45
Triple Lights or Three Lights (*san guang* 三光), 104, 304n
Triple River Crafts (*san che* 三車), 188; River Crafts (*heche* 河車), 188, 317n; Goat (*yang che* 羊車), Dear (*lu che* 鹿車), and Ox carts (*niu che* 牛車), 318n
True Fluid (*zhen ye* 真液), 74–75, 300n
True Oral Secrets on the Earthly Origin, The (*Diyuan zhenjue* 地元真訣), 45
True Solar Fire (*taiyang zhen huoli* 太陽真火力), 168
tuanjie 團結, 232
tuan ti 團體, 262
tui yinfu 退陰符, 106

tuo yue 橐籥, 164
tuxue zheng 吐血症, 48
Twelve Stacked Pavilions (*shi'er chonglou* 十二重樓), 109
Two Schools (*liangzong/liangpai* 兩宗/兩派), 133–34, 307n

unblocking (*tong* 通), 170–71, 314–15n
Union of the Psyche and Qi (*shenqi heyi* 神氣合一), 162
Unitary Qi (*yi qi* 一氣), 91, 95, 158
Upper Cinnabar Field (*shang dantian* 上丹田), 112, 187, 318n
Upper Magpie Bridge (*shang queqiao* 上鵲橋), 109

Vernacular Annotation on the Ode to the Great Way of the Numinous Origin (*Lingyuan dadao ge baihua zhujie* 靈源大道歌白話注解), 87, 93, 298n, 302–3n, 321n, 328–30n
visualization or visualizing, 111, 312n, 314n
Vitalism (*weisheng zhuyi* 唯生主義), 17, 114, 120–21
Void (*xu* 虛), 62–64, 66–67, 87, 92, 98, 102, 115, 252, 297–98n, 314n

waidan 外丹, 13, 70, 331n. See also outer (or laboratory) alchemy
waidao 外道, 247
waihu wenti 外護問題, 154
waijiao 外教, 243
waijing suo she 外景所攝, 152
waishi huici 外施惠慈, 138
waiyang neiyin 外陽內陰, 158
waiyin neiyang 外陰內陽, 158

Wang Boying 汪伯英, 319n, 332n, 335n; *Yangshan Biweekly*, 182; journey of pursuit, 192–94; cultivation community, 195, 208, 270; print culture, 240–41, 248
Wang Changyue 王常月, 35
Wang Dongting 汪東亭, 302n. See also Wang Qihuo
Wang Guowei 王國維, 295n
Wang Hongyi 王弘毅, 335n
Wang Lilian 王理蓮, 208, 322n
Wang Mingzhen 王明眞, 50, 321n
Wang Pinsan 王聘三 (h. Qiandaoren 潛道人), 88, 179, 316n
Wang Qihuo 汪啓濩, 36, 291n
Wang Quande 王權德, 251
Wang Xinde 王信德, 206
Wang Yuan 王遠 (z. Fangping 方平), 137
Wang Zhe 王喆 (h. Chongyang 重陽), 12, 208
Wang Zhen 王震 (z. Yiting 一亭), 54, 295n
Wang Zuyuan 王祖源, 287n
wan gu danjing zhi wang 萬古丹經之王, 213
Way of Alchemy, 115, 322n
Way of Lengthening Life, 242
Way of the Anterior Heaven (Xiantian dao 先天道), 136, 197–98
Way of the Perfected Void (Zhenkong dao 眞空道), 197
Wei Boyang 魏伯陽, 101, 126–27, 301n, 306n
Wei Yuan 魏源, 178
wei lü 尾閭, 106
wei renshen zhuzai 爲人身主宰, 111
weisheng 衛生, 24, 287–88n

Weisheng yaoshu 衛生要術 (Essential techniques for guarding life), 22
weisheng zhuyi 唯生主義, 17, 120
weiwu 唯物, 34
weixin 唯心, 82
wenren Daojiao 文人道教, 10. See also Literati Daoism
Wenxian tongkao 文獻通考, 4, 285n
wen xing 溫性, 149
White Cloud Monastery (Baiyun guan 白雲觀): in Beijing, 35, 56–57, 278–79, 292n, 321n; in Shanghai, 49–51, 74, 195, 206, 209–10, 267
White Origin (*bai yuan* 白元), 101
withholding the consciousness (*she nian* 攝念), 79
Wu Minzhai 吳敏齋, 197–99, 240
Wu Shouyang 伍守陽, 36, 138, 140, 170, 286n, 309n, 314n, 317n
Wu Wu 吳悞, 138, 309n
Wu Xinpeng 吳信蓬, 331n
Wu Yizhu 吳彝珠, 298n, 320–21n, 328n; early life, 67–68; pursuit of alchemy, 72, 128; inner alchemy community, 201–3; print culture, 240
Wu Yun 吳筠, 12
Wu Zhuyuan 吳竹園, 197–99
wuben zhuyi 物本主義, see materialism
wu chang 無常, 84
Wuchang 武昌, 68, 247, 304n
Wuhu 蕪湖, 67
wu li 無力, 150
wu qiao 五竅, see Five Orifices
wu se jie 無色界, 77
wushi 午時, 165

wutou xuanmiao 悟透玄妙, 130
wuxing 五行, 13
Wuxing 吳興, 67, 177
wuzang liufu 五臟六腑 (*xin zang* 心臟, *fei zang* 肺臟, *gan zang* 肝臟, *shen zang* 腎臟, and *pi zang* 脾臟), 98
wuzhi 物質, 121
wuzhi zhi jingjie 物質之境界, 85

xialou 下漏, 104
Xiandao congshu 仙道叢書, 237
Xiandao yuebao 仙道月報, *see Immortals' Way Monthly*
Xian Fo hezong yulu 仙佛合宗語錄, 286n
xian gui youxing 仙貴有形, 171
xian guo 鮮果, 149
xiantian 先天, 24, 91, 95. *See also* atemporal
xiantian dao 先天道, 136
xiantian qi 先天氣, 95, 163, 165. *See also* atemporal *qi*
xiantian shengmingli 先天生命力, 162
xianxing 現形, 171
Xianxue 仙學, *see* Immortals' Learning
Xianzhen guan 顯眞觀, 50
xiao yaowu 曉藥物, 130
xiao zhe 小謫, 229
xia queqiao 下鵲橋, *see* Lower Magpie Bridge
xibao 細胞, 117
Xie Jiyun 謝季雲, 70, 173–74, 315n
Xie Qianggong 謝強公, 240, 270, 328n, 336n
Xie Wuliang 謝無量, 200

xinben zhuyi 心本主義, *see* Mind-Centered Idealism
Xinchen geng 新陳埂, 41
xing li zuo wo 行立坐臥, 163
Xingming shuangxiu wanshen guizhi 性命雙脩萬神圭旨, 78, 97, 99, 163, 313n, 319n
xingming shuangxiu zhi shi 性命雙修之士, 87
xingshen jumiao 形神俱妙, 115
xingzhi 形質, 171. *See also* Form and Substance
xinhuo 心火, 104. *See also* Fire of the Heart
xinjing tong 心境通, 314n
Xin qingnian 新青年 (New youth), 24
xinshen 心神, 96. *See also* Heart Deity
xin xue 新學 (new learning), 48
xinyi 心意 (Heart's Intentions), 93
Xinzha Temple of the Great Kings (Xinzha dawang miao 新閘大王廟), 205
xin zheng 新政 (New Policies), 47
xiongsha zhe 凶煞者, 142
Xishan tang 習善堂, 136, 196
xiu dao 修道 (cultivating the Way), 227
xiudao jituan 修道集團, 230, 262, 327n, 335n
xiuguan 修觀 (refining the gaze), 84
xiulian 脩煉, 25, 78, 147. *See also* self-cultivation
xiulian suiyue 脩煉歲月, 165
xiushen yangxing 修身養性, 90
xiuyang 修養, 242
xixi guigen 息息歸根, 98

Xu Boying 徐伯英, 281, 286n, 338n
Xu Dede 許德得, 315n
Xu Dishan 許地山, 31, 290n
Xu Qianguang 徐乾光, 335n
Xu Rusheng 許如生, 295n
Xu Zhicheng 徐至成, 50–51
xuanguan 玄關, 101
xuan li 玄理, 73, 297n
Xuanlü jucanhui 玄侶聚餐會, 269, 337n
xuan ming 玄冥, 104
xuan que 玄闕, 103
Xuanyao pian 玄要篇, 45
xuanying 玄膺, see Dark Bosom
Xuanyuan 軒轅, 89
xueshi zhi gui 血食之鬼, 140
xu kong 虛空 (Empty Void), 115, 252. See also Pure Void; Void
xuncai 尋財, 143
xun fang 尋訪 (travels of search and inquiry), 48
xunhuan 循環, 139. See also san huan 三環
xunshi fangyou 尋師訪友, 132

Yan Fu 嚴復, 23–24, 45, 48, 61, 73, 214, 287n, 294n
Yan Hui 顏回, 213
Yan Junping 嚴君平, 173, 175, 315n
Yan Shiyu 顏士瑜, 59
Yang Fengqi 楊逢啟, 332n
Yang Shaochen 楊少臣, 239
Yang Wenhui 楊文會, 30–31, 53, 247, 289n
Yang Fire (yanghuo 陽火), 106, 109, 224, 325n
Yang Psyche (yang shen 陽神), 77, 86, 115. See also Yang Spirit

Yangshan banyue kan 揚善半月刊, see Biweekly to Promote the Good
yang shen 陽神, see Yang Psyche; Yang Spirit
yangsheng 養生, 13, 22
Yang Spirit (yang shen 陽神), 168–72, 297n, 314n
Yan Huang zisun 炎黃子孫, 129
yan jin 咽津 (saliva swallowing), 219
yanjiu 研究, 232
yanshi 驗師 (verifying the teacher), 225
yanyue tian 偃月天, 189
Yao Wennan 姚文柟, 327n
ye 液, 98
Ye Xueyu 葉學愚, 260, 331n
Yellow Courtyard (huangting 黃庭), 96–101, 103, 108, 187–89
Yellow Courtyard Scriptures (Huangting jing 黃庭經), 96, 99, 101, 104, 111, 127, 179, 274, 307n
Yellow Emperor (Huangdi 黃帝), 89–91, 242–45, 274, 302n, 308n, 311n, 323n, 329n
yi 易, 29
Yi Xinying 易心瑩, 336n
yiguan xinfa 一貫心法, 213
Yihuatang 翼化堂, 19, 69, 181, 185, 195, 234–38, 241, 251, 266, 275, 281, 298–99n, 327–28n, 331n, 335n
Yinguang 印光, 53, 193, 247
ying yang 營養, 148. See also diet
yinning zhi xing 陰凝之性, 66
yin shen 陰神, see Yin Spirit
Yin Spirit (yin shen 陰神), 170–72, 314n
Yin Talisman (yinfu 陰符), 106–7, 109, 224, 325n

yin-yang or yin and yang 陰陽, 13, 77, 91, 96, 100–101, 117, 138, 159, 161, 299n
(Yin-Yang) paired (or duo, dual) cultivation (*yinyang shuangxiu* 陰陽雙修), 153–60, 216, 254, 294n, 306n, 311–12n, 324n, 326n
(Yin-Yang) paired practice (*yinyang gongfu* 陰陽功夫), 153, 155, 157–58, 160–61, 299n
yin-yang sack 陰陽包, 77
yi qi 一氣 (Unitary Qi), 91
yishi xiang guan 義實相貫, 31
yitai 以太, 117
yiwu ermian 一物二面, 119
yixin yide 一心一德, 156
yong 用, 114
you chushi zhi zhi 有出世之志, 132
Yu Muxia 郁慕俠, 287n
Yu Yue 俞樾, 29–31, 289n
Yu Zhongjue 余仲珏, 279, 281, 293–94n, 298n, 300n, 338n
yuan 緣, 140
Yuan Jiegui 袁介珪, 281, 286n, 338n
Yuan Shikai 袁世凱, 60, 62, 290n
yuan jing 元精, 110. See also Original Trio
yuan qi 元氣, 24, 92, 110–11. See also Original Qi, atemporal *qi*, and Original Trio
"Yuanqiang" 原強 (On power), 23, 287n
yuan qi huasheng 元氣化生, 111
yuan shen 元神, 92, 110. See also Original Trio
yuan shou guijie 願守規戒, 219
yuanzi 原子, 117
yuchi 玉池, see Jade Pond

Yue lü Hu tongxianghui 粵旅滬同鄉會, 206
Yueqing 樂清, 256
Yu Garden (Yuyuan 豫園), 68, 199
yu jie 欲界, 77
Yun Ying 雲英, 228–29, 327n
yunian suo gan 欲念所感, 152
yu que 玉闕, 101
yu zhen 玉枕, see Jade Pillow

za'er duoduan 雜而多端, 4
zai Dao zhi qi 載道之器, 127
zaijia xiulian 在家修煉, 229
zai jie 栽接 (grafting techniques), 217
zaohua ku 造化窟, 95
zaxue 雜學, 31
ze di 擇地, 140. See also site selection
zhan chilong 斬赤龍, 220, 228. See also slaying the Scarlet (or Red) Dragon
Zhang Binglin 章炳麟, 289n
Zhang Boduan 張伯端, 165, 178, 207, 269, 303n, 313n, 315n, 328n
Zhang Daochu 張道初, 312n
Zhang Huasheng 張化聲, 240, 247–48, 302n, 304n, 328n, 330n
Zhang Huikun 張慧坤, 335n
Zhang Huiyan 張慧巖, 312n
Zhang Jiashou 張嘉壽, 271
Zhang Jingxu 張靜虛 (h. Zhang the Tiger-Skin 虎皮張), 286n
Zhang Junmai 張君勱, 33–34, 73, 120
Zhang Sanfeng 張三丰, 45, 133–35, 144, 310n
Zhang Weicheng 張韋承 (h. Xuetang 雪堂), 234–35, 327n

Zhang Zhide 張志德, 260–62, 334n
Zhang Zhuming 張竹銘, 277, 281, 299–300n, 308n, 310n, 316n, 323n, 327–28n, 331n, 335n; Yihuatang, 181, 185; *Yangshan Biweekly*, 194; inner alchemy community, 200, 208, 210, 265, 270–71; print culture, 235–36, 238–41; anti-Buddhism polemics, 249; science and Immortals' Learning, 251
zhan qu 斬取 (slain and plucked), 224
Zhao Bichen 趙避塵, 58, 296n
Zhao Yinhua 趙隱華, 258–59, 333n
Zhao Youqin 趙友欽, 140, 144, 309–10n
Zhejiang Academy of Letters and History (Zhejiang wenshi guan 浙江文史館), 277
Zheng Dingchen 鄭鼎臣, 70, 299n
Zheng Guanying 鄭觀應, 22–23, 47, 70, 131, 287n, 299n
zhendi 眞諦, 79
Zhen gao 眞誥, 290n
zheng shen 正神, 140. See also Orthodox Deities
zhengwen 正文, 30
Zhengyi (Daoism) 正一, 11, 35, 42–43, 45, 195, 204–5, 233, 336n
zhenkong dao 眞空道, 197
zhenkong lianxing 眞空煉形, 194
zhen qi 眞氣, 92. See also Original or True Vitality
zhenren zhi suozai 眞人之所在, 110
Zhenshanmei Press (Zhenshanmei chubanshe 眞善美出版社), 281, 305n, 331n

zhen shen 眞神, 92. See also Original Trio
Zhenyan 眞言, 82
zhen ye 眞液 (true fluid), 74
zhi duanlian 知鍛煉, 130
zhi fang 脂肪, 148. See also diet
zhiguan 止觀 (ceasing the gaze), 79
zhiguo qijia 治國齊家, 90
zhiping 治平, 267
zhi zhonghe 致中和, 268
Zhongguo Daojiao xiehui 中國道教協會, 278
Zhonghua Daojiao zonghui 中華道教總會, 267, 336n
Zhonghua guobao 中華國寶, 239
Zhonghua minzu 中華民族, 91, 129
Zhonghua xianxue 中華仙學, 286n, 338n
Zhongli Quan 鍾離權, 307n
Zhongwai weisheng yaozhi 中外衛生要旨 (Essential for protecting life from China and abroad), 23
zhongzi 中子, 117
Zhou Haixian 周海仙, 221, 325n
Zhou Minde 周敏得, 211, 239, 259–60, 322n, 334n
Zhou Zixiu 周子秀, 212, 323n, 333n
zhoutian 周天, 106–7. See also Orbits of Heaven
Zhu Changya 朱昌亞, 201–4, 229, 302n, 320–21n
Zhu Rong 祝融, 189, 191, 318n
Zhu Xi 朱熹, 4, 318n
Zhu Zumou 朱祖謀, 178
Zhuan Xu 顓頊, 311n
Zhuangzi 莊子, 4, 11, 63, 161, 242, 280, 329n

Zhuangzi 莊子, 45, 47, 200, 246, 293–94n, 302n, 319n
zhu ji 築基 (building the foundation), 168
zhusha yi li 硃砂一粒 or *yi dian zhusha* 一點朱砂 (one Grain of Cinnabar), 191, 318n
zili 自立, 232
zishi 姿勢 (postures), 163
zishi 子時, 165
zishi sike 子時四刻, 313n

Ziyang gong 紫陽宮, 206, 322n. *See also* Palace of the Purple Soleil
Ziyun dong 紫雲洞 (Purple Cloud Grotto), 210
Zizhi guan 紫芝觀 (Purple Ganoderma Monastery), 256
zong jiao 宗教, 52, 87
Zu Sheng 祖生, 134, 307–8n
zuo hua 坐化, 86
Zuowang lun 坐忘論, 327n

Harvard East Asian Monographs
(*out-of-print)

*1. Liang Fang-chung, *The Single-Whip Method of Taxation in China*
*2. Harold C. Hinton, *The Grain Tribute System of China, 1845–1911*
3. Ellsworth C. Carlson, *The Kaiping Mines, 1877–1912*
*4. Chao Kuo-chün, *Agrarian Policies of Mainland China: A Documentary Study, 1949–1956*
*5. Edgar Snow, *Random Notes on Red China, 1936–1945*
*6. Edwin George Beal, Jr., *The Origin of Likin, 1835–1864*
7. Chao Kuo-chün, *Economic Planning and Organization in Mainland China: A Documentary Study, 1949–1957*
*8. John K. Fairbank, *Ch'ing Documents: An Introductory Syllabus*
*9. Helen Yin and Yi-chang Yin, *Economic Statistics of Mainland China, 1949–1957*
10. Wolfgang Franke, *The Reform and Abolition of the Traditional Chinese Examination System*
11. Albert Feuerwerker and S. Cheng, *Chinese Communist Studies of Modern Chinese History*
12. C. John Stanley, *Late Ch'ing Finance: Hu Kuang-yung as an Innovator*
13. S. M. Meng, *The Tsungli Yamen: Its Organization and Functions*
*14. Ssu-yü Teng, *Historiography of the Taiping Rebellion*
15. Chun-Jo Liu, *Controversies in Modern Chinese Intellectual History: An Analytic Bibliography of Periodical Articles, Mainly of the May Fourth and Post-May Fourth Era*
*16. Edward J. M. Rhoads, *The Chinese Red Army, 1927–1963: An Annotated Bibliography*
*17. Andrew J. Nathan, *A History of the China International Famine Relief Commission*
*18. Frank H. H. King (ed.) and Prescott Clarke, *A Research Guide to China-Coast Newspapers, 1822–1911*
*19. Ellis Joffe, *Party and Army: Professionalism and Political Control in the Chinese Officer Corps, 1949–1964*
*20. Toshio G. Tsukahira, *Feudal Control in Tokugawa Japan: The Sankin Kōtai System*
*21. Kwang-Ching Liu, ed., *American Missionaries in China: Papers from Harvard Seminars*
*22. George Moseley, *A Sino-Soviet Cultural Frontier: The Ili Kazakh Autonomous Chou*

Harvard East Asian Monographs

23. Carl F. Nathan, *Plague Prevention and Politics in Manchuria, 1910–1931*
*24. Adrian Arthur Bennett, *John Fryer: The Introduction of Western Science and Technology into Nineteenth-Century China*
*25. Donald J. Friedman, *The Road from Isolation: The Campaign of the American Committee for Non-Participation in Japanese Aggression, 1938–1941*
*26. Edward LeFevour, *Western Enterprise in Late Ching China: A Selective Survey of Jardine, Matheson and Company's Operations, 1842–1895*
27. Charles Neuhauser, *Third World Politics: China and the Afro-Asian People's Solidarity Organization, 1957–1967*
*28. Kungtu C. Sun, assisted by Ralph W. Huenemann, *The Economic Development of Manchuria in the First Half of the Twentieth Century*
*29. Shahid Javed Burki, *A Study of Chinese Communes, 1965*
30. John Carter Vincent, *The Extraterritorial System in China: Final Phase*
31. Madeleine Chi, *China Diplomacy, 1914–1918*
*32. Clifton Jackson Phillips, *Protestant America and the Pagan World: The First Half Century of the American Board of Commissioners for Foreign Missions, 1810–1860*
*33. James Pusey, *Wu Han: Attacking the Present Through the Past*
*34. Ying-wan Cheng, *Postal Communication in China and Its Modernization, 1860–1896*
35. Tuvia Blumenthal, *Saving in Postwar Japan*
36. Peter Frost, *The Bakumatsu Currency Crisis*
37. Stephen C. Lockwood, *Augustine Heard and Company, 1858–1862*
38. Robert R. Campbell, *James Duncan Campbell: A Memoir by His Son*
39. Jerome Alan Cohen, ed., *The Dynamics of China's Foreign Relations*
40. V. V. Vishnyakova-Akimova, *Two Years in Revolutionary China, 1925–1927*, trans. Steven L. Levine
41. Meron Medzini, *French Policy in Japan During the Closing Years of the Tokugawa Regime*
42. Ezra Vogel, Margie Sargent, Vivienne B. Shue, Thomas Jay Mathews, and Deborah S. Davis, *The Cultural Revolution in the Provinces*
43. Sidney A. Forsythe, *An American Missionary Community in China, 1895–1905*
*44. Benjamin I. Schwartz, ed., *Reflections on the May Fourth Movement.: A Symposium*
*45. Ching Young Choe, *The Rule of the Taewŏngun, 1864–1873: Restoration in Yi Korea*
46. W. P. J. Hall, *A Bibliographical Guide to Japanese Research on the Chinese Economy, 1958–1970*
47. Jack J. Gerson, *Horatio Nelson Lay and Sino-British Relations, 1854–1864*
48. Paul Richard Bohr, *Famine and the Missionary: Timothy Richard as Relief Administrator and Advocate of National Reform*
49. Endymion Wilkinson, *The History of Imperial China: A Research Guide*
50. Britten Dean, *China and Great Britain: The Diplomacy of Commercial Relations, 1860–1864*
51. Ellsworth C. Carlson, *The Foochow Missionaries, 1847–1880*
52. Yeh-chien Wang, *An Estimate of the Land-Tax Collection in China, 1753 and 1908*
53. Richard M. Pfeffer, *Understanding Business Contracts in China, 1949–1963*

Harvard East Asian Monographs

*54. Han-sheng Chuan and Richard Kraus, *Mid-Ching Rice Markets and Trade: An Essay in Price History*
55. Ranbir Vohra, *Lao She and the Chinese Revolution*
56. Liang-lin Hsiao, *China's Foreign Trade Statistics, 1864–1949*
*57. Lee-hsia Hsu Ting, *Government Control of the Press in Modern China, 1900–1949*
*58. Edward W. Wagner, *The Literati Purges: Political Conflict in Early Yi Korea*
*59. Joungwon A. Kim, *Divided Korea: The Politics of Development, 1945–1972*
60. Noriko Kamachi, John K. Fairbank, and Chūzō Ichiko, *Japanese Studies of Modern China Since 1953: A Bibliographical Guide to Historical and Social-Science Research on the Nineteenth and Twentieth Centuries, Supplementary Volume for 1953–1969*
61. Donald A. Gibbs and Yun-chen Li, *A Bibliography of Studies and Translations of Modern Chinese Literature, 1918–1942*
62. Robert H. Silin, *Leadership and Values: The Organization of Large-Scale Taiwanese Enterprises*
63. David Pong, *A Critical Guide to the Kwangtung Provincial Archives Deposited at the Public Record Office of London*
*64. Fred W. Drake, *China Charts the World: Hsu Chi-yü and His Geography of 1848*
*65. William A. Brown and Urgrunge Onon, translators and annotators, *History of the Mongolian People's Republic*
66. Edward L. Farmer, *Early Ming Government: The Evolution of Dual Capitals*
*67. Ralph C. Croizier, *Koxinga and Chinese Nationalism: History, Myth, and the Hero*
*68. William J. Tyler, tr., *The Psychological World of Natsume Sōseki*, by Doi Takeo
69. Eric Widmer, *The Russian Ecclesiastical Mission in Peking During the Eighteenth Century*
*70. Charlton M. Lewis, *Prologue to the Chinese Revolution: The Transformation of Ideas and Institutions in Hunan Province, 1891–1907*
71. Preston Torbert, *The Ching Imperial Household Department: A Study of Its Organization and Principal Functions, 1662–1796*
72. Paul A. Cohen and John E. Schrecker, eds., *Reform in Nineteenth-Century China*
73. Jon Sigurdson, *Rural Industrialism in China*
74. Kang Chao, *The Development of Cotton Textile Production in China*
75. Valentin Rabe, *The Home Base of American China Missions, 1880–1920*
*76. Sarasin Viraphol, *Tribute and Profit: Sino-Siamese Trade, 1652–1853*
77. Ch'i-ch'ing Hsiao, *The Military Establishment of the Yuan Dynasty*
78. Meishi Tsai, *Contemporary Chinese Novels and Short Stories, 1949–1974: An Annotated Bibliography*
*79. Wellington K. K. Chan, *Merchants, Mandarins and Modern Enterprise in Late Ching China*
80. Endymion Wilkinson, *Landlord and Labor in Late Imperial China: Case Studies from Shandong by Jing Su and Luo Lun*
*81. Barry Keenan, *The Dewey Experiment in China: Educational Reform and Political Power in the Early Republic*
*82. George A. Hayden, *Crime and Punishment in Medieval Chinese Drama: Three Judge Pao Plays*

Harvard East Asian Monographs

*83. Sang-Chul Suh, *Growth and Structural Changes in the Korean Economy, 1910–1940*
84. J. W. Dower, *Empire and Aftermath: Yoshida Shigeru and the Japanese Experience, 1878–1954*
85. Martin Collcutt, *Five Mountains: The Rinzai Zen Monastic Institution in Medieval Japan*
86. Kwang Suk Kim and Michael Roemer, *Growth and Structural Transformation*
87. Anne O. Krueger, *The Developmental Role of the Foreign Sector and Aid*
*88. Edwin S. Mills and Byung-Nak Song, *Urbanization and Urban Problems*
89. Sung Hwan Ban, Pal Yong Moon, and Dwight H. Perkins, *Rural Development*
*90. Noel F. McGinn, Donald R. Snodgrass, Yung Bong Kim, Shin-Bok Kim, and Quee-Young Kim, *Education and Development in Korea*
*91. Leroy P. Jones and Il SaKong, *Government, Business, and Entrepreneurship in Economic Development: The Korean Case*
92. Edward S. Mason, Dwight H. Perkins, Kwang Suk Kim, David C. Cole, Mahn Je Kim et al., *The Economic and Social Modernization of the Republic of Korea*
93. Robert Repetto, Tai Hwan Kwon, Son-Ung Kim, Dae Young Kim, John E. Sloboda, and Peter J. Donaldson, *Economic Development, Population Policy, and Demographic Transition in the Republic of Korea*
94. Parks M. Coble, Jr., *The Shanghai Capitalists and the Nationalist Government, 1927–1937*
95. Noriko Kamachi, *Reform in China: Huang Tsun-hsien and the Japanese Model*
96. Richard Wich, *Sino-Soviet Crisis Politics: A Study of Political Change and Communication*
97. Lillian M. Li, *China's Silk Trade: Traditional Industry in the Modern World, 1842–1937*
98. R. David Arkush, *Fei Xiaotong and Sociology in Revolutionary China*
*99. Kenneth Alan Grossberg, *Japan's Renaissance: The Politics of the Muromachi Bakufu*
100. James Reeve Pusey, *China and Charles Darwin*
101. Hoyt Cleveland Tillman, *Utilitarian Confucianism: Chen Liang's Challenge to Chu Hsi*
102. Thomas A. Stanley, *Ōsugi Sakae, Anarchist in Taishō Japan: The Creativity of the Ego*
103. Jonathan K. Ocko, *Bureaucratic Reform in Provincial China: Ting Jih-ch'ang in Restoration Kiangsu, 1867–1870*
104. James Reed, *The Missionary Mind and American East Asia Policy, 1911–1915*
105. Neil L. Waters, *Japan's Local Pragmatists: The Transition from Bakumatsu to Meiji in the Kawasaki Region*
106. David C. Cole and Yung Chul Park, *Financial Development in Korea, 1945–1978*
107. Roy Bahl, Chuk Kyo Kim, and Chong Kee Park, *Public Finances During the Korean Modernization Process*
108. William D. Wray, *Mitsubishi and the N.Y.K, 1870–1914: Business Strategy in the Japanese Shipping Industry*
109. Ralph William Huenemann, *The Dragon and the Iron Horse: The Economics of Railroads in China, 1876–1937*
*110. Benjamin A. Elman, *From Philosophy to Philology: Intellectual and Social Aspects of Change in Late Imperial China*
111. Jane Kate Leonard, *Wei Yüan and China's Rediscovery of the Maritime World*

Harvard East Asian Monographs

112. Luke S. K. Kwong, *A Mosaic of the Hundred Days:. Personalities, Politics, and Ideas of 1898*
*113. John E. Wills, Jr., *Embassies and Illusions: Dutch and Portuguese Envoys to K'ang-hsi, 1666–1687*
114. Joshua A. Fogel, *Politics and Sinology: The Case of Naitō Konan (1866–1934)*
*115. Jeffrey C. Kinkley, ed., *After Mao: Chinese Literature and Society, 1978–1981*
116. C. Andrew Gerstle, *Circles of Fantasy: Convention in the Plays of Chikamatsu*
117. Andrew Gordon, *The Evolution of Labor Relations in Japan: Heavy Industry, 1853–1955*
*118. Daniel K. Gardner, *Chu Hsi and the "Ta Hsueh": Neo-Confucian Reflection on the Confucian Canon*
119. Christine Guth Kanda, *Shinzō: Hachiman Imagery and Its Development*
*120. Robert Borgen, *Sugawara no Michizane and the Early Heian Court*
121. Chang-tai Hung, *Going to the People: Chinese Intellectual and Folk Literature, 1918–1937*
*122. Michael A. Cusumano, *The Japanese Automobile Industry: Technology and Management at Nissan and Toyota*
123. Richard von Glahn, *The Country of Streams and Grottoes: Expansion, Settlement, and the Civilizing of the Sichuan Frontier in Song Times*
124. Steven D. Carter, *The Road to Komatsubara: A Classical Reading of the Renga Hyakuin*
125. Katherine F. Bruner, John K. Fairbank, and Richard T. Smith, *Entering China's Service: Robert Hart's Journals, 1854–1863*
126. Bob Tadashi Wakabayashi, *Anti-Foreignism and Western Learning in Early-Modern Japan: The "New Theses" of 1825*
127. Atsuko Hirai, *Individualism and Socialism: The Life and Thought of Kawai Eijirō (1891–1944)*
128. Ellen Widmer, *The Margins of Utopia: "Shui-hu hou-chuan" and the Literature of Ming Loyalism*
129. R. Kent Guy, *The Emperor's Four Treasuries: Scholars and the State in the Late Chien-lung Era*
130. Peter C. Perdue, *Exhausting the Earth: State and Peasant in Hunan, 1500–1850*
131. Susan Chan Egan, *A Latterday Confucian: Reminiscences of William Hung (1893–1980)*
132. James T. C. Liu, *China Turning Inward: Intellectual-Political Changes in the Early Twelfth Century*
*133. Paul A. Cohen, *Between Tradition and Modernity: Wang T'ao and Reform in Late Ching China*
134. Kate Wildman Nakai, *Shogunal Politics: Arai Hakuseki and the Premises of Tokugawa Rule*
*135. Parks M. Coble, *Facing Japan: Chinese Politics and Japanese Imperialism, 1931–1937*
136. Jon L. Saari, *Legacies of Childhood: Growing Up Chinese in a Time of Crisis, 1890–1920*
137. Susan Downing Videen, *Tales of Heichū*
138. Heinz Morioka and Miyoko Sasaki, *Rakugo: The Popular Narrative Art of Japan*
139. Joshua A. Fogel, *Nakae Ushikichi in China: The Mourning of Spirit*

Harvard East Asian Monographs

140. Alexander Barton Woodside, *Vietnam and the Chinese Model: A Comparative Study of Vietnamese and Chinese Government in the First Half of the Nineteenth Century*
*141. George Elison, *Deus Destroyed: The Image of Christianity in Early Modern Japan*
142. William D. Wray, ed., *Managing Industrial Enterprise: Cases from Japan's Prewar Experience*
*143. T'ung-tsu Ch'ü, *Local Government in China Under the Ching*
144. Marie Anchordoguy, *Computers, Inc.: Japan's Challenge to IBM*
145. Barbara Molony, *Technology and Investment: The Prewar Japanese Chemical Industry*
146. Mary Elizabeth Berry, *Hideyoshi*
147. Laura E. Hein, *Fueling Growth: The Energy Revolution and Economic Policy in Postwar Japan*
148. Wen-hsin Yeh, *The Alienated Academy: Culture and Politics in Republican China, 1919-1937*
149. Dru C. Gladney, *Muslim Chinese: Ethnic Nationalism in the People's Republic*
150. Merle Goldman and Paul A. Cohen, eds., *Ideas Across Cultures: Essays on Chinese Thought in Honor of Benjamin L Schwartz*
151. James M. Polachek, *The Inner Opium War*
152. Gail Lee Bernstein, *Japanese Marxist: A Portrait of Kawakami Hajime, 1879-1946*
*153. Lloyd E. Eastman, *The Abortive Revolution: China Under Nationalist Rule, 1927-1937*
154. Mark Mason, *American Multinationals and Japan: The Political Economy of Japanese Capital Controls, 1899-1980*
155. Richard J. Smith, John K. Fairbank, and Katherine F. Bruner, *Robert Hart and China's Early Modernization: His Journals, 1863-1866*
156. George J. Tanabe, Jr., *Myōe the Dreamkeeper: Fantasy and Knowledge in Kamakura Buddhism*
157. William Wayne Farris, *Heavenly Warriors: The Evolution of Japan's Military, 500-1300*
158. Yu-ming Shaw, *An American Missionary in China: John Leighton Stuart and Chinese-American Relations*
159. James B. Palais, *Politics and Policy in Traditional Korea*
*160. Douglas Reynolds, *China, 1898-1912: The Xinzheng Revolution and Japan*
161. Roger R. Thompson, *China's Local Councils in the Age of Constitutional Reform, 1898-1911*
162. William Johnston, *The Modern Epidemic: History of Tuberculosis in Japan*
163. Constantine Nomikos Vaporis, *Breaking Barriers: Travel and the State in Early Modern Japan*
164. Irmela Hijiya-Kirschnereit, *Rituals of Self-Revelation: Shishōsetsu as Literary Genre and Socio-Cultural Phenomenon*
165. James C. Baxter, *The Meiji Unification Through the Lens of Ishikawa Prefecture*
166. Thomas R. H. Havens, *Architects of Affluence: The Tsutsumi Family and the Seibu-Saison Enterprises in Twentieth-Century Japan*
167. Anthony Hood Chambers, *The Secret Window: Ideal Worlds in Tanizaki's Fiction*
168. Steven J. Ericson, *The Sound of the Whistle: Railroads and the State in Meiji Japan*
169. Andrew Edmund Goble, *Kenmu: Go-Daigo's Revolution*

Harvard East Asian Monographs

170. Denise Potrzeba Lett, *In Pursuit of Status: The Making of South Korea's "New" Urban Middle Class*
171. Mimi Hall Yiengpruksawan, *Hiraizumi: Buddhist Art and Regional Politics in Twelfth-Century Japan*
172. Charles Shirō Inouye, *The Similitude of Blossoms: A Critical Biography of Izumi Kyōka (1873–1939), Japanese Novelist and Playwright*
173. Aviad E. Raz, *Riding the Black Ship: Japan and Tokyo Disneyland*
174. Deborah J. Milly, *Poverty, Equality, and Growth: The Politics of Economic Need in Postwar Japan*
175. See Heng Teow, *Japan's Cultural Policy Toward China, 1918–1931: A Comparative Perspective*
176. Michael A. Fuller, *An Introduction to Literary Chinese*
177. Frederick R. Dickinson, *War and National Reinvention: Japan in the Great War, 1914–1919*
178. John Solt, *Shredding the Tapestry of Meaning: The Poetry and Poetics of Kitasono Katue (1902–1978)*
179. Edward Pratt, *Japan's Protoindustrial Elite: The Economic Foundations of the Gōnō*
180. Atsuko Sakaki, *Recontextualizing Texts: Narrative Performance in Modern Japanese Fiction*
181. Soon-Won Park, *Colonial Industrialization and Labor in Korea: The Onoda Cement Factory*
182. JaHyun Kim Haboush and Martina Deuchler, *Culture and the State in Late Chosŏn Korea*
183. John W. Chaffee, *Branches of Heaven: A History of the Imperial Clan of Sung China*
184. Gi-Wook Shin and Michael Robinson, eds., *Colonial Modernity in Korea*
185. Nam-lin Hur, *Prayer and Play in Late Tokugawa Japan: Asakusa Sensōji and Edo Society*
186. Kristin Stapleton, *Civilizing Chengdu: Chinese Urban Reform, 1895–1937*
187. Hyung Il Pai, *Constructing "Korean" Origins: A Critical Review of Archaeology, Historiography, and Racial Myth in Korean State-Formation Theories*
188. Brian D. Ruppert, *Jewel in the Ashes: Buddha Relics and Power in Early Medieval Japan*
189. Susan Daruvala, *Zhou Zuoren and an Alternative Chinese Response to Modernity*
*190. James Z. Lee, *The Political Economy of a Frontier: Southwest China, 1250–1850*
191. Kerry Smith, *A Time of Crisis: Japan, the Great Depression, and Rural Revitalization*
192. Michael Lewis, *Becoming Apart: National Power and Local Politics in Toyama, 1868–1945*
193. William C. Kirby, Man-houng Lin, James Chin Shih, and David A. Pietz, eds., *State and Economy in Republican China: A Handbook for Scholars*
194. Timothy S. George, *Minamata: Pollution and the Struggle for Democracy in Postwar Japan*
195. Billy K. L. So, *Prosperity, Region, and Institutions in Maritime China: The South Fukien Pattern, 946–1368*
196. Yoshihisa Tak Matsusaka, *The Making of Japanese Manchuria, 1904–1932*

Harvard East Asian Monographs

197. Maram Epstein, *Competing Discourses: Orthodoxy, Authenticity, and Engendered Meanings in Late Imperial Chinese Fiction*
198. Curtis J. Milhaupt, J. Mark Ramseyer, and Michael K. Young, eds. and comps., *Japanese Law in Context: Readings in Society, the Economy, and Politics*
199. Haruo Iguchi, *Unfinished Business: Ayukawa Yoshisuke and U.S.-Japan Relations, 1937–1952*
200. Scott Pearce, Audrey Spiro, and Patricia Ebrey, *Culture and Power in the Reconstitution of the Chinese Realm, 200–600*
201. Terry Kawashima, *Writing Margins: The Textual Construction of Gender in Heian and Kamakura Japan*
202. Martin W. Huang, *Desire and Fictional Narrative in Late Imperial China*
203. Robert S. Ross and Jiang Changbin, eds., *Re-examining the Cold War: U.S.-China Diplomacy, 1954–1973*
204. Guanhua Wang, *In Search of Justice: The 1905–1906 Chinese Anti-American Boycott*
205. David Schaberg, *A Patterned Past: Form and Thought in Early Chinese Historiography*
206. Christine Yano, *Tears of Longing: Nostalgia and the Nation in Japanese Popular Song*
207. Milena Doleželová-Velingerová and Oldřich Král, with Graham Sanders, eds., *The Appropriation of Cultural Capital: China's May Fourth Project*
208. Robert N. Huey, *The Making of 'Shinkokinshū'*
209. Lee Butler, *Emperor and Aristocracy in Japan, 1467–1680: Resilience and Renewal*
210. Suzanne Ogden, *Inklings of Democracy in China*
211. Kenneth J. Ruoff, *The People's Emperor: Democracy and the Japanese Monarchy, 1945–1995*
212. Haun Saussy, *Great Walls of Discourse and Other Adventures in Cultural China*
213. Aviad E. Raz, *Emotions at Work: Normative Control, Organizations, and Culture in Japan and America*
214. Rebecca E. Karl and Peter Zarrow, eds., *Rethinking the 1898 Reform Period: Political and Cultural Change in Late Qing China*
215. Kevin O'Rourke, *The Book of Korean Shijo*
216. Ezra F. Vogel, ed., *The Golden Age of the U.S.-China-Japan Triangle, 1972–1989*
217. Thomas A. Wilson, ed., *On Sacred Grounds: Culture, Society, Politics, and the Formation of the Cult of Confucius*
218. Donald S. Sutton, *Steps of Perfection: Exorcistic Performers and Chinese Religion in Twentieth-Century Taiwan*
219. Daqing Yang, *Technology of Empire: Telecommunications and Japanese Expansionism, 1895–1945*
220. Qianshen Bai, *Fu Shan's World: The Transformation of Chinese Calligraphy in the Seventeenth Century*
221. Paul Jakov Smith and Richard von Glahn, eds., *The Song-Yuan-Ming Transition in Chinese History*
222. Rania Huntington, *Alien Kind: Foxes and Late Imperial Chinese Narrative*
223. Jordan Sand, *House and Home in Modern Japan: Architecture, Domestic Space, and Bourgeois Culture, 1880–1930*

Harvard East Asian Monographs

224. Karl Gerth, *China Made: Consumer Culture and the Creation of the Nation*
225. Xiaoshan Yang, *Metamorphosis of the Private Sphere: Gardens and Objects in Tang-Song Poetry*
226. Barbara Mittler, *A Newspaper for China? Power, Identity, and Change in Shanghai's News Media, 1872–1912*
227. Joyce A. Madancy, *The Troublesome Legacy of Commissioner Lin: The Opium Trade and Opium Suppression in Fujian Province, 1820s to 1920s*
228. John Makeham, *Transmitters and Creators: Chinese Commentators and Commentaries on the Analects*
229. Elisabeth Köll, *From Cotton Mill to Business Empire: The Emergence of Regional Enterprises in Modern China*
230. Emma Teng, *Taiwan's Imagined Geography: Chinese Colonial Travel Writing and Pictures, 1683–1895*
231. Wilt Idema and Beata Grant, *The Red Brush: Writing Women of Imperial China*
232. Eric C. Rath, *The Ethos of Noh: Actors and Their Art*
233. Elizabeth Remick, *Building Local States: China During the Republican and Post-Mao Eras*
234. Lynn Struve, ed., *The Qing Formation in World-Historical Time*
235. D. Max Moerman, *Localizing Paradise: Kumano Pilgrimage and the Religious Landscape of Premodern Japan*
236. Antonia Finnane, *Speaking of Yangzhou: A Chinese City, 1550–1850*
237. Brian Platt, *Burning and Building: Schooling and State Formation in Japan, 1750–1890*
238. Gail Bernstein, Andrew Gordon, and Kate Wildman Nakai, eds., *Public Spheres, Private Lives in Modern Japan, 1600–1950: Essays in Honor of Albert Craig*
239. Wu Hung and Katherine R. Tsiang, *Body and Face in Chinese Visual Culture*
240. Stephen Dodd, *Writing Home: Representations of the Native Place in Modern Japanese Literature*
241. David Anthony Bello, *Opium and the Limits of Empire: Drug Prohibition in the Chinese Interior, 1729–1850*
242. Hosea Hirata, *Discourses of Seduction: History, Evil, Desire, and Modern Japanese Literature*
243. Kyung Moon Hwang, *Beyond Birth: Social Status in the Emergence of Modern Korea*
244. Brian R. Dott, *Identity Reflections: Pilgrimages to Mount Tai in Late Imperial China*
245. Mark McNally, *Proving the Way: Conflict and Practice in the History of Japanese Nativism*
246. Yongping Wu, *A Political Explanation of Economic Growth: State Survival, Bureaucratic Politics, and Private Enterprises in the Making of Taiwan's Economy, 1950–1985*
247. Kyu Hyun Kim, *The Age of Visions and Arguments: Parliamentarianism and the National Public Sphere in Early Meiji Japan*
248. Zvi Ben-Dor Benite, *The Dao of Muhammad: A Cultural History of Muslims in Late Imperial China*
249. David Der-wei Wang and Shang Wei, eds., *Dynastic Crisis and Cultural Innovation: From the Late Ming to the Late Qing and Beyond*

Harvard East Asian Monographs

250. Wilt L. Idema, Wai-yee Li, and Ellen Widmer, eds., *Trauma and Transcendence in Early Qing Literature*
251. Barbara Molony and Kathleen Uno, eds., *Gendering Modern Japanese History*
252. Hiroshi Aoyagi, *Islands of Eight Million Smiles: Idol Performance and Symbolic Production in Contemporary Japan*
253. Wai-yee Li, *The Readability of the Past in Early Chinese Historiography*
254. William C. Kirby, Robert S. Ross, and Gong Li, eds., *Normalization of U.S.-China Relations: An International History*
255. Ellen Gardner Nakamura, *Practical Pursuits: Takano Chōei, Takahashi Keisaku, and Western Medicine in Nineteenth-Century Japan*
256. Jonathan W. Best, *A History of the Early Korean Kingdom of Paekche, together with an annotated translation of* The Paekche Annals *of the* Samguk sagi
257. Liang Pan, *The United Nations in Japan's Foreign and Security Policymaking, 1945–1992: National Security, Party Politics, and International Status*
258. Richard Belsky, *Localities at the Center: Native Place, Space, and Power in Late Imperial Beijing*
259. Zwia Lipkin, *"Useless to the State": "Social Problems" and Social Engineering in Nationalist Nanjing, 1927–1937*
260. William O. Gardner, *Advertising Tower: Japanese Modernism and Modernity in the 1920s*
261. Stephen Owen, *The Making of Early Chinese Classical Poetry*
262. Martin J. Powers, *Pattern and Person: Ornament, Society, and Self in Classical China*
263. Anna M. Shields, *Crafting a Collection: The Cultural Contexts and Poetic Practice of the* Huajian ji 花間集 *(Collection from Among the Flowers)*
264. Stephen Owen, *The Late Tang: Chinese Poetry of the Mid-Ninth Century (827–860)*
265. Sara L. Friedman, *Intimate Politics: Marriage, the Market, and State Power in Southeastern China*
266. Patricia Buckley Ebrey and Maggie Bickford, *Emperor Huizong and Late Northern Song China: The Politics of Culture and the Culture of Politics*
267. Sophie Volpp, *Worldly Stage: Theatricality in Seventeenth-Century China*
268. Ellen Widmer, *The Beauty and the Book: Women and Fiction in Nineteenth-Century China*
269. Steven B. Miles, *The Sea of Learning: Mobility and Identity in Nineteenth-Century Guangzhou*
270. Lin Man-houng, *China Upside Down: Currency, Society, and Ideologies, 1808–1856*
271. Ronald Egan, *The Problem of Beauty: Aesthetic Thought and Pursuits in Northern Song Dynasty China*
272. Mark Halperin, *Out of the Cloister: Literati Perspectives on Buddhism in Sung China, 960–1279*
273. Helen Dunstan, *State or Merchant? Political Economy and Political Process in 1740s China*
274. Sabina Knight, *The Heart of Time: Moral Agency in Twentieth-Century Chinese Fiction*
275. Timothy J. Van Compernolle, *The Uses of Memory: The Critique of Modernity in the Fiction of Higuchi Ichiyō*

Harvard East Asian Monographs

276. Paul Rouzer, *A New Practical Primer of Literary Chinese*
277. Jonathan Zwicker, *Practices of the Sentimental Imagination: Melodrama, the Novel, and the Social Imaginary in Nineteenth-Century Japan*
278. Franziska Seraphim, *War Memory and Social Politics in Japan, 1945–2005*
279. Adam L. Kern, *Manga from the Floating World: Comicbook Culture and the* Kibyōshi *of Edo Japan*
280. Cynthia J. Brokaw, *Commerce in Culture: The Sibao Book Trade in the Qing and Republican Periods*
281. Eugene Y. Park, *Between Dreams and Reality: The Military Examination in Late Chosŏn Korea, 1600–1894*
282. Nam-lin Hur, *Death and Social Order in Tokugawa Japan: Buddhism, Anti-Christianity, and the* Danka *System*
283. Patricia M. Thornton, *Disciplining the State: Virtue, Violence, and State-Making in Modern China*
284. Vincent Goossaert, *The Taoists of Peking, 1800–1949: A Social History of Urban Clerics*
285. Peter Nickerson, *Taoism, Bureaucracy, and Popular Religion in Early Medieval China*
286. Charo B. D'Etcheverry, *Love After* The Tale of Genji: *Rewriting the World of the Shining Prince*
287. Michael G. Chang, *A Court on Horseback: Imperial Touring & the Construction of Qing Rule, 1680–1785*
288. Carol Richmond Tsang, *War and Faith:* Ikkō Ikki *in Late Muromachi Japan*
289. Hilde De Weerdt, *Competition over Content: Negotiating Standards for the Civil Service Examinations in Imperial China (1127–1279)*
290. Eve Zimmerman, *Out of the Alleyway: Nakagami Kenji and the Poetics of Outcaste Fiction*
291. Robert Culp, *Articulating Citizenship: Civic Education and Student Politics in Southeastern China, 1912–1940*
292. Richard J. Smethurst, *From Foot Soldier to Finance Minister: Takahashi Korekiyo, Japan's Keynes*
293. John E. Herman, *Amid the Clouds and Mist: China's Colonization of Guizhou, 1200–1700*
294. Tomoko Shiroyama, *China During the Great Depression: Market, State, and the World Economy, 1929–1937*
295. Kirk W. Larsen, *Tradition, Treaties and Trade: Qing Imperialism and Chosŏn Korea, 1850–1910*
296. Gregory Golley, *When Our Eyes No Longer See: Realism, Science, and Ecology in Japanese Literary Modernism*
297. Barbara Ambros, *Emplacing a Pilgrimage: The Ōyama Cult and Regional Religion in Early Modern Japan*
298. Rebecca Suter, *The Japanization of Modernity: Murakami Haruki between Japan and the United States*
299. Yuma Totani, *The Tokyo War Crimes Trial: The Pursuit of Justice in the Wake of World War II*

Harvard East Asian Monographs

300. Linda Isako Angst, *In a Dark Time: Memory, Community, and Gendered Nationalism in Postwar Okinawa*
301. David M. Robinson, ed., *Culture, Courtiers, and Competition: The Ming Court (1368–1644)*
302. Calvin Chen, *Some Assembly Required: Work, Community, and Politics in China's Rural Enterprises*
303. Sem Vermeersch, *The Power of the Buddhas: The Politics of Buddhism During the Koryŏ Dynasty (918–1392)*
304. Tina Lu, *Accidental Incest, Filial Cannibalism, and Other Peculiar Encounters in Late Imperial Chinese Literature*
305. Chang Woei Ong, *Men of Letters Within the Passes: Guanzhong Literati in Chinese History, 907–1911*
306. Wendy Swartz, *Reading Tao Yuanming: Shifting Paradigms of Historical Reception (427–1900)*
307. Peter K. Bol, *Neo-Confucianism in History*
308. Carlos Rojas, *The Naked Gaze: Reflections on Chinese Modernity*
309. Kelly H. Chong, *Deliverance and Submission: Evangelical Women and the Negotiation of Patriarchy in South Korea*
310. Rachel DiNitto, *Uchida Hyakken: A Critique of Modernity and Militarism in Prewar Japan*
311. Jeffrey Snyder-Reinke, *Dry Spells: State Rainmaking and Local Governance in Late Imperial China*
312. Jay Dautcher, *Down a Narrow Road: Identity and Masculinity in a Uyghur Community in Xinjiang China*
313. Xun Liu, *Daoist Modern: Innovation, Lay Practice, and the Community of Inner Alchemy in Republican Shanghai*